POWERPLAY

PRINCETON STUDIES IN INTERNATIONAL HISTORY AND POLITICS

Series Editors
G. John Ikenberry, Marc Trachtenberg, and William C. Wohlforth

For a full list of books in this series, see http://press.princeton.edu
/catalogs/series/title/princeton-studies-in-international-history-and-politics.html

Recent Titles

Powerplay: The Origins of the American Alliance System in Asia by Victor D. Cha

Economic Interdependence and War by Dale C. Copeland

*Knowing the Adversary: Leaders, Intelligence, and Assessment
of Intentions in International Relations* by Keren Yarhi-Milo

*Nuclear Strategy in the Modern Era: Regional Powers
and International Conflict* by Vipin Narang

*The Cold War and After: History, Theory, and the Logic
of International Politics* by Marc Trachtenberg

*Liberal Leviathan: The Origins, Crisis, and Transformation
of the American World Order* by G. John Ikenberry

*Worse Than a Monolith: Alliance Politics and Problems of Coercive
Diplomacy in Asia* by Thomas J. Christensen

Politics and Strategy: Partisan Ambition and American Statecraft by Peter Trubowitz

*The Clash of Ideas in World Politics: Transnational Networks, States,
and Regime Change, 1510–2010* by John M. Owen IV

How Enemies Become Friends: The Sources of Stable Peace by Charles A. Kupchan

1989: The Struggle to Create Post–Cold War Europe by Mary Elise Sarotte

*The Struggle for Power in Early Modern Europe: Religious Conflict,
Dynastic Empires, and International Change* by Daniel H. Nexon

*Strong Borders, Secure Nation: Cooperation and Conflict
in China's Territorial Disputes* by M. Taylor Fravel

The Sino-Soviet Split: Cold War in the Communist World by Lorenz M. Lüthi

Nuclear Logics: Contrasting Paths in East Asia and the Middle East by Etel Solingen

Social States: China in International Institutions, 1980–2000 by Alastair Iain Johnston

Appeasing Bankers: Financial Caution on the Road to War by Jonathan Kirshner

The Politics of Secularism in International Relations by Elizabeth Shakman Hurd

*Unanswered Threats: Political Constraints on the Balance
of Power* by Randall L. Schweller

*Producing Security: Multinational Corporations, Globalization,
and the Changing Calculus of Conflict* by Stephen G. Brooks

*Driving the Soviets up the Wall: Soviet-East German
Relations, 1953–1961* by Hope M. Harrison

POWERPLAY

THE ORIGINS OF THE
AMERICAN ALLIANCE SYSTEM
IN ASIA

VICTOR D. CHA

PRINCETON UNIVERSITY PRESS
PRINCETON AND OXFORD

Copyright © 2016 by Princeton University Press

Published by Princeton University Press,
41 William Street, Princeton, New Jersey 08540
In the United Kingdom: Princeton University Press,
6 Oxford Street, Woodstock, Oxfordshire OX20 1TR
press.princeton.edu

Cover photograph courtesy of the John Foster Dulles Papers
Collection, Mudd Manuscript Library, Princeton University
Cover design by Amanda Weiss

Fourth printing, and first paperback printing, 2018
Paper ISBN 978-0-691-18094-6

The Library of Congress has cataloged the cloth edition as
follows:

Names: Cha, Victor D., 1961– author.
Title: Powerplay : the origins of the American alliance system in
    Asia / Victor D. Cha.
Description: Princeton, New Jersey : Princeton University Press,
    2016. | Series: Princeton Studies in International History and
    Politics | Includes bibliographical references and index.
Identifiers: LCCN 2015047769 | ISBN 9780691144535 (hardback)
    | ISBN 0691144532 (hardback)
Subjects: LCSH: United States—Foreign relations—Asia.
    | Asia—Foreign relations—United States. | Alliances. |
    International relations. | Security, International. | World
    politics—1945–1989. | World politics—1989– | BISAC:
    POLITICAL SCIENCE / International Relations / Diplomacy.
    | POLITICAL SCIENCE / International Relations / Treaties. |
    POLITICAL SCIENCE / General. | POLITICAL SCIENCE /
    Public Policy / General.
Classification: LCC DS33.4.U6 C47 2016 | DDC 327.7305—dc23
LC record available at https://lccn.loc.gov/2015047769

British Library Cataloging-in-Publication Data is available

This book has been composed in Sabon Next LT Pro,
Rockwell Std, and Duke

Printed on acid-free paper. ∞

Printed in the United States of America

10 9 8 7 6 5 4

FOR MY MENTORS

*James W. Morley, Robert Jervis,
Gerald Curtis, and Han Sung-joo*

CONTENTS

List of Illustrations and Tables   *ix*
Preface   *xi*
A Note to the Reader   *xv*

1 The Puzzle   *1*

2 The Argument: Powerplay   *19*

3 Origins of the American Alliance System in Asia   *40*

4 Taiwan: "Chaining Chiang"   *65*

5 Korea: "Rhee-Straint"   *94*

6 Japan: "Win Japan"   *122*

7 Counterarguments   *161*

8 Conclusion: US Alliances and the Complex Patchwork of Asia's Architecture   *185*

Notes   *221*
Bibliography   *293*
Index   *323*

ILLUSTRATIONS AND TABLES

Illustrations

Figure 2.1. Alliance pathologies   21
Figure 2.2. Overdependence and entrapment   25
Figure 3.1. US aid to select Asian and European countries   52
Figure 4.1. Total US military assistance, obligations (historic
            dollars) (1950–1966)   86
Figure 4.2. Top ten recipients of US military assistance,
            obligations (1950–1966)   87
Figure 4.3. US military assistance, obligations (1950–1966)   87
Figure 6.1. Comparison of US aid and rest of world aid to Japan
            (1952–1956)   144
Figure 6.2. Comparison of Japanese exports to the United States
            and the world (1952–1956)   145
Figure 6.3. Japanese trade with Asia (1948–1961)   153
Figure 8.1. China-based regional architecture in Asia   199
Figure 8.2. US and regional architecture in Asia   205

Tables

Table 2.1. Abandonment and entrapment   25
Table 2.2. Bilateral versus multilateral control   29
Table 2.3. Distancing versus control strategies when faced
           with entrapment   32
Table 2.4. Powerplay   35
Table 3.1. Comparison of US aid to select Asian and European
           countries (1946–1952)   51
Table 4.1. US aircraft and naval assets deliveries to Taiwan
           (1953–1960)   89

Table 5.1.   ROK trade dependence on the United States,
            selected years (1948–1960)   114
Table 8.1.   US minilaterals in Asia   198
Table 8.2.   China-based regional institutions in Asia   200
Table 8.3.   Membership in China-based regional architecture   201
Table 8.4.   Regional institutions in Asia   212

PREFACE

The pleasure of being a professor is not found in the long summer vacations (contrary to popular opinion), but in the interaction with the students. In particular, I love the questions they ask. It shows not just how much reading they have completed for class, as evidenced by the depth of their inquiry, but what interests or motivates them. There is no greater joy for a teacher than seeing inspired students, and sometimes that inspiration infects even the jaded professor.

The initial idea for this book came many years ago after a session of my lecture course at Georgetown University on East Asian Security. That particular week's topic was "Asia after World War II," and I taught the students about the historical uniqueness of the American "hub and spokes" alliance system. An undergraduate sitting in the front row, unshaven and dressed in clothes that looked unchanged from the prior evening (it was a morning class—9:30 a.m.—which is unspeakably early for your average coed), asked a simple question: Why did the United States choose a different framework of alliances for Asia than what was pursued in Europe? I spouted all of the traditional explanations in response, having to do with geography, economics, and history. He and the rest of the class nodded attentively while tapping notes into their laptops. As the hour ended, I dismissed the class but felt as though something was missing in my answer. I realized afterward that I had missed the most important word in the student's question—that is, why did the United States *choose* a particular security design for Asia. All of the explanations I had offered to the class focused on the objective and disparate traits of the two regions, and none really addressed the issue of American volition. Did the United States build things this way intentionally, and if so, then why? Or were the outcomes determined largely by the situation on the ground in Asia and in Europe at the end of World War II? I thought to myself, there is at least a journal article to be written on this question, and maybe even a book.

My initial conversations with Chuck Myers at Princeton University Press about the project were cut short by my decision to serve on the National Security Council. The policy experiences at the White House during my public service leave from the University, particularly as they pertained to managing our alliance relationships in Asia in the context of the region's evolving security architecture, only whetted my appetite to undertake this project. When I returned to campus, two other books (*Beyond the Final Score* and *The Impossible State*) managed to distract me from the one that I had been meaning to write for years.

A book is only as good as its editors, and I am especially grateful to mine for their support of the project. Eric Crahan came to Princeton University Press with a reputation as a stellar editor for authors to work with, and I can attest to the fact that he more than lives up to the billing. His predecessor, Chuck Myers, was kind, patient, and always helpful in shepherding the project in its early iterations. My friend, Anne Routon, deserves thanks for all of the long lunches and sage advice about the publishing world.

A small army of research assistants laid a path to the book's completion. Andy Lim studiously created painstakingly difficult tables and figures for all of the chapters, which received compliments for their originality from the reviewers. Andy compiled the bibliography as well. Nick Anderson, my former research assistant and now a doctoral student in political science at Yale University, lent his unique touch to the manuscript, in particular, the chapter on Japan. I thank Shin W. David Park and Tianjing Zhang, both former students and research assistants at Georgetown, for tracking down the necessary documents from the Dulles Papers Collection at Princeton and other archives. The staff at Seeley G. Mudd Manuscript Library at Princeton assisted during my trips to track down cover art and other miscellaneous documents for the book.

John Powers and Mike Smith at the National Security Council vetted the manuscript in its entirety in a timely fashion. Jill Harris and Karen Fortgang at Princeton University Press oversaw a production process that was both flawless and swift, as did Ben Pokross and Theresa Liu. Karen Verde skillfully brought greater clarity to the manuscript, for which I am most grateful.

Many colleagues and graduate students have offered helpful comments on the project. Probably few remember they did, given the protracted timeline, including Michael Brown, Phillipp Bleek, Tom Christensen, Bruce Cumings, Gerald Curtis, John Duffield, Steve Goldstein, Michael Green, Alfred Gronquist, John Hamre, Robert Jervis, David Kang, Peter Katzenstein, Christine Kim, Robert Lieber, Sean Lynn-Jones, Galia Press-Barnathan, Jeremy Pressman, Richard Samuels, and Randall Schweller. To these and others whom I have forgotten, thank you for the insightful comments and criticisms that have made this book better. The anonymous reviewers for Princeton University Press deserve praise for exceptionally good comments that guided the revisions of the manuscript. For research support, I am indebted to the East-West Center for allowing me to spend summer months ruminating on the history of America's Pacific alliances from my favorite island in the Pacific. Director of the POSCO program, Denny Roy, and the Center's president, Charles Morrison, have been unfailingly gracious in their hosting of my research stints. This work was also supported by the Academy of Korean Studies (Korean Studies Promotion Service) Grant funded by the Ministry of Education (AKS-2010-DZZ-2102). This book was made better by all of these colleagues and by the support of these institutions. Any failings and shortcomings are entirely mine.

Parts of chapter 8 are derived from an earlier article of mine that appeared in the January 2011 issue of *Asia Policy*.

I would like to acknowledge my staff at Georgetown and the Center for Strategic and International Studies (CSIS) for allowing me the time to focus on completing the manuscript, especially in the final stages. Their teamwork—Marie, Ellen, Andy, SJ, Lisa, Robert, Jennifer, Kat, Daye, and Fay—enabled us to handle all of the administrative burdens, conferencing, student advising, and public events even as I blocked chunks of time to write.

My family has been there with me throughout. Patrick is now a freshman in college and Andrew a freshman in high school. They are both my heroes in this world. Hyun Jung has watched this book evolve over time in Washington, Hawaii, and Seoul with loving support. My mother is the source of my diligence and drive. My father-in-law has listened to me talk about the book over the years during our dinners in Seoul. The memory of my father, Moon Young Cha, is what inspires me every day to be a better scholar, father, husband, and person.

As enjoyable as it was to write this book, it was not easy. Traversing the worlds of foreign policy and academia in political science is becoming harder as the two disciplines move further apart. It is not easy to write in ways that satisfy both audiences in one piece of research, and I admire greatly my colleagues who can accomplish this. Increasingly, one has to write to two different constituencies in policy and in theory, with neither appreciating the work of the other. I hope that this book will be seen as an effort to combine international relations theory-building with rich historical archival work. In the last chapter, I try to derive the policy implications of this academic study, albeit imperfectly.

A NOTE TO THE READER

In this work I transliterate Korean words according to the McCune-Reischauer system, Japanese words according to the Hepburn system, and Chinese words according to the Pinyin system. Personal names are cited in text, notes, and bibliography with surnames first. The exception to this are names that appear as popularly Romanized in the Western language literature (e.g., "Syngman Rhee"), unless specifically cited within the context of a foreign language source. Other languages are written as conventionally found in the Western literature.

POWERPLAY

1

THE PUZZLE

We were huddled in the cramped quarters of the US Secretary of State's airplane, planning for our next stop in Sydney, Australia. The most coveted space on the Boeing C-32, the Secretary's suite, comes complete with a foldout couch and flat screen TV. But given the numbers in the room, we were all seated cross-legged on the floor like overgrown boy scouts around a campfire, in shirts and ties, rumpled from the seven-hour flight from Jakarta. We ran through the policy items for the meetings with Prime Minister John Howard and Foreign Minister Alexander Downer, with each staff person briefing on his or her area of expertise: China, UN reform, Iraq, Afghanistan, Indonesia, North Korea. The last issue was the East Asia Summit (EAS). A new organization created largely through Malaysia's initiative, EAS had gained the interest of many countries in Asia as the first true indigenously created regional institution. The Singaporeans were hosting the next meeting and the Australians and Japanese sorely wanted the United States to join this new grouping, in no small part to prevent the Chinese from dominating the organization. There were benefits to being included in the grouping. Membership would constitute a good representation opportunity in the region for the United States. At the same time, a US commitment to EAS, which still had not evinced a clear agenda or mission as a regionwide institution, would detract from the work of the other regional body, the Asia-Pacific Economic Cooperation Council (APEC). Moreover, it would be hard to convince domestic staff within the White House to send the president halfway around the world to participate in a "talk shop" among leaders with no clear agenda. In the run-up to the Sydney visit, the Australians were pushing for the United States to begin informal participation in EAS as a non-member by sending the Secretary (rather than the president) to the next meeting.

1

The State Department was leaning in this direction, but APEC proponents within the US government were against transmitting any positive signals on the issue during this trip. In the midst of the discussion, the Secretary asked one of her staff for his opinion. He sighed, and then stated in a deadpan tone, "Madame Secretary, EAS is a bad idea whose time has come."

The US official's point was that the United States could no longer eschew the new emerging architecture in Asia. Our bilateral alliance system, with treaty allies and security partners in Australia, Japan, South Korea, Philippines, Taiwan, Thailand, and Singapore, was still the most significant security architecture in the region. But the United States needed to consider transacting business in Asia through these new multilateral groupings, even if they were somewhat duplicative of work done through our exclusive relationships with the governments in the region. The United States eventually did join the East Asia Summit in 2010, but not without some trepidation.[1] Validating the new organization through US membership despite its absence of a clear agenda or mission was troubling to some who insisted that our bilateral alliances were still the most important feature of the region's architectural design.

These experiences in government led me to wonder why it has taken so long for Asia to develop inclusive political and security structures. Asia is home to the fastest growing economies in the world today. Over the next five years, 50 percent of global growth outside of the United States will emanate from this region.[2] Though many of its governments are democracies, many are not; yet this variety has not precluded high levels of regional economic, social, and political interaction. Nevertheless, multilateral structures in Asia, like EAS, emerged only in 2005, sixty years after the end of World War II. By contrast, multilateralism took hold much earlier in Europe with the creation of NATO in 1949. Rather than multilateralism, the most distinctive architecture in Asia through the end of the twentieth century and into the twenty-first has been the US bilateral alliance system—an exclusive rather than inclusive security architecture. Why did security in Asia over the last six decades evolve this way? Why has it taken so long for Asia to develop viable multilateral security institutions? And why did the United States, the preeminent power in the region after the defeat of Japan in 1945, choose to build bilateral security institutions in Asia rather than the multilateral ones it forged in Europe?

Some might respond to these questions by noting that Washington has been supportive of Asian regionalism, including organizations like APEC, the ASEAN Regional Forum (ARF), and the Trans-Pacific Partnership (TPP). But when compared with NATO and the European Union, it is fairly evident that: (1) Europe is more organized as a "region" than Asia; and (2) while the United States transacts business all over the world both through exclusive one-to-one arrangements and through more inclusive regional groupings, on balance, Europe has seen more multilateralism while Asia has seen more bilateralism.

The reason for Asia's unusual security evolution and the slow growth of multilateralism can be found in the origins of the American alliance system in Asia. In this book, I argue that a confluence of historical, political, and strategic circumstances led the United States to build a unique "hub and spokes" security network in Asia. "Hub and spokes" is defined as a set of tightly held and exclusive, one-to-one bilateral partnerships with countries in the region. Like a bicycle wheel, each of these allies and partners constituted "spokes" connected with a central hub (the United States), but with few connections between the spokes. This bilateral method of organizing Asia stood in stark contrast to Europe, where security was organized in a more elaborately designed multilateral framework (i.e., NATO). The rationale for this institutional design decision is what I term the "powerplay" in US grand strategy—the creation of these alliances to exert considerable political, military, and economic control over key countries in East Asia. In Taiwan and Korea, the bilateral alliances were created to bolster staunchly anti-communist regimes as a bulwark against Soviet influence. But an equally important, if unstated, rationale for Washington's creation of deep bilateral alliances was to constrain anti-communist leaders, embroiled in civil wars and with questionable domestic political legitimacy, from going "rogue" and recklessly pulling the United States into unwanted conflicts in Asia when the primary strategic concern was Europe. In Japan, the powerplay rationale was to create a tight, exclusive hold over the defeated imperial power to ensure that the region's one major power would evolve in a direction that suited US interests.

The powerplay strategy had a deep and enduring impact on the region's security evolution. Once created, the Cold War hub and spokes bilateral alliance system afforded the United States an informal empire of sorts in Asia. Whether this was the American intention is not the subject of this book. Rather, I seek to trace how and why the United States chose this bilateral institutional design for Asia, and to demonstrate why it has endured. While democratic values may have something to do with the longevity of the US alliance system, the fact is that democracy did not come to these East Asian players (with the exception of Japan) for de-cades after the creation of the hub and spokes system. Bilateral alliances, however, afforded the United States a powerplay advantage—it exercised near-total control over foreign and domestic affairs of its allies, and it cre-ated an asymmetry of power that rendered inconceivable counterbalanc-ing by these smaller countries, on their own or in concert with others. Not only did the United States dominate the power matrix, it also dom-inated the network matrix. That is, as the central "hub" power among disparate "spokes" as allies, the United States made itself the indispens-able power to all in Asia. Undeniably, things are changing today, but the legacies of this bilateral tradition are hard to shake. Indeed, the US-based alliance system remains the single most important security and political institution in Asia amid a plethora of recent and new regional groupings.

———

I argue that the powerplay rationale informed American intentions vis-à-vis the creation of the United States-Republic of Korea (ROK) (1953), the United States-Republic of China (ROC) (1954), and the United States-Japan (1951) alliances. The United States established mutual defense trea-ties with the ROK and ROC not only to contain communism, but also to stop the Syngman Rhee and Chiang Kai-shek governments from pro-voking conflicts with North Korea and mainland China (respectively) that might embroil the United States in a larger unwanted war on the Asian mainland when the primary theater of concern for US national security was Western Europe. The desire to use the alliance as a form of "constraint" obviated the need for a larger multilateral security alli-ance framework in Asia. Washington best exercised control bilaterally. To have tried to exercise similar control in a larger multilateral regional framework would have diluted US material and political influence. In Europe, by contrast, the United States had less concern about small ag-gressive states entrapping it in a larger war with the Soviet Union. This reduced the obstacles to designing a multilateral security organization.

The powerplay rationale for Japan was slightly different from that in-forming the US-Korea and US-Taiwan alliances. The concern was not that Japan would entrap the United States in another war; instead, it was the concern that Japan's postwar recovery would occur absent American input. The United States understood that Japan was the only candidate for great power status in the region after World War II. Washington ini-tially attempted to embed Japan in a regional framework of maritime

Asian countries for its postwar recovery, just as they were doing with Germany and its neighbors in Europe. But when this failed, the United States reverted to a tight bilateral alliance with Japan. The powerplay rationale for the alliance therefore was to "win Japan" as an ally—that is, to exercise decisive influence over Japan's transformation from a defeated wartime power into a status quo power supportive of American interests in the region. This was accomplished through the creation of bilateral security dependence within the alliance. This powerplay rationale had the effect of isolating Japan from the rest of Asia, making historical reconciliation with its neighbors difficult. Japan's lack of postwar integration with the region in turn made multilateralism difficult. The evolution of security in Asia was therefore different from that in Europe. Alliances were not just instruments of containment against the adversary; they were also instruments of control over the allies. The supplementary powerplay rationale both reduced the need for and made the prospects of organizing a NATO-like multilateral organization in Asia less likely.

The powerplay argument has implications for the recent work on multilateralism and the uses of power. It challenges the prevailing causal proposition in the literature put forward by liberal institutionalists and foreign policy internationalists that embedding a state in multilateral structures and rules is the best way to control power and dampen unilateralist inclinations.[3] Many have argued, for example, that embedding China in multilateral rules and institutions offers the most prudent path for managing the country's rise. Others have argued that America's unilateralist temptations and tendencies in an age of unipolarity are best moderated through allowing itself to be bound by the multilateral institutions and rules that it helped to create as part of the postwar order. While I do not disagree with these propositions, I show that they are highly conditional ones. Under different circumstances, the same goals of controlling others and amplifying one's own power might sometimes be more efficiently attained through bilateral rather than multilateral ties. I show that power asymmetries "select" for the type of institutional designs that work best for control. If small powers try to control a great power, then multilateralism works. But if great powers seek control over smaller ones, multilateralism is less efficient and far messier, requiring consultation and patience amid the vagaries of committee-based decision-making. Bilateral control is more effective and efficient.

The powerplay argument also has relevance for work in international relations on hierarchy. This body of scholarship acknowledges that world politics is composed of sovereign states operating under anarchy, but that in practice there is an informal hierarchical order, and in some cases an informal empire, that has always coexisted with sovereignty and anarchy. This order is based on the power of the strong states over the weak, but it is also based on the "micropolitics" of those relationships—that is, notions of the legitimacy of that order in the subjective mind-sets of both ruling powers and the subject states.[4] In this regard, the US hub and spokes system in Asia established at the beginning of the Cold War very much resembled an informal empire. Of course, all states were sovereign in this alliance framework, but the United States strode atop massive power gaps with its allies that basically muted any counterbalancing tendencies.[5] Moreover, this US-imposed order was more or less considered legitimate by all participating governments. Alliance elements like host-nation support (i.e., Korean and Japanese government funding of the costs of US bases in their countries); status of forces agreements (i.e., negotiated agreements that protect the rights of US military operating in the host country); US-imposed restrictions on allied countries' military arms acquisitions (i.e., Taiwan); the US military's right to put down "domestic disturbances" in a country without that country's consent (i.e., Japan until 1960); and even the exercise of US control over an allied government's sovereign right to use force (i.e., in Korea) all reflected and reinforced the micropolitics of an informal empire. Indeed, for political leaders in Japan, Korea, and Taiwan, closeness to the United States was an important metric of domestic political legitimacy. These are all telltale signs of an informal empire.

The powerplay argument also has relevance for the literature on network theory. One of the primary propositions of this body of literature is that an actor's power and influence are relational rather than just material. The unit of analysis is not material power capabilities, but the position one occupies in a network. Well-situated or strategically placed actors in any organization or network can exert disproportionate influence derivative of their position.[6] In this regard, the powerplay argument demonstrates how US hegemony and power was not simply material but also relational. That is, by positioning itself as the central economic and military hub among a group of disconnected states in Asia, the United States rendered itself indispensable to the region's stability and welfare. The United States made itself the exclusive partner of countries that were distrustful of one another, which afforded it a great deal of leeway and advantage in these relationships.

Network power is also sometimes operationalized as bargaining strength. A central "node" (state) with interconnections within a cluster of states and between clusters has bargaining strength granted to it solely by its position. This was where the United States sat in Asia, allowing it great leverage in negotiations with and between its Asian partners and allies. Moreover, the states in the network lacked "exit" options or the possibility to "delink."[7] The existence of outside options is an important factor in assessing the network power of any given state in a networked system. If there are no exit options for states, or few opportunities to delink from a network, the power of the strategically placed states increases. This was the position of the United States in Asia under Cold War bipolarity. With few alternative options for these non-communist states, the United States was granted a great deal of power and influence over their decisions and development, thus making the system durable. In the end, the strength and durability of the US position was overdetermined.[8] It exercised both supreme material power and network power.

The powerplay argument also challenges traditional propositions held out by international relations theory about the "alliance security dilemma" of abandonment and entrapment.[9] The prevailing causal proposition is that a country who fears that an ally might pull it into an unwanted dispute will adopt distancing strategies—such as weakening commitments, reducing aid, or even abrogating the alliance contract—to avoid entrapment. The powerplay argument shows that, on the contrary, states may *tighten* rather than loosen the alliance in order to exert more direct restraint and stop the ally from taking undesirable actions. In this regard, I highlight the active rather than passive strategies for dealing with entrapment fears.

Finally, the powerplay argument has predictive implications for the institutional design of Asia. It explains that the US alliance system, as an informal empire, has endured for so long because of material and social power. But my argument also suggests that the factors that led to the establishment of the bilateral alliance system are not as relevant today. Although the deterrence element is still important, relatively speaking, the control element of US alliances in Asia is not as compelling in modern strategic thinking. Concerns about overzealous smaller allies entrapping America in a bigger war that animated US Cold War thinking are not as operative today. Connections among the spokes in the form of bilateral and multilateral institutions have sprouted today in a way not present during the Cold War. Moreover, these interconnections are encouraged by the United States in a way that was also not the case during the Cold War. As the aide to the Secretary of State suggested, the security multilateralization of Asia is an idea whose time has come.

THE PUZZLE

What is striking about the puzzle of Asia's security bilateralism and Europe's multilateralism are the similarities in structural and substructural conditions.[10] Both regions experienced the defeat of a rising hegemonic power and witnessed a potential power vacuum at the end of World War II. Both regions faced a proximate communist threat. Both regions saw the United States extend security guarantees to allies against this threat. Both regions focused on economic development and recovery as a top postwar priority. And two dominant strategic beliefs informed US policymakers about both regions: First, the importance of constructing a multilateral world order, infused with US desires for collective security and representative institutions; and second, the importance of the domino theory—i.e., preventing the loss of even one intrinsically insignificant country to communism because of the potential cascading effect this could have on other countries falling to communism.

Despite these similar conditions and congruent intentions by the United States to design security institutions in postwar Europe and Asia, Washington acts, as one author described, with "half-hearted commitment" and "indifference" to one region while it dives into a "forceful policy" seeking "enduring peace" in the other.[11] One region turns into a collective defense organization while the other does not. By the early 1950s, a twelve-member multilateral security organization is institutionalized in Europe with all the bells and whistles—a bureaucratic apparatus, integrated military planning, and central command structure. Security in Asia, however, is characterized by a series of bilateral alliances—known as the "San Francisco system" or hub and spokes—centered on the United States with no apparent connections between them. The United States independently inked bilateral security treaties with the Philippines (August 1951), Japan (September 1951), South Korea (October 1953), Formosa/Taiwan (December 1954), and a single trilateral arrangement with Australia and New Zealand (September 1951). The exception to this in form was the Southeast Asian Treaty Organization (SEATO), created in 1954 as an inclusive regional security apparatus. But in substance there was no collective security provision (such as NATO's Article V) regarding an attack on one member as constituting an attack on all members, and the power disparities between the United States and these small Southeast Asian nations rendered irrelevant the notion of a multilateral institution with all members sharing a seat at the table with America. Because each state preferred bilateral relations with the

United States, experts assessed that SEATO was "little more than a traditional alliance, embodying none of the multilateral features of NATO."[12] These American-Asian bilateral alliances were not only discrete, but on the whole they each exhibited little institutional structure and enjoyed less joint military planning than their European counterparts.[13]

Two questions emerge from this puzzle. First, why does bilateralism take hold in Asia as opposed to a more sophisticated form of multilateralism as the dominant security structure? And second, if the answer to the first question is that the United States intended for there to be two disparate designs, this still raises the question of *why* the United States preferred bilateralism rather than multilateralism in Asia?

EXPLANATIONS

Power and Threats

Realist arguments trace the differences in the institutional designs of Asia and Europe to the explanatory variables of threats, geography, hegemonic power, and relative costs.[14] With threats and geography in particular, the nature of the external threat faced in Europe determined the type of alliances that were needed. The United States and its allies faced 200 Soviet ground divisions, realists might argue, on a contiguous continental piece of territory, with a clear dividing line between the two sides on the German front. This combination of threat and geography required a collective, multilateral response—the United States had neither the resources nor the manpower to prepare for such a contingency on its own. The nature of the military-operational imperatives therefore determined the shape of the alliance. In Asia, by contrast, there was no similar military contingency in the Soviet Far East as that in Western Europe.[15] There were land contingencies in Northeast Asia (Korea) and in Southeast Asia (Indochina), but there was also a maritime theater in Northeast Asia (the Taiwan Straits) as well as allied responsibilities as far as the South Pacific Ocean. Such a situation was not conducive to a single overarching collective umbrella alliance.

Realists may also point to regional hegemony as an explanatory variable.[16] The United States had no feasible incentive for building multilateralism in Asia, having established itself as the supreme power in the region at the end of World War II. It had just forced an unconditional surrender by the rising challenger in the region, Japan; militarily occupied the country; and established itself as a key underwriter of security

for Asia. Subjecting this hegemonic position to a multilateral committee of powers was neither desirable (given all the costs borne by the
United States) nor feasible (given the absence of any comparable power
equivalents).

Realism could also point to relative cost concerns regarding nuclear
weapons and military doctrine to explain bilateralism in Asia.[17] In particular, the Eisenhower administration sought to bolster America's security guarantees embodied in the Truman Doctrine with a "New Look"
strategy that featured the deterrent threat of massive retaliation. This
doctrine, combined with a mandate for fiscal conservatism, inclined the
United States away from the need for a costly and major integration of
the regional security architecture in Asia. Bilateral alliances were cost-
efficient in a way that multilateralism was not. They did enough to show
the US commitment to defend and deter, reinforced by the doctrine of
massive retaliation.[18]

These realist explanations are persuasive; however, they tend to reinforce the puzzle rather than solve it. First, if external threats are the primary determinant of the alliance's design (i.e., multilateral or bilateral),
then this should have had a somewhat uniform rather than disparate
effect across the two regions. Granted, the Soviet threat was much more
in the face of Europeans on the ground than in Asia, where the threat
was diversely continental and maritime.[19] But as Adlai Stevenson noted,
the United States clearly saw the alliance network in Asia as focused on
the Soviet Union as well.[20] While there was no geographic dividing line
in Asia as clear as that in Germany, the United States did draw—in Dean
Acheson's famous 1950 "defense perimeter" speech—a clear line of defense across the continental and maritime areas, defining American strategic interests in Asia. Moreover, the United States faced another threat
in China. Not only did the Chinese present a ground contingency that
the United States had to prepare for, but the threat was an existential one
for US allies, demonstrated by the Chinese intervention in the Korean
War. The point here is that arguments about large operational ground
contingencies determining the collective shape of alliance designs in Europe should have yielded similar predictions in Asia, where a ground war
was *actually fought* rather than just planned for.

In this regard then, the Korean War poses an extremely perplexing
puzzle. The Korean War was the one place where the budding Cold War
turned hot. By the fifth month of the war in 1950, the United States
found itself fighting a ground contingency on the Asian continent. This
crystallized the existential communist threat for the United States and

prompted a wide-ranging security multilateralization in Europe, reinte-gration of Germany, and militarization of NATO. Yet it did *not* lead to a similar multilateral design in Asia. The realist irony therefore is that the one military contingency that deepened the coherence of NATO as a collective defense body took place in Asia, not Europe. Furthermore, if the predominant fear among US planners across *both* regions was the domino theory, then the attack against South Korea should have led to somewhat similar responses in the two regions. Yet the United States re-sponded to the same core security event in disparate ways across the two regions. Realism is certainly helpful, but there appears to be more at play in understanding these differences than just threats.

Finally, if realists point to the cost-effectiveness of the massive retalia-tion strategy during the Eisenhower years or to US regional hegemony as the reasons that multilateralism did not take root in Asia, this begs the question as to why a similar outcome did not obtain in Europe where both variables were also present. If the United States thought that secu-rity bilateralism was the more affordable option, then why was this not the case for Europe as well, where the United States was underwriting huge costs associated with the Marshall Plan and European reconstruc-tion? From the end of the Second World War, through the Marshall Plan, and up to 1953, the United States poured nearly $25 billion into Europe. Given that in Asia the corresponding figure was just shy of $6 billion, it is hard to argue that the United States was primarily concerned with relative costs.[21] Realists might respond that it served US hegemonic in-terests to administer bilateralism in Asia and multilateralism in Europe. But this still begs the question as to *why* the United States perceived this balance to be optimal.

Economic Development and Institutions

A liberalist interpretation would likely trace the variation in security structures in Asia and Europe to several variables, such as economic development, regime type, and the absolute gains-motivated interests of states in the region.[22] First, levels of economic development in Asia were very low. Despite the destruction of the war, Europe was still a global economic powerhouse. The combined GDP of the twelve largest Western European countries was equivalent to $967 billion in 1946, and would reach $2.1 trillion by 1960.[23] The comparative figure of the United States' East Asian allies and partners was just $140 billion in 1946 ($28 billion without Japan), rising to $492 billion in 1960 ($117 billion without

Japan).[24] These figures show that although there was a fair amount of growth in Asia, aside from Japan there was very little economic heft. This was not conducive to an intraregional trading order which would have been an important spur to greater multilateralism in the region. In Europe, the European Coal and Steel Community (ECSC) was created in 1951 with the distinct purposes of revitalizing the member economies, of eventually creating a single market, and of peacefully uniting the continent more generally. In Asia, these sorts of multilateral economic groupings proved to be a much harder sell.

Low levels of economic development in Asia, liberals may also argue, reinforced bilateralism because most of the regional powers were able to secure their material needs from the United States alone. For example, between 1948 and 1960, US-Japan trade annually averaged nearly 28 percent of Japan's total.[25] Between 1953 and 1960, US trade comprised nearly 32 percent of Taiwan's total and approximately 45 percent of South Korea's.[26] There was neither an incentive nor any likelihood of success in venturing outside the bilateral relationship to others in the region for help. In Western Europe, for instance, the intraregional trade volume steadily increased from $8.5 billion in 1948 up to more than $29 billion by 1960. Intraregional Asian trade, by comparison, started out at a paltry $167 million and capped out at just over $1.2 billion over the same period.[27] The total volume of aggregate trade during these years was nearly twenty-five times greater in Europe than in Asia.[28] The priority of Asian countries at the end of World War II was economic reconstruction, and only one partner mattered.[29]

Augmenting this disincentive was the wide variety of regime types in the region. Unlike the liberal democracies of Western Europe, the types of domestic political systems in Asia ranged widely from authoritarian to democratic. Japan, for starters, was a full-blown constitutional democracy by the end of the occupation in 1952. Korea and Taiwan, on the other hand, were fairly repressive authoritarian regimes right up until the 1980s and 1990s. Thailand's record was mixed in this period, but it tended to lean toward authoritarianism. And the Philippines was similarly mixed, but it leaned toward democracy.[30] Unlike the community of liberal democracies in Europe, the diversity of regime types in Asia made it that much more difficult to organize in a multilateral fashion.[31]

Liberal theorists would also note that any regional institution's success rests on the enthusiasm or shared interests of its membership. Arguably while this existed in Europe, no similar support was exhibited by Asian nation-states. The reasons for this ambivalence were many, but the most prominent was postcolonialism. That is, governments that had just been liberated from Japanese colonial rule, and prior to that European colonial rule, were in no mood to surrender their newly won sovereignty to some larger regional body. Asian states also harbored a deep distrust of re-integrating Japan into the region, which naturally would have had to play a large role in any regional security organization.[32]

Liberalism is useful in understanding the complexities of postwar security institution-building in Asia, but there is the issue of relative consistency—that is, many of the impediments to multilateral cooperation in Asia cited could be equally applicable to Europe, yet we see dissimilar outcomes. For example, Europe lay in total destruction after the war and sought a great deal more support from the United States than its Asian counterparts. As noted previously, from the end of the war up until 1953 the amount of US aid to Europe was more than four times greater than that to Asia. In addition, the distrust of postwar Germany by Europeans was no less vehement than that experienced in Asia vis-à-vis Japan. As French Foreign Minister Robert Schumann told his National Assembly in 1949, the question of German accession to NATO "cannot be raised. . . . Germany has no army and may not have one. She has no weapons and will not be allowed to acquire them."[33] Some in Britain were equally wary, with the Chancellor of the Duchy of Lancaster arguing in 1948 that a rearmed West Germany would constitute "the greatest danger to world peace."[34] But Germany saw far more successful reintegration in a regional security organization.[35] It eventually acceded to NATO in 1955 and would go on to become the conventional fulcrum of European defense, maintaining about 500,000 troops from the mid-1960s onward—among the greatest forces in Western Europe.[36]

Contrary to the conventional wisdom, the absence of multilateralism in Asia was not for lack of supporters of the idea. There were countries in the region that were interested in building some form of regional security. Regional players voiced proposals during the Vietnam War in the late 1960s and early 1970s, for example, to turn the Vietnam War allies' conference as well as a regional cultural organization known as the Asian-Pacific Council (ASPAC) into a "PATO-like" organization.[37] The fact that such proposals never took root is puzzling. Finally, regime theory would predict that hegemonic concentrations of power should be conducive to multilateralism.[38] But this argument also lacks relative consistency. While it can explain the creation of NATO, the European Common Market, and GATT, a similar if not more concentrated distribution of power existed in Asia without similar outcomes.[39]

But what is most puzzling is the question of American volition.[40] While many assert that the United States chose to pursue one form of security in Europe and not in Asia, they cannot explain why the choice was made. John Ruggie, for example, writing in 1997 on the origins of multilateralism, stated that the United States chose not to pursue multi-lateralism in Asia because "the situation on the ground there made that impossible," but does not delve deeper to explain this American choice.[41] Robert Gilpin (though not a liberal) wrote in 1989 that the United States always subordinated the Pacific to the Atlantic in every aspect of economic and political affairs.[42] Liberalism argues that multilateralism is a higher form of social organization that offers efficiency gains (e.g., transparency, reduced transaction costs, economies of scale, credible commitments, rules, and information).[43] If this requires on the part of the United States more cost, more input, and more attention, then this begs the question: Why did the United States pursue this laborious effort in Europe and not Asia? John Ikenberry's answer is that the United States made the effort in Europe because it wanted more out of the European experiment than it wanted out of Asia. The United States therefore was willing to construct multilateral institutions in Europe that would allow its power to be constrained by these institutions in return for more benefits from Europe. This was not the case in Asia: "Conditions did not favor Atlantic-style multilateralism. . . . the United States was dominant in East Asia yet wanted less out of the region, so the United States found it less necessary to give up policy autonomy in exchange for institutional cooperation there. . . . To get what it wanted, the United States had to bargain with the Europeans, and this meant agreeing to institutionally restrain and commit its power."[44]

Ikenberry is correct in explaining how postwar multilateralism in trans-Atlantic relations required more effort and compromise on the part of the United States. In this sense, the United States exercised a deliberate form of self-restraint as the wartime victor, which enabled it to create a stable, rule-abiding order. His depiction of the postwar strategy in Asia deserves closer examination, however. Did the United States really pursue bilateralism in Asia because it "wanted less" from Asian countries? The tradable "commodity" in building postwar order that Ikenberry describes is essentially control. He argues that the United States surrendered some of this political control in order to gain institutional cooperation from European allies. The obverse of this logic is that the United States chose bilateralism in Asia not because it "wanted less" from Asia but because it wanted and needed *more* political control than in Europe.

Why then was the United States willing to concede a degree of policy autonomy in Europe but not in Asia? It is this aspect of America's postwar order-building that requires further attention.

Distrust and Racism

Constructivism would attribute the absence of a NATO-like security organization in Asia not to issues of power, but to identity.[45] In particular, countries held a deep historical distrust of Japan as part of their postwar, postcolonial, nationalist identity that trumped all incentive-based arguments for re-integrating the former adversary as part of a regional order.[46] Even if there was American interest in cultivating regional security institutions in Asia, as John Foster Dulles observed in a *Foreign Affairs* article in January 1952, Asian states "have memories of Japanese aggression which are so vivid that they are reluctant to create a Mutual Security Pact which will include Japan."[47]

Undeniably, Asian nations were wary of working with Japan after World War II; however, again like both the realist and liberal arguments, there is the issue of relative consistency. Europeans faced a similar situation regarding Germany in 1945, as one author described, where a capitalist union of democracies was "unimaginable" and Franco-German cooperation as its pillar was "even more remote."[48] But there, the postwar regional re-integration project was a priority of the United States. Germany had to be brought back into the fold in Western Europe for the sake of stability and order. Why not a similar priority for Japan in Asia? Second, as noted earlier, while not denying that Asian countries certainly distrusted Japan after the war, this did not stop some countries like Taiwan and South Korea from advocating an Asian form of NATO during the Cold War years. During the Korean War, for example, Taipei offered to join forces with the United States, the ROK, and Japan in a collective anti-communist alliance. But, as Miles Kahler and others have observed, rather than adopt the idea, the United States decidedly resisted it.[49]

Constructivists and social historians offer race as a related explanation for the disparity in security structures. Although Europe and Asia lay in ruins after World War II, what distinguished the former theater was an expectation or belief that one was dealing with "grown-ups" in Europe rather than the "children" in Asia. European powers were assumed to re-emerge eventually as great powers with which the United States still shared a common civilization, and therefore these states would be able to manage a more complex organizational design that assumed responsibilities and sophistication on the part of member states.[50] No such expectations, however, existed with regard to states in Asia.[51] As Blum describes, Americans viewed postwar Asia as "foreign," almost alien, and further down on the international relations food chain:

> American politicians and diplomats, who were of European ancestry, who had occasionally traveled to Europe, and who were familiar with its languages and culture, felt much more comfortable dealing with the problems of Western Europe. Their images and understanding of Asia were much more vague . . . They watched Asia, and especially China worriedly, but held back from taking an activist role.[52]

The small, postcolonial powers were not perceived to be capable of handling the responsibilities of multilateralism. A State Department memo from 1953 encapsulates these views:

> [T]he plain fact is that any Western joint action in Asia must carry with it the clear implication that we do not take the Asians very seriously and in fact regard them as inferiors. We should not be able to avoid this implication because that is indeed our attitude.[53]

For constructivists and social historians, racism could not be disentangled from distrust in these views. Europe was devastated, yet would rise from the ashes again. As Assistant Secretary of State Will Clayton stated unabashedly in a 1949 testimony on NATO, "my idea would be that in the beginning the [postwar] union would be composed of all countries that have our ideas and ideals of freedom and that are composed of the white race."[54] Those with a common civilizational rooting could be trusted to work with the United States. Asia, by contrast, was devastated and in need of direction: "The image of Asia, racist and utterly uninformed, was of a region with vast resources and opportunities, populated by dutiful and cringing peoples who followed white leadership."[55] The idea of small, yellow and brown, uneducated people sharing a multilateral table as equals with Ivy League–educated East Coast intellectuals was beyond comprehension (Acheson once testified that the United States was contending with "simple and mostly illiterate people" in Asia).[56] As Hemmer and Katzenstein note, "In the case of Asia, these various affinities [shared with Europeans] and trust were absent, religion and democratic values were shared only in a few cases, and race was invoked as a powerful force separating the United States from Asia. The US preference for multilateral or bilateral security arrangements followed from these different constellations."[57]

There is no denying racism in these early views of Asia and the idea that this racism may have fed deep-seeded feelings of Asians as distrustful partners.[58] The problem with this argument, however, is that the puzzle it explains is *not* the multilateralism puzzle. Arguments about racism help to explain why the "Europe-firsters" carried the day over "Asia-firsters" inside of the US government. But there is not necessarily a direct causal link between this relative prioritization of regions and the design of security institutions that follow. Social historians have utilized the race argument to explain, for example, why Dean Acheson as Secretary of State was unapologetic about his Atlanticist leanings and his conspicuous dearth of interest in Asia. To the extent that he cared about Asia, it was only to beat back Republican criticisms that his State Department had botched China policy. Acheson made eleven trips to Europe but none to Asia during his term, and those within the US government who pleaded for greater attention to Asia in postwar planning went unheard. Nevertheless this variable does not explain why multilateralism was preferred in Europe but not Asia. The fact that Western Europe was prioritized over Asia does not logically mean that a different type of security institution was to emerge in each part of the world. After establishing their argument about the collective identities of the two regions, Hemmer and Katzenstein even admit that "available evidence is relatively sketchy and permits only cautious inferences,"[59] and at best one could surmise that the institutional variation in security design may have flowed from these disparate identities.[60] Despite these best efforts by astute scholars, ignorance or prejudice as causal variables only gets as far as regional priorities of the United States between Europe and Asia.

Finally, while all of these explanations are helpful, none of them speak to the fundamental and human element of uncertainty that the United States faced in Asia after World War II. The future path seemed very unclear. The United States had just fought a bloody war in the Pacific with a brutal enemy in Japan to an unconditional surrender in August 1945, but lacked any clear direction or conviction about what was to follow in terms of the relationship between Asia's only great power and the region. A plethora of new nation-states were emerging out of an era of European and Japanese imperialism without a clear organizing structure for the region. Unlike in Europe, the United States had to contend with two significant actors in East Asia—the Republic of China and Republic of

Korea—both of which were divided countries with authoritarian leaders embroiled in civil wars (against mainland China and North Korea respectively). Because leaders are much less likely to compromise in civil conflicts than in international ones,[61] Washington could predict with less certainty whether these countries would follow the dictates of a multilateral grouping, especially when their interests were far from those of the coalition.[62] The most proximate counterpart in Europe was a divided Germany, but there was less concern about adventurist leaders who might take unauthorized actions. The process of dealing with a postwar Germany was much more carefully considered by the European powers than was the case for China or Korea after 1945. Further clouding the picture in Asia was the problem of Japan. Washington knew that the loser in the Pacific War would eventually re-emerge as the region's only great power; yet, how to deal with this eventuality was unclear, especially when most of Japan's former colonies in the region harbored intense distrust, if not hatred, of the country's playing a larger role again.

The point of this exposition is not to argue that all prior explanations are incorrect. On the contrary, they all contribute pieces of an eclectic answer to the puzzle.[63] My effort is to use the powerplay variable to help complete the story of why disparate postwar institutional designs emerged in the Asian and European regions. The United States would deliberately choose a unique design for Asia based on a desire to control the environment and reduce uncertainty. This story will be told in the pages that follow, but understanding why states use alliance institutions to manage risk in their external security environment is important, and will be dealt with in the next chapter. Chapter 3 will provide an overview of US grand strategy in Asia after the Second World War. This chapter provides the context for the three case study chapters on Taiwan (chapter 4), Korea (chapter 5), and Japan (chapter 6). Chapter 7 is devoted to addressing counter-arguments and alternative explanations to my powerplay thesis. Chapter 8 first looks at the generalizability of the powerplay argument. It then takes the story of US alliances in Asia to the present day, assessing the resiliency of the American hub and spokes network in the context of new forms of regional architecture emerging in Asia.

2

THE ARGUMENT: POWERPLAY

I argue that bilateralism rather than multilateralism emerged in Asia as the dominant security design because of the "powerplay" strategy behind US alliance formation. At the broadest level, the powerplay relates to strategic choices made by states about what types of institutional designs best achieve their security goals. Every state will have a set of priorities in managing their security needs. One assumes that at the top of this list is protection of the homeland, but the priorities that follow are not necessarily uniform across states. Some states, for example, may see base access from allies as a critical goal. Others might see preservation of economic ties, security of natural resources, or political reputation as critical in managing security. How such priorities figure into the design of security institutions will depend on a host of factors including geography, ambition, economics, and the domestic politics of the countries.[1] The powerplay relates to a state that sees *control* of its environment and, in particular, control of its ally as critical to its security needs. The key condition for control to be a top priority, as discussed throughout this book, is when a state must hedge against *overdependence* and *entrapment*. This priority of control, in turn, will shape the choice of institution (bilateral or multilateral) that states prefer to manage their security.

Paul Schroeder once described alliances as *pactum de contrahendo* (pacts of restraint).[2] Powerplay is the creation of an alliance tie for the purpose of inhibiting the ally's unilateral actions. I argue that in East Asia, the United States created alliances not just for containment, but also for the constraint of potential "rogue" allies from undertaking adventuristic behavior that might drag the United States into an unwanted larger military contingency in the region.[3] In this sense, the powerplay highlights how alliances are multifaceted institutions that protect one's homeland, but also constitute tools of risk management.[4] Particularly for great powers, alliances can be used to deal with uncertainty; to mitigate mistrust of potential partners; to create norms and rules of behavior among its security partners; and to impose a pseudo-hierarchical order conducive to the needs of the state.

Bargains and control have a symbiotic relationship. We seek bargains to benefit ourselves, but the deals we make also generate a desire for control so that there are no ill effects of the bargain. Similarly in alliances, when states make security bargains with other allies, the bargain creates dual types of pathological behavior by allies—undercommitment and overdependence.[5]

Alliance Pathologies

Undercommitment is behavior by an ally that suggests it will not uphold its end of a bargain.[6] Undercommitment sounds like abandonment as the concept was first introduced by Snyder in 1984, but the two are different.[7] Undercommitment precedes abandonment, and is the compulsive and generally undesirable behavior of one ally, which creates abandonment fears in the other. Different variables impact undercommitment and the credibility of an ally's signals, including regime type (democracies tend to make more credible commitments than non-democracies), leadership, and reputation (leaders who value reputation will make more credible commitments).[8]

Undercommitment in one ally engenders anxieties of abandonment in the other. Nation-states suffering abandonment fears cope with this anxiety through a variety of strategies. They might try "adhesion strategies"—that is, to draw closer to the under-committed ally and elicit reciprocity. They might revert to internal balancing, or in extreme cases, exit the alliance rather than be caught in an abandonment scenario. States might also hedge by using adhesion strategies with the ally and appeasement strategies with the adversary in order to avert an abandonment scenario. In all cases, undercommitment displayed by one ally would be accompanied by "whining" or complaints by the other that the ally is not fully committed to the relationship.[9]

The other pathological behavior created by the alliance bargain is overdependence. Sometimes states enter into security pacts that generate overzealous alliance commitments. Of course, there is a degree of reciprocity in security obligations in an alliance treaty. Without such a norm, an alliance compact would not be worth its weight in paper.

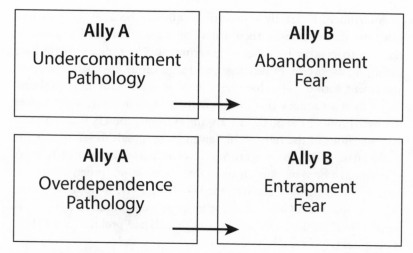

FIGURE 2.I. Alliance pathologies

Displaying a credibility of commitment is not just beneficial to a partner; it is beneficial to one's own security as it will likely translate into a sturdier commitment from the partner, which then enhances deterrence and defense against the adversary.[10]

But even good and trustworthy allies may become overly dependent on a relationship. This creates a moral hazard problem where the ally expects maximal commitments from its partner, thus pressing the partner into a bigger operation than the partner signed up for. Overdependence is different from entrapment and precedes it. It is compulsive and undesirable behavior that manifests itself in adventuristic, difficult, or expensive actions by the overdependent state that might partially or wholly discount the value of the alliance for the partner. Figure 2.1 displays the relationship between alliance pathologies and abandonment/entrapment fears.

Determinants of Overdependence

There are several drivers of overdependence pathologies. In general, the more one invests in an alliance, for example, the more likely one will exhibit overdependence. These investments could be in the form of political capital, large-scale military commitments, or massive economic stakes such that one has poured so much equity into the partner that one cannot allow the alliance to fail. Similarly, if a particular branch

of government is heavily vested in the alliance because the pact provides specific advantages, then it may be more committed to the relationship than other branches of government. The military might have
basing rights, overflight privileges, and a generous host nation support
agreement with the ally that might make it more committed to the alliance than an agency that does not enjoy the same privileges. Before
the overthrow of the Shah in Iran, for example, the US Pentagon was
very solicitous of the relationship given its proposals to sell fighter jets
to the Shah. USAID by contrast was less committed because of Tehran's
reluctance to heed its calls for development assistance programs for the
country.[11] During the Cold War, the US military's desire for basing privileges in Spain and Greece made it much more committed to these relationships than the State Department, which had problems with these
governments' policies.[12]

The character of your ally can generate overdependence pathologies
in the relationship. A greedy ally who is unafraid to make grand claims
of your obligations to it; an ally who is emotionally hog-tied to the alliance rather than rationally motivated; an ally who has "penetrated" your
system, enlisting domestic lobbies, big business, ethnic groups, or other
social actors—these all reflect overdependent behaviors that create entrapment fears in the other ally.[13] Regarding the penetration factor, the
US-Israeli relationship is cited by some as an example of this, or the Taiwan lobby in the 1950s in the United States (discussed in the next chapter).
These activities may be a natural part of alliances between democracies
with their porous political institutions, and can serve to give a security
alliance a deeper foundation in the socioeconomic roots of both countries, but such penetration could also be a driver of overdependence.[14]

Overdependence may correlate positively with power asymmetries
in alliances, all other variables held equal.[15] Because smaller states are
less concerned about how their actions affect the international system,
they may be more willing to use the alliance to pursue narrow-minded
agendas that put commitment pressures on the larger partner. Smaller
states may have more at stake in the alliance and therefore try to suck all
they can out of the larger power. Smaller states may also have the leeway
both at home and in the international system to behave more rashly,
knowing that they can rely on the patron and thus tax the patron's commitment capacities.[16] As discussed in chapter 5, South Korea undertook
deliberate efforts to sabotage US armistice negotiations with the communists during the Korean War out of the leadership's parochial desires
to reunify the peninsula. But the United States was focused on ending

hostilities in Korea and focusing its Cold War priorities on defending Western Europe. Washington therefore countenanced some outrageous behavior by the South prior to formation of the alliance in 1953 in order to achieve its broader goals. In general, big patrons are more concerned about such compulsive overdependent pathologies by small allies, while small allies are more concerned about undercommitment pathologies by big allies.[17] Patron allies are less worried about undercommitment behavior by the smaller ally because the benefits of this commitment are marginal. In some extreme cases, small, desperate countries can use the threat of their own collapse to compel inordinate political and economic commitments from a larger patron. This "blackmail out of weakness," as Keohane once described it, can be effective when the patron state believes that the smaller state's demise is intrinsically unbeneficial to the patron or is somehow strategically compromising.[18] The quintessential example of this has been China's tortured relationship with North Korea since the end of the Cold War in which Pyongyang has used its weakness and possible collapse as leverage to extort assistance from Beijing.

The obverse of the "blackmail out of weakness" pathology that can generate overdependence in alliance politics is when an ally becomes obsessed with amassing as many alliance contracts as possible. Once referred to as the "collector's approach," an ally seeks these commitments based on the premise that the more states that the ally can sign on, the more countries that become committed to the ally's well-being, principles, and policies in the international system.[19]

Another condition under which a larger patron might exhibit overdependence to a smaller ally is when the patron holds beliefs that the ally is a critical piece of a larger strategic equation. In certain instances, the demise of that smaller ally could be seen as connected to a broader chain of alliance failures. During the Cold War, this strategic belief was known as the domino theory, and in some quarters of international relations, as the "interdependence of commitments theory."[20] In either case, the idea is that overdependence occurs because of the perceived need to hold on to every ally, lest the loss of one leads to challenges by the adversary against the others.

It should be noted that overdependence is different from loyalty. Loyalty is when an ally supports the policies, statements, or actions of its partner. For any state, a good ally is a loyal one. A loyal ally, even if she has diverging policies, will try to suppress criticism, support the partner, and play down any perceived differences in positions. Loyalty does not equate with overdependence in security bargains.[21] Rather, attribution errors related to perceived loyalty or disloyalty can be a source of over-dependence. Every alliance bargain has a different psychology attached to it. If one ally consistently mistrusts her partner, then she might discount signs of alliance loyalty as being situationally motivated. That is, she interprets loyalty signals by the ally as being merely compelled by the circumstances (e.g., "the ally had no choice but to be loyal"). The distrustful ally might attribute signs of allied disloyalty as being dispositionally motivated. That is, disloyalty signals by the ally register more strongly because she perceives these as reflecting the true intentions of the ally (e.g., "disloyalty signals are not compelled by the situation but reflect her true intentions"). The permeation of an alliance relationship by such attribution errors carry the potential for overdependence as the ally must constantly prove loyalty in the face of these biases.[22]

Overdependence is different from free-riding. Free-riding occurs when a security bargain is afflicted by one or several allies not contributing to the alliance even though they need it.[23] When both allies do this, you have free-riding, but not overdependence. When one ally free-rides while the other provides, then you have the potential for overdependence.

Overdependence and Powerplay

Overdependence in one partner creates anxieties of entrapment in the ally (figure 2.1). Entrapment is when a security commitment pulls an ally into contingencies that do not overlap with or only partially overlap with the ally's security interests.[24] Figure 2.2 shows how a state becomes entrapped by overdependence pathologies of the ally. First, the state's entry to the ally's conflict is compelled by the letter and deed of the treaty obligation. Second, the state's entry is compelled by credibility and reputational needs that may have been put at stake by the ally's overzealous behavior toward the adversary.[25] Third, the state may become a target of the ally's adversary because of the ally's overzealousness.[26] Fourth, the state may find itself pushed into the ally's conflict by domestic lobbying groups friendly to the ally's cause, even if it is not in the state's immediate interests.[27] The literature is mixed on how often entrapment occurs. Some believe that alliances reduce entrapment because they deter adversaries and reassure allies, thereby preventing any latent conflicts from escalating.[28] But others believe alliances can be misinterpreted by allies and adversaries as blank checks, thereby creating more insecurity, preemptive or preventive incentives by either the ally or adversary to act first, and misperception spirals.[29] Table 2.1 summarizes the alliance

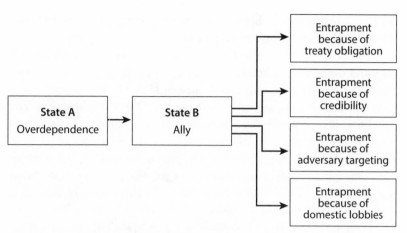

FIGURE 2.2. Overdependence and entrapment

TABLE 2.1. ABANDONMENT AND ENTRAPMENT

	OVER-DEPENDENCE BY B	UNDER-COMMITMENT BY B
Entrapment fear by A	High	Low
Abandonment fear by A	Low	High

pathologies as I have described them, and how they generate abandonment and entrapment anxieties in alliance relationships.

How do states deal with the entrapment anxieties that arise from overdependence? According to the literature, states deal with entrapment in several ways. They may seek any combination of distancing strategies that include abrogation, voice, or hedging strategies. Distancing generally means to attenuate the alliance obligation through "loopholes" or "escape clauses" that set out conditions under which the ally would not receive support.[30] Abrogation or "side-stepping" is an extreme action meant to cut cleanly from the alliance or decline to offer support in order to shed any unwanted security commitments.[31] Voice strategies mean criticizing the ally privately for its actions, and, if necessary, also going public with the complaint. Hedging means to strike a deal with the adversary in order to balance out an overzealous ally. This is a risky strategy because it might also embolden the adversary if the adversary feels that the state's alliance commitment is weak.[32]

This book introduces another strategy to deal with entrapment anxieties and over-reliance, known as the powerplay strategy. That is, sometimes a state will deal with entrapment anxieties not by distancing or hedging, but by drawing even closer to the ally. The purpose of this "doubling down" on an overdependent ally is to exercise control over the ally's actions. The core idea is to leverage the dependence of the overzealous ally to insure against one's entrapment. Distancing may alleviate one's entrapment fears, but it also carries the risk of losing control over the overzealous ally's actions. Deepening the alliance tie creates more dependence, and also more control over the ally.

The literature on alliance control and overdependence is not terribly deep.[33] Morrow explained how asymmetric alliance bargains between larger and smaller allies usually entail an exchange of security (provided by the patron) for a degree of autonomy (given up by the smaller power), which make alliance institutions instruments of control.[34] During the Cold War, when the United States associated all security challenges in the periphery with challenges in the core conflict with the Soviet Union, there was a body of work that spoke to how small states exploited alliance commitments of big power patrons precisely because the bipolar structure compelled big states to overvalue these small alliances.[35] In the post–Cold War, Ikenberry, Lake, and a few others looked directly at the choice of different institutional forms to manage or control security relations.[36] Beckley has studied how alliances can both restrain the great power patron from entanglement in some instances and permit the great power to restrain its allies in other cases.[37] There has also been a small body of statistical work looking at the efficacy of alliances as conflict management mechanisms.[38]

Taken together, these authors and I show that alliances are multidimensional security bargains in which alliance managers deal with multiple competing tendencies. Every alliance manager must be attuned to overdependence pathologies. On the one hand, one does not want to be entrapped by the partner. On the other, one does not want to convey too weak or conditional a commitment such that it weakens the deterrent effect of the alliance (vis-à-vis the adversary), causes the partner to exit the alliance, or causes the partner to appease the adversary. What the powerplay argument adds to this conversation is that it highlights a counterintuitive method of dealing with an ally's overdependence pathology that is often overlooked. If the general tendency is for states to distance themselves from an overzealous ally, according to Snyder, the powerplay argument shows that states may actually do the opposite when sensing overdependence. That is, they may draw closer to the ally in order to restrain and control its behavior precisely to avoid an entrapment scenario. Under what conditions does this happen?

Three simple conditions are necessary for a state to choose "adhesion" (control) rather than distancing to manage the risks associated with entrapment and overdependence: (1) external threat; (2) domestic legitimacy of the target state; and (3) power asymmetries between the allies. There must be an external threat against which the alliance is directed, which provides the raison d'être for the alliance. The powerplay motive, however, operates implicitly rather than explicitly in the alliance contract. And it does not apply to all alliances. The nature of the ally's domestic politics and leadership is an important condition. Simply put, if the ally has a propensity to get herself into trouble or undertake reckless actions, then the powerplay motive becomes operative. This propensity for trouble could be a function of domestic legitimacy problems, civil conflicts, and economic difficulties, among other issues.

In America's European alliances, for example, the defense and deterrence rationales were operative, but the powerplay rationale was not because there was no concern about smaller countries lashing out against the Soviet Union and entrapping the United States in a larger, perhaps nuclear, war. In Asia, by contrast, there were real concerns about unpredictable authoritarian leaders dragging the United States into a larger war with either China or the Soviet Union. As will be discussed in later chapters, this variable was especially salient in Asia because there were two allies who were embroiled in civil wars that were embedded in a larger Cold War context. President Dwight Eisenhower's exasperated debate with one of his Asian allies in the early 1950s captured the nature of this US concern: "when you say that we should deliberately plunge into war, let me tell you that if war comes, it will be horrible. Atomic war will destroy civilization. . . . The kind of war I am talking about, if carried out, would not save democracy. Civilization would be ruined . . . That is why we are opposed to war."[39]

Powerplay rationales become operative in alliances with large power disparities. As Schroeder, Altfeld, Morrow, and other scholars have argued, states entering into alliances contend with a tradeoff between autonomy and security. That is, the security savings achieved through alliances must always be discounted by the costs of giving up some autonomy.[40] Control, therefore, is a part of alliance dynamics.[41]

For two major allied powers of equal capabilities, control is usually negotiated through some form of mutual accommodation; however, Otto
von Bismarck noted long ago that the best alliances are when one ally
is the horse and the other is the rider, not when you have two horses.[42]
If the alliance is between unequal partners, then an alliance becomes
potentially a powerful instrument of control over the smaller ally.[43] The
smaller ally does better in the sense that it receives security, but it also
becomes heavily dependent on the ally in ways that award the larger
patron a great deal of leverage.[44]

The larger power's desire for control may be even more acute when
it sees strategic value in the smaller ally's allegiance—that is, the larger
power perceives a loss of the ally to the other side as a major defeat. If the
smaller ally understands this situation, then it will be immune to threats
of distancing by the larger power.[45] The only way the larger can influence
the smaller power is through adhesion and control.

Large powers may cut different bargains to control different players.
The smaller partner in theory always has an exit option if the relationship becomes too overbearing, but sometimes the asymmetry is so large
that the dependence afforded by the bargain makes exit difficult to contemplate; moreover, it renders outright counterbalancing behavior obsolete.[46] Smaller powers may do soft balancing in such situations, using
coalitions of diplomatic resistance or deliberate abstention policies to
stymie the ally's agenda.[47] But in total, this ability to control by cutting
different deals with different players gives the larger power authority that
approximates informal empire-building (discussed below).

Bilateral versus Multilateral Controls

The notion of bilateral alliances as instruments of control complements
neoliberal institutional arguments about multilateralism in contemporary international relations theory and foreign policy.[48] If the objective is
to control a target state, liberal institutionalists and foreign policy internationalists assume that this is best achieved by embedding the target in
multilateral structures. As Ikenberry argues, multilateralism's logic centers on a set of agreed upon rules and principles that require participants
to trade some reduction in policy autonomy in return for predictability
and transparency.[49] Whether the state in question is a rising China or
even a unilateralist America, liberals advocate multilateral mechanisms
to exercise control. Tying the subject into a myriad of rules, obligations,
and procedures subject to the consensus of a committee of members is
the best means of control.[50]

What differentiates the liberal conception of control and the power-play is power—and in particular who seeks control over whom.

As a general rule, multilateralism is the preferred strategy for exercising control over another country. For example, if control is sought by a small power over a great power, then the Lilliputian strategy of control makes sense (table 2.2, quadrant II). Multilateral constraints, whether in the form of membership in collective alliances or international institutions, are necessary to "bind" the great power, discourage unilateralism, and afford the small powers effective voice and vote opportunities as a group that they would not otherwise have.[51] This is why Southeast Asian nations prefer to deal with China through the structure of ASEAN or why some Europeans have described the postwar construction of NATO as an assurance of multilateral constraint on American power within the western bloc as much as it was an alliance against the Eastern bloc. Multilateralism has the effect of equalizing power asymmetries to the advantage of the smaller players, as everyone gets only one vote.

Similarly, if control is sought by a great power over another great power (quadrant IV), then multilateral controls may still work best. The great power could seek control through bilateral ties, but this will be costly and will require bargaining and a degree of compromise with the other great power. Embedding the target state in multilateral ties reduces the costs borne by the power seeking control, and at the same time offers the same "binding" benefits of the Lilliputian strategy over the target state. When the United States sought to control the actions of two major powers—Britain and France—in the 1956 Suez crisis, it used a combination of multilateral and bilateral measures. The United States looked to the UN to implement a ceasefire and to put in a police force, but it also made clear to London and Paris that it would not approve the flow of interim oil supplies to the countries (through approval of the Middle East Energy Committee plan) until they withdrew their forces from Egypt.

If a small power seeks control over another small power (quadrant I), multilateralism may be the only feasible choice since small powers rarely

TABLE 2.2. BILATERAL VERSUS MULTILATERAL CONTROL

	SMALL TARGET STATE	LARGE TARGET STATE
Small state seeking control over target	Quadrant I **Multilateralism**	Quadrant II **Multilateralism**
Large state seeking control over target	Quadrant III **Bilateralism**	Quadrant IV **Multilateralism**

have the resources to exert control on their own. In 1964, for example, Egypt sought multilateral controls through the convening of two Arab summits in order to restrain Syria from a military confrontation with Israel over its water diversion project. As Pressman notes, Nasser viewed the multilateral forum of Arab leaders as the best means to address Arab concerns about Israel's project as well as demonstrate to Syria that Arab countries were not ready for a military conflict with Israel.[52]

If control is being sought, however, by the great power over a smaller one, then this is best done bilaterally rather than multilaterally (quadrant III). Multilateralism gives the advantage to the small power, but bilateralism maintains or even *amplifies* a great power's capabilities (the conditions under which powers seek to do this are elaborated in the next section). As authors on hegemonic control and unipolarity have argued, great powers can maximize leverage by forging a series of bilateral deals with allies rather than have that leverage diluted in a multilateral forum.[53] As Robert Kagan notes, those who are weak seek multilateralism as a way to constrain the strong. But those who are strong avoid universal rules and multilateral constraints.[54] John Foster Dulles was known to have liked the hub and spokes concept of bilateral alliances because it gave the United States more leverage while depriving allies of other mediators or rule-makers.[55]

The history of European alliances is littered with illustrations of this dynamic. In the early 1800s, the secret Austro-Neapolitan alliance (June 1815) was formed in lieu of a larger Italian league. This afforded Metternich direct, bilateral control over the smaller entity. Austria provided security and in return received commitments from Naples that it would not change its form of government without Austria's permission. Slightly more than three decades later, Austria's bilateral treaties (1849–1850) with smaller powers in Italy gave it control over rulers in Tuscany, Modena, and Parma. In 1866, Bismarck's alliances with Bavaria, Wurttenberg, and Baden aimed to exert maximum control to prevent the smaller states' formation of a South German union and to promote Prussia's leadership through these states' allegiance to a North German confederation.[56] While the world seeks to embed a rising China in multilateral institutions in order to constrain its hard power capabilities and shape its preferences, China much prefers cultivating deep bilateral relationships. In Southeast Asia, for example, Beijing prefers to deal with ASEAN nations on a bilateral basis over territorial disputes in the South China Sea where it can "divide and conquer," exercising maximum leverage with each rather than contending with the group as a whole.[57] At the end of the Second World War, when the United States contemplated the security architecture for smaller Southeast Asian nations, Washington expressly rejected the idea of a framework including any of the European great powers who were former colonizers in the region precisely because Washington did not want its influence diluted. Arguably, the George W. Bush administration's foreign policy penchant in Iraq and Afghanistan was not for multilateralism or even unilateralism, but for intense bilateralism. Rather than going it alone or going it with others, intensive one-on-one relationships with hand-picked countries maximizes the US capacity to give what they must in order to get what they want.[58] In sum, bilateralism affords the great power efficient control. Every issue does not need to be put to a committee vote. Moreover, the more materially dependent the small power becomes, the more control exercised by the great power.[59]

The control exercised by the larger ally can take various forms. It could control the domestic policies of the smaller ally. During the 1820s–1830s period of the German Confederation, for example, Metternich used the confederation more as a means to exercise bilateral control over the internal policies of member states than he did for defense against an external security threat. Similarly, as Stephen David noted, the larger power's control over domestic policies is enhanced by the legitimacy gains bestowed on the smaller ally's leadership by the alliance itself.[60]

The larger ally could seek control through securing access to strategic resources or territories proximate to the smaller ally.[61] In 1833, Russia's alliance with Turkey, for example, provided security to its ally from the Egyptian threat even though Russia was not directly threatened by Egypt. This was because Russia wanted not security, but control from the alliance—not only in terms of better treatment of Orthodox Christians in Turkey, but also in terms of access to vital straits, and the exclusion of the Black Sea to potential competitors.[62] Another control motive for the larger ally is to decrease the probability of independent action by the smaller power deemed inconvenient to the larger one. Germany's Dual Alliance of 1879 with Austria-Hungary provided security against the Russian threat (security commitment borne inordinately by the German side), but for Bismarck, the value-added of the alliance was to slow the growth of Slavic federalism and keep the junior partner from moving off in an autonomous direction. In similar fashion, Bismarck's "powerplay" in his alliances with Italy (in the Triple Alliance, 1882), Rumania (1883), and Serbia (through the Austro-Serb treaty of 1881) was an exchange of security (for the smaller ally) for control (by the bigger ally).[63]

In terms of alliance strategy, the powerplay rationale or control strategy represents more of a "take the bull by the horns" approach to entrapment.[64] Rather than distancing, the strategy invests more in the alliance, ironically, because of fundamental distrust of the ally. Koremenos, Lipson, Snidal and other authors have argued that higher levels of distrust in international relations foster institutional arrangements that are more hierarchical in nature.[65] Such is the case with the powerplay: it is a proactive means by which large states can deal with distrust of an ally through establishing more authoritative controls.

Conditions for "Distancing" versus "Control" Strategies

In this section, I will derive when states choose distancing versus control (or adhesion) strategies in an alliance. Table 2.3 shows that the intensity of the entrapment fear will determine when states will choose one strategy or the other.

> *Definition 1*: Entrapment fears are *moderate* for ally A when it *might* have to intervene and get dragged into a conflict started by ally B.

> *Definition 2*: Entrapment fears for ally A, on the other hand, are *intense* when it *must* intervene and get dragged into a conflict started by ally B.

Allies experience entrapment fears with varying degrees of intensity. If a captain must go down with his ship, then his entrapment fears,

TABLE 2.3. DISTANCING VERSUS CONTROL STRATEGIES WHEN FACED WITH ENTRAPMENT

	LARGE POWER	SMALL POWER
Low-moderate entrapment fear re: ally's actions	Quadrant I **Distancing** strategy (to alleviate entrapment fear)	Quadrant II **Distancing**
Intense entrapment fear re: ally's actions	Quadrant III **Control** strategy (to alleviate entrapment fear)	Quadrant IV **Distancing***

*A control strategy is preferred, but because the costs of such a strategy may be prohibitively high for small powers (i.e., creating material dependence of target state on the alliance), the only feasible choice is distancing.

figuratively speaking, are more intense than a captain who can bail out in a lifeboat at the last minute. Similarly, if an ally estimates that the consequences of abstaining from aid to the ally are life-threatening, then its entrapment fears are, relatively speaking, more intense. There are generally five conditions under which entrapment fears are intense:

1. Structure—if A is locked in a zero-sum confrontation with the adversary where every piece of territory becomes contested.
2. Strategic and intrinsic value of the ally—if losing the ally is of unacceptable strategic and/or intrinsic cost.
3. Credibility vis-à-vis the adversary—if A's not responding to ally B's call for help may communicate a lack of resolve to the adversary over a different conflict where the stakes are even higher for A.
4. Reputation as a trustworthy ally—if A feels that the reputational costs vis-à-vis other allies of not coming to B's aid, however wasteful the conflict, are so burdensome that it must act.
5. Cost of intervention—if the expected cost of sending troops in to help an ally (in terms of political capital or blood and treasure) are inordinately higher than the marginal benefit.

Proposition 1: Control strategies are generally more costly than distancing strategies in dealing with entrapment fears.

The prevailing means by which states deal with entrapment fears— reducing material support; weakening commitments; castigating the ally—are generally not costly in material terms. These strategies may have reputational costs (e.g., reduce goodwill between allies, greater mistrust, signal weakness to the adversary) associated with them, but the material costs are not high. For this reason, they are often the preferred strategies among allies. The costs of a control strategy, on the other hand, are high. They usually require the ally to expend more military assistance, expand defense commitments, offer political support, and provide more economic cooperation. The purpose of these increased expenditures is to make the ally more dependent on oneself such that one's control is enhanced.

Proposition 2: If ally A experiences *moderate* fears of entrapment regarding ally B, then A will employ *distancing strategies* to discourage B from acting.

Proposition 3: If ally A experiences *intense* fears of entrapment regarding ally B, then A will employ *control strategies* to restrain B from acting.

In proposition 2, distancing strategies are more appealing than a control strategy to deal with entrapment fears because: (1) the stakes are not as high (i.e., if the ally chooses not to get dragged in, then the consequences are not that great); and (2) the costs of a control strategy (in terms of providing resources that create a dependence by ally B on ally A) are high (table 2.3, quadrants I and II).

In proposition 3, however, the incentives for employing a control strategy over a distancing one are high (table 2.3, quadrant III). This is because ally A does not have an exit option. It knows that regardless of the nature of its relationship with ally B, it must intervene and get dragged into a conflict started by B. If this is the case, then ally A is better off trying to exercise a proactive strategy of restraint over B's actions to minimize its fear of entrapment rather than a more passive distancing strategy. Ally A, by drawing closer to B and creating B's dependence, can effectively control B's actions more than would otherwise be the case.[66] This is a more costly way of dealing with entrapment fears than employing a distancing strategy.[67] But these preventive costs are acceptable compared with the actual costs of being dragged into the ally's war.

Table 2.4 summarizes my argument about the types of alliance design and the type of strategy that states will choose when faced with entrapment concerns. The liberal institutionalist literature covers explanations for quadrants (II) through (VIII)—i.e., that states seek to manage others through the use of multilateral structures. And the alliance theory literature explains the dynamics of quadrants (III), (IV), (VII), and (VIII)—i.e, that states faced with entrapment anxieties will utilize distancing strategies including abrogation, hedging, and voice strategies to address their anxieties. The powerplay strategy helps to explain quadrants (I) to (IV)—i.e., that the relative size of the allies and the intensity of the entrapment fear will determine the manner of risk management (control vs. distance) and the choice of security institution (bilateral vs. multilateral); and in particular, large powers with intense entrapment anxieties will "double down" on the alliance partner and seek to manage the risk bilaterally.

US-Israeli relations with regard to arms sales to China offer an example of how a great power employed control strategies on a smaller ally to change behavior. On two different occasions the Israelis hatched plans for military sales to China (in 2000, the Phalcon airborne early

TABLE 2.4. POWERPLAY

POWER	ENT INTENSE/ SMALL TARGET	ENT INTENSE/ LARGE TARGET	ENT MODERATE/ SMALL TARGET	ENT MODERATE/ LARGE TARGET
Large power	Control bilaterally (I)	Control/ multilaterally (concert) (II)	Distance/ bilaterally (III)	Distance/ multilaterally (IV)
Small power	Control/ multilaterally (V)	Control/ multilaterally (VI)	Distance/ multilaterally (VII)	Distance/ multilaterally (VIII)

warning system, and in 2005, upgrades to the Harpy anti-radar drone). And in both cases the United States strongly opposed the actions, and both the administration and Congress threatened to suspend assistance packages and to deny Israeli participation in development of US weapons programs. And in each case, the Ehud Barak and Ariel Sharon administrations canceled the deals. United States-Israel interaction fits into quadrant (I) in table 2.4: entrapment fears by a great power were intense with regard to a smaller ally, and so it exerted control, not through distancing, but through the bilateral exercise of power within the alliance.[68]

Adversary versus Alliance Games

As Glenn Snyder has noted, the alliance and adversary games are inextricably intertwined.[69] Actions taken within alliances naturally have effects on relations with adversaries, and so alliance partners must keep one eye toward alliance management and the other toward coercive diplomacy in navigating the "composite" alliance security dilemma. Sometimes the signals sent by alliance actions are linear—that is, the action in the alliance game registers in its intended coercive message in the adversary game. And sometimes, the signals sent by alliance actions create unintended and nonlinear reactions in the adversary game. This dynamic could be the result of many different variables, as explained by Robert Jervis among others. The impact of alliance signals on adversary games could also be a function of the cohesiveness of the adversary bloc and/or the alliance bloc.[70]

In this regard, control or "adhesion" strategies in the alliance game can create reactions in the adversary game that have a feedback effect. These feedback loops tend only to reinforce the powerplay preferences of the stronger ally. For example, adhesion to an adventurous junior ally for purposes of control might register with an adversary, not as a powerplay (i.e., great power restraint), but as emboldening support for further adventurism by the junior ally. While the great power might see some deterrent benefit to such perceptions, it certainly does not want its adhesion strategy to have the opposite effect, causing the adversary to escalate the conflict with the junior partner. Thus, the adversary game creates additional feedback incentives for the great power both to exercise control over the ally as well as to signal restraint to the adversary as part of the powerplay.

Does Powerplay Work?

How effective are alliance control strategies? Methodologically, there are difficulties in isolating the causal effect of alliance institutions as control tools. This is because a successful instance of control could stem not just from the powerplay but also from the common interests that brought the alliance together in the first place. For example, I may tell my ally to vote with me in the UN, but my ally's compliance may have naturally flowed from the common interests we share as allies regardless of my influence attempt. Christopher Gelpi's model circumvents this problem by looking at the effect of a patron state's influence to mediate between two disputants, one of which is the patron's ally.[71] In such instances, the patron's lack of commonly shared interest in the ally's dispute with the third party helps to isolate the causal importance of the alliance as an influence tool. The patron state's directive to the ally is a credible influence attempt because the patron does not share the same interest as the ally in the dispute. Thus, the ally must deal with the fear of abandonment if it does not listen to the patron. The behavior of the third party disputant vis-à-vis the ally is not influenced by the patron (i.e., the disputant is not emboldened) because the patron still sends credible signals that it will intervene if the disputant oversteps.

Based on a dataset of 117 cases between 1918 and 1988 that fit the preceding description, the primary empirical finding is that alliances are indeed effective instruments of intra-alliance control.[72] Specifically, a state is 50 percent more effective (81 percent success rate) at controlling the behavior of another if it is allied to that state rather than unaffiliated.[73] Moreover, as per our theory, power asymmetries are a significant indicator of effectiveness. Great powers are 71 percent more successful at controlling an ally's behavior in a dispute than non-great powers. In addition, when states use coercive actions to pressure allies, they are 53 percent more successful at controlling behavior (all other variables held constant). Gelpi also controls for the quality and closeness of the alliance tie by coding for level of institutionalization and finds that the deeper the tie, the greater success there is in the influence attempt.[74]

In a similar vein, Michaela Mattes's study of 230 cases from the Alliance Treaty Obligations and Provisions (ATOP) database reached similar conclusions. She focused on the degree to which abandonment fears within an alliance affect the degree and type of institutionalization.[75] One of her primary findings was that symmetric alliances show a high degree of military institutionalization as a way for partners to address abandonment anxieties by delineating more clearly the terms of the alliance contract. But an incidental finding of the study was that asymmetric alliances between major and minor powers show a high degree of similar institutionalization even when neither member of the alliance has a history of abandonment behavior. Mattes attributes this to the motives of the major power to equate institutionalization of the alliance with better control of the junior partner.[76] A recent study that further confirms the powerplay finding through three-party formal modeling is by Fang, Johnson, and Leeds.[77] These scholars note that more than 50 percent of military alliances that include a mutual defense commitment also include an explicit mechanism for consultation and coordination in the event of a crisis. They find that most partner states use this consultation mechanism to successfully control the ally in a dispute with a challenger, if the ally strongly values the alliance.[78] A 2015 study on the downside risk of US alliance obligations by Beckley also offers evidence of the powerplay dynamic.[79] Utilizing a database of militarized interstate disputes involving the United States from 1948 to 2010, Beckley's primary finding is that America's sixty-plus postwar alliance commitments have not resulted in many cases of entanglement (contrary to popular perception). However, an incidental finding of his study is that the United States on several occasions restrained its allies from conflicts to avoid entanglement. Pulling all of these findings together, therefore, the most successful cases of intra-alliance control occur when a great power forcefully imposes constraints on an ally with which it has deep institutionalized alliance ties—the exact conditions of the powerplay strategy.

Powerplay and Empires

Alliances are institutions designed by powers not just to defend against threat but to manage broader risk.[80] The more power a state accumulates in the system, the more it likes to have control over its environment. The powerplay in this regard is appealing to great powers who want to control risk. As noted earlier, employing a powerplay strategy allows a great power to cut different deals with each party in ways that maximize its interests and control. A collection of such pacts starts to approximate an informal empire.[81] If the great power can create insurmountable power differentials within each relationship, then (according to the literature on unipolarity), it can string together a set of relationships in which no one partner can counterbalance within the alliance.[82] These smaller allies could of course band together against the great power, but if the powerplay strategy is successfully implemented, the importance of that bilateral tie with the patron weakens the attractiveness of other multilateral groupings so that they do not pose serious competition to the bilateral tie. Thus, the most extreme form of counterbalancing would take the form of "soft balancing" within the alliance rather than outright counter-coalitions.

Finally, the powerplay strategy amplifies the great power's capabilities by affording it "positional power" in addition to its hard power. That is, the great power not only commands control and suppresses counterbalancing, it also positions itself as the central link in a network of relationships. In this regard, position can be as important as power in determining outcomes in international relations.[83] Creating a set of bilateral relationships in which the patron sits at the center affords it a position of supremacy where all need to answer to it rather than to one another. This is not just the view of social network theorists like Kahler, but also that of liberal institutionalists. Ikenberry argues that the durability of a hegemonic order depends in part on the creation of "an organizational hub around which other states connect and operate."[84] In this regard, the powerplay strategy allows the state to position itself as the "Grand Central Station" of its alliance network.[85] It is the central connection point through which the system operates. In Ikenberry's analysis, the great power is not just a power pole but a "hub" that provides the organizing infrastructure, security and stability, rules and normative principles, and dictates how the system interacts with each other.[86]

———

The powerplay theory therefore connects to a wide variety of conversations ranging from alliance theory to social network theory to unipolarity. With regard to policy, to the extent that big powers like control (and they do), the powerplay is always preferable. China today, as the rising power in the international system, would much rather deal with each power in its neighborhood on bilateral terms than as a group. It prefers to deal with South Korea, for example, bilaterally where it can exercise greater influence rather than negotiate with a Korea embedded in the United States-Korea-Japan trilateral framework. Similarly, in Southeast Asia, where Beijing has territorial and maritime disputes with many of the smaller nations, it would much prefer to negotiate with each one bilaterally rather than negotiate a Code of Conduct with ASEAN nations as a group. For smaller powers, negotiating as a group gives them more leverage. But China's power is amplified when it cuts individual deals with each. Eventually China would like to create a network where it is indispensible to all based on the individual deals it cuts with each party. Such an arrangement would amplify their power in the region (discussed in chapter 8).

If China were to do this in the future, it would have taken a page from America's Asia strategy at the end of World War II. Holding more power than any other actor in the region, the United States would set out to design a security architecture for Asia that contained the communist threat but also managed the risks associated with these newfound commitments to Asia. It is this story to which we now turn.

3

ORIGINS OF THE AMERICAN ALLIANCE SYSTEM IN ASIA

At the end of World War II and in the early days of the Cold War, the United States confronted two strategic questions in Asia: How committed should the United States be to this region? And what form should this commitment take? For policymakers like Dean Acheson, George Kennan, John Foster Dulles, and others, Asia was a blank slate in need of a master plan. The challenge for US strategy in these early years was to design a security institution that contained communism, secured US preeminence, but did not lead to overextension. In the end, the institutional design selected by the United States to meet these needs in Japan, Korea, and Taiwan was very different from that used in Europe. The tight bilateral hub and spokes design—the powerplay—that became exclusive to the East Asian region evinced not just American power but American vulnerability. It amplified Washington's control, essentially giving the United States decisive say over another nation's sovereign right to use force. These neo-imperial arrangements, however, also reflected a core American anxiety—to guard against an unwanted conflict in Asia when the priority was defending Western Europe. This duality of strength and vulnerability was informed by a deeply rooted strategic ambivalence toward Asia, the story of which is told here.

EARLY AMBIVALENCE

American disinterest in major military commitments in Asia had long been a hallmark of US global strategy. Before US imperial ambitions took

root in the Philippines and Hawaii, American pre-twentieth-century interests in Asia were largely restricted to securing commercial opportunity (the "Open Door"), promoting missionary activity, and restricting
the region's immigration to the United States, unlike European powers
that sought to carve out spheres of influence in the Pacific. Otherwise,
the United States practiced political detachment. As prominent historian
and president of Yale University, A. Whitney Griswold observed in 1938:
"It should be noted that up to 1898—indeed to 1900—the American
policy of respect for the territorial integrity of the Far Eastern nations
had the effect of a purely self-denying ordinance. It did not enjoin on the
United States the obligation of defending this territorial integrity from
others. The United States was thus able to keep free of serious involvement in the politics of Eastern Asia."[1]

Even as the United States became more engaged in the region from
the twentieth century, it consciously restricted this role to an offshore
maritime one based largely in Guam, Hawaii, Japan, and the Philippines.
Americans saw no strategic purpose that could justify US military commitments to the Asian mainland, and this mind-set was reflected in the
absence of intervention against Japan's occupation of the Korean peninsula in 1910 and Japan's aggression against Manchuria in 1932.[2]

The story was very different for Europe. At the end of the Second
World War, the United States reluctantly accepted the emergence of a
bipolar power competition with the Soviet Union. By February 1947,
Truman realized that the British could no longer be counted on as a partner in dealing with the Soviets given the weak economy, coal shortages,
and massive defense cuts.[3] But Washington was terribly conflicted on
both the imminence of this threat and the proper policies to deal with
it. Some believed that war with the Soviets could come in a matter of
months, while others thought Moscow was too weak to contend with US
industrial capacity and nuclear monopoly. An NSC paper in 1948, for example, stated that the Soviets might resort to immediate war if it served
their needs, yet in 1949, the American embassy in Moscow believed that
Stalin would remain quiescent and seek several years of peace to rebuild.
Dean Acheson, too, concluded from his own reading of Soviet history
that Moscow was risk-averse when it came to military adventurism and
would focus instead on the political game in Europe. As Robert Jervis
describes, a number of questions thus energized US postwar strategy for
Europe. Was US industrial capacity enough to deter Soviet military actions? How long would the nuclear monopoly last and what could it
deter? Did the United States need a military force large enough to win a

war over massive Soviet forces or just enough to evince a political commitment to defend the line in Western Europe?[4] Amidst these debates, Washington slowly but deliberately enhanced its security plans for Europe, eventually culminating in large and unambiguous commitments with the Marshall Plan and then NATO.[5] By May 1950, the latter became an established multilateral institution, with a formal membership, and with a permanent executive decision-making committee to address issues of US-European defense.

This caliber of concern and discussion simply did not take place when it came to Asia. As one scholar noted, the British retrenchment in Europe caught Acheson and Truman off guard.[6] It was in this context that as the United States tried to craft a postwar strategy for Europe, it was at the same time making the "biggest *non*intervention of the entire Cold War—in Asia. There, the United States decided it would not attempt to keep communism from taking over China."[7]

Dean Acheson's "Salutary Neglect"

Dean Acheson, the fifty-first US Secretary of State who served President Harry Truman from 1949 to 1953, had virtually no interest in Asian affairs. He was an Atlanticist to the core. Trained as a lawyer at Harvard, Acheson joined the State Department under Franklin D. Roosevelt in 1941 and became undersecretary of state during the Truman administration for Secretary of State James Byrnes and his successor, George Marshall. Acheson saw America's main priority after World War II to be reconstruction of Western Europe, which he termed "the keystone of the world."[8] He wanted to restore a stable balance of power on the European continent and contain the Soviet threat, and he knew this would be extremely expensive and politically taxing. Stopping communism in the Pacific was also a desired goal, but given the priority of Europe, as historian Waldo Heinrichs observed, "East Asian problems must have seemed an unwelcome distraction."[9] While the United States was undertaking precedent-breaking aid to Greece and Turkey, administering the Marshall Plan, creating NATO, and bolstering an independent West Germany, happenings in Asia were viewed as "remote and nebulous."[10] Warren Cohen observed that Acheson was moved by the simple conviction that "American interests on the Asian mainland would be served best by a policy of salutary neglect."[11] Little could sway the Secretary of State from this view, much to the consternation of key advisors including Dean Rusk, his deputy undersecretary (and later assistant secretary for Far Eastern affairs), W.

Walton Butterworth (Rusk's predecessor as assistant secretary), Philip C. Jessup, ambassador at large, George Kennan, policy planning chief, and John Patton Davies, China specialist on the policy planning staff.

Acheson was not moved to action by the fall of Chiang Kai-shek and the Kuomintang (KMT) on mainland China. Despite nasty attacks from large segments of the Republican Party for having "lost China," Acheson wanted to cut off all support for the KMT, and to seek some type of latent accommodation with the Chinese to keep them unaligned with the Soviets (discussed more in the next chapter). Acheson shrugged off all his critics as "primitives" who were uniformly ignorant of delineating broader US strategic interests (or, more crudely, as shills for Chiang Kai-shek).[12] He viewed the outrage expressed by some in Congress about left-wing sympathizers in the State Department as knee-jerk, highly emotional, and uninformed. Indeed, in one meeting with congressional leaders in 1949, as the KMT's fate on the mainland hung in the balance, a flu-ridden Acheson responded to what he viewed as fiery but inane questions from Republican House members by abruptly stuffing his papers in his briefcase, pushing away from the table, and declaring "we are not getting anywhere" as he walked out of the chamber.[13] Acheson's speeches were replete with references to Asia's strategic unimportance. This ambivalence was also rationally and logically laid out in internal State Department memoranda. American commitments to Asia should be at best "symbolic," the Secretary thought, designed to address domestic-political criticisms, and to assuage those in Congress who linked their support of European assistance packages to some help for Asia, but should show no genuine engagement with Asia.[14] As notes from the Secretary's meetings on the topic in 1949 recorded, Acheson's mind had been made up on Taiwan, and the majority of the discussions focused on managing the public optic vis-à-vis the Republicans.[15] A larger-than-life figure, Acheson impressed his views upon all around him, including the president.

Maritime, not Continental—The Defense Perimeter

Acheson's views on the peripheral importance of Asia became enshrined in a speech at the National Press Club in January 1950, entitled "Crisis in China—An Examination of United States Policy." Enunciating a new US strategy for the region in the aftermath of the Chinese communist victory, Acheson delineated a US defense perimeter that excluded all of continental Asia and its extremities (i.e., Korean peninsula and Formosa) and proclaimed that US interests solely resided in maritime Asia:

What is the situation in regard to the military security of the Pacific area, and what is our policy in regard to it?

In the first place, the defeat and the disarmament of Japan has placed upon the United States the necessity of assuming the military defense of Japan, so long as that is required, both in the interest of our security and in the interests of the security of the entire Pacific area and, in all honor, in the interest of Japanese security. We have American—and there are Australian—troops in Japan. I am not in a position to speak for the Australians, but I can assure you that there is not intention of any sort of abandoning or weakening the defenses of Japan and that whatever arrangements are to be made either through permanent settlement or otherwise, that defense must and shall be maintained.

The defensive perimeter runs along the Aleutians to Japan and then goes to the Ryukyus. We hold important defense positions in the Ryukyu Islands, and those we will continue to hold. In the interest of the population of the Ryukyu Islands, we will at an appropriate time offer to hold these islands under trusteeship of the United Nations. But they are essential parts of the defensive perimeter of the Pacific, and they must and will be held.

The defensive perimeter runs from the Ryukyus to the Philippine Islands. Our relations, our defensive relations with the Philippines are contained in agreements between us. Those agreements are being loyally carried out and will be loyally carried out. Both peoples have learned by bitter experience the vital connections between our mutual defense requirements. We are in no doubt about that, and it is hardly necessary for me to say an attack on the Philippines could not and would not be tolerated by the United States. But I hasten to add that no one perceives the imminence of any such attack.

So far as the military security of other areas in the Pacific is concerned, it must be clear that no person can guarantee these areas against military attack. But it must also be clear that such a guarantee is hardly sensible or necessary within the realm of practical relationship.[16]

Acheson's "defense perimeter" speech has been famously framed as the strategic miscommunication and miscalculation that invited North Korea's invasion of the South only six months later. What is often forgotten is that this had been the consensus view of the top strategic thinkers inside the US government for quite some time.[17]

George Kennan, head of policy planning at the State Department, was one of the most influential thinkers for Acheson's predecessor, George C. Marshall.[18] Kennan was a young, ambitious, Princeton-educated diplomat at the US embassy in Moscow when he penned the "Long Telegram" and unwittingly set the course of US grand strategy for the following half century. The following year, Kennan expanded upon these original ideas in an article in *Foreign Affairs* under the pseudonym "X," in which he argued for a strategy of "long-term, patient but firm and vigilant containment" to deal with the Soviet Union.[19] He was thereafter plucked from his position as a lecturer at the National War College by then-Secretary of State George C. Marshall, and became the inaugural Director of the Policy Planning Staff at the US State Department. The architect of Cold War containment strategy, Kennan assigned greater strategic value to Asia than Marshall's successor, and therefore did not advocate "salutary neglect" of the region. However, his bottom line did not differ hugely from his secretary's in that he was deeply ambivalent about any military interests on the Asian mainland.

Kennan's thinking about Asia was heavily influenced by John Patton Davies, the son of missionary parents in China and one of the few China experts in the State Department, who eventually joined Kennan's small staff in policy planning.[20] In a 1948 letter to then-Secretary of State Marshall, the Soviet specialist opined, "Today, so far as I can learn, we are operating without an overall strategic concept for the entire western Pacific area,"[21] so Kennan took it upon himself to design one. The quintessential realist, Kennan argued that there were five great power centers—the United States, Soviet Union, Britain, Germany, and Japan. In Kennan's estimation, the balance of power among these did not require a strategic stake on the Asian continent.[22] The primary task of the United States, instead, was to ensure that no major power from the Eurasian landmass could dominate the region. In March 1948, he proposed this strategic concept to Acheson. Kennan believed US forces should be immediately evacuated from Korea, and that Formosa/Taiwan,[23] while valuable, would not be worth defending. The United States, instead, should occupy strategic maritime positions limited to areas west of the Japan-Okinawa-Philippines line of defense.[24] Kennan explained his thinking succinctly in a speech in October 1948:

> [Y]ou do not need to hold land positions on the Eurasian land mass to protect our national security. If that is true, you can theoretically content yourself with permitting most of these land areas to be

in the hands of people who are hostile to ourselves as long as you exercise that power of inhibiting the assembling and launching of amphibious forces from many Asian ports.[25]

For this reason, Kennan did not see the Truman Doctrine as applicable to China in the way it was applicable to Greece and Turkey. In Kennan's words, "[T]he deterioration of the situation in China did not seem to constitute in itself any intolerable threat to our security."[26] This was because Communist China was not the primary threat from the Asian continent, as it did not have the capacity to project power off its shores. The real threat was the Soviets, but any projection of Soviet power from the Eurasian landmass did not have to be met with a US foothold on the ground; rather, it could be contained from the sea with a strong maritime defense perimeter, in which case Japan was key, not mainland Asia. Kennan lays out the algorithm in his own words:

> Americans, laboring under that strange fascination that China has seemed to exert at all times on American opinion, tended to exaggerate China's real importance and to underrate that of Japan. I considered then, and hold to the opinion today, that if at any time in the postwar period the Soviet leaders had been confronted with a choice between control over China and control over Japan, they would unhesitatingly have chosen the latter. We Americans could feel fairly secure in the presence of a truly friendly Japan and a nominally hostile China—nothing very bad could happen to us from this combination.[27]

Second, in power politics terms, continental Asia's underdevelopment made it unattractive as a potential partner against Moscow. In unpublished personal papers, Kennan wrote that China "could never become a first class military power," and that its culture was "not conducive to any rapid technical or economic development." He also once wrote, "It is just unbelievable what amounts of stuff you can pour into that country and still have it spread too thin to really accomplish much, even if it were well used, but actually an awful lot of it seems to get out of control."[28]

Kennan's views were shared by many in the military. The Joint Chiefs of Staff had no desire to be militarily engaged on the continent. Because Asia's distance from the heart of Soviet power was so vast, it made the mainland an unfavorable way to advance on the Soviets.[29] The terrain and long supply lines made it an unfriendly environment logistically.

Moreover, war planners believed that the same military operational dis-
advantages applied to Moscow as well: Conquest of mainland Asia would
not provide Moscow with a significant advantage: "The inability of the
USSR to rapidly extend lines of communications, base development
operations, and military and political control through the vast areas
of Siberia and into Communist-dominated China appears to preclude
military exploitation of this area, to our detriment, in the immediate
future."[30] This was not to say that having a foothold in Taiwan or on the
Korean peninsula was completely worthless to the military, but maintaining such positions were not worth the candle. In testimony before
the Hill one year prior to the fateful North Korean invasion, US generals
responded to a question about giving up South Korea to the communists
by assessing, ironically, that such a scenario would amount to a "very,
very minor disadvantage."[31]

The strategic irrelevance of the Asian continent became enshrined in
policy through a series of NSC meetings in December 1949. At issue was
the direction of US policy following the CCP victory. The State Department believed that Taiwan should be let go aside from providing some
token economic assistance. The Joint Chiefs of Staff and defense secretary Louis Johnson believed that there was some value to Taiwan as a
base of military operations off the Chinese coast, and that economic aid
should be supplemented by some military assistance. In the end, NSC
48/2 of December 30, 1949 read that the United States could not prevent
the inevitable fall of Taiwan to the communists and that instead it should
consolidate its maritime position by "mak[ing] every effort to strengthen
the overall US position with respect to the Philippines, the Ryukyus, and
Japan."[32] Thus, as John Lewis Gaddis observed, when Acheson in 1950
laid out the defense perimeter excluding all of continental Asia, including Korea and Taiwan, he was channeling the consensus view of a US
government that harbored deep ambivalence to engagement in Asia.[33]

Resource Scarcity

Resource scarcity also informed American strategic ambivalence toward
Asia. US military planners in the postwar and early Cold War years faced
a budget and military dilemma: They knew that European countries
could not devote large amounts of money to defense spending during
their postwar recovery. They also knew that it was far too early to expect
the region to countenance a re-growth of Germany's military to fill the
gap in Europe's defense. So the burden fell to the United States, yet both

Eisenhower and Truman operated under the belief that the American public and the national economy could not countenance growing defense budgets in the early Cold War years. In part, this constraint was imposed by a still-strong isolationist strain in American foreign policy after the war. From late 1945 to early 1950 a palpable desire for demobilization pervaded the American general public. Troops were standing down at an unprecedented rate of more than 15,000 per day.[34] Gallup polling in late 1949 showed a public unwilling to countenance higher taxes and desirous of cutting foreign assistance.[35] Truman did not want to be remembered as the first American president in recent memory to ask for large military outlays in peacetime following a world war. Moreover, he did not want to finance this through public borrowing or higher taxes to give the advantage to Republicans thirsting for the opportunity to run on a platform of tax cuts. These concerns grew even stronger when the Republicans won both the Senate and the House of Representatives in November 1946.

The atmosphere of resource scarcity was not just political, but informed by basic economics. In 1949, the effects of a wartime economy dissipated as growth slowed, unemployment increased from 3.5 percent to 6 percent, and industrial production declined by 13 percent. Budget hawks feared a $5 billion deficit in fiscal year 1950 and as high as $8 billion in 1951 and 1952. Moreover, the priority in spending had to be in domestic programs that had been underfunded during the war. The only place where substantial spending cuts could happen was in the defense budget.[36] The imperative to economize on security was amplified by the advent of nuclear weapons. The American nuclear monopoly created the political pressure to demobilize now that the United States had the ultimate weapon. The US Commander during the Korean War explains the impulses at the time:

> We had faith in the United Nations. And the atomic bomb created for us a kind of psychological Maginot Line that helped us to rationalize the national urge to get the boys home, the armies demobilized, the swords sheathed, and the soldiers, sailors, and airmen out of uniform . . . But would any political candidate in that era have been able to survive had he urged keeping the nation still under arms and large forces still posted 8000 miles from home?[37]

Thus, in September 1949, the Council of Economic Advisors recommended against a $2 billion increase in defense spending because of the deleterious impact such deficits would have on the economy. As several scholars have described, these pressures on the administration to "economize" were great and fiscal conservatism would affect thinking about all security commitments abroad.[38] Nowhere was this more apparent than in the drafting of NSC-68. The national security document was meant to delineate a comprehensive US response to the growing Soviet challenge, as evidenced most recently in Moscow's breaking of the American nuclear monopoly. But when completed in April 1950, the document was effectively shelved because it met with a domestic-political environment unwelcoming of large defense expenditures. As noted in one of the better treatments of the domestic politics of national security during Truman's presidency as it related to Asia:

> Regardless of the mobilizing rhetoric of the March 1947 Truman Doctrine regarding the defense of "free peoples everywhere," the United States could not realistically create a global defense commitment to counter all forms of communist aggression in all places around the world. That is the main reason why in April 1950 Truman shelved NSC-68, the National Security Council's dramatic call for a more expensive and assertive US security policy. . . . [there was] little sense that the requisite defense budgets, foreign aid allotments, and security commitments would be marketable domestically.[39]

The first place the belt-tightening hit was in Asia. George Kennan recollected as he was about to embark on a trip to Asia in February 1948, "the view that we were greatly overextended [in the Far East]. Things looked bad, and there was little we could do about it. We would have to show great restraint."[40] In November 1948, the Joint Chiefs of Staff told Secretary of Defense James Forrestal that "[C]urrent United States commitments involving the use or distinctly possible use of armed forces are very greatly in excess of our present ability to fulfill them either promptly or effectively."[41] As one military memoir describes, every branch of the armed services felt the "surgeon's knife," with the navy short of combat ships and minesweepers, the air force short of fighters and heavy lift transport, and munitions dwindled to a "hatful" as productions factories were mothballed.[42] On the Korean peninsula, where the United States began a process of drawing down, and ultimately withdrawing, all of its 45,000 forces, every one of the Eighth Army's four divisions were undermanned below its authorized strength of 12,500 troops; every division was short 1,500 rifles, had no anti-tank guns, lacked one firing battery out of every three in the divisional artillery, and had no regimental tank companies.[43] In March 1949, the Joint Chiefs again advised that the United States should not squander valuable resources on Asia as opposed to Europe.[44]

This way of thinking also pervaded views on Indochina in 1949. Even as the threat of Soviet-backed communism arose in Southeast Asia, the United States was terribly ambivalent about engagement. Few had confidence in the French as a partner that could maintain military control, and many believed that Ho Chi Minh's communist-backed nationalism could not possibly be won over by French colonial appeals to the Vietnamese people. In October 1949, CIA estimates judged that French expulsion from its former colony by Vietnamese nationalists was inevitable, and could happen within as early as two years.[45] Kennan advised on limiting US commitments to the region, both militarily and economically. He believed that Southeast Asian nations were uncivilized, incapable of governing and developing themselves, and though susceptible to communism, they were not strategically valuable.[46] Moreover, he believed that nationalism in these countries—more harshly opposed to Western colonialism than communism—did not bode well for US intervention, or for intervention on the part of European allies. An internal State Department memo in 1950 laid out the problem: "To continue to pour treasure (and perhaps eventually lives) into a hopeless cause in which the French have already expended about a billion and a half dollars and about fifty thousand lives—and this at a cost of alienating vital segments of Asian public opinion[?]"[47]

The issue was not simply military forces, but also pertained to assistance programs. Even as the economic hegemon after World War II, purveyors of US assistance voiced deep concern about America spreading itself too thin. Kennan recalled in his memoirs that European recovery and the Marshall Plan sucked all of the time and attention of planners that precluded them from "com[ing] up for air" to take stock of other issues around the world like Asia.[48] NSC 48/1 and 48/2 decided that at best, the United States would pursue a defensive position in Asia, using the "minimum expenditure of military manpower and material."[49] Table 3.1 and figure 3.1 illustrate the prioritizing of Europe and ambivalence toward Asia.

US ambivalence in its policies toward Taiwan and Korea in this period was evident not only to allies but also to adversaries. By the spring of

TABLE 3.I. COMPARISON OF US AID TO SELECT ASIAN AND EUROPEAN
COUNTRIES (1946–1952)

	TIME PERIOD			
	1946–1948		1949–1952	
ASIAN COUNTRIES	Economic	Military	Economic	Military
Burma	5	0	10.2	3.1
India	39.9	0	248.7	0
Indonesia	67.7	0	107.5	4.1
Japan	979.7	1,220.7	0	0
Pakistan	0.1	0	11.1	0
Philippines	256.7	72.6	564.2	148.3
South Korea	181.2	0	485.6	12.5
Taiwan	502.3	141.4	467.8	275.3
Thailand	6.2	0	16.1	88
Total	2,094.6	1,434.7	1,911.2	531.3
Combined total	3,529.3		2,442.5	
EUROPEAN COUNTRIES				
Belgium	31.4	0	559.9	713.5
France	709.1	0	2,714.80	3,186.1
Germany	1,344.4	0	2,491.7	462.4
Greece	510.5	198.4	733.4	593.7
Italy	1,171	0	1,516.7	846.1
Netherlands	36	0	982.1	823.2
Norway	25	0	255.2	403.1
Turkey	12.2	68.8	225.1	553.2
United Kingdom	3,836.9	0	3,190.1	618.4
Total	7,676.5	267.2	12,669.0	8,199.7
Combined total	7,943.7		20,868.7	

All contributions in millions, current $US
Source: Compiled from U.S. Agency for International Development (USAID), "U.S. Overseas Loans and Grants: Obligations and Loan Authorizations," July 1, 1945–September 30, 2012, at http://pdf.usaid.gov/pdf_docs/pnaec300.pdf, accessed November 4, 2014.

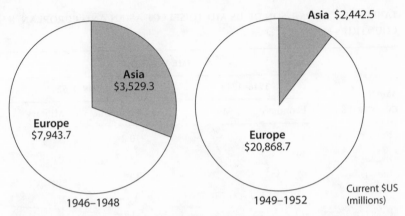

FIGURE 3.1. US aid to select Asian and European countries
Source: Compiled from US Agency for International Development (USAID), "U.S. Overseas Loans and Grants: Obligations and Loan Authorizations," July 1, 1945–September 30, 2012, at http://pdf.usaid.gov/pdf_docs/pnaec300.pdf, accessed November 4, 2014.

1949, as Christensen details in his study of deterrence signaling in the early Cold War years, Soviet intelligence received reports from the field regarding US intentions to pull forces out of Korea. The Chinese military judged that the United States would not intervene in the Taiwan Straits. Mao and Stalin incorrectly assessed that a remilitarized Japan might step into the void left by the United States. But this news came atop clear signals of American disinterest in intervention in the Chinese civil war and the drawing down of assistance to Chiang. Soviet and Chinese judgments about the United States would only be further confirmed with Dean Acheson's January 1950 Press Club speech.[50]

One of the most outspoken critics of US strategic ambivalence was General Douglas MacArthur. The Commander in Chief of US Forces— Far East, and Supreme Commander of Allied Powers in Japan (SCAP) believed that when it came to the fight against communism, the United States could not afford to bifurcate and prioritize its strategic interests. He argued that the "Europe-firsters" in Washington had fundamentally misread the nature of the military challenge. Precisely because the United States was signaling a dedicated effort to contain the Soviet threat in Europe, Moscow would shift its offensive to the Asian theater, where the United States was woefully unprepared.[51] In December 1949, as the NSC was reaching the conclusion to disengage from Taiwan, MacArthur rallied allies from the Joint Chiefs of Staff and Republicans on Capitol Hill to press the administration to channel $75 million in defense assistance to Chiang. In May 1950, the general described Taiwan's strategic value to the United States as an "unsinkable aircraft carrier" in the region. Two months later, he made headlines with a visit to Taiwan with three squadrons of jet fighters where he criticized policies of "appeasement and defeatism in the Pacific," and called "threadbare" the argument that support of Taiwan would be backed by no one in Asia.[52] The following December MacArthur derided Washington as a group of "Europhiles" who:

> just will not recognize that it is Asia which has been selected for the test of Communist power and that if all Asia falls Europe would not have a chance—either with or without American assistance. In their blind and stupid effort to undermine public confidence in me as something of a symbol of the need for balanced thinking and action, they do Europe the gravest disservice and sow the seeds to its possible ultimate destruction.[53]

MacArthur's actions eventually led to his dismissal, but they demonstrated that not all in the US government supported the policy of strategic ambivalence. Others including Secretary of Defense Louis Johnson and then-State Department Undersecretary Dean Rusk also supported a more proactive Asia policy. Johnson, in particular, was openly critical of State's weak China policy and considered it ill-advised, based on the wrong strategic assumptions, and narrow-mindedness. Like MacArthur, he pushed for a "carefully considered and comprehensive plan" to contain Asian communism.[54] But these entreaties consistently ran into the same problem: How was the United States to flow the necessary resources into such a plan in Asia?

Plotting global strategy was therefore a finite-sum game. The United States had to choose carefully where it would invest its resources. A memo from the director of the Pentagon's Mutual Defense Assistance Program to Acheson in 1950 about giving more aid to Indochina evinced the gravity of the situation:

> We have reached the point where the United States, because of limitations in resources, can no longer simultaneously pursue all of its objectives in all parts of the world and must realistically face the fact that certain objectives, even though they may be extremely valuable and important ones, may have to be abandoned if others of even greater value and importance are to be attained.[55]

Significantly for the powerplay rationale, the Europe-first mentality meant that any commitments made by the United States in Asia were subject to intense entrapment fears. As one scholar noted, at issue was not US political resolve but basic capabilities. American and European strategic thinkers believed that the United States had to "save its best punches" for the defense of Europe.[56] What little they could invest in Asia in terms of material and manpower could under no circumstances metastasize into a larger problem that required even more time, attention, and resources. The anxiety that fueled the control aspect of America's alliances in Asia therefore was not just rash actions by irresponsible smaller allies (discussed below), but the inherent material constraints on American power.

Predominant Strategic Beliefs

Another factor fueling American ambivalence toward commitments in Asia pertained to strategic beliefs. In these early Cold War years, the concept that smaller wars in the periphery could become the proxy battleground for US-Soviet superpower competition never animated strategic thinking. The predominant view was that war, should it come with the Soviet Union, would be massive and all-out. Thus, US energy had to be focused on defending a contingency in the core (i.e., Europe) rather than on the periphery (i.e., Asia). One study by Jervis of the internal NSC and JCS memos, policy documents, and congressional hearings in 1948 and 1949 concluded that while limited war was occasionally mentioned as a possible scenario, "[n]owhere was the belief in the possibility of limited wars spelled out with an analysis of what could cause them, keep them limited, and how they might be fought. . . . it was not a danger decision makers worried about or even a concept that they fully grasped."[57] A corresponding strategic belief in this regard centered on China. Despite the 1949 revolution, most decision makers saw this as a sui generis event (i.e., not tied to a broader movement in the region), and few perceived any concerted alliance forming between Beijing and Moscow. On the contrary, Acheson assessed that while the Russians may have played some role in the revolution, eventually Sino-Soviet tensions would emerge given the difficult history of the relationship and the rise of nationalism. Ironically, the minority views who grasped the concept of limited wars as well as the significance of the communist takeover in China were the Asia specialists in the US government (discussed below). Given these dominant strategic beliefs, however, it is not surprising that strategists saw no need for Korea or, more broadly, mainland Asia. Were a war to break out there, the United States would not fight because it was a peripheral conflict unrelated to core US interests, and at most, it might be one small front in a much larger world war to come with the Soviets. And so, JCS plans called for the withdrawal of all forces from the Korean peninsula, even as Central Intelligence Agency reports assessed that the North "would probably" invade the South.[58] It was only after North Korean forces poured into the South in June 1950 that limited war, and its logical corollary, the domino theory, predominated strategic thinking.

THE KOREAN WAR

When the principals in the NSC meetings in December 1949 crafted NSC 48/1 and 48/2, none of them anticipated that Kim Il-sung would invade South Korea only six months later. Indeed, in the period between the fall of 1949 and summer of 1950, US strategists would be confronted with the Soviet nuclear test (August 1949), the consolidation of communist rule in China, and the consummation of the Soviet-Chinese defense treaty in February 1950. These events prompted the Truman administration to craft a new strategy on paper, NSC-68, in April 1950 to contend with the Soviet threat, but it was the Korean war that sparked the implementation of the document. As Gaddis observed, this string of events, capped by Kim Il-sung's invasion, would in effect turn on its head the core principles that informed the administration's Asia strategy that were so carefully crafted over the prior two years, "when that country was attacked on June 25, 1950, the United States, with a rapidity that surprised both itself and its adversaries, committed air, naval, and ground forces to repel the invasion. Five months later, Washington found itself in an undeclared war there with Communist China as well."[59]

Before the invasion, there was no debate within Washington circles that Korea should be written off. In Kennan's words, and in rare agreement with the Joint Chiefs, he wrote, "Our policy should be to cut our losses and get out of there as gracefully but promptly as possible."[60] Korea was an appendage of the Asian continent that did not figure in US grand strategy. It was not a good launching point for offensive operations against the Soviets, and any forces needed to protect Korea would necessarily detract from those needed to protect Japan.[61] The last US armed military unit left Korea on June 29, 1949, leaving only a 500-man advisory group.[62]

And yet the North Korean invasion was such a blatant act of aggression, Truman felt compelled to respond. Within ten months of the decisions made in December 1949, the United States found itself in contravention of its three key strategic principles on Asia: (1) do not engage in a ground war on the Asian continent (the United States would commit 1.8 million forces in theater [5.7 million overall] to the Korean conflict); (2) do not divert resources and assistance from the primary theater in Europe to peripheral areas in Asia (the United States would spend $341 billion on the conflict); (3) do not lose the opportunity to seek an accommodation with the newly established regime in China, at minimum to ensure against potential Sino-Soviet alignments (China's fall 1950 intervention in the Korean War would extinguish over the next two decades any residual American embers for recognition and coexistence with the PRC).[63]

Perhaps the best explanation for why the United States contravened its own strategic principles on Asia by going into Korea had less to do with strategy and more to do with credibility. Truman was outraged and angered by the attack. The nature of the act—an all-out armored invasion against a weak partner—triggered the Munich analogy.[64] He reportedly told his Secretary of State on the day of the attack that he would stop those "sons of bitches no matter what."[65] Policymakers were concerned that Korea was a diversionary tactic and a test of American resolve in order to advance communist interests in the primary theater on the other side of the world. For this reason, as Truman initiated a re-evaluation of US strategy that would eventually lead to NSC-68, the focus of this review remained on how to bolster European defense. By the end of 1950, General Eisenhower was put in the newly created position of Supreme Commander of NATO forces, and the United States committed six divisions of troops to deter conventional war.

Moreover, despite its seeming innocuousness, Korea now mattered in certain respects. First, it was the location of a direct head-to-head Cold War confrontation between two rival regimes, each backed by a superpower. As the Joint Strategic Survey Committee noted, "[Korea] is the one country within which we alone have for almost two years carried on ideological warfare in direct contact with our ideological opponents, so that to lose this battle would be gravely detrimental to United States prestige, and therefore security, throughout the world."[66] Second, it was a place where the credibility of the UN was also at stake given the UN-administered elections in the South just two years earlier (a service declined by the North). Korean administration had thus become one of this new postwar institution's first important actions. A bipartisan group of senators told Truman that South Korea was "the UN's baby," and if it failed to act, it was effectively done.[67] In a famous moment during Truman's meetings in Blair House on the day of North Korea's invasion, the president shouted with animation, "We can't let the UN down! We can't let the UN down!"[68] The reputation of the United States and the UN were therefore both on the line in this small country, as a then-top US diplomat for UN affairs, John Hickerson, noted:

> From the standpoint of military security, Korea is of no particular importance to the United States or, I suppose, to any of the other 52 [UN] members. But as a symbol, she is of tremendous significance—a symbol of determination of all free nations that aggression will be firmly resisted, that an attack upon the United Nations will not be countenanced.[69]

Truman, Acheson, and the great strategic minds in Washington could no longer separate US prestige and credibility in the world from defending remote South Korea.

The Domino Theory

Perhaps the most important consequence of the Korean War on the next four decades of American strategic thought in Asia was the domino theory: the idea that if one regime in the periphery fell to communism, this would set off a chain of dominoes, ultimately threatening to the core. Statements by key decision makers in June 1950 all reflected this thinking. John Foster Dulles sent a telegram to Acheson on the day of the invasion, stating that "To sit by while Korea is overrun by unprovoked armed attack would start a disastrous chain of events leading most probably to world war."[70] Secretary of Defense Johnson said in June 26 meetings at Blair House with Truman and Acheson: "The fairest statement I can make as to the general approach was that if you let this one happen, others would happen in more rapid order; that the whole world looked to the majesty and strength of the United States to see what we were going to do about this picture."[71] Acheson agreed: "The governments of the rest of the world, especially in Western Europe, were in a state of jitters and near panic, wondering whether the United States would take this lying down. If we let this pass, other aggressions would occur one after another, leading on to a third world war."[72] MacArthur put it even more succinctly: "Victory is a strong magnet in the East."[73] Truman's internalization of the domino theory was clear. He told his advisors on

June 26, 1950, that if he did not help the Koreans, then he was convinced that the "rest of Asia would go down."[74] In the recorded minutes of his remarks to a group of congressional leaders brought to Blair House on June 27, 1950, he was reported to say:

> If we let Korea down, the Soviets will keep right on going and swallow up one piece of Asia after another. We had to make a stand some time, or else let all of Asia go by the board. If we were to let Asia go, the Near East would collapse and no telling what would happen in Europe. Therefore, the President concluded, he had ordered our forces to support Korea as long as we could . . . it was equally necessary to draw the line at Indo-China, the Philippines, and Formosa.[75]

Asia scholars outside of government, too, worried about the region's vulnerability to falling dominoes. First, Asia consisted of postcolonial political regimes that were seen as weak and unstable. Second, these societies suffered from deep economic deprivation, making them susceptible to influence by any offer of outside assistance. The third factor was proximity. The United States was literally on the far side of the earth, while the Soviet Union and communist China were in the neighborhood. Japan was the closest non-communist Great Power patron, but was hated after the war. And fourth, the people in these postcolonial societies lacked an ideology or inspiration to animate their thinking. In this regard, the 1949 communist revolution in China suddenly offered a model for newly liberated Asian regimes. As Harvard scholar John King Fairbank warned in 1950, what the West saw as an unfortunate turn of events on mainland China had the potential to be seen as a watershed moment of national liberation and self-determination by postcolonial Asian societies. Fairbank believed that the appeal of this vision—the notion that communism with its promise of food, education, and independence could be accepted as the way to national salvation and human salvation for underdeveloped Asia—could become the valid idea of the twentieth century: "An insecure peasantry and a frustrated intelligentsia, the hope for economic improvement and national regeneration, are ready at hand to be organized in the Communist pattern."[76]

Although counterfactuals are impossible to prove, the attack on Korea alone in 1950 might not have elicited the US response that it did had it not been preceded by the successful Soviet nuclear test in August 1949, the October 1949 CCP revolution, and the February 1950 Soviet alliance with China. The loss of China and then Korea to communism might precipitate a formulaic string of tumbling dominoes, starting with Indochina, then stretching south to Indonesia and the Philippines and west to India and Pakistan, effectively undermining the US defense perimeter in Asia. Even if not by outright attack like in Korea, the precedent of two communist victories, the end of the US nuclear monopoly, and a newfound Sino-Soviet alliance might be enough to tip the balance and convince others to yield to an inevitable trend. Kennan was deeply moved by the turn of events, and wrote to Acheson the day after the North Korean invasion that he saw Korea not just as the beginning of a chain of dominoes that started with China, but as potentially having ramifications for the globe: "There will scarcely be any theater of the east-west conflict which will not be adversely affected thereby, from our standpoint."[77] The US enthusiasm for a response first took the form of saving the South from extinction following the initial invasion, but then transformed into a more proactive effort to fight a protracted land war all the way to the Yalu River after the successful landing at Incheon. In both the pre-Incheon phase of the war and the post-Incheon phase (i.e., rollback or advancing north of the 38th parallel), it had been decided that this Korean domino could not fall. The stakes were too large. The Joint Chiefs concurred on the domino effect and the global stakes at play in Korea. They told the defense secretary, "this loss [of the peninsula] would have widespread political and psychological repercussions upon other non-communist states throughout the world."[78]

Strategic Entrapment

If the vision of falling dominoes strengthened the arguments for US military engagement in Asia, then fears of entrapment reinforced the tendencies toward strategic ambivalence. The two impulses were not necessarily inconsistent. Even as Truman and Acheson prosecuted the war in Korea, they did not want partners or adversaries to view US boots on the ground as a "blank check" for Asian leaders or those inside of the US government to exploit the war for their own purposes. I will discuss Korean overdependence and US fears of entrapment in much greater detail in the ensuing pages. Here, I shall offer some preliminary evidence of US strategic "wartime" ambivalence toward Asia, even as Truman and Eisenhower were prosecuting a full-scale war in the theater.

At a meeting on the evening of June 25 at Blair House, where all players were expected to give President Truman their "honest-to-God opinion on the [Korean] situation," Defense Department officials opposed the extension of ground troops because they would be needed if the war spread to Europe.[79] Even as the army shipped out to the peninsula, Secretary of Defense Johnson and the Joint Chiefs of Staff were concerned about how this new deployment would weaken defenses in Japan as well as troop rotations to Europe. Some military leaders, including JCS Chairman General Omar Bradley, opposed sending too many forces as late as three days after the invasion.[80] John Foster Dulles, the Republican brought into the administration to provide Truman with some cover from rabid critics on the Hill, understood the need to supply air and naval support to Korea, but also did not want the United States to get drawn into a ground war on the Asian continent, as the Chinese and Russians could supply North Korea forever and win through attrition.[81] Dulles told influential journalist Walter Lippmann, "I had doubts as to the wisdom of engaging our land forces on the Continent of Asia as against any enemy that could be nourished from the vast reservoirs of the USSR. I expressed that doubt to the military as soon as I returned and before our decision was made."[82]

Dulles and the military were not alone in their ambivalence toward committing too much in Asia. Paul Nitze, one of the principal architects of NSC-68 and head of policy planning, advised against an expansive and deep military campaign, instead calling for the United States to consolidate a postwar division slightly north of the 38th parallel that would leave the shortest and most defensible line north of Seoul.[83] Nitze's ambivalence was striking given his willingness, espoused in NSC-68 and elsewhere, to take the fight against communism globally.

As the war progressed in the summer of 1950 and Western forces gained a foothold on the peninsula and started pushing back the North, George Kennan advised that US objectives in Korea should be limited strictly to recovery of the status quo antebellum. He explicitly warned that "when we begin to have military success, that will be the time to watch out. . . . Anything may then happen, entry of Soviet forces, entry of Chinese Communist forces, new strike for a UN settlement, or all three together."[84]

Why was there such strategic ambivalence in the summer of 1950? Clearly, American overextension and distraction from the European theater (e.g., Kennan's concerns); and overvaluing Korea's strategic importance (e.g., Nitze's view) contributed to the concern.[85] But there were two additional interlocking concerns. First, the United States wanted to avoid creating a moral hazard problem in Korea or Taiwan because of its military actions on the peninsula. US leaders did not think that the

Soviet Union or China really wanted to engage in an all-out war with the United States as a result of Korea, but this did not assuage concerns about escalation because Taiwan and South Korea constantly sought to leverage US support to pursue popular irredentist agendas.[86] Chiang would do almost anything to draw the United States into a war to retake mainland China. Rhee would do the same to "March North" and reunify the Korean peninsula.

Second, within the United States, significant groups wanted to use the war to escalate the US fight against Asian communism. General MacArthur and those of his ilk saw Korea as an opportunity to blockade mainland China, use KMT forces in the Korean War, bomb industrial facilities in China, and generally expand the Korean War into a war against the mainland with both Rhee's and Chiang's help.[87] In addition to MacArthur, politicians friendly to the KMT and a vast network of lobbyists sought to pressure the US government to do more in Asia, linking intervention in Korea with a wider anti-communist campaign at home. Even after the Incheon landing and the US decision to advance to the Sino-North Korean border, Senator H. Alexander Smith (R-NJ), Congressman Walter Judd (R-MN), Senator William Knowland (R-CA), Senator Robert Taft (R-OH), and even former president Herbert Hoover castigated the administration for being "soft" in Asia and violating the basic tenets of Truman's own doctrine. Knowland's statement on the Senate floor in 1950 typified the political pressures to do more: "Are we to take the position that human freedom is less worth supporting in Asia than it is in Europe?"[88] Witch hunts led by Wisconsin Senator Joseph McCarthy stirred up anti-communist frenzies in Washington, and ruined the lives of several US specialists on Asia, including Kennan's trusted Asia advisor, John Patton Davies.[89] Groups like Alfred Kohlberg's American China Policy Association, Frederick McKee's Committee to Defend America by Aiding Anti-Communist China, and the Committee of One Million held posh dinners, inviting prominent politicians and opinion-makers like Time-Life publisher Henry Luce and Joseph Alsop to make the case for taking back the mainland and opposing the recognition of Communist China.[90]

Even after MacArthur's September 1950 Incheon landing changed the course of the war and persuaded Truman, Dulles, Nitze and others to roll back communism on the Korean peninsula for good, the limited nature of the US commitment was still evident.[91] Specifically, MacArthur was given the go-ahead to advance to the Yalu River based on the condition that it would not spark a wider war on the Chinese mainland.[92] US decision makers did not want to feed overdependence pathologies of Taiwan and Korea, which might then embolden them to action and to embroiling the United States in multiple conflicts on the mainland. Hence, even after MacArthur pushed north of the 38th parallel in October 1950, officials went to extraordinary lengths to convey the message that Korea was not reflective of a larger doctrinal shift. Washington instructed the American ambassador in Seoul, John Muccio, for example, to stop Syngman Rhee from making any public statements about a "new" US rollback doctrine.[93] Truman and Acheson did not want US actions in Korea to be viewed as a blank check for Taiwan to move against China. Truman officials went out of their way to state that there was no doctrinal link between US actions in Korea and US defense of Taiwan. Indeed, Acheson sent Averell Harriman as a special envoy to the Pacific with specific orders to stop General MacArthur from encouraging the Nationalists (which MacArthur had been doing from July 1950).

Thus, even with the commitment to intervene to save Korea in June 1950, and then to push north of the 38th parallel in September 1950, the United States experienced a degree of "wartime ambivalence." That is, it prosecuted the war against the North Koreans, but was hypersensitive to becoming involved in a wider confrontation with China over Taiwan or with the Soviet Union in Asia that would somehow leave them unprepared in Europe. As historian Melvyn Leffler described, Washington believed that "every effort should be made to localize the conflict. . . . substantial efforts would be made to avoid a direct confrontation [with the Soviet or Chinese communists]."[94]

Similarly, the Korean War highlighted the potential communist threat to Indochina, but the United States remained ambivalent about devoting more resources there too. The need to help Southeast Asia was reflected in a memo by the Joint Chiefs of Staff to Marshall in November 1950: "The United States should take action, as a matter of urgency, by all means practicable short of the actual employment of United States military forces, to deny Indochina to communism."[95] But this imperative did not dampen the deep ambivalence surrounding a perceived strategic catch-22: Because of the military commitment in Korea and overall resource needs in Europe, the United States could only devote as much assistance to Indochina as to help the French maintain a foothold. This, however, would have the effect of perpetuating an incompetent colonial system that had made Indochina vulnerable to communism in the first place.

Truman's impulses for strategic ambivalence in Asia occasionally faded—as they did in September 1950, when the president and the majority of his advisors chose to roll back communism in Korea. The president rationalized this as the need for a uniform application of his anti-communist doctrine to Asia in order to bring the American public around to supporting NSC-68 and a strong defense. But with the Chinese intervention in October, the retreat back down the peninsula, and the ensuing stalemate, Truman was reminded constantly by his European allies of the need to cut his losses in Korea and opt for containment over rollback.[96] The Truman-Attlee meetings in late 1950 offer useful insights. British Prime Minister Attlee traveled to Washington after rollback was met in Korea with the massive Chinese counteroffensive. He was deeply concerned about the United States avoiding overextension in Asia when the main fight was in Europe. In Christensen's words, the British, who had once been fully supportive of a US response to the June 1950 invasion, were now "near panic" that the United States was expending valuable resources in a "strategic backwater," sapping its raw power to defend Europe.[97] The British even brought forward proposals for a peace settlement, not caring much whether it would look like a Western defeat after the Chinese counteroffensive, because some "lost face" in Korea was worth the price of concentrating scarce resources on Europe's defense against the Soviets. Acheson understood the problem and instructed embassies in Europe to assure allies that the United States was aware of avoiding entrapment in Korea and would fight only a limited war that would not be to the detriment of European defense.

The dilemma was obvious. In an address to the nation in April 1951, Truman explained to the American public the logic of limited war. In the second sentence of the speech, Truman stated that his objective was not to start another world war in Asia. But this was followed by impassioned clauses throughout about standing down communist aggression. The president was trying to counter a multitude of cross-cutting pressures. He needed to be strong in Korea in order to deter further aggression, win the American public's support for his global anti-communist stance, and appease congressional critics who accused him of losing China. At the same time, he needed to show restraint in order to avoid an escalatory war, becoming entrapped in a strategic backwater, and avoid provoking even tighter Sino-Soviet ties. The distillation of this was strategic ambivalence in Asia. The speech probably sounded strong, but it reflected preoccupation about how much war was enough to win, and how little war was needed to avoid out-of-control escalation.[98]

By the end of 1950, it became clear that containment would be applied differently in Europe and in Asia. In Asia, the question facing US strategy thinkers was how to contain without overcommitting to a region about which Washington exercised deep ambivalence. Truman and Eisenhower knew that they could not abandon Asia (especially after the North Korean invasion in 1950), because of the fear of falling dominoes, but they could not offer to write a blank check either, given the priority placed on the European theater. American strategic thinkers also became wary of wily and ambitious Asian leaders, domestic lobby groups, as well as some of its own military generals, capitalizing on American military commitments to drag the United States into a wider war with China. The nub of the institutional design problem would be how to construct alliance institutions that not only conveyed credible strength to the enemy, but did so in a way that also restrained the ally from entrapping the United States. The answer was the powerplay strategy.

4

TAIWAN: "CHAINING CHIANG"

US policy initially was to abandon Taiwan even before the Chinese Communist Party (CCP) victory in October 1949. When George Marshall became Secretary of State in January 1947, he had already spent one year in China trying to mediate the Chinese civil war in hopes of creating a coalition government. He left that year-long effort thoroughly skeptical of the Chinese nationalists, but informed by the views of George Kennan and John Patton Davies, assured that the Chinese communists were largely independent of the Soviets. His best recommendation to President Truman at the time was for the United States to disengage from China because any further involvement could spur anti-American attitudes and push Beijing closer to Moscow. By mid-1947, Marshall's advisors told him that funneling assistance to the KMT was effectively a no-win situation: The massive amounts needed to make a difference, including fundamental reform of the KMT, might not work, and it would deeply entangle the United States in the civil conflict. The fact that these recommendations ran completely counter to the Truman Doctrine's mandate to stem the tide of communism everywhere (enunciated in March 1947) did not matter. Despite critical members of Congress pointing out the contradiction (i.e., Marshall Plan for Greece and Turkey but not for the anti-communist Chinese Nationalists), by 1948 Marshall saw no other alternative. In his mind, the KMT would eventually lose out, and China's victory ultimately would not create a significant shift in the balance of power between the United States and the Soviets.[1] The United States in these early postwar years still provided limited assistance to the KMT, largely to appease Republican critics, to counter domestic charges of appeasement, and to barter for passage of large assistance packages for Europe, but a 1,054-page US government report in mid-1949 concluded that US aid could delay but not forestall an inevitable communist victory.[2]

This line of thinking continued after Marshall left office. His successor Dean Acheson, seeking to preempt a closer alignment between the Chinese communists and the Soviets,[3] did not want to renew the 1949 China aid bill as a way to signal accommodation to Beijing.[4] He responded to irate congressional leaders like Vandenberg and fifty others who called for an independent review of China policy in February 1949 by urging that they all wait for the "dust to settle" in the civil war before doing anything else.[5] Acheson, like his president, did not want to do anything that could entrap the United States in a civil conflict in China, when the real fight could be with the Soviets in Europe. As far as they were concerned, this issue was the "sideshow" and decisions taken here could not be allowed to have negative political or material ramifications for core American grand strategy in Europe.[6] Moreover, after the CCP victory in October 1949, the CIA judged that the KMT situation was so dire that anything short of all-out US military intervention and a full-bore aid program would be a futile effort.[7] The Secretary was open to the idea of a prompt recognition of the Beijing government and the use of carrots to keep them unaligned with Moscow in the hopes of promoting "Titoism" in Beijing.[8]

This "Titoist hypothesis" was most evident in the State Department even as the military establishment and even President Truman thought it held little water. In Congress, the Democrats were ambivalent while the Republicans were strongly opposed. Nevertheless, Acheson held fast to this view even as Mao signed a treaty of friendship with Stalin and seized US consular property in early 1950.[9] In testimony before the Senate Foreign Relations Committee in March 1950, Acheson stated confidently his hypothesis that the Chinese would "inevitably" come into conflict with Moscow because of differing objectives, if the United States was careful not to alienate Beijing. Moreover, even if this were not the case, Communist China was still too much of a "morass" to ever be a springboard for communist power projection.[10] Taiwan was not worth fighting for, the Secretary argued, ("why should we . . . fight the Chinese for an island that is not vital?")[11] and its greatest significance could only be measured in the degree to which the Nationalists, who displayed a "genius for misgovernment," could muck up broader strategy and objectives regarding mainland China.[12]

George Kennan, head of policy planning under Secretary Marshall and then for a period under Acheson, likewise saw little need for Taiwan in order to achieve the balance of power in Asia. He believed that the communist revolution in China did not make it a serious regional power given Beijing's underdevelopment.[13] He believed that supporting Chiang was at best a gamble not worth the wager, and would play squarely into Soviet hands. And even if Beijing allied with the Soviets, this would not significantly augment Moscow's capabilities. Thus, Kennan advised that the United States should "liquidate as rapidly as possible our unsound commitments in China and to recover, vis-à-vis that country, a position of detachment and freedom of action."[14]

The fundamental corruptness of the KMT and its unpopularity on the island also fueled American distaste for Taiwan. Kennan (along with Marshall and Truman) despised the characters making up the KMT, describing Chiang to a group of CIA officers in late 1949 as "sitting on Formosa with a group of extraordinarily stubborn and demoralized and selfish and rather pathetic people around him."[15] Acheson's aides observed him to have "utter contempt" for Chiang and loathed the Kuomintang, which the Secretary saw as both deceitful and incompetent.[16]

For all of these reasons, by the end of 1949, the best that US policy could do for Taiwan was to put it on slow life support. NSC 48/2 (December 30, 1949) limited US support only to economic and diplomatic means, with full acknowledgment that this might not prevent a communist takeover. Acheson sent confidential instructions that same month to foreign posts, with talking points anticipating the fall of Taiwan, coupled with what one scholar described as a "massive propaganda effort" to downplay Taiwan's importance to US interests (MacArthur leaked the memo, which gained Republican outrage).[17] President Truman gave a speech to this effect on January 5, 1950 when he reaffirmed the Cairo Declaration's commitment to return Taiwan to China and stated clearly that he would not send troops or substantial military aid.[18] A week later, Secretary of State Acheson's "defense perimeter" speech at the National Press Club excluded Taiwan (and Korea) from US areas of interest.[19]

"Saved from Extinction"

All of this changed with the North Korean invasion of South Korea on June 25, 1950. As historian Nancy Tucker wrote, the Korean War "miraculously saved Chiang Kai-shek's government from extinction," because the communists were now perceived to be testing the West's resolve in

Asia as part of a broader challenge in the world.[20] The impact of the Korean crisis on China policy could not be overestimated, as Robert Blum describes: "When North Korea invaded the South, administration officials who had championed the tattered Titoist policy for the previous eighteen months kicked it over in an evening, without much apparent regret and with full public support."[21] Internal NSC documents described the value of that which only months ago was considered expendable:

> [The] significance of Asia arises from its resources, geography, and the political and military force which it could generate. The population of the area is about 1,250,000,000. . . . The resources of Asia contribute greatly to United States security by helping to meet its need for critical materials . . . the area produces practically all of the world's natural rubber, nearly 5% of the oil, 60% of the tin, the major part of various important tropical products, and strategic materials such as manganese, jute, and atomic materials. . . . Therefore, it is important to US security interests that US military and economic assistance programs be developed in such a manner as to maximize the availabilities of the material resources of the Asian area to the United States and the free world.[22]

But more important than the intrinsic value of raw materials, Korea and Taiwan had to be kept out of communism's grasp in order to preserve the US strategic position in Asia.[23] The loss of Taiwan would "endanger the offshore defense line, Japan-Ryukyus-Philippines-Australia and New Zealand," as NSC 48/5 noted. In addition, "the inheritance of military supplies of United States origin by Communist conquerers of Formosa would increase the threat to our Pacific position."[24] US policy now inched from resolute resignation to reluctant support.

Washington made the decision on June 27, 1950 to interpose the Seventh Fleet in the Taiwan Straits; this "neutralization" still reflected some hope on the part of Washington (and the Democrats) that a modus vivendi could be reached with Beijing, but it also represented the sober judgment that the Seventh Fleet would discourage any malign intentions on China's part. NSC 48/5 in May 1951 called for new military training for Taiwan, and contingency plans to launch guerilla operations from Taiwan to the mainland.[25] It further authorized the Seventh Fleet's mission in the Strait for an indefinite period.[26] Among other actions, Washington concluded arms sales to Taipei and sent a Military Advisory Assistance Group to begin regular consultations between the two militaries. By 1951, nearly $100 million had been allocated for military equipment and economic aid. In 1952, the Mutual Security Appropriations Act increased aid to some $300 million. Between 1951 and 1953, the US official community in Taiwan increased from 119 to more than 1,200.[27] Truman, however, remained ambivalent about the commitment to Taiwan. Echoing a theme that would recur throughout his presidency, Truman did not trust Chiang and reportedly said "that we were not going to give the Chinese a nickel for any purpose whatsoever. [Truman] said that all the money we have given [Chiang] is now invested in United States real estate."[28] Until his last days in office, the president who had committed the United States to a ground war to repel the North Korean communists saw his support of Taiwan to be temporary, "occasioned by war but soon to be terminated by peace."[29]

The new Republican administration under Eisenhower in 1953 raised Taiwanese hopes that a more supportive US stance was forthcoming. Eisenhower wanted to re-orient the US military position around the globe by increasing the capabilities of indigenous forces in regions faced by communist threats while redeploying American forces back home. NSC 146/2 in November 1953 formally included Taiwan in the US western Pacific defense perimeter, in contrast to Truman (NSC 48/5 in May 1951),[30] and Eisenhower was in favor of utilizing Taiwan as a base of operations against the mainland.[31]

On September 3, 1954, heightening Cold War tensions over Korea, the brewing struggle in Indochina (where the PRC supported the Vietminh war against the French), and the tightening of US-Taiwan relations led the Chinese to commence shelling of Quemoy (Jinmen) and Matsu (Mazu) islands, held by the Nationalists approximately one mile and ten miles, respectively, off the Chinese coast near Xiamen.[32] The first of what became three offshore islands crises, this Chinese attack was followed two months later by Chinese bombing of Nationalist KMT positions on the Dachen island group, and in January 1955 Chinese troops overtook Yijiangshan. The United States responded by signing a mutual defense treaty with Taipei in December 1954 (ratified in March 1955); and Congress passed the Formosa Resolution the following January authorizing the use of military force to defend Taiwan and the offshore islands. This new alliance commitment was couched in the language of Cold War containment of the adversary; however, the relationship with Taiwan was much more complicated than this one dimension. Indeed, as alliance managers soon found out, Washington's enthusiasm for the alliance would be tempered by deep anxieties about overextension.

RECKLESS CHIANG

In Chiang Kai-shek, the United States had a potentially dangerous partner. The leader was at times delusional in his desire to reverse the tide of events that had befallen the Nationalists. As Steven Goldstein describes, Chiang behaved as if Chinese history had stopped before the CCP revolution.[33] Denying the political realities of the time, he spoke openly of returning to the mainland and defeating the communists. Chiang maintained that Taiwan was not his new home, even after most of the cities on the mainland had been overrun by CCP forces. "Fangong Dalu" (counterattack the mainland) and "Guangfu Dalu" (recover the mainland) were favorite slogans bandied about the KMT as reminders of Chiang's ambitions even as he set up a government on the island.[34]

Chiang's irredentist ambitions were driven not just by a dose of megalomania but also by his tenuous domestic political circumstances. The Nationalist government was not popular among native Formosans; moreover, Chiang needed to maintain the rhetoric of retaking the mainland as the best way to keep the military loyal to him, many of whom also wanted to return. Rallying disparate political opinions around this overarching cause therefore justified Chiang's authoritarian rule on the island. Chiang set provocative public timelines for when he would invade, and was unafraid to undertake escalatory military actions. In February 1950, Chiang ordered his forces to bomb Chinese cities, including American-owned facilities in Shanghai with US-supplied planes and munitions in flat defiance of US orders.[35] In June 1950, the Nationalist leader offered three divisions of KMT forces (33,000 troops) to the United States for use in the Korean conflict with the plan to leverage a wider war against Asian communism.[36] Chiang once proposed a large-scale amphibious assault on the mainland, a coastal blockade of China, and bombing of Chinese facilities with US planes in 1952 if the truce in Korea failed.[37] The Nationalist leader openly defied the Seventh Fleet "neutralization" of the Straits by conducting periodic raids with Nationalist forces on the mainland.[38] He ordered his air force to bomb Shanghai and drop leaflets boasting of the "Tiger Airforce Squadron" which looked like the US "Flying Tigers" Air Force, suggesting American support. Chiang even hired Japanese mercenaries to fight for the Nationalist army to give China the impression that the United States was sending occupation forces from Japan to help the war in China.[39] Chiang told Eisenhower in 1953 that he could mobilize 500,000 ground forces as the "spearhead" to an invasion, and in 1954 he proposed an expansion of his military through the so-called Kai plan, tailored to undertake an invasion of the mainland.[40] During the 1958 offshore islands crisis, Chiang increased his forces on the islands to 100,000 as a provocative ploy to invite Chinese shelling in hopes of escalating a wider war.[41] In the 1962 Quemoy-Matsu crisis Chiang informed Washington that there were millions of loyalists ready to rise up in China after the failed Great Leap Forward, and advocated openly for invading China. The Generalissimo even instituted a new "war tax" in order to raise $60 million for the invasion.[42] Though his fiery anti-communism was sometimes appealing to Truman, Eisenhower, and Kennedy, this Nationalist leader was a loose cannon and potentially very dangerous.

Chiang Kai-shek and his wife also sought to manipulate domestic politics in the United States by cultivating relationships and by lobbying different elements of the US government. Chiang maintained a channel of communication, without State Department or White House input, with General MacArthur in Tokyo, who encouraged Chiang's revisionist agenda. The KMT also had a relationship with the CIA which, operating under the cover of different US agencies, supported covert operations on the mainland.[43] The CIA recruited a force of nearly 100,000 Nationalist troops by 1951 to perform guerilla operations on the mainland, and itself grew to more than 600 personnel.[44]

The US Congress was a fat target of these lobbying efforts.[45] Madame Chiang Kai-shek set up offices in Riverdale, a suburb of New York City just ten minutes outside of Manhattan, and worked outside embassy channels, much to the consternation of officials. She pushed her husband's agenda by befriending Secretary of State George Marshall and other influentials in the New York-Washington, DC power corridor.[46] These efforts were not without success during her stay from December 1948 to January 1950. In September 1949, for example, Mrs. Chiang got Congress to oppose the nomination of W. Walton Butterworth as Assistant Secretary of State for East Asian affairs because he was viewed as leaning in the direction of accommodating the CCP's imminent victory on the mainland. The Nationalists befriended high-profile senators like Alexander Smith (R-NJ), William Knowland (R-CA), Styles Bridges (R-NH), Patrick McCarran (D-NV), and Robert Taft (R-OH), hosting their lavish trips to Taiwan. In the House, Walter Judd (R-MN), John Vorys (R-OH), and John Davis Lodge (R-CT) among others attacked the administration for their weak support of Taiwan. Other prominent supporters of the cause were Henry and Clare Boothe Luce of *Time*, journalists Joseph and Stewart Alsop, former US official Stanley Hornbeck, former Harvard Law School Dean Roscoe Pound, and retired Major General Claire Chennault (who led the "Flying Tigers" squadron in China). Frederick McKee, an industrialist from Pittsburgh, led a group called the "Committee to Defend America by Aiding Anti-Communist China"; and Alfred Kohlberg and William Loeb, also businessmen with roots in China, led the American China Policy Association, which accused the State Department of harboring pro-communist sympathizers.[47] Between 1950 and 1954, the Taiwan lobby circulated fraudulent documents suggesting that Americans like Owen Lattimore, John Service, and Eleanor Roosevelt were pro-communist sympathizers and anti-KMT. Chiang's lobbying efforts even enlisted the support of former presidents like Herbert Hoover.[48] The Generalissimo was never interested in US support of a government in exile; instead, he wanted Washington's commitment to take back the mainland.

THE DILEMMA OF DUAL DETERRENCE

Chiang's pathologies generated for the United States what Robert Jervis called the dilemma of "dual deterrence"—it had to defend Taiwan but not embolden it.[49]

US Anxieties about Chiang

Top US policymakers openly expressed concerns about Taiwan's dangerous behavior. US support for the Nationalists during this period entailed a military advisory group that provided support on strategy issues and training of troops; a naval advisory group with a large element of the US Western Pacific Fleet based at Tsingtao; and aid provided through the China Aid Act. Truman's secretary of state, George C. Marshall did not trust Chiang's efforts to use these elements to drag the United States into a war of "uncertain magnitude and indefinite duration."[50] His successor, Dean Acheson, was equally concerned. One of the first actions taken by Washington that evinced fears of entrapment pertained to the disposition of the Tsingtao naval unit. Acheson became concerned that the navy might attempt to protect the city from the communist advance and embroil the United States in hostilities with China. In December 1949, the NSC sent explicit instructions to the Tsingtao naval commander, Admiral Oscar Badger, to avoid engagement and to liquidate all shore facilities.[51]

Acheson genuinely despised the KMT leader; so much so that prior to the policy turnaround that occurred with the Korean War, Acheson had a more than casual interest in ousting the Generalissimo and the KMT. Acheson in early 1949 had his close aide Livingston Merchant contact the governor of Taiwan, Chen Cheng, about encouraging islander participation in the local government. The not-so-subtle message was that American ambivalence toward Taiwan might change to active economic assistance if Chiang and his cronies were ousted.[52] In February 1950, one week after Chiang bombed Shanghai, hitting some US-owned facilities with US-supplied munitions, Acheson asked his experts internally whether this blatantly provocative act could give the United States the chance to cut off ties.[53] Newly appointed as Assistant Secretary of State in March 1950, Dean Rusk, like his boss, saw the Generalissimo as dangerous. He hatched a plan to send Chiang to the Philippines, but Manila did not want him. He then suggested to the KMT the elements of better future relations with the United States: "[Rusk] indicated to Chinese representatives that Chiang was an obstacle to American aid to Formosa. Koo and Hollington Tong came away from the discussions with Rusk and Dulles persuaded that, however obliquely, the Americans were saying that Acheson might be won over to aiding a reformed, i.e., Chiang-less regime."[54]

Avoiding Entrapment in the Straits and Korea

Anxieties about entrapment led the United States to systematically restrain Chiang. This took the form of private communications, public proclamations, as well as direct warnings (and even threats) that leveraged US support for Chiang's good behavior. Washington improvised in terms of how it would do this, but the predominant practice that emerged was the powerplay—to utilize whatever bilateral defense statements, military assistance, political commitments, and economic aid the United States proffered as a tool to restrain Chiang from starting a broader war. Dean Rusk characterized the "front end" of the powerplay strategy: "A little aid to strengthen the island's defenses would be forthcoming, but nothing more—nothing for the recovery of the mainland."[55] Moreover, the "back end" of the powerplay was the restraint angle—i.e., should Chiang behave offensively, the United States made clear that this aid would dry up.

The Seventh Fleet's neutralization of the Taiwan Straits, in this regard, was as much about avoiding entrapment by the client state as it was about containment of the adversary. When Truman authorized the operation, Acheson sent a private letter to Chiang on June 27, 1950, stating plainly

that the KMT leader should stop all actions against the mainland and
seek no unauthorized advantage based on the US defense commitment:

> The United States Seventh Fleet has been ordered to prevent any
> attack from the mainland against the island of Formosa. . . . Your
> Excellency will understand that a continuation of air and sea op-
> erations by forces under Your Excellency's command against the
> Chinese mainland or against shipping in Chinese waters or on
> the high seas would not be compatible with the discharge by the
> Seventh Fleet of the mission assigned to it. The US Government is
> therefore confident of your full cooperation in the issuance of the
> orders necessary to effect the termination of such operations, and
> its forces have been instructed to proceed on the assumption that
> such orders have been issued.[56]

In internal meetings, Truman was preoccupied with the back end of the
powerplay. He wanted explicit acknowledgments from the Taiwanese
that Chiang would not provoke in ways to "avoid reprisals by the Reds
that might enlarge the area of conflict."[57] Heeding US direct pressure,
Foreign Minister George Yeh announced on June 30 that the government would stop all navy and army actions against the mainland. The
US determination to avoid entrapment in the Straits was formalized publicly in the president's statement on July 3, 1950:

> The occupation of Formosa by Communist forces would be a di-
> rect threat to the security of the Pacific area and to United States
> forces performing their lawful and necessary functions in that
> area. Accordingly, I have ordered the Seventh Fleet to prevent any
> attack on Formosa. As a corollary of this action, I am calling upon
> the Chinese Government on Formosa to cease all air and sea op-
> erations against the mainland. The Seventh Fleet will see that this
> is done.[58]

Even after the neutralization operations were no longer necessary, US
military officials in Taiwan worried that once they left the Strait, they
would lose all leverage and have "practically no control over the Nationalist forces on Formosa."[59] In early 1953, Eisenhower in NSC meetings
noted the "real trouble and danger [is] that Chiang Kai-shek might go
on the warpath," and instructed the US Pacific commander "to expedite
obtaining a commitment from the Chinese Nationalist government that

Chinese Nationalist Forces will not engage in offensive operations considered by the United States to be inimical to the best interests of the United States."[60]

Stopping Chiang's Efforts to Widen the War

The US objective in the Korean War was, of course, to repel the North, but an equally important objective was to prevent a wider war in Asia. In the very first set of instructions sent to MacArthur four days after the invasion, the JCS authorized the general's operational command of the Seventh Fleet, his use of army combat forces to defend the Pusan perimeter, and limited authorization to bomb north of the 38th parallel. But the JCS also made clear that "[You] will insure that Formosa will not be used as a base of operations against the Chinese mainland by Chinese Nationalists."[61] In this context, Chiang's proposal in June 1950 to lend 33,000 troops for the conflict was seen as an attempt to drag the United States into a general war with China.[62] Chiang promised to send an infantry division under the command of General Sun Li-jen, and an armored division commanded by none other than one of Chiang's sons, General Chiang Wei-kuo.[63] Chiang even established ties between his agents in Burma (discussed below) and ROK president Syngman Rhee in hopes of opening a second front.[64] An internal State Department memo aptly summed up US thinking: "The introduction of Chinese Nationalist troops into Korea would immediately throw Korea into the Chinese civil war and would make it much more difficult, if not impossible, for US to maintain the position that we have so far maintained that in any political talks on Korea after an armistice there would be no discussions of any matters outside of Korea."[65] Chiang's offer gained the support of US commanding generals in Korea, but Truman went against their advice. Within two days of the receipt of Chiang's offer, Acheson responded to the Taiwan ambassador that a transfer of forces to Korea might be premature given the island's own defense needs, and suggested that Taipei host defense consultations with MacArthur.[66] Even after the United States' refusal, Chiang remained undeterred; he made the same offer to the UN Secretary-General three days later, and colluded with MacArthur to keep the idea alive.[67]

Acheson had little patience for Chiang's mischief over Korea. In July 1950, the Secretary of State got personal approval from Truman to tell MacArthur and defense secretary Louis Johnson to stop encouraging Chiang's ideas.[68] That same month, Truman declared in a message to

Congress on the Korean situation that there should be "no doubt in any quarter" that the United States will not become embroiled in any offensive military actions from Taiwan to the mainland as a result of the Korea conflict.[69] Truman also demanded that MacArthur retract his public characterization as "defeatist" of Washington's disinterest in Chiang's offer in the summer of 1950.[70] To end the discussion, in August 1950, the president dispatched esteemed diplomat and former US Secretary of Commerce Averell Harriman to the region to clamp down on both Chiang and MacArthur.[71]

Even after the United States in October 1950 moved to roll back communist forces north of the 38th parallel, it evinced no interest in advancing Chiang's agenda, and as one historical account put it, the United States put "every obstacle" in the way of allowing Taiwan's offensive operations against the mainland.[72] In messages to the Chinese through Indian intermediaries in the first days of rollback, the United States made clear that it saw rollback as a Korea-only operation, not the spark of a wider move against China. One of many internal communications from the State Department to its embassy in India in the early days of rollback operations in October 1950 captured the United States' intended message to China:

> Up to now this Govt's sole channel communication with Chi Commies, except for public statements by officials, has been dubiously reliable intermediary Panikkar. Given latter's predispositions and free-wheeling proclivities, we cannot be sure what Chou En-lai says or hears in conversations with him. . . . even though fol[lowing] may consist to some extent repetition what you have already said to Bajpai, . . . Dept feels you might seek some opportunity through Bajpai to meet Chi Amb and put directly to him this Govt's position re Korea. . . . Summary might take fol[lowing] line: "As shld be abundantly clear, US has no desire whatsoever that hostilities develop between UN and Chi forces. Such eventuality would be tragedy for world and particularly for China. . . . Therefore, fol facts shld be understood beyond shadow of doubt:
>
> 1. UN operations constitute no threat whatsoever to Korea's neighbors.
> 2. As evidence of good faith US is prepared accept . . . neutral unbiased investigation and assessment damages arising out of charges of bombing incidents brought by Peiping authorities.
> 3. US has no desire to extend conflict or to establish bases in Korea.
> 4. US does not seek any special position whatsoever in Korea.

... Authorities in China shld not underestimate historical sympathy Am[erican] people toward those seeking to maintain territorial integrity and genuine political independence of China.[73]

US anxieties about becoming entrapped by Chiang grew stronger, not weaker, after a ceasefire was reached in Korea in 1953. Chiang despised the armistice (and the end to Seventh Fleet patrols of the Straits) as a sign of US weakness. This emboldened the Generalissimo to push the envelope even further. Nowhere was this dynamic more apparent than in Burma and the offshore islands. In the case of Burma, Chiang had use of a remnant force after the PLA expelled Nationalist troops numbering 45,000 from neighboring Yunnan province in 1950. Truman, in response to China's intervention in the Korean War in late 1950, initially approved a CIA plan, known as "Operation Paper," to covertly supply these Taiwanese forces under the direction of General Li Mi, and fund a guerilla war against Yunnan to help distract and disadvantage Chinese efforts on the Korea front.[74] Arms and munitions were sent from Okinawa and money was funneled through a front company in Thailand.[75] General Li's forces eventually more than tripled in size and occupied bases in different parts of the Yunnan-Burma border. Chiang was authorized to engage in cross-border guerilla operations through 1953, killing many PLA troops, but also eliciting crushing responses from the Chinese. These CIA-backed operations reached their height in the first half of 1953.[76]

However, with the Korean War armistice in July 1953, what had previously been a convenient side operation to sting and distract the Chinese had now under General Li's actions become a liability in the fragile ceasefire, as well as in US relations with Burma. The latter was a country with which Taiwan did not have diplomatic relations, but one that Washington wanted to keep in the non-communist camp. From 1951 Rangoon had asked the United States to stop supplying Taiwanese guerilla operations in its country, and sought to terminate its receipt of bilateral assistance from the United States in March 1953, appealing to the UN in protest.[77] Washington did not deny the existence of these guerilla forces in Burma, but it obscured any US involvement.[78] However, as Operation Paper increasingly looked like a freelance operation by Chiang designed to provoke war with China, Washington sought to restrain Chiang directly.

The Eisenhower administration in January 1953 gave "unequivocal orders" to stop the raids into China.[79] Chiang resisted the demarches, insinuating that the State Department's view was not necessarily the view of the CIA, which had been his true partner in the operations. Chiang used other excuses as well, such as the inability of Taipei to control the operations of Li Mi's guerilla forces, the offer of partial withdrawals, and later complaints that Burmese forces were harassing his troops as they were trying to stand down operations and exit through Thailand.[80] Eisenhower officials pushed harder to terminate the operations. In March–April 1953, Karl Rankin, the US point person, told Chiang that Washington might reevaluate its aid packages to Taipei as well as its support in the UN if the raids did not stop. In a March 1953 meeting between Secretary of State Dulles and ROC Ambassador Wellington Koo, Dulles interrogated the ambassador, bluntly asking, "When are you going to get your troops out of Burma?" Koo was so taken aback by Dulles's outburst that he later followed up with Assistant Secretary Allison, who stated that prompt withdrawal was the "best possible thing" that the ROC could do.[81] The following month, Dulles blocked authorization of supply planes into Burma for General Li's forces. In a tersely worded eyes-only cable to the ambassador in Taipei, Dulles instructed Rankin,

> [Y]ou will promptly take all necessary steps to prevent commandeering CAT planes or flights by any other planes to Li Mi's forces. . . . You should immediately bring matter to attention of Foreign Minister, . . . that no clearance will be given to any further flights from Formosa to KMT forces Burma.[82]

Finally, in September 1953, Eisenhower intervened with a personal communication to Chiang and a face-to-face meeting with his son, Chiang Ching-kuo, calling for the end to operations in Burma at the earliest possible date.[83] Presidential intervention in such a delicate issue reflected the US concerns with becoming entrapped in Chiang's antics. In spite of these entreaties, Chiang would continue to send forces into China from Burma during the 1958 crisis, and it would take eight more years before the Generalissimo would relent to their removal in 1961.[84]

Offshore Islands

The United States was extremely concerned about Chiang's use of the offshore islands to provoke China. A small cluster of islands off the coast of the mainland, Quemoy and Matsu were the most important of them. Universally recognized as part of Fujian province on the mainland, they were not part of the Formosa/Pescadores formations, and so the ROC's occupation of them during the civil war was legitimized as Chiang's proverbial bridge to the mainland, while the PRC saw them as axiomatic with Chinese prevention of Taiwan's independence.[85] Chiang occupied the islands during the civil war, but mainland Chinese forces were in the process of taking these back when the United States interposed the Seventh Fleet in the Straits in June 1950. The United States acquiesced in Chiang's holding these islands, deeming these as useful as a first line of defense against the mainland, a staging point for a future mainland invasion and/or guerilla raids, a point from which to harass Chinese shipping, and a psychologically important symbol of the KMT's irredentist ambitions given the proximity of its presence to the mainland. The use of these islands as a base for offensive operations to pressure the mainland and to disrupt maritime commerce increased under the Eisenhower administration (NSC 146/2 in November 1953 authorized such operations but without the commitment of US forces). However, the line between whether these islands were an asset or a liability became increasingly blurred. The United States was happy to use the islands for small-scale operations, but at a tempo and time of Washington's choosing. Chiang, on the other hand, sought to take full advantage of these proximate positions to carry out his irredentist agenda as well as compel US commitments in his goals. It became increasingly clear that the proximity of the offshore islands allowed Chiang to take military actions without US help, which confounded the US ability to control the situation.

In September 1954, the Chinese commenced heavy artillery bombardment of the islands. Eisenhower and Dulles wanted no part in defending them. Dulles told the NSC he objected to getting "sucked into the offshore islands."[86] Defense Secretary Charles Wilson and Treasury Secretary Humphrey had the same view.[87] Eisenhower wanted to avoid a conflict with China over the islands at all costs, cognizant of letters he received from average Americans pleading with him not to send American boys to war again.[88] Furthermore, no one wanted to take on the defense of the islands, which would require neutralization of PLA artillery and airfields on the mainland, large-scale ground troop commitments, or possible escalation to the nuclear level.[89]

The crisis eased in February-March 1955, but the United States would remain concerned about Chiang. In order to de-escalate the crisis, Eisenhower provided a secret pledge to Chiang for US defense commitments to Quemoy and Matsu in return for a withdrawal of Nationalist troops from these and other island groups. Chiang became emboldened by the US defense assurance; he refused to reduce his troop presence on the islands, and instead upped deployments to more than 100,000 men and to one-third of his military equipment by mid-1956.[90] After the 1958 crisis, in which the United States sent substantial military assets to the Straits to deter further Chinese aggression, the United States experienced heightened fears of entrapment. Washington sought dialogue with Beijing, it looked for face-saving ways for Chiang to draw down his forces, it proposed demilitarization of the islands under the auspices of the UN or the international court. But most of all, the anger at Chiang was palpable.[91] Internal State Department memos in 1958 openly assessed that Chiang's objective was to pull the United States into a nuclear war with China.[92] Eisenhower in internal meetings remarked that he wanted the Generalissimo to leave office, and wanted to put someone in place who would evacuate the islands.[93] Chiang, in response, dared the United States not to stand with him in facing down the Chinese from the islands, leveraging US anxieties about preventing dominoes from falling in Asia. The two were engaged in a game of chicken with neither side offering an exit ramp.

"Unleashing Chiang"?

A counterargument to this historical treatment of US policy to Taiwan might point to the many statements of support by the United States, and in particular, from the Eisenhower administration, for Taiwan's defense. Taking office in 1953, the Republicans sought to differentiate their Asia policy from the Democrats. During the 1952 presidential campaign, the Republican Party platform boasted that it would "end neglect of the Far East" and cast the incumbent's policies as "Asia Last" in contrast to Stalin's "Asia First" scheme.[94] Candidate Eisenhower attacked the Democrats for being weak on communism and promised to liberate countries from behind the "bamboo curtain," using the Republican campaign slogan of K1C2 (Korea, communism, and corruption).[95]

As a symbol of this new commitment, Eisenhower in his 1953 State of the Union speech, famously instructed the Seventh Fleet to abandon its dual deterrence mission under Truman, and to "no longer be employed to shield Communist China."[96] Newspapers headlined that the new president was taking the "handcuffs" off of Chiang in contrast to the "timorous and apprehensive" policies of Truman.[97] NSC 146/2, approved by Eisenhower in November 1953, formally included Taiwan in the US defense perimeter in Asia, unlike Truman's handling of the same. Chiang praised the change of tone out of Washington and probably hoped that

MacArthur's aspirations of Taiwan as an "unsinkable aircraft carrier" might be realized.[98]

These stated policy positions raise legitimate questions about whether the front end of the powerplay (i.e., security commitment) was the meat of US policy under the new Republican White House, and anxieties about entrapment (i.e., back end of powerplay) of the previous administration had become just a peripheral concern.

I believe that at the start of the Eisenhower administration, Washington undeniably signaled strong support. The reasons had to do with US domestic politics and the state of the war in Korea. On domestic politics, differentiating this White House's Asia policies from the previous one was of paramount importance. Moreover, anti-communist witch hunts under the banner of McCarthyism created an atmosphere welcoming of strong, unconditional statements of support for Taiwan.[99] Regarding the Korean War, Eisenhower inherited a stalemate, and promised to the electorate that he would end hostilities by compelling the Chinese to sue for peace. Eisenhower still supported some level of Taiwanese activity against the mainland, but only as a diversionary tactic, never as part of a plan to re-take the mainland.[100] Furthermore, there was reputational significance to demonstrating US support for Taiwanese stability. As Dulles said, "If all hope of a Nationalist return to the mainland were to be destroyed the United States would lose the whole show in the Far East."[101]

Thus, Eisenhower emphasized rhetorically the front end of the powerplay, and this made headlines. However, administration officials harbored many of the same concerns that their predecessors had about Chiang's overzealous behavior and overdependence pathologies. They sought actively to curtail the Generalissimo's ability to provoke a conflict with the mainland. Indeed, after Eisenhower achieved the objective of a Korean War armistice, the back end of the powerplay became a major concern and preoccupation of John Foster Dulles. Nowhere was this more evident than in the hard-headed exchanges between Secretary of State Dulles and the Nationalist leader.

Although the new administration talked about "unleashing Chiang," Dulles pointedly relayed to Taipei that this sound bite should not be publicly presented as American support for aggressive actions against mainland China.[102] In addition, Dulles supported secret curtailment of arms transfers until Chiang committed to US demands:

I have your memorandum of March 31 with reference to the worries of the JCS arising from the delivery of US F-84 aircraft to Formosa. I share these worries. . . . we are attempting to get an agreement with Chiang Kai-shek that he will not use the new equipment we give him against the China mainland without our prior consent. . . . I believe that the Defense Department should suspend any deliveries of aircraft capable of attacking the mainland until we get the political agreement we want.[103]

Dulles worried about Rhee (discussed in the next chapter) and Chiang colluding in their opposition to the 1953 armistice negotiations to keep the United States at war. He sent instructions to the US embassy to let Chiang know the consequences of such a plan:

In view of G'mo's apparent backing of Rhee you should quickly in your own words informally and in highest secrecy let G'mo know that Rhee's attempts to force US troops to fight indefinitely in Korea . . . will not succeed. Plans are being formulated so that if Rhee persists responsibility for Korea will be left wholly to ROK forces. . . . this will be disastrous for Korea. . . . possible withdrawal from Korea would doubtless require reconsideration of US-Formosa policy with result now not predictable.[104]

During the first offshore islands crisis (1954–1955) as well, Dulles met with Chiang (in March) and although not publicly released, the memoranda of conversations detailed how the Secretary of State chided Chiang for his openly provocative "target dates" to invade the mainland. Initiating such actions, Dulles argued, would make Taiwan look like the aggressor, and the United States could not be blamed for that. Dulles even opened a secret channel with China in 1955 with the hope of negotiating a renunciation of force agreement over Taipei's head. The idea failed, but it was a sign of how much of a problem Dulles considered Chiang.[105]

During the second offshore islands crisis in 1958, Dulles wrote an internal paper that laid out four key imperatives the United States must impress upon Chiang: (1) that the Nationalist government must act as though there were an armistice in place with the mainland; (2) that Chiang must publicly reaffirm that he will not attempt to forcibly retake the mainland; (3) that Chiang must refrain from commando raids, provocations, and overflights; and (4) that the offshore islands should not be used as a "jumping off" point to conduct attacks against the mainland.[106] Regarding the last point, Dulles admonished Chiang's ambassador in Washington, George Yeh, of the military madness of putting so many armed forces on Quemoy. He said these forces served no military function whatsoever, and either would entrap the United States in a war with China or become hostages to Chinese communist aggression.[107] Dulles was even more blunt in expressing his distaste for Chiang's tactics in personal correspondence with US Ambassador Drumright in Taiwan: "[Chiang] should equally realize that we are up against the charge that we are being dragged into a world war by Chiang, that we have put the destinies of the American people at his disposal, and that we have no flexibility in our position because Chiang is stubborn and will not agree because he feels that his only real hope is to precipitate world war."[108]

Thus, while Eisenhower's statements about unleashing Chiang sent clear political and tactical signals of support for Taiwan's defense, it was equally clear that the core strategic imperative remained the same. Dulles could never be so public about this concern, and had to be sensitive to congressional views. But he and Eisenhower knew they had to implement successfully the back end of the powerplay against Chiang's antics.

The 1954 Defense Treaty

Chiang Kai-shek once complained that the 1954 mutual defense treaty with the United States, which he had wanted so dearly, had the effect of binding the Republic of China by "hand and foot."[109] An exaggeration, certainly, but not by much. The treaty formalized a defense commitment to Taiwan that eliminated ambiguity about US resolve in China's eyes. It provided a legal basis for US military use of the island in future military contingencies. The treaty also gave legitimacy to the Chiang regime in Taipei, which enhanced domestic stability. But the dilemma was that Chiang might abuse a treaty commitment as a blank check, and create more security liabilities for the United States. In the end, Eisenhower and Dulles decided to triangulate the problem—that is, employ the treaty as a restraint on Chiang. Neither of them trusted Chiang and both worried about the problems that a foreign, uncouth Asian leader, who leveraged a civil war conflict as the only mantle of domestic legitimacy, could create for the United States. As Goldstein observed, "Washington sought to use the treaty to limit the ROC military to defensive actions, and to spin a web of restrictions that would prevent Taiwan from using the alliance to pursue its mainland ambitions and entrapping the United States in an unwanted conflict."[110] The United States, of course, had a policy of restraint on Taiwan before, but now with the pro-offering of a security treaty, the United States had powerful tethers, both security and economic, with which to bind Chiang from mischievous behavior in a way that would not have been possible without such a treaty.

NSC 146/2, approved by Eisenhower in October 1954, laid out the objectives of the treaty negotiation (concluded in December 1954 and ratified the following March): (1) Taiwan should be kept independent from communism; (2) the United States would support Taiwan militarily and diplomatically; however, this commitment would not be a blank check in support of actions from the offshore islands; and (3) any military coordination with Taiwan would be "subject to the commitment taken by the Chinese Nationalist Government that its forces will not engage in offensive operations considered by the United States to be inimical to the best interest of the United States." Furthermore, the treaty would "avoid any implication of US obligation to underwrite the Government or to guarantee its return to power on the mainland."[111] In the course of the treaty negotiations, Assistant Secretary of State Walter Robertson consistently opposed Foreign Minister George Yeh's efforts to win some wiggle room for Taiwan's actions. Yeh sought, for example, to expand the US defense commitment to include all of the offshore islands in the treaty terms, as well as the right for Taiwan to intercept Chinese shipping. But Robertson made clear that such commitments would not be ratified by Congress and that the president opposed the proposals as unnecessarily provocative.[112]

Washington essentially sought a treaty that could be used to exercise veto power over Taipei's sovereign right to use force. It also sought through the treaty to cement a neutralization of the Strait (i.e., no attempts to disrupt the status quo by either side). This was an extraordinary level of control. Chiang strongly resisted on the grounds that this was effectively sanctioning a two-China policy and would delegitimize the core of Chiang's political mandate to return to the mainland. In order to navigate these political delicacies, Washington consented to not writing this "binding" element into the body of the treaty. Instead it was carried in a separate private minute exchanged by Dulles and Foreign Minister Yeh a week after the signing on December 10, 1954. Taipei wanted the note to be kept secret from the public, which remained so until the 1980s. The key clause read:

> In view of the obligations of the two Parties under the said Treaty and of the fact that the use of force from either of these areas by either of the Parties affects the other, it is agreed that such use of force will be a matter of joint agreement, subject to action of an

emergency character which is clearly an exercise of the inherent right to self-defense.[113]

The United States also hedged its defense commitment by intentionally excluding the offshore islands by name in the treaty, instead referencing "such other territories as may be determined by mutual agreement." This omission was designed to avoid giving Chiang the justification to claim that America backed his actions on the islands closest to the mainland.[114] In public, Dulles pushed back against any accusation that the treaty somehow limited Chiang's freedom.[115] But in truth, Washington had designed a defense commitment to the Nationalists inseparable from that same commitment's capacity to restrain the regime. The powerplay strategy—as Doak Barnett observed—was unmistakable, "Washington took steps to restrain the Nationalists from embarking on military adventures against the mainland. In an exchange of notes, the Nationalists agreed that the 'use of force' from Taiwan required joint agreement. . . . Chiang was obviously leashed."[116]

One could argue that the conditional nature of the US commitment was not unusual, and was in fact prudent policy. But this appeared to be more than routine diplomatic practice. As noted earlier, the United States exhibited far less conditionality in its defense commitments to Europe when the communist threat in Asia arguably was more immediate. In a note to the president right after he initialed the draft treaty with Yeh, Dulles assured Eisenhower of the treaty's extraordinary quality:

> The Treaty covers an attack directed against Formosa and the Pescadores. The [diplomatic] note will in substance recognize that the Chinese will not use force from either Formosa, the Pescadores or the offshore islands without our agreement and will not transfer military equipment and the like from Formosa to the offshore islands without our agreement. This has been a difficult negotiation but the result, I believe, stakes out unqualifiedly our interest in Formosa and the Pescadores and does so on a basis which will not enable the Chinese Nationalists to involve us in a war with Communist China.[117]

In Senate testimony, Dulles referenced this diplomatic minute in response to senators' concerns that Article 1 of the treaty gave the impression that the United States would back Taiwan's attack on the mainland. The Secretary testified that Chiang would not under any circumstances be able to manipulate the defense commitment into affording Taiwan a privileged sanctuary for offensive attacks on the mainland. Chiang would not be able to launch offensive military operations and could not divert US military assistance, weapons, or equipment without US consent.[118] On the contrary, Dulles said the treaty would "frustrate Taipei's dream of retaking the mainland."[119]

The Powerplay

Massive amounts of assistance flowed into Taiwan, all facilitated by the defense treaty. As figures 4.1, 4.2, and 4.3 show, Taiwan became the third largest recipient of US military assistance globally, and the largest in Asia. Economic and military grants and loans amounted to $3.7 billion and $1.3 billion respectively between 1949 and 1963.[120] The United States was responsible for 43 percent of gross investment in Taiwan and an astounding 90 percent of capital inflows.[121] Taiwan's growth was entirely dependent on the United States, and US military assistance relieved Taiwan of the costs of a large defense budget.

Through all that it gave, the United States could micromanage Taiwan. The US military provided guidelines on what types of military

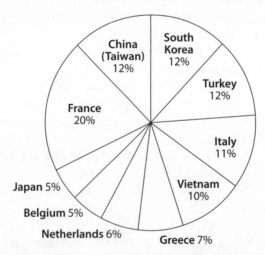

FIGURE 4.1. Total US military assistance, obligations (historic dollars) (1950–1966) *Source*: Compiled from US Agency for International Development (USAID), "U.S. Overseas Loans and Grants: Obligations and Loan Authorizations," July 1, 1945–September 30, 2012, at http://pdf.usaid.gov/pdf_docs/pnaec300.pdf, accessed July 25, 2014.

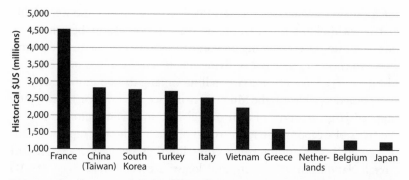

FIGURE 4.2. Top ten recipients of US military assistance, obligations (1950–1966)
Source: Compiled from US Agency for International Development (USAID), "U.S. Overseas Loans and Grants: Obligations and Loan Authorizations," July 1, 1945–September 30, 2012, at http://pdf.usaid.gov/pdf_docs/pnaec300.pdf, accessed July 25 2014.

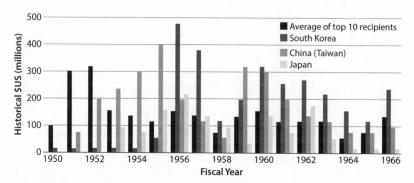

FIGURE 4.3. US military assistance, obligations (1950–1966)
Taiwan, South Korea, Japan, and average of top ten recipients.
Taiwan (3): 2,411,000,000; Korea (4): 2,391,000,000; Japan (10): 902,000,000
Source: Compiled from US Agency for International Development (USAID), "U.S. Overseas Loans and Grants: Obligations and Loan Authorizations," July 1, 1945–September 30, 2012, at http://pdf.usaid.gov/pdf_docs/pnaec300.pdf, accessed July 25, 2014.

actions Taiwan could take. Small-scale offensive pinpricks were acceptable, but indiscriminate bombing of mainland targets or other actions that could be construed by the Chinese as incendiary were ruled out. In the event of a provocation by the mainland, all military responses had to be approved by US commanders,[122] including whether Taiwanese planes could follow Chinese adversaries in hot pursuit and what parts of the Chinese southern coast (if any) the Taiwanese could attack. The United States surveilled Taiwan to make sure that they were abiding by the guidelines; whenever it determined that the Taiwanese were deliberately withholding information, overstating the severity of a situation, or surreptitiously conducting provocative actions (e.g., aggressive patrols closer to the Chinese coast or flying unauthorized routes over communist territory), it issued directives telling Chiang to stop immediately.[123]

As noted in table 4.1, the Military Assistance Advisory Group (MAAG) supplied large amounts of arms to Taiwan, and Washington calibrated the types of weapons systems it would provide. It did not supply systems that could be used for force projection, limiting the number of transport aircraft, landing naval vessels, and logistics capabilities.[124] The MAAG supplied small-, but not large-scale landing craft (indeed, the majority of those were supplied during the 1958 offshore islands crisis in order to allow Chiang to supply his forces on the islands). It focused on bolstering defensive capabilities such as anti-submarine warfare and minesweeping capabilities. Washington, largely through the CIA, would dictate details such as the type of operation and the size of the force (e.g., 20 or 200 men), which led to complaints of American heavy-handedness.[125] When Chiang chafed at Eisenhower's requests to clear all offensive operations against the mainland with him, the United States simply withheld further shipment of jet aircraft, fuel, or artillery until the assurances were received.[126]

Contingency Planning and Second Offshore Islands Crisis

The restraint aspect of the Taiwan alliance permeated all levels of US policy from talking points to operational plans. Internal policy guidance to CINCPAC and the American Embassy instructed officials to always incorporate in all demarches that Taiwan had a sovereign right to self-defense, but that the American defense commitment explicitly did not involve the unilateral use of force against the mainland.[127] Military contingency plans, moreover, exhibited operational guidelines that were phased in ways that would enable the United States opportunities to decipher whether a bona fide Chinese attack was under way without any Taiwanese provocation. Phase 2 was premised on an overt Chinese attempt to take one of the islands, in which case US forces would directly assist in defense of offshore isles, including attacks on enemy artillery positions and local airfields. Phase 3 was premised on a Chinese attempt to capture Taiwan or the Penghus, which would elicit a direct US response on China, possibly including nuclear weapons. But most interesting in the context of the powerplay argument was phase 1, which was premised on the most likely scenario—a Chinese action short of major military

TABLE 4.1. U.S. AIRCRAFT AND NAVAL ASSETS DELIVERIES TO TAIWAN
(1953–1960)

TYPE OF EQUIPMENT	QUANTITY	AIR OR NAVAL	DEFENSE OR OFFENSE
C-119	16	Air	Defense
F-100 F/A	90	Air	Offense
F-104 A/B/G	20	Air	Offense
F-47	150	Air	Offense
F-84G	245	Air	Offense
F-86F/D	433	Air	Offense
H-19B	4	Air	Defense
HU-16A/B	9	Air	Defense
P4Y	35	Air	Offense
PBY5A	11	Air	Defense
SA-16	2	Air	Defense
T-28	26	Air	Defense
T-33A	67	Air	Defense
Sub Chasers	17	Naval	Defense
Destroyers	4	Naval	Defense/Offense
Mine Sweepers	4	Naval	Defense
Utility Landing Craft	17	Naval	Defense
Auxiliary Floating Dock	1	Naval	Defense
Landing Ships for Tanks	13	Naval	Defense/Offense
Landing Craft Repair Ship	1	Naval	Defense
Medium/Large Support Landing Ships	8	Naval	Defense/Offense

Source: Adapted from Garver, *The Sino-American Alliance*, pp. 67–69 (page 50).

attack. In this scenario, direct US military action would be expressly held in abeyance pending evidence that Chinese aggression was unprovoked. In the interim, the United States would only provide material support and logistics.[128] In retrospect, this was an extraordinary statement. The scenario posited some Chinese hostility (at the height of the Cold War, no less), but did not give the Taiwanese the benefit of the doubt regarding who was the instigator.[129]

For obvious political reasons, the United States could not so boldly display such a heavy hand, so the treaty contained a "mutual consultation" clause, which technically permitted Chiang to undertake whatever he wanted as long as the United States agreed. Chiang attempted to invoke this clause on more than one occasion in Eisenhower's second term and into the Kennedy administration. After Eisenhower's re-election in November 1956, for example, Chiang sent a personal communication the following month calling on the American president to be more like Lincoln and accomplish the herculean task of "emancipation of the captive peoples in Europe as well as in Asia." After essentially urging Eisenhower to start World War III, Chiang then wished the president and his wife a Merry Christmas.[130]

Each and every time, the United States beat down Taipei's entreaties. Eisenhower stated in NSC meetings and in conversations with Chiang that he saw these 100,000-strong force deployments on the islands as an attempt to provoke communist hostilities and thereby embroil the United States in a third world war.[131] The United States had to fulfill its alliance obligations, and so it mobilized air and naval forces to break China's attempted blockade of the island. The United States even hinted that it would use nuclear weapons to defend Taiwan, but discussions at an August 29, 1958, White House meeting showed contempt for Chiang's recklessness and anxieties that he might draw the United States into war:

> The discussion then turned to the fact that Chiang Kai-shek, despite our advice, had put such a large proportion of his strength on the Off Shore Islands and now came "whining" to us. . . . Admiral Burke and Governor Herter both indicated that Chiang was seeking to find out if we were really behind him. The President remarked that in effect he had in fact made his soldiers hostages on those islands. Admiral Burke said that this had been done deliberately and in fact made Taiwan virtually a hostage. Mr. Quarles added that Chiang's policy in this respect was designed to put leverage on us.[132]

For these reasons, the United States withheld any public statement of support for Taiwan for a full two weeks after China's initial shelling of the islands on August 23. It was not until September 1 that Eisenhower committed publicly to defending the islands, but only in a highly conditional manner:

> It has been our policy not to commit the United States to assist in the defense of the off-shore islands unless it is clearly demonstrated that the CHICOM attack is a prelude to attacks on Taiwan and the Penghus. We hope by our actions to convince the CHICOMs that we will come to the assistance of the GRC, without at the same time, inviting the GRC to create a situation which will cause our immediate involvement. *We intend to assist the GRC to hold the major off-shore islands, but the manner and timing of this assistance must remain under U.S. control.* (emphasis added)[133]

The fact that the United States felt the need to make clear its restraints on Taiwan even at the height of a crisis when engaged in defensive actions clearly attests to the concerns about avoiding entrapment.

During the John F. Kennedy administration, Chiang constantly pressed for a "revision" of the mutual consultation clause in the treaty, complaining that it was outdated. He urged the White House to support a large-scale invasion. In 1962, during the third Quemoy-Matsu crisis, Chiang believed that the combination of domestic dislocation in China caused by the Great Leap Forward and a series of floods and droughts in northern and southern China provided a golden opportunity to incite instability. Chiang prepared troop deployments, and invoked the mutual consultation clause to suggest a Bay of Pigs–like invasion plan with a covert landing of Taiwanese forces designed to look like a domestic uprising. President Kennedy rebuffed Taipei's request, reminding that the 1954 treaty required all action by Taiwan to be subject to US approval, and that there were no "blank checks" for action against the mainland.[134] In a private statement made through the Warsaw ambassadorial talks in June 1962 to the Chinese, Kennedy also said that the United States would not support a Taiwan offensive operation on China.[135]

Mutual Hostages

Two questions naturally arise when thinking about US policy toward Taiwan during the Truman and Eisenhower years. Why didn't the United States simply abandon Chiang? After all, if the Generalissimo's antics raised such fears in Washington of being baited, deceived, and sucked into Chiang's ambition of a nuclear war with the mainland, wouldn't

Washington have been better off just cutting ties and minimizing risk? Second, why were US leaders so obsessed with the notion that Chiang's antics would spark a general war with China? If Washington just abrogated ties with Taipei, then the regime would not have been seen to possess the capabilities to invade the mainland and Chiang's pinpricks through Burma or the offshore islands would not have been enough to provoke Beijing into war. Distancing strategies are often invoked by states as a reaction to an ally's overdependence pathologies and one's own entrapment anxieties.

The answer stems from core strategic beliefs held by the United States at this time. First, American leaders judged that Chiang was not bluffing in his desires to retake the mainland. The Generalissimo staked his political legitimacy on this goal above all else. Moreover, even if he did not have the capabilities to provoke an all-out war with China, the vulnerability of his regime if abandoned by the United States might incentivize Beijing to retake the island. In this latter respect, US officials were constantly worried about "morale" on the island. A restrained Taiwan was important, in American eyes, but a demoralized one that could raise the specter of regime instability or communist infiltration was also dangerous. In short, Taiwan could not de-align or "defect" from the US relationship, but it could collapse. Chiang regularly raised this possibility with the ambassador in Taipei whenever he grew frustrated with US heavy-handedness.[136] Thus, the US intelligence community, when it was not spying on Chiang, was doing elaborate analytic estimates of the domestic strength of the regime and its morale. While Washington sought to bind Chiang from carrying out his ambitions, US planners were careful that the optics of its directives looked like mutual decisions between Washington and Taipei, and that Chiang had more independence in decision-making than he really did. Finally, as noted in chapter 3, the domino theory pervaded US strategic beliefs at the time. Even if Americans assessed that Taiwan was not worth the candle, its collapse—either because of US abandonment or because of Chiang's war with China—would set off the collapse of other smaller states to communism. As Dulles told Eisenhower in a 1957 NSC meeting, losing Taiwan would lose "the whole show in the Far East."[137]

Thus, Truman and Eisenhower were inexorably tied to Chiang and other anti-communist Asian leaders as much as those leaders tried to tie down Truman and Eisenhower. They were in effect mutual hostages. To distance from the regime would have only engendered a teetering domino, which would have been strategically damaging in Washington's eyes.

The only answer was to bolster these small Asian nations, but use these deep bilateral ties to control all downside risk from unpredictable leaders.

The powerplay was about defending Taiwan, but at the core, it was about fundamental distrust and risk management. Truman, Eisenhower, and Kennedy did not trust Chiang one iota, and they needed to manage risk if the Taiwan leader went rogue. The most appropriate institutional design the United States could build to minimize these two concerns was a deep US bilateral tie that awarded unprecedented control over the sovereign choices of another state. Washington designed a security institution with the island that allowed the United States to prosecute the Cold War at a tempo of its choosing. The neo-imperial culture of this relationship was reflected in subtle but telling gift-giving practices omnipresent in diplomacy with Asian nations. At the end of a 1962 meeting between President Kennedy and Chiang Kai-shek's son and envoy, Chiang Ching-kuo, the Taiwanese presented Kennedy with a Chinese translation of Kennedy's inaugural speech and a translation of the book, *Profiles in Courage*. In return, Kennedy presented Chiang with an autographed picture of himself. The relationship was entirely about what the United States wanted.[138]

5

KOREA: "RHEE-STRAINT"

The Republic of Korea's first president, Syngman Rhee (served 1948–1960), made no secret of his aspirations for unifying the Korean peninsula. The ROK leader despised the competitor communist regime in the north, and viewed Korea's national division as a historical aberration. The First Republic's official policy was "pukch'in t'ongil" (unification by marching north), but privately Rhee more colorfully talked of "unification or death!" This was explicitly a policy of taking the North by force that was intolerant of the concept of peaceful coexistence between the two regimes.[1] Rhee, who once said, "An armistice without national unification was a death sentence without protest," did not want the Korean War to end, and when it looked like it might, he wanted to fight on without the United States and the UN if necessary.[2] Washington's welcoming of such rabid anti-communist partners in these early Cold War years was laced with palpable anxiety about Rhee's overzealousness. Pukch'in t'ongil could very well drag the United States into unwanted wars on the Asian mainland. The strategic mandate was therefore to help Rhee, but also to restrain him.

Rhee's Belligerence

The United States contended with a mixed blessing in the first ROK head of state. Rhee was a known quantity to Americans relative to the other non-English-speaking Koreans who vied for political power in Korea after Japan's surrender in 1945, ending thirty-six years of colonial rule. Rhee was fluent in English, Princeton-educated, a staunch anti-communist, and a true patriot who, as the first US ambassador to Korea John Muccio recalled, had dedicated forty-five years of his adult life to fighting for Korean independence from the hated Japanese.[3] As a young man, he traveled to Portsmouth, New Hampshire, in 1904 to appeal to President Theodore Roosevelt not to surrender Korean sovereignty to Japan as part of a postwar settlement ending hostilities between Japan and Russia. And in 1933, he again pleaded the Korean case for independence at the League of Nations, to no avail. After that, he led the Korean provisional government in exile located in Shanghai. Rhee lived in the Theological Seminary at Princeton, and was allowed free board there as the Seminary's first-ever Korean student. Most of his coursework was within the Department of History, Politics, and Economics, and he wrote his doctoral dissertation on the international-legal concept of neutrality. Rhee was hard working as a student, with an uncommonly heavy workload, as he also spent summers at Harvard finishing up a master's degree he had started there.

Attaining the presidency of South Korea through UN-administered elections in 1948, Rhee ruled in a far-from-perfect fashion, presiding autocratically over what was nominally a constitutional democracy. The country was dirt poor and war-ravaged, which did not make governance an easy task. Rhee compensated for the glaring imperfections of his leadership and sought legitimacy through two practices that were mirror images of each other. First, playing off of his regime's inherent weakness, he constantly extorted aid from the United States through the threat of its imminent collapse at the hands of the communists. And second, boosting the ROK's military strength, he defined the legitimacy of his presidency in terms of the national goal of overthrowing the enemy regime in the North by military force.

It was in this latter respect that Rhee knew no restraint. As one American official who had nearly daily interaction with the ROK president remembered,

> [Rhee's] advanced age made him humanly impatient to achieve his lifetime ambition to become the first president of a unified, free Korea. Anything that helped him attain that goal was good; anything that impeded or postponed it . . . was bad . . . although I personally liked the man, I still found him as exasperating an ally as anyone could have.[4]

Like Chiang in Taiwan, Rhee's desires to defeat the communists and retake territory were pursued with a single-minded fervor. His actions and statements were often unpredictable, provocative, and, at times, completely unreasonable. In the immediate post–World War II years, for example, he urged US occupation commander Lieutenant General John R. Hodge to capitalize on America's temporary nuclear monopoly and threaten nuclear use to force the Soviets to withdraw from their half of the peninsula.[5] In February 1949, Rhee told the Secretary of the Army, Kenneth C. Royall, that he wanted the US Army to help strengthen and expand the number of South Korean army divisions to facilitate an invasion of the North.[6] This was not just expensive and dangerous, it was particularly annoying to Washington because of reports from the field that ROK army units readily abandoned hundreds of thousands of dollars of US-supplied equipment when in retreat from the enemy.[7] Rhee, moreover, was unafraid to commit US interests to his goals. In May 1949 he released a surprise press statement declaring that the United States had provided a security guarantee to his country. When US Ambassador John Muccio demarched the ROK president about the inflammatory impact such uncoordinated statements could have on rising peninsular tensions, he recalled Rhee's belligerent response: "Rhee asserted over and over his government would fight to the last man against Communist aggression no matter what help might be received from the United States."[8]

Later that year, when the DPRK celebrated the one-year anniversary of its founding (September 9, 1948), Rhee complained about US and UN fecklessness. During a stopover in Tokyo en route to Lake Success, New York, where Rhee was to join UN deliberations on Korea, the outspoken South Korean president responded with disdain to news that the UN sought to extend the stay of the UN Commission on Korea to help his country. Rhee derided the help as too little too late, complaining that if only the UN and United States had helped him take over the North a year earlier, he could have established his own "iron curtain" along the Korean-Manchurian border. When UN members sought to encourage more dialogue between the two Koreas, Rhee was defiant, eliciting anger from some UN members at the South Korean's "uncompromising" and belligerent attitude.[9] He instead proposed that the US pool Taiwanese and South Korean forces for a ground assault on mainland China, backed by US airpower, to roll back communism.

Rhee shared his unification rhetoric with the body politic in South Korea, effectively equating anti-communism and anti-Japanism with a postcolonial concept of nationalism. This set off a vicious cycle—Rhee's provocative acts gained popular support, which only reinforced the man's tendency to continue them. As one Southeast Asian newspaper reported in covering the growing animosity between the two Koreas in the years leading up to the Korean War, ROK society felt confident that it could challenge the North. The mentality was "Hold it back? We'll push it back!"[10] As US Ambassador Muccio recalled from his many meetings with Rhee, the ROK president suddenly interjected threats to invade the North in otherwise sedate press conferences. Muccio stated bluntly, "[W]e had recurring problems with old man Rhee. We just couldn't shut him up."[11]

The Korean War

In the early morning hours of June 25 1950, Korean People's Army (KPA) troops poured southward across the 38th parallel, making easy work of the ROK defense forces and taking the capital, Seoul, in just four days, and pushing ROK forces back to a toehold at the southern tip of the peninsula. This prompted quick action in Washington and at the UN in New York. On June 27, Truman decided to deploy elements of the Seventh Fleet into the Taiwan Straits. Three days later he approved the commitment of US forces under the auspices of the UN and the leadership of General Douglas MacArthur. In one of the most memorable plans in military history, MacArthur landed forces at Incheon on September 15, splitting advancing North Korean forces in two and turning the tide of the war. The capital city of Seoul was retaken by US/UN forces on September 27, 1950, and on October 7–8 1950, Western forces advanced north of the 38th parallel to roll back North Korean forces, capturing Pyongyang on October 18. On October 1, Beijing received a formal request from Pyongyang for help, and conferred with Moscow in a decision-making process that took nearly two weeks between the two poorly coordinated allies.[12] The Americans incorrectly perceived that Chinese forces, which had been amassing in the hundreds of thousands in Manchuria since July, did not intend to set foot in Korea and were there largely for defensive purposes to ensure the war would not cross into China. Chinese forces eventually crossed the Yalu, first engaging UN forces in late October and early November, supported by Soviet airpower, and pushed American and UN forces back once again, retaking Seoul in January 1951. By June 1951, with neither side wanting to escalate the war further, a stalemate ensued and armistice talks began.[13]

From the outset of the war through to its ceasefire, Rhee consistently saw the conflagration as an opportunity to fulfill his ambitions of unifying the peninsula. In the summer of 1950, even when backed up to the southernmost tip of the peninsula, Rhee boasted that he would advance north of the 38th parallel once UN forces broke out of the Pusan perimeter.[14] He aggressively pressed the United States to increase Korean fighting forces by upwards of twenty divisions. One author described Rhee's attitude as "tenacious" in urging Truman to take the "victorious march north."[15] He criticized Truman for being weak on communism, a mantle that the Republican Party eventually latched on to in criticizing the president's foreign policy.[16] As the ultimate symbol of America's budding informal empire in Asia, but also a sign of Rhee's aggressiveness and willingness to fight to the end, he conceded sovereign control of ROK military forces to the United States. But these actions, designed to increase interoperability and an efficient fighting force with the Americans, were often accompanied by downright outrageous proposals, such as the one floated by Rhee in March 1953. Even though the battlefield stalemate left no chance for the United States to consider another drive north of the 38th parallel, Rhee called for the US military to establish a buffer zone *north* of the Yalu River (i.e., in Chinese sovereign territory) in order to keep the Chinese off the peninsula permanently.

By September 1950, after months of grueling battle and great losses, UN and ROK forces were bottled up around the port city of Pusan, when on September 15 MacArthur orchestrated the amphibious landing of two divisions at Incheon, dividing the already extended North Korean forces and reasserting control of all ROK territory by the end of the month. From this position of strength, the fateful decision was made to push north of the 38th parallel, in an attempt to rout the Korean People's Army and to reunify the peninsula under the leadership of the South. Rhee, predictably, was a big supporter of rollback. As early as July 1950, months before the US decision to cross the 38th parallel, Rhee's position was clear: North Korea's June 25 invasion had rendered moot the legality of the 38th parallel as a sovereign boundary.[17] It was now incumbent upon the United States to retake the whole peninsula just as the communists had hoped to do with their invasion. A personal letter to Truman in July 1950 captures Rhee's enthusiasm:

> It would be utter folly to attempt to restore the status quo ante, and then to await the enemy's pleasure for further attack when he had had time to regroup, retrain, and reequip. The time has come to cut out once and for all the cancer of imperialist aggression, the malignant growth artificially grown within the bosom of our country by the world communists. . . . The Government and the people of the Republic of Korea consider this is the time

to unify Korea, and for anything less than unification to come out of these great sacrifices of Koreans and their powerful allies would be unthinkable. . . . Daily I pray for the joint success of our arms, for clear skies so that the planes of the United States Air Force may search out and destroy the enemy, and for the earliest possible arrival of sufficient men and material so that we can turn to the offensive, break through the hard crust of enemy forces and start the victorious march north.[18]

As North Korean forces were put on the defensive after Operation Thunderbolt in 1951 (a counteroffensive by US forces to push north of the Han River), Rhee wrote in exclamatory terms: "If the United States wants to save democracy for the world, it had better do it now [in Korea]. . . . Do not be weak. Do not turn back. Democracy must not go backwards. Some day the United States will have to fight alone. Do not wait for that day."[19]

Rhee threatened to pull his forces out of United Nations Command and attack the North on his own, if the United States did not comply. As UN Commander Mark Clark recalled, Rhee's threats to pursue a war on his own against the North Koreans and Chinese was tantamount to a declaration of suicide. But there was a messianic quality to Rhee's bluster. He believed it was better for Korea under his leadership to die than to suffer the fate of other countries like Czechoslovakia, which surrendered to communism without a fight. As General Mark Clark recalled, "Through suicide, [Rhee] argued, Korea at least would go down in history as a nation of great honor and the sacrifice of Korea might be a lesson to the rest of the free world."[20]

Dangerous Quirks

Rhee had a habit of practicing over-the-top, anti-communism antics for domestic consumption (and for his own ego). This predilection had the unnerving effect of increasing military liabilities for the United States. One good example of this occurred in August 1952 after Rhee was inaugurated for his second term in office. He declared publicly, and then lobbied the United States to help him return the capital to Seoul from Pusan, where the enemy had forced the initial retreat of the ROK. The United States was against such a move because it would endanger critical government facilities near the border with the North while fighting was still under way (Seoul is only about 35 miles from the 38th parallel). This was not only dangerous, but also potentially escalatory as it would entice the North and the Chinese to attack such proximate high-value targets. Despite US objection, Rhee moved his personal offices back to Seoul, which effectively compelled officials and then thousands of civilians to do the same. The action so worried General Mark Clark that he personally intervened to stop Rhee, exercising his authority as head of the UN Command. Rhee continued nonetheless.[21]

Rhee also trampled over democratic rights enshrined in the constitution in ways that irked the United States, but with a recklessness that created security problems. In order to enforce martial law and upend efforts by the National Assembly to seek constitutional revision in 1952, Rhee pulled ROK army units from the front lines without seeking US approval. This prompted formal protests from not just the United States, but also from the embassies of nations participating in the UN Command. Rhee's actions created true vulnerabilities at the war front, and were among the key motivators for covert US plans to depose Rhee if necessary (discussed below).[22]

Though not directly related to national security, Rhee's obstinate behavior was evident in economic policies. The ROK president consistently pushed to keep the value of the Korean currency (won) overly inflated in order to maximize dollar amounts of US assistance. This, of course, did nothing to help the price of Korean exports on the world market, but Rhee did not care. Despite strong opposition from the United States, Rhee maintained this policy at the expense of developing an export-oriented economy.[23]

Another example pertained to the employment of Japanese during the war. US authorities found that Korea was poorly equipped in terms of human capital and technology to help support the war effort. As Clark recalled, the Koreans were "long on courage but short on everything else needed to fight a war."[24] Thus, equipment from Japan, as well as Japanese operators, had to be brought into the country as an essential part of the US and UN defense of Korea. Approximately 3,000–4,000 Japanese were performing various war industry jobs. Rhee, who was vehemently anti-Japanese, was preparing to run again for the presidency in the 1952 elections. He protested these measures in the strongest possible terms. He told the Americans that South Korea would unilaterally impose a trade embargo on goods from Japan, even if they were part of US assistance packages.[25] Regarding the Japanese workers, he said that he would rather surrender to the communists than have hated Japanese colonizers set foot again on Korean soil. The United States tried to comply with Rhee's concerns by training Koreans as replacement workers and by even taking the extraordinary measure of having Japanese work in Korea during the day and sleep on offshore ships at night. But this did not stop Rhee from imprisoning some of these workers, which was both embarrassing for the United States and detrimental to the overall war effort.

To demonstrate his patriotic credentials at home, Rhee made other outrageous demands such as seeking a veto over the US usage of war items from Japan. Rhee did not want anything from Japan in his country, and wanted to approve every US purchase, "right down to the last nut and bolt."[26] When General Clark tried to invite Rhee to his headquarters in Japan as a way to forge better relations with Japanese Prime Minister Yoshida, Rhee arrived with a press statement that was so hateful of Japan in tone that it would have worsened overall bilateral and US-Japan-Korea trilateral relations. These emotional outbursts exasperated US officials. As Clark recalled, "with a volatile character like Rhee there rarely is a time without incident."[27]

Sabotaging the Armistice

By the spring of 1953, the nearly-three-year war had reached a stalemate. The drive north toward the Yalu River in October 1950 had prompted the intervention of Chinese "volunteer" forces in November, who drove UNC and ROK forces back, south of Seoul. Though the two sides entered armistice negotiations in July 1951, territorial and prisoners-of-war disagreements led to deadlock, as the war churned on, with neither side gaining or losing much ground. In April 1953, however, Washington sensed greater receptivity from the communists on a ceasefire to end the hostilities on the peninsula, due in part to US suggestions that use of nuclear weapons was not off the table as part of the Eisenhower administration's emerging "massive retaliation" doctrine. Introduced by Secretary of State John Foster Dulles in 1954, massive retaliation was the notion that the United States would rely on disproportionate response to deter the adversary from considering any military attack. The doctrine leveraged the short-lived US nuclear monopoly, and focused US global strategy on deterrence rather than on local defense.[28]

Rhee was against the negotiation of an armistice agreement and constantly pressed the United States to take the war to China. When MacArthur's successor, General Matthew Ridgway, first raised the issue of a truce, the cantankerous Rhee took him by the arm and said, "General, you're a very persuasive talker, but you have not convinced me that you cannot go to the Yalu if you want to."[29]

Eisenhower recalled Rhee's intransigence in detail. Rhee wrote a "frank letter of protest" to him, calling communist peace gestures duplicitous. The ROK leader asked how "you can win from a political conference by persuasion, what you could not win on the battlefield by force?"[30] He argued that it was morally unjustifiable for free nations like the United States to negotiate with communists, and he accused the United States of having "cold feet" in not prosecuting the war to its end.[31] Eisenhower described Rhee's communication as "drastic in tone" and "extreme in its terms," which the US president felt needed to be restrained.[32]

In these letters to Eisenhower, Rhee constantly blustered that the South would fight alone if need be. On one occasion, he warned that if the Chinese remained in the North, "South Korea would feel justified in asking all her allies to get out of the country except those who would be willing to join in a drive northward to the Yalu."[33] To follow through on this threat, in April 1953 Rhee's ambassador in Washington formally notified the White House of the ROK's plans to remove its troops from the UN Command. The threat was taken seriously enough by the United States to warrant a trip by UN Commander Mark Clark from his Tokyo headquarters to Pusan.[34] Rhee's threats constituted a ridiculous proposition given the vastly superior Chinese military compared with the fledgling forces of the ROK. There was no way the ROK could win. But it could create a great deal of trouble for the United States. South Korea held two-thirds of front-line troops on the peninsula. This meant that Rhee could easily have removed his forces from the UN Command and authorized an attack. Clark described this scenario as a "nightmare" possibility and a "frightening" action that would wrest control of the war away from the United States while at the same time embroiling it in an escalation.[35] In short, Rhee's words amounted to a threat to entrap the United States. Such an offensive would have failed but at the same time provoked the Chinese to re-engage in hostilities. "As the unofficial leader of the free world, the United States could have ignored Rhee's [actions]," as one author observed, but "only at the risk of jeopardizing her own ideological posture vis-à-vis the Communist world. Any military engagement by Rhee with the communists would obligate a US response."[36]

Once truce negotiations resumed, Rhee continued to act like a loose cannon. On May 30, 1953, he wrote Eisenhower of his concerns that an armistice agreement would allow the Chinese to remain in North Korea. He pleaded with Eisenhower to allow the fighting to continue as this was the "universal preference of the Korean people to any divisive armistice or peace."[37] In June 1953, Eisenhower invited Rhee to visit Washington to help persuade him of the benefits of an armistice. The ROK president declined the great honor to be hosted at the White House, saying that demonstrations in South Korea *against* the armistice negotiations kept him at home to manage an unstable situation. Once again, Rhee said that he reserved the right to use his forces to attack the North regardless of US policy preferences.

Later that month, the communists finally agreed on the most difficult issue in the armistice talks—the voluntary repatriation of prisoners of war. This breakthrough all but ensured that an agreement could be reached soon. Rhee wrote a June 17 letter to Eisenhower again complaining about the dangers of a truce. This last letter worried the president deeply. He described its tone as "highly emotional" and noted that Rhee's behavior caused much "uneasiness" among US decision makers.[38]

The Ultimate Gambit

Eisenhower's concerns proved right. In a deliberate attempt to undercut armistice negotiations, on June 18, 1953, Rhee released 27,000 prisoners of war being held in the South. The release was hardly random; rather, it was a carefully coordinated plan hatched by Rhee with a small number of Korean military commanders. Overnight, ROK guards at prison camps simultaneously opened the gates and released the prisoners into the population. American forces tried to stop the escape with tear gas, but with only one officer and a handful of administrative personnel at each camp guarding thousands of released prisoners, their efforts were thwarted by active local civilian and police cooperation. Prisoners were told where to go. Families were asked to hide them. Local police were told to warn citizens of the American soldiers searching for the prisoners. In some cases, ROK soldiers drew their guns on US soldiers until the prisoners could get away. As the UN Commander put it, "all hell broke loose" with Rhee's actions.[39]

The danger of the action was not the security concerns posed by these released prisoners because most were anti-communists who wanted to be in the South anyway. Rhee's actions instead undercut the principle that all repatriations should be voluntary and should be facilitated through a processing arrangement observed by both sides. The United States had been steadfast in pressing this issue despite communist opposition, and so the decision by communist truce-negotiators to give in on this point was considered a major step forward. Rhee negated with one action all of the work that had been done to that point to reach a truce agreement.[40]

Rhee's actions were testament to how much of a renegade partner he was. Eisenhower described the POW release as a "bombshell" event that was completely unexpected. He worried about the emotional stability of the ROK leader.[41] Rhee's unpredictable actions bewildered the administration and caused considerable awkwardness for the US president. He recalled, "The Communists asked at this juncture and, I must confess, with some right—whether the United States was able to live up to any agreement to which the South Koreans might be a party." At a July 1 news conference, Eisenhower felt the need to correct popular perceptions "as to the identity of the real enemy" on the peninsula and to remind the press that the true enemy "is still in *North* Korea."[42]

Rhee's actions had their intended effect. The communists responded to the POW release by resuming large-scale attacks on US and UN positions. A two-division offensive along the east coast pushed ROK frontline divisions back four to six miles.[43] The Chinese launched a major six-division offensive across the central front that engaged six ROK and one US division in major hostilities. The ceasefire that had seemed so close was once again ruptured. Rhee's actions had resulted in some ten thousand casualties. Though a truce would eventually be reached in July 27, 1953, Rhee's POW release was the ultimate gambit in his brinksmanship efforts to force the United States into a war to retake the entire peninsula. Washington had to find a way to restrain further unilateral actions by the ROK leader.

POWERPLAY

The United States faced a similar entrapment dilemma with South Korea as it had with Taiwan. On the one hand, it appreciated Rhee's anticommunist fervor and vigilance in standing toe-to-toe with the Chinese and North Koreans. On the other, as hostilities in 1953 looked as though they would subside to a ceasefire, the United States saw absolutely no use for further conflagrations in Asia. Washington could not trust Rhee, who like Chiang was a foreign Asian leader invested deeply in winning an unwinnable civil war as his mantle of political legitimacy. It became clear that Rhee's willingness to throw his entire country over a cliff to achieve his "march north" objective could drag the United States into an unending hostile mire in mainland Asia when the primary Cold War theater of concern was Western Europe. This dilemma was accentuated by a belief in the domino theory—which would obligate Washington to respond to any renewal of hostilities on the peninsula (even if instigated by the South) because Korea had now become the front line of the Cold War in Asia, and by association, the world. US planners had to provide a defense commitment to Korea to deter further aggression, but at the same time, not give President Rhee the impression that a new US commitment gave him carte blanche to pursue his irredentist agenda.

The United States could not abandon the ROK; rather it had to support it, but at the same time, control it. The best way to do so was to execute a tight bilateral relationship that would deter the communists, but just as important, exercise absolute hegemony over its ROK partner to avoid entrapment. This hegemony was exercised through the creation of an asymmetric security dependency of the ROK on the patron ally. Secretary of State Dean Acheson in early 1950 referred to this as the American "civil war" deterrent, giving equal weight to the control of the ally and the confrontation of the enemy: "[T]he US troops are there to block a North Korean invasion, but also to restrain the South. . . . because of the revolutionary challenge presented by the new North Korean government, and the volatility of the [South Korean] government with its frequent threats to march north."[44]

Successive American administrations consequently viewed the alliance relationship with South Korea in three ways. First, the alliance was part of a network of alliances and military installations connected with Taiwan, Japan, the Philippines, Thailand, New Zealand, and Australia, designed to contain the Soviet threat in the Pacific. Second, it was an alliance aimed at deterring a second North Korean invasion, with US ground troops in-country as the "tripwire" guaranteeing US involvement. And third, the alliance implicitly bound and restrained the South from adventurism.

Underwrite or Overthrow?

This restraining rationale became evident immediately in US postwar planning. Both US Ambassador to Korea John Muccio and Secretary of State Dean Acheson were acutely aware of the need to control Rhee, given his incessant chatter about "unification or death." Muccio's cables to Acheson in 1949 framed the problem: "We were in a very difficult position, a very subtle position, because if we gave Rhee and his cohorts what they wanted, they could have started to move north the same as the North started to move south. And the onus would have been on us."[45]

US General Mark Clark was so concerned about ROK unilateralism that he complained about being engaged in a two-front diplomatic battle—with the communists at Panmunjom and with Rhee in Seoul—and that the "biggest trouble came from Rhee."[46] The dilemma for US planners was that they could not simply ignore Rhee's antics. By virtue of the three-year war effort, the United States was now wedded to the fate of Korea in a broader Cold War context. Clark called it the "psychological whammy" that the South Korean president had on the United States —"He knew that no matter what happened we could not, after three years of war, after all the blood and treasure we lost, let Korea go to the Reds by default because of a quarrel 'in the family.'"[47]

The fact that Rhee placed all of his military forces under US command authority (discussed further below) in 1950 did little to allay Washington's concerns. As Ambassador Muccio recalled, Rhee had a habit of issuing orders to his military (particularly to those forces fighting north of the 38th parallel) through non-military channels that was maddening to US officials.[48] Dulles was equally worried and plainly told the ROK leader the dangers inherent in such an idea: "Any 'little war' as proposed by Rhee would not only turn world opinion against the US but also would inevitably escalate into a general, full-scale war with the Soviet Union, 'unleashing such terrible weapons' . . . that it would destroy civilization."[49] President Eisenhower summed up US fears of entrapment regarding the ROK: "[Rhee] wants to get his country unified, but we cannot permit him to start a war to do it. The consequences would be too awful. But he is a stubborn old fellow, and I don't know whether we'll be able to hold him in line indefinitely."[50]

Prior to the formation of the 1953 mutual defense treaty, the United States government initially contemplated an overthrow of Rhee as an option for dealing with his intransigence. Plan EVERREADY was devised in 1952 in the event that Rhee took unilateral actions such as the withdrawal of his forces from US and UN operational control to enforce martial law. Metrics for Rhee's uncooperativeness were described as: Unresponsiveness on the part of ROK forces to UN directives, outright independent ROK military actions, or overt signs of hostility by ROK forces against the UN Command.[51] Under such circumstances, the Eighth Army Command in Korea recommended that EVERREADY call for draconian measures to stop Rhee. These included the securing of key transport and communications installations, the end to all supplies and assistance to ROK units, discontinuation of fuel and munitions support, control of all radio, telegraph, bus, and railways facilities, and the arrest of Rhee and declaration of martial law in the name of the United

Nations.[52] But the Americans soon learned that the only way to restrain the ROK was to threaten the very thing that Rhee valued most—the relationship with the United States.[53] American officials initially did this by threatening to withdraw from the United Nations Command. Robert Bowie, the State Department's director of policy planning at the time of the armistice talks, observed the dangers of not adopting such a tactic: "[not to] threaten Rhee with the possibility of UNC withdrawal eliminates the most effective weapon at our disposal for dissuading Rhee from taking unilateral action."[54] While some members of the Joint Chiefs like Admiral Duncan believed "it might be well worth giving Rhee such a [mutual defense] pact in order to keep him in line," others like General Collins believed that "we should be prepared to take Rhee into personal custody rather than try to sweeten him up with [a] security pact." Policymakers wrestled with how to control this loose Korean cannon.[55]

For similar reasons, US planners sought to strengthen the ROK but were never certain how much was too much. Dean Acheson and Secretary of State John Foster Dulles, though supportive of enhancing Korea's defense capabilities, were wary of the United States providing any tanks or other offensive weaponry to Rhee.[56] Dulles in particular opposed the transfer of jet aircraft as part of the US-sponsored military modernization program in Korea on the grounds that these "mobile instruments of war" should not be given to a country that "has a vested interest in starting a third world war."[57] Dulles wanted Rhee to commit—as Chiang Kai-shek had done—to not using the planes against the North without explicit permission from the United States. Similarly, as the United States withdrew four divisions from the peninsula at the end of the war, the question arose as to how much equipment would be left behind as part of Korean military modernization. The Koreans, naturally, wanted it all, but defense secretary Charles Wilson stated in blunt terms the prevailing US concern: "Well, we will try to figure out what we think you need, what we think we can let you have, and tell you what it is. . . . Of course, frankly, we don't want to give you enough equipment so you start the war up again."[58] In response, Rhee expressed frustration at a lack of US resolve: "Our border clashes are increasing in number and intensity, but we are told that if we move one inch over the 38th parallel the Americans will pull out."[59]

"Rhee-straint"

The notion of using the bilateral defense treaty as a tool of restraint on Rhee was, ironically, raised early on by Rhee himself. On May 30, 1953, as the ROK defied all US entreaties to support an armistice, the ROK president for the first time raised the idea that the only acceptable quid pro quo for his acquiescence was a defense treaty with Washington.[60] This offer allowed Washington to view a bilateral treaty as an appropriate tool to exercise restraint on Rhee in a multifaceted way. First, it might get him to abide by an armistice. Second, it might prevent him from fulfilling his incessant threats to "march north." And third, Washington would enjoy general veto power over Rhee's actions in a way that would not be apparent if there were security independence from the United States. General Clark's internal instructions from Washington clearly laid out the quid pro quo:

> The President has authorized you and Briggs to inform Rhee that US is prepared immediately to undertake negotiations for a mutual defense treaty with the ROK . . . Our willingness to negotiate and enter into such a treaty is subject to receiving the following assurances from Rhee: A. The Korean Govt will refrain from opposition to and agitation against an armistice along the lines presently proposed by the UNC and use its influence to restrain the Korean population from engaging in such agitation and opposition. B. The ROK will cooperate in the implementation of an armistice agreement. C. The armed forces of the ROK will remain under operation control of CINCUNC until US and ROK mutually agree such arrangements no longer necessary. . . . Upon receipt of such firm assurances the US will be prepared immediately to undertake formal negotiations.[61]

In a response to Rhee on June 17, Eisenhower stated that he "was prepared promptly, *at the conclusion of an acceptable armistice*, to negotiate with [Rhee] a mutual defense treaty along the lines of the treaties heretofore made between the United States and the Republic of the Philippines, the United States and the Commonwealth of Australia, and the United States and the Dominion of New Zealand."[62]

As noted earlier in the chapter, Rhee's release of the POWs later that month endangered the entire armistice negotiation. But after this last-gasp action, the ROK slowly but surely became socialized to the new terms of a bilateral relationship with the United States in the driver's seat. Washington told the Korean president that a mutual defense treaty would purchase security for Seoul, but for Washington, it afforded the promise of no further homegrown South Korean unilateralism.

The Robertson Trip

The core agreements and understandings that comprised the powerplay in Korea were made during an 18-day trip to Korea by Assistant Secretary of State for Far Eastern Affairs Walter Robertson, from June 26 to July 12, 1953. Originally from Blackstone, Virginia, a small town about 50 miles southeast of Richmond, Robertson was a pursuit pilot for the US Army Air Service during the First World War. After establishing a successful career in investment banking, he entered government service in 1943 as a lend-lease administrator in Australia, and then in 1945 as chargé d'affaires at the US Embassy in Chongqing, China. Shortly after Eisenhower was elected, in January 1953, Robertson was appointed to the assistant secretary position, where he was regarded as a persuasive and skillful negotiator, as his Korea visit would bear out.[63] Participants' descriptions of this trip offer a dramatic picture of all the variables at play as the Americans and Koreans sought to forge a new treaty relationship. Both sides, in a sense, knew that a defense treaty was the inevitable outcome of their negotiations given the necessity of building a Cold War front in Asia against the Soviets and Chinese. But each tried to maximize its advantage using the treaty as a tool of influence over the other.

For the Koreans, the treaty was to buy them national security and assistance, but also a US promise to get the Chinese off the peninsula as a condition of an armistice ceasefire, and a political conference at a future date to discuss unification. Rhee went to not-so-subtle lengths to hammer the latter point home with his American guest. As the assistant secretary arrived in Korea, Rhee gave an impassioned speech at a rally of more than 500,000 people on the third anniversary of the war, in which he opposed the armistice and called for Koreans to fight on for unification.[64] Driven through the streets of Seoul, Robertson was subjected to dozens of banners strewn from buildings, conveniently written in English, with phrases opposing the armistice. Thousands of demonstrators chanted "Pukch'in t'ongil! Pukch'in t'ongil!" Hundreds of mobilized schoolgirls cried hysterically in the streets, "Don't Lose Korea [to the communists]" in plain view of the visiting assistant secretary. As observers recalled, these visual and oratory messages became the boisterous backdrop of the negotiations. They were a daily reminder of the needs of a soon-to-be-treaty ally—a country written off by US planners like Kennan and Dulles only three years earlier—which the United States could no longer ignore now that it was committed to Korea.

For Robertson, the defense treaty was about deterring communist aggression, protecting Japan against communism, and positioning US bases and forces in the theater. But there was another objective for the assistant secretary. Rhee's leverage up to this point had always been the threat to entrap the United States in his grand schemes to retake the peninsula. Such threats had compelled the UN commander Clark to scurry to Seoul from his headquarters in Tokyo on more than a few occasions to pacify the Korean leader. Rhee had used these threats to foul up armistice negotiations. And he had used them to extort support from the United States. So for Robertson the defense treaty was about ending this vulnerability for the United States as much as it was about deterring the North. In his own words, "The essential point is that President Rhee cannot dictate the global policy of the United States or the basic decisions of the UN."[65]

Robertson met with Rhee every day of his stay in Seoul. Rhee was emotional and at times angry as he voiced his concerns. But once his entourage of cabinet ministers left the room for one-on-one meetings requested by Robertson, Rhee's tone grew calmer and more pragmatic.[66] The two worked through numerous sessions to hammer out an agreement in the form of an aide-mémoire. The United States would provide a mutual defense treaty, but only after the armistice was signed. It would provide $200 million in economic aid and distribute ten thousand tons of food as an immediate sign of America's commitment. Washington would also work closely to help the ROK field a 20-division-strong, well-equipped military.

The return on this investment in a new security treaty was a loyal ally for Washington, but also one that could be assured not to create commitment traps for the United States. This meant: (1) control over Seoul's actions regarding the armistice (i.e., the ROK would support it/abide by it); (2) control over Seoul's "march north" agenda; (3) operational control over the ROK military; (4) control over ROK actions vis-à-vis China (i.e., stop demanding the Chinese leave the peninsula as a condition of the armistice); and (5) control over Rhee's contemplation of any military action, however small (i.e., required permission of the United States).[67] Robertson was authorized to give Seoul assurances of a treaty only if these conditions were met. Time was of the essence because Washington wanted to respond soon to a June 20 letter from the communists on moving forward with the final stages of the armistice dialogue, but needed ROK assurances that it would abide by the ceasefire in order for the communists to deem the US commitment as credible.

Rhee delayed his response, which frustrated Washington. At one point an exasperated Robertson cabled to Washington that his negotiating counterpart was a "highly emotional, irrational, illogical fanatic [who was] fully capable of attempting to lead his country into national suicide." At the same time, the US negotiator knew that the United States could not abandon a country in Asia that had "a determination and will to fight Communism, probably unmatched by any other country in the world, [and that] his army, equipped by us is [the] largest and most effective anti-Communist army in Asia and we badly need it on our side."[68]

On June 28 in Seoul, the ROK president finally answered in defiant fashion: He wanted a mutual defense treaty negotiated between the two sides *before* the signing of an armistice. He also said that if the post-armistice political conference on Korea did not result in unification "under its only legal government" (i.e., the South) within ninety days, that the ROK would withdraw from the armistice, would re-start the war, and would pull ROK military forces from US operational control.[69] Rhee's new negotiating position was effectively laying another trap for the United States. Seoul demanded a US alliance before the armistice was signed, and then called for renewal of hostilities and breaking of the armistice once the political conference failed to achieve unification.

Secretary Dulles sensed the trap immediately and rendered Rhee's argument moot by explaining that such a renewal of hostilities would be a violation of the armistice and thus would not be sanctioned by the UN. Moreover, the US president cannot "promise" to go to war for any country, including his own, without a congressional declaration of war.[70] Though Robertson and Clark contemplated telling Rhee that further uncooperativeness would result in US withdrawal from Korea, they both knew that was a spurious threat (i.e., the United States was indeed now committed to Korea), and that the suboptimal alternative would be to negotiate the armistice with the Chinese and North Koreans without South Korean consent. But this alternative could hardly guarantee success, as the first question from the Chinese would be whether the South Koreans were on board. The only path was to "double-down"—to draw closer to Rhee through the treaty as a way to control him.

The Eisenhower administration mobilized Rhee's friends in Congress (Senators William Knowland and Alexander Smith, Congressman Walter Judd, and General James Van Fleet) to urge him to accept the terms of the American offer. The hope was that positive soundings from the Hill would assure Rhee that such a treaty would face a swift ratification vote in the Senate. But Robertson also warned Rhee that his continued intransigence was starting to wear on the patience of the American public and the Congress, and the longer the negotiations dragged on, the less goodwill he would find among US politicians.[71] Internally, Robertson grew angry at Rhee's efforts to undermine his negotiating authority by leaking to the Korean press on a daily basis the false rumor that a higher-level American envoy was to follow the assistant secretary. The United States provided a draft treaty text and Dulles informed Robertson that he had vetted this successfully with key members on the Hill.[72] As only a couple of days remained before Robertson's departure, Eisenhower on July 8 sent a personal letter to Rhee imploring him to move forward.[73] Rhee finally relented in an eleventh-hour response given to Robertson as he departed Seoul on July 11, which put in writing for the first time that he would not obstruct the armistice if the United States could produce a ratified defense treaty.[74] In their final meeting, Robertson and Rhee agreed that a joint statement to the press would show the degree of unity between the two countries, and make public Rhee's commitment to abide by the armistice and avoid unilateral actions. Rhee acknowledged that he had been "a thorn in the side of the State Department,"[75] but that in the end, the United States had prevailed: "Mr. Robertson, you have come to Korea and it is you who have conquered. I am left in a ditch. Please pull me out."[76] The US objective of restraint had been accomplished.

As soon as the agreement was reached, however, Rhee was quick to test the waters. After Robertson's departure, Rhee backtracked publicly in his commitment to the United States, suggesting to journalists that he would only commit to a ceasefire for 90 days if the planned post-armistice political conference did not result in unification. The stern and blunt nature of Washington's response reflected the new control it exercised in this emerging informal hierarchical arrangement between two sovereign nations. Dulles wrote to Rhee on July 24, 1953:

> We believe that your country can feel confident that the treaty we propose will deter aggression. . . . Never in all of its history has the US offered to any other country as much as is offered to you. . . . many countries have been slandering you and alleging that such promises as you have given the President and me could not be depended upon. . . . [we] have insisted that we had complete confidence that you would adhere to the position which you communicated to us. . . . My final plea is that you should share this sentiment.[77]

After the signing of the armistice (July 27, 1953), Eisenhower dispatched Dulles to Seoul to negotiate the final terms of the defense treaty. Dulles's four-day trip to Seoul (August 4–8, 1953) and six meetings with Rhee were once again filled with the ROK president's efforts at providing ROK autonomy in the defense treaty text.[78] Rhee asked to include a new paragraph in the treaty acknowledging Korean sovereignty over its domestic affairs, which Dulles agreed to. But in a last-ditch ploy on Dulles's final day in Korea, Rhee sought to include the ROK's sovereign right to drive Chinese communists off the peninsula (i.e., an attack on North Korea) as part of the definition of ROK sovereignty over domestic affairs. Dulles refused outright, and Rhee relented.[79] Eisenhower recalled in his memoirs that his strategy of restraint had worked—Rhee was sufficiently deterred from doing anything untoward to entrap the United States.[80]

Why did the United States obsess so much in these high-level treaty negotiations about Rhee's commitment to restraint? Prior to the 1950 invasion by the North, the United States knew that Rhee was authorizing his military to undertake attacks along the 38th parallel, but could do little in response. As discussed in chapter 3, Kennan, Acheson, and others wanted nothing to do with Korea as they were in the midst of withdrawing from the peninsula under NSC 7, leaving the postcolonial territory under UN auspices. Thus, Washington had little influence over ROK actions, even if it had concern that fighting might break out on a larger scale. As then-ambassador Muccio recalls, he had no tools with which to influence Rhee. The United States was positioned neither to help Rhee nor to punish him given its disengagement plan. All he could do was to tell Rhee that Washington knew he was provoking some of the altercations. Muccio summed up the dilemma, "Beyond that I don't know what could be done unless you could hit him over the head with a baseball bat."[81] This is why the treaty was so important as a tool. During negotiations, General Clark told Assistant Secretary Robertson the control elements of the treaty were critical. "If we could get a commitment out of Rhee not to violate truce or to take other action to obstruct armistice, and to leave ROK army under [UNC] command without specifying a time limit, that such an agreement would be 'worth a million dollars.'"[82] After the Robertson-Rhee negotiations concluded, Clark explicitly conveyed to the Chinese at Panmunjom that the United States now had control over Rhee and could assure his compliance with the armistice.[83]

The mutual defense treaty that was signed on October 1, 1953 was between two sovereign nations,[84] but its arrangement was tantamount to that of an informal empire. The level of security and economic dependence of the ROK on the United States during the Rhee years was absolute. Eisenhower sought to use the money saved from the cessation of hostilities in Korea for economic programs to the South since he believed

TABLE 5.I. ROK TRADE DEPENDENCE ON THE UNITED STATES,
SELECTED YEARS (1948–1960)

	U.S.-ROK TRADE VOLUME, MIL. USD (% OF TOTAL ROK TRADE)	U.S.-ROK AID, MIL. USD (% OF ROK GDP)
1948	71 (31.6%)	134 (—)
1953	123 (27.5%)	206 (15.8%)
1954	106 (39.7%)	165 (11.8%)
1955	131 (36.5%)	237 (16.9%)
1956	202 (49.1%)	325 (23.2%)
1957	281 (60.6%)	304 (17.9%)
1958	218 (55.2%)	220 (11.6%)
1959	141 (46.7%)	223 (11.7%)
1960	158 (43.8%)	211 (10.6%)

Sources: Trade statistics from *Yearbook of International Trade Statistics, 1955, 1958, 1960* (New York: United Nations, 1956, 1959, 1962), 701; 18–19, 550; 14–15, 580 (respectively). Aid statistics from *Statistical Abstract of the United States, 1954, 1958, 1961* (Washington, DC: Department of Commerce, 1954, 1958, 1961), 902; 872; 875 (respectively). ROK GDP statistics from the Bank of Korea Economic Statistics System (2013), http://ecos.bok.or.kr/EIndex_en.jsp, accessed August 2, 2013.

the world would be watching Korea in the context of the Cold War.[85] As table 5.1 shows, in the three years after the treaty, US trade comprised an average 34 percent of ROK total trade, and US aid comprised an average 15 percent of the ROK's gross domestic product. And the United States had no problem with leveraging this assistance to assure absolute control over Rhee's actions. Internal NSC documents also made clear that the program of economic assistance (based on a study led by Henry J. Tasca, also known as the Tasca Report) that would accompany the new treaty would be entirely contingent on Rhee's restrained behavior and compliance with the armistice:

> The United States has already warned the Republic of Korea that economic aid is dependent upon cooperation in connection with an armistice. Furthermore, an important factor in deterring the Republic of Korea from taking action to frustrate or violate an armistice will be the immediate undertaking of an enlarged program of economic assistance. If, however, despite its assurances, the Republic of Korea takes actions to frustrate or violate an armistice, or fails to cooperate with the United States in developing

and carrying out satisfactory economic and financial programs, the United States should reconsider the program of additional economic aid, and should be prepared to cut off such aid if it is deemed advisable to do so.[86]

At times, Rhee tried to leverage the aid to extract more concessions from the United States. In particular, he did so by leaking to the press that the United States was effectively bribing his government to acquiesce to a stalemate with the communists. But this was a double-edged sword for Rhee as it risked delegitimizing his own leadership, not to mention the risk of losing the US aid.[87]

Vice President Nixon and Rhee

The United States never really considered a multilateral treaty organization in the region that would include Korea in lieu of a bilateral defense treaty. I discuss this in much greater detail in chapter 7, but I believe one of the primary reasons for this decision had more to do with control than deterrence. That is, a network of bilateral defense treaties involving Taiwan and South Korea probably netted Washington no less deterrence than a multilateral arrangement involving the same parties. But the former arrangement permitted much better control of two overzealous allies. Designing a hub and spokes arrangement where all transactions took place inside of exclusive bilateral arrangements maximized US power. A multilateral arrangement could give opportunities for collusion between Taipei and Seoul to create commitment traps, which could weaken US control and increase the possibility of entrapment. For its own needs, Seoul too preferred dealing face-to-face directly with the United States, as Muccio recalled, because Rhee had little patience for the prolonged consultations and multilateral coordination of the UN.

Once the defense treaty was signed, the United States made a regular practice of leveraging this new tool to restrain Rhee from unilateral acts against the North. Washington constantly reminded Rhee that his calls for renewal of hostilities ran counter to a world that wanted peace. More concretely, though, the United States positioned the alliance to reduce ROK capacity for independent military action. In coordinating with ROK forces, the United States ensured that they were equipped, but only enough to deter an initial attack by the North, with no more than six days' supply, thus rendering a sustained offensive by the ROK (counter-offensive or unilateral offensive) impossible.[88] Moreover, the contingency plan EVERREADY, which was the ultimate metric of US restraint on

Seoul, was revised in late 1953 to consider the following extreme measures if Rhee re-started the Korean war: (1) arrest ROK commanders to
prevent implementation of such orders; (2) withdraw all logistics support
for ROK military; (3) ground the ROK air force; (4) seize transportation
nodes; and (5) bomb ROK ammunition supplies.[89] The NSC meeting on
these restrictive contingency measures referenced that both State and
Defense agreed that the removal of Rhee from the presidency was also an
option.[90] These were extraordinary measures, codified in NSC 167/2 (November 6, 1953) and NSC 170/1 (November 20, 1953), that contravened
the sovereignty of another country.[91] But the key point in the context
of my argument is that such control could not have been exercised if
the United States did not create the levels of asymmetric security dependence afforded by the 1953 bilateral defense treaty.

In November 1953, the US grew increasingly concerned that Rhee
would fulfill his threat to pull his forces from the UNC and undertake
some sort of military action to sabotage the armistice and restart hostilities. In addition to the NSC revision of EVERREADY, Vice President
Richard Nixon went to Seoul with the explicit purpose of shutting Rhee
down. Nixon delivered a letter from Eisenhower reiterating that under
the armistice, the United States would not resume hostilities on the peninsula. Furthermore, he warned that Rhee's treasured mutual defense
treaty with the United States would not be ratified by Congress unless
Nixon received "explicit confirmation" that Seoul would not act independently. An excerpt from Eisenhower's letter follows:

> [T]his treaty will actually promote peace and mutual defense. If
> I should be forced to conclude that after the coming into force of
> the Treaty, you might unilaterally touch off a resumption of war in
> Korea, I could not recommend its ratification and I am certain that
> the Senate would not ratify it.

Eisenhower reinforced the point later in the same letter:

> If you were to plan to initiate military action while the Communist
> forces are complying with the Armistice, my obligation to both
> United States forces and other United Nations forces would be to
> plan how best to prevent their becoming involved and to assure
> their security. . . . I must have explicit confirmation from you, in
> order to reach my own decisions and to be able to answer ques-
> tions which the Senate and the Congress will properly ask before
> [ratification].[92]

Nixon arrived in Seoul on November 12, 1953 and held a two-hour-long private conversation with Rhee after the general introductory meetings. The vice president delivered the letter to Rhee, who then read the strongly worded missive out loud. As Nixon's telegram to Washington noted that evening, Rhee was deeply affected by the letter. All he could muster upon finishing it was, "That is a very fine letter."[93] In that meeting and in subsequent ones, Rhee obediently provided such assurances to Nixon.[94] Rhee wrote a personal letter to Eisenhower in which the ROK president promised no unilateral action. Rhee requested that no copies of this letter be made and Nixon complied. A copy of the letter does not exist in State Department archives nor in the Eisenhower library, but NSC and other internal US government declassified documents made numerous references to the commitment to restraint made in this letter.[95] Nixon further made the point about South Korean restraint in an address to the Korean national assembly where he cleverly spun the Korean slogan of "unification or death" with an encapsulation of the US position: "unification *without* death."[96]

Operational Control in the US-ROK Alliance

Skeptics might view US actions to restrain the ROK as I have described them in this chapter as not atypical of alliances. Tensions between allies, particularly smaller ones seeking more autonomy from their patrons, are part and parcel of healthy alliances. American archives, however, reveal the extent to which this preoccupation with restraining the ally went beyond routine alliance management. The need to restrain ROK leaders from acting on their ambitions of pukch'in t'ongil was inextricably tied to the US obsession with maintaining operational command authority of Rhee's military forces within the alliance.[97]

The origins of operational command authority date to the outset of the Korean War. After the United States and UN committed troops to the peninsula, ROK president Rhee handed over control of his troops to General MacArthur in a simple letter on July 15, 1950:

> In view of the joint military effort of the United Nations on behalf of the Republic of Korea, in which all military forces, land, sea and air, of all the United Nations fighting in or near Korea have been placed under your operational command, and in which you have been designated Supreme Commander of the United Nations forces, I am happy to assign to you command authority over all land, sea, and air forces of the Republic of Korea during the period

of the continuation of the present state of hostilities; such command to be exercised either by you personally or by such military
commander or commanders to whom you may delegate the exercise of this authority within Korea or in adjacent seas.[98]

In the aftermath of the mutual defense treaty (October 1953), the two
governments signed a memorandum of understanding codifying operational control authority over ROK forces by the UN Command (November 1954). In 1961, this understanding was revised to pertain only to
control authority over forces to defend against an external communist
invasion. In the late 1970s, the Combined Forces Command (CFC) was
created (November 7, 1978) to create a structure in which the United
States could gradually transfer authority over to the Koreans.[99] Operational control authority was put in the hands of the CFC commander,
and the UNC body's duties extended only to maintaining the terms of
the armistice. Pursuant to the goals of creating the CFC, in October
1994, peacetime operational control of Korean forces was transferred to
Korea, giving the deputy CFC commander (a Korean) peacetime authority over a range of activities including unit management, movements,
precautionary actions, patrols, combined tactical training, and troop
readiness. Even under these conditions, however, the authority of the
peacetime commander is greatly curtailed not only in wartime but also
at peacetime readiness levels beyond Defcon 3. In 2006, it was agreed
that operational control would be handed back to the South Koreans
by 2012. But after the sinking of the ROK Naval Corvette *Cheonan* in
2010, this was pushed back to December 2015. And with tensions on the
Korean Peninsula continuing to rise in the years that followed, the two
countries agreed in 2014 to another delay of the transfer.

The rationale for the United States holding operational command
authority in the early Cold War years was not just for warfighting efficiency, but also to keep a leash on unilateral offensive acts by the South
Koreans. The fact that South Korea was and continues to be the sole US
ally with this sort of arrangement lends support to this interpretation.
With the establishment of United States Forces Korea (USFK) during the
Eisenhower years, US officials worried about ROK entreaties for command authority. It was standing policy that any unilateral ROK military
actions would prompt Washington to the severest of actions, including
the immediate cessation of economic and military aid, disassociation of
the UN Command from support of ROK actions, and even the use of US
forces to impose martial law.

I discussed some aspects of US contingency planning for Rhee's antics above (Plan EVERREADY). The fact that the Eisenhower administration continued to deliberate on these plans after the signing of the mutual defense treaty in 1953 shows how integral they were to the alliance. NSC 5817 "Statement of U.S. Policy Toward Korea" (August 11, 1958) stated that if the ROK unilaterally initiated military operations against Chinese or North Korean forces in or north of the Demilitarized Zone, then: (1) UN Command ground, sea, and air forces will not support such operations directly or indirectly; (2) The United States will not furnish any military or logistic support for such operations; (3) All US economic aid to Korea will cease immediately; and (4) The UN Commander will take any action necessary to prevent his forces becoming involved in the renewal of hostilities and to provide for their security.[100] In White House deliberations in the late 1950s, President Eisenhower went so far as to say that the United States would covertly support new leadership, forcibly remove Rhee, or even threaten abrogating the alliance. In conversations with his cabinet, Eisenhower argued,

[I]f we became aware that President Rhee was moving north to attack North Korea, we would simply have to remove Rhee and his government . . . Such a move would simply have to be stopped. Again Secretary Herter agreed with the President but asked how we proposed to keep the Communists from counter-attacking and seizing South Korea. The President stated with emphasis that everything possible must be done to stop a unilateral South Korean move on North Korea before it started, including deposing Rhee. Thereafter, if South Korea wanted to go on to commit suicide, we would say go ahead and do it. . . . If ever this attack on North Korea occurred, the President said that the military alliance between the US and the Republic of Korea would be broken at that moment.[101]

The provision regarding covert support of alternative leadership to Rhee (in the event he planned unilateral action) was first contained in a president-approved revision of a 1953 NSC policy document on Korea (NSC 170/1 Annex A).[102] Earlier NSC policies document extraordinary measures designed to restrain Rhee and his military: the arrest of ROK military commanders; withdrawal of US air support; grounding of the ROK air force; blockading the ROK navy; bombing of ROK ammunition depots; securing US military control of transport and communication nodes; cutting off all economic assistance; de-recognizing Rhee; blocking ROK dollar-sterling accounts; initiating an anti-propaganda campaign against Rhee; and declaring martial law.[103]

The 1958 revision contained a clause that stated:

> d. To select and encourage covertly the development of new South Korean leadership prepared to cooperate in maintaining the armistice, and if Rhee initiates or is about to initiate unilateral action, assist such new leadership to assume power, by means not involving overt US participation until and unless US overt support is necessary and promises to be decisive in firmly establishing such new leadership.

This provision was considered extremely sensitive and circulated only to the Secretaries of State and Defense, Chairman of the Joint Chiefs of Staff, and Director of Central Intelligence. Subsequent NSC policy reviews on Korea made reference to the annex (later known as Annex F) as regular practice, but the actual contents were kept separate. The internal instructions noted, "This revision is being disseminated only to [selected] addressees . . . and it is requested that special security precautions be observed in the handling of this memorandum and that access to it be very strictly limited on an absolute need-to-know basis."[104] The provision about US unilateral abrogation of the treaty took place in the context of deliberations a couple of years later on revising NSC 5817, which was then standing policy on Korea (revised as NSC 5907).[105]

Retaining operational control of ROK forces therefore was arguably as much a tool of alliance restraint as it was a tool of deterrence and warfighting.[106] The US concern about South Korean preemptive attack has abated considerably over the years (particularly after democratization in 1987) and the United States transferred peacetime authority to the South in 1994, and plans eventually to transfer wartime operational. But the point remains that the US role in inter-Korean relations during the Cold War was a dual one that featured not only containment of the North, but also restraint of the South.

"Doubling Down" in Asia

The powerplay rationale informed the formation of both the Taiwan and Korea alliances. The United States faced acute entrapment fears that overzealous allies might try to take the fight to the communists with the hope that the United States would feel obligated to come to their aid. One US commanding general in the theater recalled the mind-sets that allowed countries like Korea and Taiwan to leverage US commitments and raise fears of entrapment. He spoke about Rhee, but this was equally applicable to Chiang.

> Rhee was, of course, supremely confident that the United States, at least, would have to support him in any crisis. It is inconceivable to the Koreans that the United States would fail to back Korea in any trouble with the Communists. Their feeling is that Korea, by its resistance to communism, has become a showpiece for the world. Other small nations, the Koreans are convinced, will judge the profit in resistance to communism through the fate of the republic [*sic*] of Korea.[107]

The United States could not afford to abandon these countries because of the prevalent strategic belief in the domino theory. At the same time, it could not mount an effective anti-communist front if Taiwan and Korea "felt free to run a private little war with [their] neighbor[s] that could disrupt the whole system of security the free world was striving to create."[108] US architects of a postwar Asia policy needed to design a security institution that would maintain deterrence against further communist advances while minimizing entrapment fears. The answer was essentially to "double-down"—that is, to deal with overdependence by deepening the commitment and asserting control. The anxiety that one of these anti-communist, East Asian leaders might pull the United States into another war was assessed to be real, and the decision was made to form alliances not just to contain communism, but also to constrain their allies.

This control was best exercised bilaterally. Opting for multilateralism in the region had little marginal benefit (in terms of enhancing containment) and significant marginal cost—i.e., diluted control, and putting decisions to committees rather than by fiat. Neither was appealing with regard to the powerplay rationale. This assessment of Asia is not to deny that in Europe, the United States was also interested in control. But this was not on the same scale as in Asia, nor with similar distrust and suspicions of smaller allies entrapping the United States through unilateral actions in a larger war with the Soviet Union or China.

6

JAPAN: "WIN JAPAN"

The powerplay in US strategy operated differently for Japan than it did for Korea and Taiwan. In the latter cases, the strategy was about minimizing overdependence pathologies and entrapment fears by Washington. In Japan's case, the powerplay was not about entrapment, but about control of the only major power in the region, whose postwar rise was inevitable in American eyes. After Japan's unconditional surrender in 1945, the United States conducted its military occupation with the goal of permanently demilitarizing Japan and making it forever safe from fascism. The advent of the Cold War compelled the United States to think more strategically and long-term about the Japan project. And when the Cold War turned hot with the outbreak of hostilities on the Korean Peninsula, the United States had to contend with Japan as a frontline state in the war against communism. For thinkers like Douglas MacArthur, George Kennan, John Foster Dulles, and Presidents Truman and Eisenhower, the institutional design choices for a relationship with Japan were wide. At one end of the policy spectrum was a neutralization approach, which amounted to a protracted occupation and complete demilitarization and political neutralization of Japan. At the other end was a rearmament approach, which called for the early signing of a peace treaty and encouragement of rebuilding Japanese security capabilities such that it could balance against the emerging communist threat. Neither worked for US interests, which focused on three immediate needs—to prevent Japan from becoming a revisionist power again; to deny it to communist influence; and, not unlike its plans for Korea and Taiwan, to ensure that the United States had absolute control over Japan's postwar disposition. Strategic thinkers ultimately determined that the best sort of security institution to achieve these objectives was a tight bilateral alliance with Japan.

Washington "reversed course" in its occupation of Japan, focusing more on rebuilding the country than on emasculating it. It contemplated a reintegration of Japan in Asia by embedding it in a multilateral grouping of states including Australia, New Zealand, Philippines, and Indonesia.[1] This short-lived effort failed as some members were not yet ready to enter into a pact with the wartime aggressor. Japan, too, was less interested in tying itself to this committee of countries (the idea lasted about eight weeks). This confluence of preferences eventually pushed Washington in the direction of tight bilateral bonds with Tokyo. Tying Japan to the United States reduced regional fears of a resurgent revisionist power. It also allowed the United States to oversee the postwar development of a politically stable state that would act consistently in the advancement of American interests. As George Kennan aptly described, Japan was the key to Asia, just as Germany was the key to Europe. The American objective was therefore to align Japan with the United States for the long term—it was "to win Japan as an ally."[2]

The Occupation

The story of America's strategic choices on Japan begins with the 1945 surrender and military occupation of the country. In the initial stages of the occupation, US planners were chiefly concerned with demobilization of the Japanese military, democratization of its political system, and the rooting out of its ultra-rightists. The occupation was headquartered in the Supreme Command for Allied Power (SCAP) under the sixty-five-year-old General Douglas MacArthur. MacArthur, who came to be known as the "blue-eyed Shogun" in Japan, was the third-born son in a southern military family from Little Rock, Arkansas. After graduating as valedictorian at the West Texas Military Academy and finishing top of his class at West Point, MacArthur served in the First World War, where he received thirteen combat medals and seven silver stars for exceptional valor.[3] By the time of the Second World War, MacArthur, now as military advisor to the newly semi-independent Philippines, was promoted to Supreme Commander for the Southwest Pacific Area, and despite criticism from some quarters, was awarded the Medal of Honor for his service in the Philippines. By the end of the war in the Pacific, MacArthur had taken on a legendary status among the American public, so when it came time to select an overseer for the occupation of Japan, the general seemed the inevitable choice.[4] In his memoirs, MacArthur recounts relaying the initial policy to his staff in late August 1945:

First, destroy the military power. Punish war criminals. Build the structure of representative government. Modernize the constitution. Hold free elections. Enfranchise the women. Release political prisoners. Liberate the farmers. Establish a free labor movement. Encourage a free economy. Abolish police oppression. Develop a free and responsible press. Liberalize education. Decentralize political power. Separate the church from state.[5]

And it was these very orders, in almost this sequence, that would basically define the first three years of the occupation.

According to Japan historian Kenneth Pyle, "never in the history of any modern nation has there been a greater external impact on a nation's domestic institutions than what Japan experienced following its surrender."[6] Initially, Japan's 4.5 million person military was disarmed and disbanded. This was followed by the International Military Tribunal for the Far East, with the United States trying 1,344 individuals as Class A, B, and C war criminals.[7] There were also vast purges, with some 2.5 million Japanese investigated for possible purging and more than 200,000 from the Japanese military, government, business, and civil society consequently being removed from their positions and having their political rights revoked.[8] From the standpoint of the occupation, these purges were deemed absolutely necessary. As General MacArthur put it at the time, "It was these very persons . . . who held the lives and destiny of the majority of Japan's people in virtual slavery, and who . . . geared the country with both the tools and the will to wage aggressive war."[9] Political reform and democratic elections then took place, first in April 1946, followed by elections the next year. Japan's 1889 Meiji Constitution, whose first article states that Japan "shall be reigned over and governed by a line of Emperors unbroken for ages eternal," and refers to the Japanese people as "subjects,"[10] was also replaced with a document that retained the emperor as a national figurehead, but rooted Japanese politics in parliamentary democracy, and guaranteed full civil and human rights to all Japanese citizens. The 1947 Constitution's most controversial aspect was, and continues to be, Article 9, in which Japan agrees to "forever renounce war as a sovereign right," and therefore promises that "land, sea, and air forces, as well as other war potential, will never be maintained."[11] With the guarantees of civil and human rights came the release of hundreds of political prisoners and the abolition of the *Tokkō*, the imperial government's secret police, who were widely referred to as the *shiso keisatsu*, or "thought police." Church and state were also separated, with all government funding being cut off for the Shinto religion and Emperor Hirohito abdicating his position of divinity in a dramatic New Year's Day address in 1946.[12] Japan's education system too, was reformed, with textbooks, teachers, and curricula being replaced or revised to promote Japan's newfound liberal democratic values.

Yet in spite of all these changes, the Japanese economy was in shambles. Though General MacArthur's first directive from Washington for the occupation stressed that he not "assume any responsibility for the economic rehabilitation of Japan or the strengthening of the Japanese economy,"[13] the hand of SCAP was soon forced by the dire necessity of the situation. The war had destroyed one quarter of the Japanese economy. Production in 1946 was a mere 30 percent of what it had been ten years earlier. Against the orders of SCAP, the Japanese government repeatedly expanded the monetary base, leading to hyperinflation rates of nearly 25,000 percent between 1945 and 1949. The unemployment rate hovered around 17 percent, with some 13 million Japanese out of work. In 1948, Japan's trade deficit stood at $426 million, up nearly $75 million from the previous year.[14] Compounding these effects was the ongoing return of some 3 million Japanese civilians and soldiers from Korea, Manchuria, and Southeast Asia, putting a greater strain on state and occupation resources. And with a pitiful 1945 harvest of only 60 percent of prewar levels, the very real possibility of famine and mass disease cast a frightful shadow over the occupation. Early on in his role as SCAP commander, an exasperated MacArthur entreated Washington, "Give me bread or give me bullets."[15] It was clear that something had to be done.

SCAP therefore initiated a massive humanitarian aid and economic development program. Occupation forces were reduced from 600,000 to 200,000, with SCAP diverting approximately $500 million in surplus food supplies to the Japanese populace. Mass inoculation programs against communicable disease were instituted, and fields were sprayed to stave off water-borne disease. Between September 1945 and June 1948, the United States sent in excess of $1 billion in humanitarian aid to the Japanese archipelago, and roughly $400 million annually thereafter.[16] US occupiers also initiated land reform, which in effect turned Japan's approximately 40 million poverty-stricken peasants into landowning, middle-class, politically conservative farmers.[17] Labor reform also took place, with unions being legalized, along with collective bargaining rights and the right to strike being guaranteed under law. A 1947 law was also passed which enshrined a six-day, 48-hour workweek, 25 percent overtime premiums, women and child labor protection, safety and sanitation guarantees, and accident and sick leave compensation.[18] SCAP also attempted to break up Japan's massive industrial conglomerates, known as *zaibatsu*, but was ultimately unsuccessful in this venture.

While the economic reforms enumerated above staved off the threat of famine and large-scale domestic unrest, they did little to set the Japanese economy on a trajectory of stability and growth. Unemployment remained high and inflation continued to soar. Uncertainty over possible reparations payments and the future of the zaibatsu meant Japanese industrialists had little incentive to invest in capital, and banks had little incentive to lend. Reluctance on the part of regional states to accept Japanese goods meant Japan's trade deficits continued to swell. Undersecretary of the Army William H. Draper complained that MacArthur was turning the Japanese economy into a "morgue," and *Fortune* magazine derided US policy in the country, referring to it as "SCAPitalism."[19] The disarmament and democratization program was losing steam, and consensus began to build on the need to have Japan stand on its own two feet sooner, rather than later.[20] As an October 1947 memo by Undersecretary Draper notes, a "shift of emphasis" in occupation policy was becoming increasingly desirable.[21]

The "Key to Asia"

Complicating American strategic thinking on the occupation of Japan was the larger geostrategic environment emerging in Europe and Asia. The Cold War competition with the Soviet Union compelled the United States to reassess its goals in the military occupation of Japan. While MacArthur may have wanted to demilitarize the country, end the occupation, sign a peace treaty, declare victory (and run for nomination as the next president of the United States), his bosses in Washington needed to take the longer view. American planners understood that postwar Japan was the only country in Asia that had the chance of emerging as a great power. As historian Bruce Cumings's critical treatment of American postwar Asia strategy recounts, Japan was considered ". . . an honorary European country, clean and fastidious, long the repository of a high culture, and most important, it deployed an industrial base and thus military might."[22] However, to leave Japan as a militarily weak and economically floundering version of "Switzerland" in Asia could make the population prone to the growing and proximate Soviet communist threat.

An additional complicating factor was whether the United States should bet on Japan or China as the key interlocutor in the region. The consensus view among most influential US grand strategists (though not all) was that the American postwar position in Asia should lie with Japan.[23] George F. Kennan's views in this regard were fundamental. If one had to fall to communism, as he put it, "[Japan] was more important than China as a potential factor in world-political developments. It was . . . the sole great potential military-industrial arsenal of the Far East."[24] Kennan believed that Japan was the key to Asia, just as Germany was the key to Europe, which he affectionately termed the "most important pawns on the chessboard of world politics."[25] "It was essential" as he put it, "if any sort of a tolerable balance of power was to be established in the postwar world, that they be kept out of Communist hands."[26]

Kennan envisioned a postwar multipolar world with five power centers "where the sinews of modern military strength could be produced in quantity": the United States, Britain, Germany and central Europe, the Soviet Union, and Japan.[27] It was therefore vital that West Germany and Japan become tightly aligned with the United States; otherwise the loss of these two power centers would turn the current four-to-one ratio in favor of the United States and the West into a three-to-two ratio in favor of the Soviet Union. Secretary of State Dean Acheson largely concurred with Kennan's views. "[A] grim fact of international life," stated Acheson in a May 1947 speech, "is that two of the greatest workshops of Europe and Asia—Germany and Japan . . . have hardly been able even to begin the process of reconstruction because of the lack of a peace settlement." What was needed, claimed Acheson, was to immediately "push ahead with the reconstruction of those two great workshops."[28] The peace and stability of the Asia-Pacific, and the emerging Cold War balance in the region, hinged upon the economic recovery of Japan. Or, as MacArthur's successor assessed, "There was and is no question in my mind that Japan is a vital link in our system of defense in the Far East and in the free world's system of security against the Communist drive for world domination."[29]

Kennan had these ideas truly crystallize when, as Policy Planning Director, he traveled to Japan on a fact-finding mission "of the utmost delicacy" in March 1948.[30] In what turned out to be quite an odyssey, Kennan and two aides departed Seattle, stopped to refuel in Anchorage, then made a second, "terrifying" refueling stop on the island of Shemya in the North Pacific, and finally arrived in Tokyo some 30 hours later in the wee hours of a snowy Sunday morning.[31] What Kennan saw upon arrival to Japan only strengthened his belief that change was necessary. Even before his trip to Tokyo, Kennan was resolutely opposed to the reparations program, and this visit only hardened these convictions, with him variously referring to the program as "absurd," "deleterious" to Japan's recovery upon which the entire region would depend, and "without overstatement—sheer nonsense from [a] practical standpoint."[32] Kennan also saw the zaibatsu decartelization policy as counterproductive, writing in a cable during the visit that the deconcentration program was simply an unjustifiable level of interference into the Japanese economy and in Japanese affairs.[33] The war crimes trials too, Kennan claimed, were "profoundly misconceived from the start" and were working at cross-purposes to the Allied aims in the country.[34] But more than anything else, he found the purges abhorrent. Looking back, Kennan noted that SCAP policy in this respect "had proceeded on a scale, and with a dogmatic, impersonal vindictiveness, for which there were few examples outside the totalitarian countries themselves."[35]

In sum, Kennan saw the trajectory of the occupation as profoundly off course. In a note he penned to General MacArthur before they were to meet, Kennan wrote that from then on, emphasis should be placed on a "firm" US security policy for the region, an "intensive" program of economic recovery, and a relaxation of SCAP controls.[36] Without these, the occupation, as he saw it, could make little progress. But more than simply perpetuating the stagnation of Japanese economic and political development and wasting billions of US dollars, he saw the direction of the occupation as being most favorable to the Soviets. In Kennan's mind, many of the occupation policies enacted thus far bore an uncomfortably striking resemblance to the "softening up" policies which Russia pursued in what eventually became Soviet-occupied Eastern Europe.[37]

Upon his return to Washington, Kennan forcefully argued in a Policy Planning report for a drastic change in the occupation's approach. A general and non-punitive peace treaty, the curtailing of the purges and reparations programs, long-term US military control of Okinawa, increased flows of American educators and culture, and the gradual loosening of SCAP controls were all part of his proposal, but above all, Kennan urged that "Economic recovery should be made the prime objective of United States policy in Japan for the coming period."[38] In the broader scheme, Kennan believed that Japan occupied the strategic and economic center of East Asia; thus it would never emerge as a neutral power in the region; it would either fall into the US or Soviet orbit.[39] Kennan conveyed all of these views to Secretary of State George Marshall. Within six months, an almost verbatim version of Kennan's recommendations were adopted by the National Security Council (NSC) 13/2 on October 7, 1948, and two days later President Truman signed off on them as the new direction of US policy in Japan.[40]

Kennan's impact on the reversal of US policy in Japan was undoubtedly profound. Looking back years later, he noted in his memoirs: "I consider my part in bringing about this change to have been, after the Marshall Plan, the most significant constructive contribution I was ever able to make in government."[41] And while Kennan's primary motives and rationale for this policy reversal were based on objective, strategic calculation on his part, they were likely not his only ones. Kennan had an appreciation for the Japanese, whom he viewed as intelligent, industrious, and thoughtful. By contrast, he found the Chinese to be uncouth, arrogant, and self-centered.[42]

The United States had now inherited the Japan project for the long term. Thus began what became known as the "reverse course" of US policy in Japan. While much of the objective of pre-1948 occupation policies was to preserve Allied Powers' security from future Japanese aggression, the new priority was to make provisions for Japan's security from outside aggression.[43] Punitive measures were replaced by regenerative efforts. An overly intrusive, domineering stance was displaced by a more passive, supporting role. An emphasis on reform was substituted for one on recovery. And the idealistic, neoliberal aims of the early occupation years were discarded for hard-nosed realism. Rather than simply trying to punish Japan or fundamentally change Japan, a new concern arose of trying to "win" Japan. Kennan's two central objectives of keeping the Japanese away from the Soviets and friendly to the West became the pillars of US policy in the country. "The essential objectives of the United States from both the political and the military standpoints," says just one of hundreds of similarly inclined documents of the time, "are the denial of Japan to the USSR and the maintenance of Japan's orientation towards the Western powers."[44]

For the attainment of these two objectives, nothing was as initially crucial as ensuring the recovery of the Japanese economy. During an early 1948 speech, Secretary of the Army Kenneth C. Royall stated that for Japan's "political stability to continue and for free government to succeed in the future, there must be a sound and self-supporting economy."[45] And so Washington went to work. In December 1948, MacArthur received a directive for the economic stabilization of Japan. It called for the balancing of the budget; a strengthening of tax collection; greater price controls; greater control of foreign trade and exchange; a more effective rationing system; increased production of raw materials; and a more efficient food collection program.[46] To oversee the implementation of these changes, the White House sent Detroit banker Joseph M. Dodge to Tokyo as an advisor with the rank of Ambassador in February 1949. Dodge became the face of the new economic policies in Japan, and his ultimately successful efforts to balance the budget, combat inflation, attract investment, and promote trade led to these policies being unofficially dubbed the "Dodge Line." By May 1949, the reparations program was officially brought to a halt. And by June, many of the zaibatsu decartelization policies had been successfully reversed. With these changes, Japan finally began to emerge from its dilapidated economic state of the previous four years.

A second imperative was of lightening the US military and administrative footprint in the country. Nothing, with the exception of severe economic stagnation, was seen as so sure to isolate and disillusion the Japanese populace as an extended, overly intrusive occupation of their country. NSC 13/2 stated that "Every effort . . . should be made to reduce to a minimum the psychological impact of the presence of occupational forces on the Japanese population."[47] And by moving off of center stage, the US occupiers tried to assume a less offensive, less intrusive role as a general observer of Japanese affairs and counselor to the Japanese government. By 1949, SCAP personnel had been greatly reduced, with headquarters employees declining from a peak of 3,660 to 1,950. Civil affairs teams too, which were stationed in Japan's prefectural capitals, went from about 3,000 to about 300. And most importantly, military personnel were reduced from 600,000 all the way down to 150,000, though this figure would again climb up slightly in the 1950s.[48] As a 1949 State Department document makes clear, it was understood that the United States could "neither impose nor enforce a pro-Western orientation on any people, including the Japanese."[49] This orientation would have to be attained more subtly. Denying Japan to the Soviets was seen as dependent not simply on military might, but on the attitude and emotional orientation of the Japanese people. But to some, it wasn't simply the fate of Japan that was at stake during these incipient stages of the Cold War, but the United States' own ideals. As if taking a page out of Thucydides' history, *The Peloponnesian War*, Secretary of State Dean Acheson wrote that in the long run, the US role in Japan "rested upon the consent of the Japanese. Force can overcome force, but a free society cannot long steel itself to dominate another people by sheer force."[50]

The third and perhaps most important issue to emerge in the shift in occupation policy concerned the end of the war and the future of

Japan's security. For the first three years of the occupation, US policy had been to sign a treaty of peace with Japan and to restore its full sovereignty in relatively short order. This changed with the reverse course. Rather than simply free Japan to the vagaries of early Cold War East Asian international relations, it was thought more prudent to proceed incrementally with peace negotiations, to ensure a favorable outcome for the United States and the West. As NSC 13/3, the polished and finalized version of Kennan's original recommendations, notes, through bilateral diplomatic channels, the goal was to have the United States seek agreement among participating states on the main points of the treaty before actually entering into a peace conference.[51] Once there was consensus on the fundamentals, the peace conference itself would be little more than a signing ceremony. Moreover, internal State Department planning documents noted that Washington should have little tolerance for any disagreements among the Allied powers on what Washington wanted in a peace settlement, in which case, the United States should move forward with a bilateral settlement. As historian Paul Heer observed, "Japan was simply too strategically important for the United States to surrender any control over deciding its fate."[52]

A second shift in this respect was around the idea of a permanently disarmed Japan, one that would be vastly accelerated by the outbreak of the Korean War in June 1950.[53] As early as 1947, discussion had begun to arise of the possibility of Japanese rearmament, and a 1948 State Department document refers to a "general trend" in War Department thinking regarding the need for a small, defensive, post-occupation military force in Japan.[54] A Joint Chiefs of Staff memorandum in early 1949 advocated "anticipatory measures" to allow some military potential in Japan, and a late 1949 draft peace treaty included a provision allowing for Japan's rearmament five years after the treaty was signed.[55] But these rearmament proposals all came with one important, implicit catch—the requirement of some form of military alliance between Japan and the United States, and the retention of at least some US troops on Japanese soil. The idea was that allowing Japan to minimally rearm under the aegis of a bilateral alliance with the United States or within a US-led regional collective security arrangement would not only ameliorate the fears of suspicious regional partners, but would allow the United States to shape Japan's future security orientation. "We are absolutely confident," notes a State Department memorandum of the time, "that if Japan is basically committed to the free world and accepts US troops in and about its territories we will have complete control over any rearmament plans Japan may adopt."[56]

For these reasons, American planners tied Japan's postwar recovery with US national interests in Asia. This was elucidated in Dean Acheson's famous January 12, 1950 Press Club speech: "The defeat and disarmament of Japan have placed upon the United States the necessity of assuming the military defense of Japan so long as that is required, both in the interest of the security of the entire Pacific areas and in the interest of Japan's security."[57] Assuming this responsibility also meant that the United States sought to build a politically stable post-imperial Japan that, "however constituted, consistently acted in ways that would advance United States interests."[58] A November 1949 strategy paper for the president stated this in no uncertain terms: "[Regarding Japan] make every effort to see to it that political and economic progress in Japan is such as to demonstrate the advantages of close association with the United States and our ability as a democracy to deal with the [development and security] problems in Asia."[59] The objective of the alliance was to mold Japan into becoming the Britain of Asia.[60]

The "Beta" Strategy

The powerplay rationale for Japan was similar to those for Taiwan and South Korea in that it was still about control. But the control sought by the United States was more subtle. It was not explicitly tied to fears that Yoshida Shigeru, the first prime minister of postwar Japan, might have revisionist intentions like Chiang or Rhee. At the same time, though, controlling Japan did not mean wholly curtailing its postwar development. Instead the vision was to shape Japan through a "beta" strategy.

State Department and White House foreign policy documents offer a window into the American strategy. With the reverse course of the occupation now in place, Washington had to decide in what direction it wanted to take the relationship with Japan. Unlike Korea and Taiwan, Japan did not present a "civil war" problem in the sense of domestic leaders potentially entrapping the United States into unwanted conflicts. Nevertheless, the problem was complex with multiple dimensions. It had to extend the occupation and delay a peace treaty, but not for too long as this would alienate the Japanese people. The Pentagon wanted to maintain bases in Japan to fight the Cold War, but the Soviets were sure to oppose any final peace settlement on Japan with US forces still in the country. Allies like the Australians, British, and New Zealanders worried that the end of the occupation might lead to a resurgence of Japanese militarism. At the same time, worries abounded among some in Washington that a weak Japan might end up bandwagoning with the Soviet Union. The United States had to locate an institutional design for the relationship with Japan amid these cross-cutting pressures—not leave Japan too weak such that it could be overrun by the Soviets, but not leave it too strong such that it would be threatening to its neighbors.

The United States rejected a design that would leave postwar Japan fully disarmed as a long-term goal. Known as the "alpha" option, this visualized a harsh treaty settlement, with the confinement of the defeated power to her home islands and with only modest defense capabilities. This was essentially the consensus left over from the wartime conference at Potsdam, where the allied powers agreed that the destruction of Japan's war-making potential, the occupation of its territory, the disarmament of its military, and the meting out of "stern justice" to those responsible for its militarism, were essential for the maintenance of peace in the region.[61] General MacArthur believed in these principles of Potsdam. He told Acheson that the only effective permanent solution for Japan was complete demilitarization under international security guarantees.[62] He valued the alpha principles as setting a clearly defined endpoint to the occupation with a peace treaty that would then allow the general to pursue larger political aspirations back home. The Chinese and British also leaned toward this strategy, manifest in the form of various proposals for the three countries (United States, Britain, China) to guarantee the long-term disarmament of Japan.[63] These principles basically defined the initial, pre–"reverse course" years of the occupation of Japan. But as the occupation wore on, this strategy was increasingly considered undesirable for three reasons. First, it was based on the assumption that Japan would not reemerge as a major power in the region, which few in the US government accepted as a valid assumption of strategy. Second, it assumed that Japan would welcome such blatant controls. And third, the alpha option would be detrimental to US longer-term regional interests as a totally emasculated Japan would not provide a base for US influence in the region.

Kennan's opposition to the alpha option was clear in his discussions with MacArthur. The policy planning chief believed in particular that the Russians could not be trusted to honor a demilitarization treaty arrangement for Japan.[64] To the contrary, Soviet forces were already in Sakhalin and the Kurile Islands and Vladivostok effectively placing the threat only miles away from Tokyo. Ominously, Kennan warned that Korea would be overrun in a matter of months, and that it was "obvious that the Russians would exercise a good deal of pressure against a demilitarized Japan."[65] It was these geostrategic realities and the aspirations for what could be gained from a stronger Japan that turned American planners away from the alpha option.

The obverse to the alpha strategy was the "gamma" strategy. This called for the encouragement of a militarily independent Japan capable not only of defending itself against communism, but also projecting force in the region. This strategy acknowledged Japan's position in the region as the only great power that could play a stabilizing role friendly to US interests. A strong Japan as a bulwark of anti-communism could balance the threat posed by the Soviet Union. A stable and strong Japan was also needed to contend with the uncertainties posed by the Communist party's revolution in China. Proponents of this view were found throughout the US government. At the State Department, John Foster Dulles wanted Japan to play a somewhat larger military role and therefore supported some form of Japanese rearmament.[66] MacArthur's successor, General Matthew Ridgway at SCAP, was another proponent, as were secretaries Forrestal and Johnson at the Pentagon. In the end, however, the gamma option was rejected on the grounds that a rapidly reconstituted Japan might be destabilizing to the region. It would raise the specter of Japanese armed aggression again. It would also create fears of abandonment among countries in the region as the United States might be seen as buck-passing security responsibility for Asia to Japan. These concerns would be particularly detrimental to US interests if Washington were perceived as explicitly exerting pressure for such a policy as a way to disengage from the region while focusing on Western Europe's defense.[67]

The aversion to the extremes of the alpha and gamma strategies was candidly reflected in internal discussions in the Truman and Eisenhower administrations. Once Truman decided on the reverse course for occupation policy and began to contemplate Japan's path after a peace treaty, his strategic thinkers believed that the alpha option was not viable in the face of Soviet threats. For Kennan, furthermore, the gamma option was only plausible in that it would deter Soviet aggression, but would "be contrary to our solemn most international commitments and basic principles of SCAP policy, and would be impractical from the military-economic point of view."[68] NSC 13/2 reflected Kennan's ambivalence toward the two strategies. It laid out one path for Japan's future that entailed an early end to the occupation, the signing of a peace treaty, and the creation of multilateral security guarantees for a demilitarized Japan. It laid out another path entailing an early end to the occupation, peace treaty, and a militarily independent and strong Japan. But both of these paths, the report opined, meant releasing Japan from US control prematurely.[69]

If US planners believed that Japan would remain a great power in Asia, why were they so concerned about it falling into the communist orbit? The answer lay in fears that the alpha option would spur bandwagoning dynamics in a weak Japan. And such anxieties were exacerbated by the policies of the Soviet Union, and, ironically, Britain. In Moscow, Nikita Khrushchev was embarking on his own détente initiatives in Asia, and in London, the British, having recently recognized communist China, were supportive of better Sino-Japanese economic relations (in part to keep the Japanese out of British markets in Southeast Asia). Informing these concerns were also somewhat racist preoccupations with Japan as being genetically incapable of absorbing Western values and ways of thinking. US ambassador to Japan John Allison warned Washington in mid-1952 that the Japanese were culturally distinct and predisposed to believe American values and influence were superficial and transitory. John Foster Dulles once stated before a French audience that Japan "had a unique capacity for good *or* evil (emphasis added), and that the people had been historically susceptible to militarism."[70]

Eisenhower's appreciation of the problem and his penchant for finding the middle path for Japan was evident in his discussions with officials like Secretary of the Treasury George Humphrey. Humphrey, a fiscal conservative and one of the president's confidantes, had strongly held views on maintaining stringent emasculation of a defeated Japan. Eisenhower resisted, however, saying that if the United States only sought to clamp down on Japan with a tough postwar settlement and occupation without assisting its recovery more broadly, then it would eventually turn Communist, and "then instead of the Pacific being an American lake, believe me it is going to be a Communist lake."[71] Eisenhower in a later exchange during a National Security Council meeting noted that one of the problems with Japan was that the United States had "licked [Japan] too thoroughly." When asked whether this meant the president had some longer-term strategic view to see the restoration at some level of Japan's empire, Eisenhower responded, "No," and stated that that "seemed to be going too far."[72] Nonetheless, Eisenhower knew that the United States would need allied support in Asia in the long term against the communists and that Japan was to play an important role in this respect. The challenge therefore was to find an institutional design for the relationship between the alpha and gamma extremes.

The sweet spot was the "beta strategy"—America's powerplay to control, craft, and temper Japan's postwar recovery in the context of an alliance with the United States. The powerplay rationale was to formulate deep and robust ties and thereby create a Japanese reliance on the alliance to channel growth and development in a controlled direction beneficial to US interests. This collaboration's scope would be wide, across all sectors of politics and economics.

John Foster Dulles's 1951 Mission and the Peace Treaty

John Foster Dulles was brought into the government as a consultant to the Secretary of State on April 19, 1950. Bringing Dulles in not only gave the administration an able and experienced diplomatic hand for the peace negotiations, but Dulles being a Republican contributed to the bipartisan image that President Truman was trying to project in foreign policy.[73] Truman still remained mildly peeved with Dulles for his criticism of the president's Fair Deal policies during Dulles's failed New York Senate election bid the previous fall, but accepted him nonetheless.[74] But this bipartisan gesture from the White House did little to ameliorate the interdepartmental conflict that would plague the initial steps on the path to peace with Japan. Between MacArthur and SCAP's position of an early peace treaty/neutralization of an unarmed Japan, and Defense Secretary Johnson and the JCS's desires for a protracted occupation to oversee a rearmed Japan, sat Dulles, Secretary of State Dean Acheson, and the Department of State.[75] Their belief was that a non-punitive peace treaty should be negotiated and entered into in a reasonable amount of time, and that a post-treaty security system suited to the United States should come into effect along with the signing of the treaty.[76] From the perspective of State, MacArthur's plan of Japanese neutrality was a non-starter, with Acheson calling it "illusory" and Dulles claiming it "did not make any sense."[77] And pushing for a treaty too soon, it was thought, would leave an unarmed and unprepared Japan a vacuum of power—unacceptably vulnerable to Soviet encroachment. The Joint Chiefs' position, on the other hand, was seen as ignoring the growing Japanese hostility toward the occupation, insensitive to the regional anxieties about Japan, and threatened to inadvertently feed the Japanese archipelago directly into the jaws of the Soviet bear. This is, in fact, an analogy of Dulles's. In describing the Soviet territorial holdings and satellites in the region, such as the Sakhalin Islands to the north and much of the Korean Peninsula to the south, he remarked that Japan was "between the upper and lower jaws of the Russian Bear."[78] The JCS were particularly intractable in their position, with State officials even referring to them as "the Pentagon hurdle" in internal documents.[79] And so after MacArthur's views were cast aside fairly early on (he would be replaced by General Matthew Ridgway in April 1951), State eventually emerged victorious in its bureaucratic battle with the JCS,[80] with President Truman's endorsement of its policy direction on September 8, 1950.[81]

With this mandate, Dulles was sent to the region to conduct preliminary negotiations for the eventual treaty of peace. Before departing, he was given a letter from President Truman designating him Special Representative to the President, with the responsibility of carrying out the negotiations on the part of the US government.[82] Dulles headed out for the region armed with the firm belief that a punitive treaty settlement would do more harm than good in the long term. He noted that it was in US interests to "avoid the humiliations and the discriminations which victors usually impose upon the vanquished either because passion supplants their reason or because they think that is the way to discourage a defeated nation from going to war again. History shows that such a course in fact spurs the vanquished to seek revenge."[83] Dulles's lessons from history were personal. In 1907, at nineteen years of age, he took time away from his studies of philosophy at Princeton to accompany his grandfather, former US Secretary of State John W. Foster (1892–1893), to the Second Hague Peace Conference as a secretary-clerk for the delegation.[84] Twelve years later, this time as a young lawyer, Dulles accompanied his uncle, Secretary of State Robert Lansing (1915–1920), to the Palace of Versailles for the Paris Peace Conference. These experiences, but more poignantly Versailles, had a profound effect on Dulles, as he expressed in an October 1951 address in Gatlinburg, Tennessee, just after having signed the Japanese Peace Treaty. "In our dealing with the Japanese," Dulles explained, "we recognized their personal dignity and worth . . . I had witnessed the treatment of the Germans at Versailles. It was so humiliating that the treaty never had the chance to make real peace . . . We were not going to repeat that blunder in the case of Japan."[85]

Accompanying Mr. and Mrs. Dulles was Assistant Secretary of the Army Earl D. Johnson, Dulles's deputy John M. Allison, Major General Carter B. Magruder, John D. Rockefeller III, Colonel Stanton Babcock, and Secretary of the Mission Robert Feary. The first stop of the ambassador, his wife, and his six-man delegation (known collectively as the Dulles Mission) was Tokyo, where they arrived on the evening of January 25, 1951. In a statement upon arrival in Japan, Dulles set the tone of his mission, pointing out that the US government looks "upon Japan as a party to be consulted and not as a vanquished nation to be dictated to by the victors."[86] Without wasting a moment, the courtship had begun. During his seventeen-day stay in the country, Dulles met with government leaders, parliamentary opposition officials, and groups representing business, trade, finance, education, and labor. The Dulles Mission sought public opinion through mass petitions and the reading of thousands of letters from ordinary Japanese (during a press conference back in Washington, Dulles read two of these letters out—one from a disgruntled bar owner's son complaining about liquor licensing laws; the other from a frustrated train passenger who insisted that all public clocks should always tell the correct time).[87] They also met with allied diplomatic officials in the country, to exchange views on the progress of Japanese peace. Just before leaving the country, Dulles released a statement in which he claimed that his mission was leaving with a "gratifying measure of understanding" with the Japanese regarding the direction of the process.[88]

From Japan, the Dulles Mission carried on to the Philippines, then to Australia, closing out the trip with an impromptu stop in New Zealand. In the Philippines, Dulles held extensive talks with President Elpidio Quirino and Acting Foreign Minister Felino Neri, where the concern was centered on the prospect of reparations payments from the Japanese.[89] After two days in Manila, Dulles and his mission carried on to Canberra, Australia, where they were greeted by Prime Minister Robert Menzies, Foreign Minister Spender, and other members of the Australian government. Here the primary concern was of a resurgent Japanese military, with the Australians pushing for a militarily restrictive settlement.[90] Present during these discussions was New Zealand Foreign Minister Frederick Doidge, whose government had a similar position, and was somehow able to convince Dulles to make a stop in Wellington before his return to Washington. What all of these allied positions had in common was that they bore a striking resemblance to the punitive occupation policy of the United States before the "reverse course." But Dulles and his delegation were nearly four years beyond this point, and the well-institutionalized process of winning Japan as an ally was not going to be derailed by the anxious clamor of regional allies. As he explained to his somewhat skeptical counterpart, "Japan might revive as Germany had after the last war. But we do not wish to try to prevent this by the methods which failed so signally for Germany. . . . Such restrictions, however, are just an incitement to a nation to break them in order to show that it is as good as any other."[91]

As a result, the eventual settlement after six years of American occupation was one of the most generous ever offered by a victor over a defeated enemy. As Dulles explained at a December 1951 luncheon in Tokyo, "never before in all history has a peace treaty restored the vanquished to such a status of equality with the victors."[92] The formula for reparations was extremely beneficial to Japan. Dulles proposed an arrangement in which Japan would pay "reparations" to countries it had invaded after 1931, but in the form of funds that would be tied to the purchase of Japanese products. This arrangement enabled Japan's recovering economy to "penetrate the very markets that Japan had failed to seize or hold militarily not long before."[93] The purges of Japanese elites was stopped, with many reintegrated in the new government. Full sovereignty was restored to Japan with the exception of Okinawa, which the United States kept but granted residual sovereignty to the Japanese. Japan renounced claims to all former colonies, but former President Herbert Hoover, who saw Japan as a future ally against Russia, even urged Truman to allow Japan to keep Korea and Taiwan as colonies as part of the settlement.[94] These favorable terms were the subject of protests by several countries in the run-up to the treaty's signing in San Francisco. South Korea, for example, pressed the United States for much harsher treaty terms, but to no avail.[95] President Quirino and other leaders in the Philippines were adamant about retrieving their claim of $8 billion in war reparations, but this also proved impossible. In an address just a few weeks after meeting with the Philippine president, Dulles expressed that "the United States does not question the inherent justice of the proposition that Japan should make good the damage done to others by its aggression. Reparation is, however, not merely a matter of what is just, but of what is economically practicable without disastrous consequences."[96] Similarly and also mentioned above, the Australians and Kiwis initially took issue with the US position on the treaty. Being two regional states that had, as Dulles put it, "felt the hot breath" of the Japanese military machine, leaders in Canberra and Wellington pushed for a treaty that enacted severe rearmament restraints on the Japanese government. But here again, the ambassador drew upon his personal past, pointing out that "the Versailles experience indicated that the surest way to induce rearmament is to forbid it."[97] Dulles further cited Plato in his defense with *Newsweek* right after the peace settlement in San Francisco:

Twenty-five centuries ago, Plato wrote a treatise on the "conduct of victors in war." He said that wars will never cease so long as the victors execute vengeance on the vanquished. The way to bring warring to an end, he says, is for victors "to exercise self-control, drawing up equitable terms that are designed to favor them no more than the defeated party." We try, in the Japanese peace treaty, to follow that good advice. [98]

Even the British—thousands of miles away—had their own issues with the treaty. Aside from their belief that the peace agreement should include the recently victorious communist government in Beijing (as opposed to the nationalists on Taiwan), the British government largely feared Japanese economic competition in world trade. Officials in London therefore hoped to limit Japanese shipbuilding and textiles production, to confiscate Japan's gold and other precious metals reserves, and to seize their assets in neutral countries. With an eye to their colonial holdings and established trade links, they additionally wanted to freeze Japanese trade and investment out of India, Malaya (now Malaysia and Singapore), Indonesia, and several central African states.[99] But Dulles, Acheson, and the negotiating team would successfully fight off all of these grievances. To their minds, the San Francisco conference was about ceremony, not substance. There would be no further negotiation or change to the US plan to ensure a smooth recovery and reintegration for Japan in the region.

An Alliance of Two, Not Many

Along with the peace treaty, the United States had to contemplate the nature of its postwar alliance with Japan. Initially the institutional design favored by many was to have some sort of collective-security arrangement for the region. In President Truman's appointment letter to Ambassador Dulles, this was precisely what was called for, with the president stating his government's willingness to "make a mutual assistance arrangement among the Pacific island nations."[100] And yet as the Dulles Mission's journey progressed, the idea of a Pacific Pact came to be seen as less and less plausible (covered in great detail in chapter 7). As then-Australian Foreign Minister Sir Percy Spender aptly put it, "the idea of a Pact seemed to have dissipated in the course of Ambassador Dulles' travels."[101]

By the end of the mission, Dulles came to see that the multilateral institutional design used for Europe would not accomplish US objectives in Asia. Rather, they would be better accomplished through a tight bilateral alliance where the United States would "permanently assume the principal responsibility for sea and air defense of the Japan area."[102] As long as the peace and security treaties were carefully negotiated and arranged, it was thought, the United States should have no problem maintaining and perhaps even enhancing its influence in Japanese foreign and security policy. "In the post treaty period," notes a 1949 State document, "there is no apparent reason why the United States . . . should not increase its influence over Japan's foreign policy and thus align Japanese policy to parallel our own."[103]

Even if Spender, Doidge, and others Dulles encountered on his sojourn had not spoken in favor of tight US bilateral control over Japan rather than a Pacific Pact-type solution, it is highly likely that Dulles would have reached a similar conclusion. Indeed, the American penchant for bilateralism over multilateralism became evident as soon as the reverse course was implemented. Between 1948 and 1951, the United States operated in an increasingly unilateral fashion while marginalizing the Far Eastern Commission (FEC). Set up as a multi-nation body (United States, UK, China, and Soviet Union) for administering Japan's surrender, the FEC had two primary functions: (1) formulate the policies, principles, and standards to ensure Japan's fulfillment of its obligations; and (2) review any directives issued to the SCAP Commander involving policy decisions regarding Japan. But as the United States began formulating the reverse course and the beta strategy, it avoided bringing any proposals before the FEC. Indeed, one of the few things that MacArthur and Kennan agreed on during the latter's 1948 trip to Japan was marginalization of the FEC. Kennan believed Japan was simply too important to leave to a committee decision, and MacArthur reportedly slapped his thigh in approval.[104] Allies like Australia, Britain, and Canada complained about the unilateral issuing of SCAP press releases on the "reverse course" in Japan policy without clearance through the FEC channels. Australians and New Zealanders filed formal protests over the US decision to allow Japanese coastal patrols, fishing expeditions (outside of regional waters near Australia), and travel abroad for Japanese nationals without seeking approval of the FEC.[105] The formal US response to these complaints was to reiterate the division of responsibility between the broad principles for administering Japan by the FEC and the daily implementation duties carried out by the SCAP. But Washington's desire to take control of the operation, and its disdain for a larger multilateral decision-making process, were barely concealed in its defenses. Citing the "unique position" of the United States vis-à-vis Japan's recovery, the State Department's formal response to FEC member complaints stated unapologetically:

> It would be manifestly undesirable and impracticable for an eleven-nation body in Washington to attempt to do more than set the broad framework within which the Japanese occupation should proceed. . . . it is necessary that the Supreme Commander should have broad discretionary powers to take action with regard

to problems arising in Japan which must be promptly and decisively dealt with if the occupation purposes are to be successfully accomplished.[106]

In internal NSC policy directives, moreover, the emphasis on circumventing any messy rule by committee was clear. The instructions were to take an "aggressive and positive attitude," with the FEC firmly and "forcefully backing" US needs, and that if agreement cannot promptly be reached, then SCAP should act on its own accord.[107]

For example, in the formulation of the Japanese constitution and the defense treaty, the FEC wanted the right to review the draft (largely drawn up by the United States) and, upon reading the text, questioned whether the document represented the will of the Japanese people. The FEC proposed that some type of referendum be taken on the draft constitution. Washington's response was clearly disdainful of any attempt to dilute American decision-making power. NSC 13/2 stated clearly that "[The United States] should not at this time propose or consent to any major change in the regime of control. SCAP should accordingly be formally maintained in all its existing rights and powers."[108] In subsequent instructions to the US representative to the FEC, the State Department demanded that the FEC should: (1) "inconspicuously" and with "minimum debate" review and accept the draft constitution; (2) judge that the constitution meets the full requirements agreed at Potsdam; and (3) refrain from any calls for amendments or a public referendum. The instructions end gratuitously, acknowledging, "The United States would be glad to hear the opinions of the other members on this topic."[109] But in truth, there was no such intention. This was made even clearer with regard to the peace treaty when Dulles gave an off-the-record press briefing at the State Department after his return from his 1951 trip to Asia. The Secretary fielded questions about the FEC's role in definitive terms, "I want to make clear when I refer to the Far Eastern Commission that that does not mean that we are negotiating with the Commission itself. . . . The Far Eastern Commission has no responsibility for the Japanese Peace Treaty."[110] Japan had become an exclusive American project.

THE POWERPLAY

The United States proceeded to conclude an arrangement that legitimized and enshrined America's near-absolute control over Japan's internal and external affairs. The arrangements were neo-imperial in nature.

In military terms, the United States sought to retain "long-term strategic control" of the Ryukyu chain. Okinawan air and sea bases were critical to the US strategic position in Asia. The United States could not have fought the war in Korea (nor would it be able to fight the war in Vietnam) without the outposts in Okinawa for staging, logistics, repairs, hospitals, and secure sanctuaries. The United States had 169 bases, 45,000 military personnel, 54,600 dependents, 3,300 civilian employees, and nearly 70,000 Japanese employed on the islands. It negotiated a status-of-forces agreement over the heads of the Japanese government regarding the extraterritorial rights of US soldiers, which allowed 97 percent of the 14,000 crimes committed by US servicemen in Japan between 1953 and 1957 to be tried outside of Japanese courts.[111] The official language of Japanese air force and navy was English, not Japanese.[112] The security treaty even had a provision for allowing American forces to quell internal riots and political disturbances with the approval of the Tokyo government, leading critics to say the United States was basically able to use force anytime and anywhere in Japan. Dulles once confided to British officials that the 1951 treaty amounted to a voluntary continuation of the military occupation, but in the guise of a normal political relationship between two nation-states. Internally, Dulles told cabinet secretaries that the goal was a postwar institutional design that "gave the United States the right to maintain in Japan as much force as we wanted, anywhere we wanted, for as long as we wanted."[113] The famed Ambassador to Japan and Harvard professor Edwin Reischauer, who would later be seen as critical to improving relations between Tokyo and Washington after the 1960 treaty crisis, observed that the primary goal of this unprecedented US fixation with controlling Japan was to "insure that this country [Japan] does not fall or gravitate into Communist hands or into a neutralist position."[114]

US bilateral control over Japan was not merely in the military sphere. In the economic arena, the powerplay objective was to develop Japan's postwar economy as a bulwark against communism, but one wholly dependent on the United States. Joseph Dodge, the architect of the "reverse course," believed that this was the most effective means of assuring Japan's pro-US alignment in the long term. As figure 6.1 illustrates, Washington was the dominant aid provider, which war-torn Japan—a country with little food, high inflation (prices increased twelve-fold in the immediate postwar years), no exports, and no savings—could not refuse. Between 1952 and 1956, US military assistance (both outright assistance and planned purchases of Japanese products) financed 25 percent of Japan's total commodity imports.

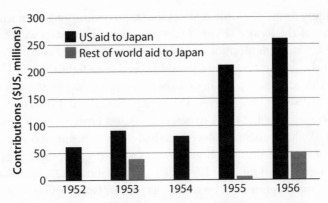

FIGURE 6.1. Comparison of US aid and rest of world aid to Japan (1952–1956)
Source: Compiled from US Agency for International Development (USAID), "U.S. Overseas Loans and Grants: Obligations and Loan Authorizations," July 1, 1945–September 30, 2012, and Ministry of Finance, Japan, "Fiscal and Financial Statistics."

The US domestic market also absorbed a large portion of Japanese exports, as figure 6.2 shows.

The Korean War was a major factor in early US-Japan economic cooperation. During the war, US procurements of Japanese goods accounted for a whopping 70 percent of the country's total exports, totaling some $200–$300 million annually.[115] These American purchases provided Japan with much-needed hard currency, which enabled modernization and infrastructure growth, hence prompting Yoshida's famous remark that the Korean War was a "gift of the gods" for Japan's recovery. These funds also reduced Tokyo's need for foreign capital from other sources that might create external influence in Japan beyond the United States.[116]

One manifestation of this economic strategy was the relatively lopsided interaction that took place between the United States and different branches of the postwar Japanese government. American authorities found themselves dealing more with the Ministry of Finance in Japan than with the foreign ministry, given the large sums of assistance being provided. The foreign ministry was largely emasculated as most of the foreign policy decisions for Tokyo were being shaped in Washington. The flow of monies to Japan did not stop with official assistance or military payments, moreover. The CIA provided financial support to the conservative political elements in Japan and to the LDP in order to ensure that domestic politics did not move in a direction inimical to US interests. Some of this money was passed through private sector surrogates

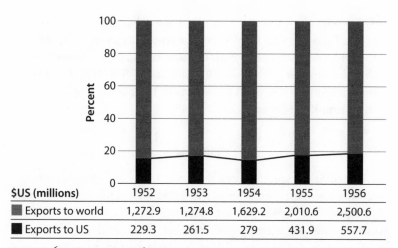

$US (millions)	1952	1953	1954	1955	1956
■ Exports to world	1,272.9	1,274.8	1,629.2	2,010.6	2,500.6
■ Exports to US	229.3	261.5	279	431.9	557.7

FIGURE 6.2. Comparison of Japanese exports to the United States and the world (1952–1956)

Source: Compiled from US Department of Commerce and UN Yearbook of International Trade Statistics (1955 and 1956).

like Eugene Dooman, a former OSS operative who paired the American need for scarce strategic metals in Japan (e.g., tungsten for munitions) with CIA payments of millions of dollars to Japanese conservatives during the Korean War.[117] As historian Walter LaFeber recounts, key Japanese politicians such as Eisaku Sato approached US embassy officials in Tokyo with requests for financial assistance to counter apparent campaign funding of the leftist political elements and the Socialist Party by the Soviets and Chinese. While the State Department did not accede to these requests, the CIA undertook the task, according to statements by former operations officers.[118] This decision was apparently authorized at the very top of the US government, according to some historians, and was communicated quietly during a June 1957 visit by Prime Minister Kishi to the United States, during which he addressed a joint session of Congress and threw out the first pitch at a New York Yankees baseball game. The money was provided through private American citizens to aides of Kishi and other conservatives within the LDP and amounted to about $10 million annually between 1958 and 1960.[119] The Kennedy administration reviewed this covert funding but decided against stopping it, and the practice carried forward throughout the 1960s. CIA and other Americans infiltrated opposition parties and the major trade union, Sohyo, to advantage the conservatives. LaFeber writes,

These operations were overseen by a Special Group (SG), chaired by the President's national security advisor. It met in Room 40 of the Old Executive Office Building next to the White House, and thus was known as the "the 40 Committee." The SG guided the most important US covert operations in Japan and elsewhere into the Nixon-Kissinger era of the 1970s.[120]

"Soft Bind"

The United States saw the mutual defense treaty with Japan, therefore, as serving two purposes. One was to build a bulwark against communism and defend Japan. But the other was to "bind it" by controlling, managing, and promoting Japan's reintegration into the world. In conversations with Australian and New Zealand foreign ministers, Dulles, an avid fisherman of Lake Ontario salmon, encapsulated the "soft bind" of Japan. He noted that the objective of winning Japanese favor, of "attracting Japan" as he put it, "is one which must be dealt with extreme delicacy, the type of delicacy one would have to employ in landing a big trout with a light tackle. If too much strain is put on the tackle it will break and the fish will get away."[121]

Rather than disillusioning the Japanese population and embittering its leadership with hundreds of thousands of pairs of boots on the ground, the United States sought to quietly shape preferences from the periphery through a variety of means. And in these endeavors, the "soft bind" strategy proved as effective as any other. Writing in 1965, more than a decade after the signing of the peace treaty, Edwin O. Reischauer noted that "American influence and leadership [in Japan] . . . while now dependent on persuasion and negotiation rather than dictation, has been almost as marked these past few years as during the declining days of the occupation."[122] Before Reischauer, in a famous 1952 *Foreign Affairs* article laying out the US postwar strategy for Asia, Dulles elaborated on the "front-" and "back-end" of the powerplay.[123] He wrote that the alliance kept Japan safe from communism (front end), but also was legitimized in a regional context because it provided a "shield" for former colonies against a resurgent Japan. At the same time, however, Dulles wrote that it was imperative for the United States to utilize the alliance to shape Japan's postwar recovery. This was the back end of the powerplay—the goal was a reformed, politically stable, economically prosperous Japan, without its colonies, that would become the linchpin of US influence in the region. US military protection under the alliance was, in effect, insurance against losing Japan to the communist bloc and keeping it aligned with the West. As he wrote in a moment of candor to Acheson while the former was in Tokyo seeking a commitment from premier Yoshida that Japan would not pursue relations with Communist China, the goal of control was to make it "inconceivable that Japan should pursue foreign policies which cut across those of the United States."[124]

Ultimately, through this powerplay, the United States foresaw Tokyo playing an important role as an American proxy in the region. American views on the disposition of Korea were particularly instructive in this regard. In October 1949, George Kennan told Dean Rusk that the United States should have "no objection" to eventually delegating influence over Korea to Japan.[125] Kennan's view was to establish the status quo ante on the peninsula and then allow a rehabilitated Japan under American influence to be responsible for Korea.[126] Dulles too, was aware of the challenge for US policy: "The problem is," Dulles noted just weeks before the treaty was signed, "you have got to find a way whereby the Japanese can play their proper and necessary part in collective security . . . without recreating a militaristic machine within Japan." "I think that way will be found," he added, "but it is a delicate matter."[127]

When it came time to sign the Japanese Peace Treaty in the fall of 1951, the mechanisms for winning Japan were all in place. Dulles and his team had successfully negotiated, not one agreement, but four: a general treaty of peace between Japan and fifty-two allied states; a bilateral security agreement with Japan; a mutual defense treaty with the Philippines; and a trilateral security treaty with Australia and New Zealand (known as ANZUS). On August 30, just days before the opening of the conference, Presidents Quirino and Truman signed the US-Philippine mutual defense treaty.[128] Two days later, Ambassador Dulles and Secretary Acheson, along with Foreign Minister Spender and New Zealand Ambassador to the United States Carl Berendsen, signed ANZUS.[129] And for the main event, representatives from fifty-two nations met in San Francisco between September 4 and 8 for the "Conference of the Conclusion and Signing of the Treaty of Peace with Japan." In the opening address of the conference, the first ever nationwide televised speech in US history, President Truman called on all parties to "be free of malice and hate, to the end that from here on there shall be neither victors nor vanquished among us, but only equals in the partnership of peace."[130] And after much pomp and ceremony, and a series of lofty speeches, the treaty was signed by forty-nine countries on the conference's final day (with the Soviet Union, Czechoslovakia, and Poland refusing to sign).[131] But less conspicuously, the United States was putting its primary powerplay mechanism into place. Later that day, in a discreet ceremony, Acheson, Dulles, and Prime Minister Yoshida gathered for the signing of the US-Japan Security Treaty. The two sides had agreed in advance to keep the details of the bilateral pact as far from the public eye as was possible, and quietly released the text of the treaty to the press shortly before its signing.[132]

Tokyo's Embrace of Powerplay

The powerplay rationale for the US-Japan alliance was implicit. Its purpose was never formalized or enshrined in a document. And yet its force was felt very strongly in Tokyo by Japan's first prime minister. Yoshida Shigeru was the stocky, bespectacled, barely five-foot-tall, first prime minister of postwar Japan. After graduating from Tokyo Imperial University, Yoshida entered the Japanese diplomatic corps in 1906, and had an illustrious career which included ambassadorial appointments in Rome and London. Largely as a result of being locked up in the waning months of the Pacific War for his opposition to it, he was exempted from SCAP's postwar purge and emerged as prime minister after his Japan Liberal Party won 140 of the Diet's 466 seats in the April 1946 election.[133]

Yoshida's opposition to the war, his fluency in English and diplomatic savvy, and most importantly, his anti-communist, pro-American perspective, made him a perfect partner for Washington's powerplay strategy. And the policies he would put in place as Japan's leader for more than seven years have largely defined Japanese foreign policy to this very day, eventually being anointed "the Yoshida Doctrine." It held that Japan would maintain a small self-defense force limited to protection of its home islands and would focus the majority of its national efforts on postwar economic development.[134] Miyazawa Kiichi, an aide to Prime Minister Yoshida (who would later become Prime Minister himself [1991–1993]), noted in his memoirs that Yoshida once told him: "the day [for rearmament] will come naturally when our livelihood recovers. It may sound devious, but let the Americans handle [our security] until then. It is indeed our Heaven-bestowed good fortune that the Constitution bans arms."[135] This formulation of Japan's grand strategy during Yoshida's government from 1948 to 1954 signified Tokyo's embrace of the powerplay rationale for the alliance. From his perspective, these policies were "warmly welcome[d]" as the greatest guarantor of what he saw as "winning by diplomacy after losing in war."[136] When faced with objections over turning his country into a de facto colony of the United States, Yoshida half-joked to an American official, "I tell our people . . . just as the United States was once a colony of Great Britain but now is the stronger of the two, if Japan becomes a colony of the United States, it will also eventually become the stronger!"[137] The United States, of course, wanted Japan to play a larger military role than Yoshida was willing to commit, but Yoshida's focus on industrial development in the postwar liberal economic order and his designation of Japan's place within the US sphere of influence constituted commitments consistent with the powerplay rationale. As Dulles pointed out during a speech in Australia at the time, the Japanese "like it better if the American troops stay there because the American troops give them invisible dollars."[138] But these invisible dollars were not simply flowing into a black hole. They enabled the United States to exert the influence necessary to advance its interests in the region. In Chalmers Johnson's terms, this was an informal empire arrangement, but one in which Japan fared well: "From approximately 1950 to 1975, the United States treated Japan as a beloved ward, indulging its every economic need and proudly patronizing it as a star capitalist pupil."[139]

In the years that followed the signing of the peace and security treaties with Japan, Kennan's dual objectives of keeping Japan away from the Soviets and in the arms of the West remained central to US policy in the region. The courtship process that had begun in 1947 continued on. Although Japan had been "won" in the peace process, its allegiance now had to be kept by convincing it that the West's side was the best side. At times, Washington used sweet diplomacy, but at other times it strong-armed Tokyo into accepting its control. Now that the United States had invested in Japan as its primary partner in Asia, it had no tolerance for a weak return on that investment.

Economic Engineering

The United States' exercise of control over Japan had ripple effects throughout the region. The objective was to grow Japan economically by reuniting it with regional markets, but in a direction that fit with the emerging Cold War interests of the United States. One target of US control was Japan's postwar relationship with China. Wartime procurement orders from the Korean conflict gave a significant boost to the Japanese economy, basically covering the country's annual trade deficit of $575 million, but what was really needed was sustained, long-term economic growth.[140] One of the ways this would be achieved and maintained was through trade. China had long been a critical source of raw materials for the Japanese archipelago, supplying 50 percent of its coal, 25 percent of its iron ore, 75 percent of its soybean, 17 percent of its imports, and 27 percent of its exports in 1941.[141] But the loss of the Japanese empire and its territorial holdings in Manchuria, Shandong, and the Korean Peninsula meant Japan's mainland imports dried up, going from an average of $600 million per year in the early 1940s, to just $7 million by 1948.[142] Though the United States allowed Japan to continue some trade with China in the beginning of 1950 in order to spur the economy, many in Washington, including Dulles, feared that Japan would want to renew fully economic relations with China, which might create Japanese dependence on communist China and push Japan in the direction of neutrality.[143] The concerns about a Sino-Japanese rapprochement were also shared by a pro-Taiwan (then called pro-China) group of fifty-six US senators, led by William Knowland (R-CA) who did not want to see Japan sign a peace treaty with Communist China and threatened that the Senate would not ratify the bilateral United States-Japan security treaty. Moreover, Yoshida believed that Japan's natural market was mainland China, and that US Cold War policy toward Beijing was doomed to eventual failure. As the premier famously stated in 1948, "I don't care if China is red or green. China is a natural market, and it has become necessary for Japan to think about markets."[144] The British also supported Sino-Japanese rapprochement because they did not want Japanese economic competition moving further to Southeast Asia.

And so the United States exercised some draconian control. In December 1951, Dulles flew to Tokyo to elicit from Japan an explicit commitment that it would not improve ties with Communist China, would recognize Taiwan, and would trade with it. He said that Japan's lack of cooperation would undercut support in Congress for the treaty, which would in turn make US protection of the Japanese archipelago and the proffer of preferential trade arrangements more difficult for the American public to swallow. Two senators from the "pro-Taiwan" lobby and the highest ranking members of the Senate subcommittee on East Asian affairs, John Sparkman and H. Alexander Smith, accompanied the Secretary of State in this mission, which all hoped could be wrapped up in time to return home for Christmas. In a rambling press conference upon their arrival that covered everything from the delegation's planned visit to a Kabuki performance to Hawaiian statehood, the senators offered a message with the subtlety of a billy club:

Assuming something that we certainly do not anticipate, that Japan should show signs of executing a peace treaty with Communist China and of recognizing Communist China and opening up trade relations with Communist China, that certainly would constitute a very formidable roadblock toward ratification [of the peace treaty].[145]

On December 24, 1951, Yoshida signed a letter stating that Tokyo had "no intention to conclude a bilateral treaty with the Communist regime in China." This so-called Yoshida Letter was an extraordinarily powerful exercise of US control over its ally, the true scale of which did not become fully known until it was later revealed that the document signed by the Japanese prime minister was drafted by Dulles himself.[146]

Not only did Washington seek to control Japan's official ties with China, it also sought control over private sector ties. A little less than six months after the Yoshida letter, Japanese business conglomerates began signing a series of trade agreements with China that had the effect of more than doubling bilateral trade by 1953 and increasing it again by 75 percent in 1954. Yoshida regarded these activities as private sector, beyond the purview of government, but these activities deeply concerned US officials. American economic advisors sent contradictory messages to the Japanese, telling them that on the one hand, China in the midst of a communist revolution would not be as good a trading partner as it was during the 1930s; at the same time, US officials warned that trading with China could make Japan vulnerably dependent on the communists.[147] Dulles wanted to stifle all Sino-Japanese ties, defending such demands before foreign policy bodies like the Council on Foreign Relations as necessary to apply maximum containment against Communist China. The Japanese business community complained about US heavy-handedness. They blamed high production costs at home on the requirement to import raw materials like coking coal and iron ore from North America rather than from China, and chafed at having to seek approval from SCAP (and later MITI) for every export application to China.[148] In July 1952, the US government called upon Japan to join COCOM as well as CHINCOM, both bodies aimed at coordinating allied trade in certain goods and services with communist countries (the latter body was explicitly aimed at sanctions on China). Washington sent envoys to Tokyo in August 1952 aimed at "forc[ing] Yoshida to accept a secret agreement imposing even harsher restraints on Japan in its China trade than other CHINCOM members had accepted."[149]

Washington had to facilitate access to new markets for the Japanese in lieu of China. And that is precisely what they did. In an NSC document that was approved by President Truman in August 1952, it was recommended that the United States "Encourage Japanese contribution to the economic development of countries of South and Southeast Asia through . . . trade and investment."[150] As an alternative to the massive reparations program, which was largely abandoned by 1949, the United States devised a regional economic system in which increased US aid would be sent to Southeast Asia on the condition that it be used to buy Japanese goods and services.[151] Under this scheme, Southeast Asian states would ship raw materials to Japan to be processed and manufactured into final goods using Japanese labor, in Japanese factories. SCAP authorities removed price controls on Japanese items in 1949 in order to allow for greater export competitiveness. Other schemes to promote trade between Japan and South and Southeast Asia (India, Pakistan, and Ceylon, and India) included a plan hatched in 1949–1950 for Japan to sell textiles to Britain and then use the pound sterling to purchase food. This food would then be "bought" by the United States, which would then be given to Japan as assistance, thus enriching the country with both food and dollars. Japan would then use these dollars to buy cotton.[152] US negotiators went to Burma on behalf of Japan to negotiate a $50 million trade agreement for rice exports to Japan in return for textiles. They did the same with Thailand, inking a $90 million barter agreement of Thai rice for Japanese steel and machinery.[153] Yoshida resented the effort, saying that Southeast Asia lacked the capacity to absorb Japanese exports and complaining about having business counterparts for Japan who were not "rich men," but "beggars."[154] Nevertheless, he was forced to comply with the system which America argued had the fourfold effect of developing the region, of appeasing Southeast Asian states in their demands for large reparations payments, of getting Japan's manufacturing and trade sectors up and running, and importantly, of keeping Japan away from too close a trade relationship with China. And, while the United States could never completely cap Japanese trade with mainland China, it did successfully foster the emergence of alternatives in South and Southeast Asia.

For instance, as figure 6.3 shows, in 1948 Japanese trade with the noncommunist countries of Asia[155] totaled just $196 million. In just two years this figure had reached $570 million, by 1955 it was at $1.3 billion, and by 1961, nearly $2.2 billion. Over the same period, trade with the communist countries stagnated.[156] In 1948, Japanese trade with these countries sat at a paltry $18 million. By 1950 it had jumped to $55 million, but

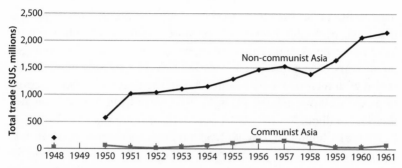

FIGURE 6.3. Japanese trade with Asia (1948–1961)
Source: UN Statistics Yearbook, 1960, 1961.

would dip back down to just $15 million in 1952. Japanese-China trade would peak at just $152 million in 1956, before receding back to $32 million after the Great Leap Forward.[157] Admittedly, there are far more states in the non-communist category, but it is the trajectory, rather than the volume, that is most important (see figure 6.3).[158]

Thus, the United States sought to assemble a regional economic formula that would rejuvenate Japan, provide trade ties with South and Southeast Asia, and divert economic interaction away from China. This effort did *not* reflect an American penchant for multilateralism in Asia, however. Consonant with the powerplay, this was done with a heavy US hand that engineered all the regional agreements on behalf of Japan. The flavor of this institutional design was not one in which there would be a regional economic community without the United States. Instead, it tasted of an American engineering of regional trade solutions for Japan that would enhance *US control* over building an anti-communist economic bulwark in the country and delimiting its interaction with mainland China.

The United States also made itself a vital trade partner to Japan.[159] Despite the objections of domestic labor and industrial groups, the government initiated "buy Japanese" campaigns and allowed Japan nearly unfettered access to the American market while tolerating Japan's numerous trade barriers. One indication of how far the government was willing to go was the "dollar blouses" controversy. In the early 1950s Japan's textiles sector rebounded rapidly, and with a wide-open US market of willing importers, Japanese exporters had a field day. In 1955 alone, 4 million one-dollar, Japan-made blouses were sold in the United States, up from zero just three years earlier, effectively capturing one quarter of the entire market. But rather than immediately erect protectionist barriers to Japanese imports, Washington instead pressured Japan to "voluntarily" limit its textiles exports, and carried out extensive negotiations which dragged on for years.[160] And it wasn't just textiles that the United States willingly traded with their new Japanese ally. Across the board, the trade relationship expanded through the 1950s. In 1948, Japan-United States trade was just $390 million. Yet by 1952 it had risen to more than $850 million, by 1955, $1.1 billion, and by 1961, $2.8 billion.[161] The irony in all this, as Japan historian Marius Jansen points out, is that "with an open field for the import of raw materials and access to foreign markets, Japan seemed to have achieved its chief war aims in defeat."[162]

The United States manipulated the value of the Japanese currency as another instrument of control. The purpose was to maintain an undervalued yen as a means of spurring continued economic growth. Back in 1949, as part of the "Dodge Line" economic reforms, Japan's currency was revalued to 360 yen to one US dollar, a level low enough to ensure that Japan's exports were competitive internationally. It remained fixed at this level for the following twenty-two years. In the course of these two decades, the Japanese economy grew rapidly, at an average of 10.8 percent per annum between 1955 and 1971.[163] And because the Japanese economy grew at a significantly greater rate than that of the United States (which averaged 6.6 percent in the same period),[164] each year brought the value of the yen lower and lower, and made Japanese exports increasingly competitive. And, in stark contrast to current debates regarding the renminbi, with policymakers in Washington griping about China undervaluing its currency, the US government actually encouraged Japan to do so.

Not all US controls on Japan were harsh. Part of this informal empire arrangement required the United States to become Japan's biggest advocate on the international stage. Washington lobbied for and sponsored Japanese entry into the global economy, often in the face of strong opposition. In August 1952, in no small part due to US efforts, Japan was admitted into the International Monetary Fund (IMF) and the World Bank's International Bank for Reconstruction and Development (IBRD). In September 1955 it signed the General Agreement on Trade and Tariffs (GATT), and in July 1956 joined the World Bank's International Finance Corporation (IFC). This was followed in 1960 with its accession to the International Development Association (IDA) and in 1964, with its admittance to the Organization for Economic Co-operation and Development (OECD). Beyond organizational membership, the United States actively encouraged individual governments to lower tariffs and other trade restrictions and to accept Japanese goods.[165] The goal, as an NSC document phrased it, was to "seek to prevent Japan from becoming dependent on China and other Communist-dominated areas . . . through stimulation of Japan's trade with other free nations and through implementation of programs designed to develop sources of supply for Japan among the free nations."[166]

With these economic measures, the Japanese economy absolutely exploded, multiplying itself thirteenfold between 1955 and 1973.[167] And yet, economic growth was seen as a necessary but not sufficient condition for keeping the Japanese on side. The United States would also have to make Japan as acceptable politically as it was becoming economically.[168] And so, at America's initiative, Japan was accepted into the Universal Postal Union in 1949 and the World Health Organization (WHO) and the United Nations' Food and Agricultural Organization (FAO) in 1951. In December 1956, with the help of US support, Japan became a full-fledged member of the United Nations, and just two years later, sat as a rotating member on the Security Council (Japan has since been a UNSC rotating member a total of ten times, matched only by Brazil among all non-permanent members).[169] In July 1957, Japan was one of fifty-six states to ratify the International Atomic Energy Agency (IAEA) and bring it into force,[170] and by 1961, Japan had its first judge sitting in the International Court of Justice (ICJ). Japan's regional diplomatic relations followed a similar path. It established full diplomatic relations first with India and New Zealand (1952), then Australia and Cambodia (1953), followed by Burma (1954), Laos (1955), the Philippines (1956), Malaysia (1957), and Indonesia (1958). By 1965, Japan had normalized relations with the Republic of Korea, and by the early seventies, with China (1972) and Vietnam (1973). In all of these instances, Japan's political trajectory was, at least in part, steered by the United States—constantly working in the background, cutting deals and lobbying foreign leaders. The political reintegration of Japan into the region and the wider world was seen as crucial to maintaining Japan as an ally.[171]

But in addition to economics and politics, there was a third pillar to the retention of Japanese favor in the early Cold War years—the provision of Japan's external security. This is where the United States' impact was undoubtedly most profound. In 1954, the United States had more than 200,000 personnel stationed in and about Japan. Through most of the sixties this number would stay above 80,000, and only in the late seventies would it fall to around 45,000.[172] These troops were stationed in more than 300 individual US military facilities stretching from Naha on the southern tip of Okinawa (26°12'N) up to Wakkanai on the very northern tip of Hokkaido (45°25'N). The United States also provided Japan with large amounts of military aid, totaling $866 million between 1954 and 1965.[173] Under the watchful eye of the US military, the Japanese government was free to concentrate on rebuilding the Japanese state and achieving and sustaining high levels of economic growth.

America's Heavy Hand

With Japan's economic, political, and security fortunes secure, the process of ensuring Japan's loyalty was complete. Japan had, in effect, been "won." But the effort to win Japan was not simply a bean-counting exercise in early Cold War competition. There were real domestic-political consequences. The powerplay generated local resistance to all of these practices of American heavy-handedness, particularly in the military sphere. US officials dismissed these complaints almost flippantly, which further instantiated the degree of US control. In the early 1950s, for example, Japan tried unsuccessfully to resist US efforts to change Japan's small police reserve into a defense force. Eisenhower wanted Japan to expand its postwar rearmament at the height of the Korean War, given his domestic-political imperatives to reduce government spending (Eisenhower ran on a campaign of how the Democrats were spending the United States into bankruptcy). In 1953, as Vice President Nixon explained before hundreds of Japanese leaders Eisenhower's "New Look" doctrine, he also called on Japan to grow its military and stated his view that the United States had made a mistake to include Article IX in Japan's constitution. Yoshida was fearful that Washington would drag Japanese troops into the war on the Asian mainland, but could not resist US calls because they came with the promise of $150 million in military equipment and hundreds of millions in agricultural assistance. In the end, Japan grew its police reserve from 75,000 to 110,000, passed legislation in 1954 to create a Defense Agency, and renamed the police reserves as the Self Defense Forces. Yoshida also crafted legislation that ensured civilian control of Japan's military, but American heavy-handedness once again won the day.

One of the primary manifestations of the powerplay in Japan in these early postwar years was growing anti-American sentiment. The United States may have tried to be a benevolent hegemon, but the scope of American control was so vast, it was bound to incur negative sentiments.

This was often catalyzed by individual events. Yoshida complained to Washington that Article 22 of the Administrative Agreement would undercut his domestic legitimacy as it basically gave the US military unlimited authority to do whatever it pleased in and around Japan.[174] The United States made regular practice of moving nuclear weapons through Japan even after the end of the military occupation and despite Japan's self-professed non-nuclear principles.[175] In 1954, a Japanese fishing boat (*Lucky Dragon*) sailed too close to a nuclear test site in the South Pacific and the crew died days later of intense radiation poisoning. This prompted widespread panic and anger in Japan that their fishing stock was irradiated, and many citizens demonstrated against the United States. A couple of years later, a US soldier shot an elderly Japanese woman in the back who was picking up spent shell casings near a military base. Both events engendered widespread protests in Japan, and in each case, American authorities acted quickly to resolve the issue. They provided an apology and a $2 million indemnity in the former case, and consented to the trial of the US serviceman (Sergeant Girard) by a Japanese court in the latter case. But the feeling of being so squarely under the American thumb were palpable. US ambassador to Japan John Allison cabled Washington warning that Japanese cooperation stemmed not from benevolence but from brute force of US economic, political, and military muscle.[176] In the end, being perceived in a benign light mattered less to US alliance crafters than did maintaining absolute and deep control. When the Hatoyama government (successor to Yoshida) tried to push back against the American movement of nuclear weapons on ships to Japan without Tokyo's consent in 1955, the response from Washington could not have been clearer: John Foster Dulles told foreign minister Shigemitsu Mamoru that Japan could raise a renegotiation of the terms of the alliance when it could pay for its own military, defend itself, and help the United States abroad; otherwise, it should basically shut up.[177]

The control Washington exercised over its ward state was so pronounced that it raised concerns among American friends about potential blowback consequences. The British ambassador to Japan Sir Esler Dening in 1955 cabled home that the Americans were overdoing it. They were treating respected Japanese ministries like a PX and were asking too much of its leaders. Dening believed that because of these actions, the United States risked suffering the same fate as the British did in Egypt.[178]

Japan's resistance to US hegemonic control of the bilateral relationship came to a head with the 1960 treaty crisis. The intense Japanese desire to gain greater autonomy through a revised treaty arrangement was evident not only in the proclamation and complaints of the short-lived governments of Hatoyama Ichiro (November 1955 to December 1956) and Ishibashi Tanzen (December 1956 to February 1957), but also in the complaints of the Kishi government, which was sympathetic to US plans. Unhappy with the depth and breadth of US control, Kishi sought to end US obstruction of Japan's trade relations with China, reversion of Okinawa, and the right of prior consultation for US military movements in Japan. The cry for greater Japanese independence swelled onto the streets when hundreds of thousands of students (*Zengakuren* or Federation of Students for Self-Government) protested against American policies.[179]

Despite these efforts, the treaty revision negotiation fell in line with US preferences. Kishi did not achieve any of the things he wanted. Moreover, the treaty now committed Japan to defense of the "Far East," including the potential use of its bases for US operations and military contingencies on the Korean peninsula and across the Taiwan straits. Unknown to the public at the time, treaty revision also included a secret verbal agreement to allow the United States unfettered movement of nuclear weapons through Japan.[180] US Assistant Secretary of State Graham Parsons privately bragged that the "treaty gave Washington everything it wanted."[181] For many Japanese, Dulles's claim that the bilateral alliance was the continuation of the occupation by other means started to ring true. Incensed that Kishi had completely caved to US pressure, former Prime Minister Yoshida boycotted the Diet ratification sessions and the Socialist party mobilized to stop the vote. The country reeled in crisis as six million workers went on strike, and demonstrators attacked the prime minister's home. Following ratification of the treaty on June 19, the protests were still so virulent that Eisenhower was forced to cancel his visit to Japan. Kishi was stabbed by a right-wing fanatic the following month, and left office five days later. The United States was unapologetic about the domestic havoc wreaked by these events. The treaty was considered too valuable an instrument through which the United States could execute its powerplay over Japan.

Another critical mechanism of the powerplay strategy was the United States-Japan "Administrative Agreement," signed in early 1952.[182] This agreement was essentially the nuts and bolts of the 1951 security treaty, and it included some powerful clauses for the United States. First, it officially granted the United States the "rights, power and authority" within and adjacent to the facilities it controlled, including land, airspace, and territorial waters. This meant that the US military could station troops and materiel, collect intelligence, and stage regional military exercises when and how it saw fit. Second, the agreement guaranteed the United States access to Japanese ports and airports, and gave the US military the right to use all public utilities and services in Japan. Third, in the event of imminent or actual hostilities, the Japanese government was obligated to consult the US government "with a view to taking necessary joint measures for the defense of that area." These administrative agreement clauses meant that, while Japan was sovereign, it didn't have a true monopoly on the legitimate use of force within its territory.[183] This monopoly was ceded, in part, to the US government.

The renegotiated alliance agreement of 1960 contained more evidence of a powerplay strategy on the part of the United States.[184] By 1960, with Japan's economic growth in full swing, US negotiators were able to get even more from their ally. For instance, the treaty explicitly addressed the need for *both* parties to continuously maintain and develop their capacity to resist armed attack. While the treaty text does state "subject to their constitutional provisions," the intent is clear. Second, the 1960 treaty strengthened mutual aid and defense, stating that in the event of an armed attack on either party in Japan's territory, the other would "act to meet the common danger." While this article also notes that this action must be "in accordance with [the state's] constitutional provisions," it is clearly a step further than the 1951 treaty. Finally, the renegotiated treaty was more binding than the 1951 version. It essentially locked the Japanese into the alliance for a minimum of ten years, and thereafter required a one-year notice for alliance termination.

———

Postwar planners in the United States faced multiple pressures in designing the right security institution for its relations with Japan. The choice of bilateralism in the form of the US-Japan treaty alliance served dual rationales. The first was the front end of the powerplay strategy—traditional security protection in terms of deterring communist threats. The second was the back end of the powerplay rationale—to control the ally's postwar development and shape its return to the region as a major power congruent with American interests. This newfound institution both shielded the region still fearful of a militarily independent Japan, and gave Japan enough autonomous capabilities such that it could serve as a bulwark for US interests in the region.

This powerplay rationale for the alliance is different from standard explanations of the dual nature of the alliance. One popular version states that the alliance is not only to defend Japan but also to contain it. This latter rationale refers to the alliance as the "cork in the bottle" of renewed Japanese militarism, or as the *gobanken-sama* (honorable watchdog).[185] The problem with this analogy, however, is that the United States has historically supplied and encouraged a more modern Japanese military. It sells more advanced weapons to Japan than to any other country except Saudi Arabia and Taiwan.[186] America's powerplay rationale for the US-Japan alliance was more subtle than the cork in the bottle. It called for a reconstituted Japan, but one dependent on, and made in, the American image.

7

COUNTERARGUMENTS

The United States faced cross-cutting pressures as it emerged as an Asia-Pacific power at the dawn of the postwar era. Truman and Eisenhower needed to defend against dominoes falling in Asia; at the same time, Washington's best thinkers believed that US military engagement in the region should be delimited to the maritime perimeter. The United States had to manage these security concerns amidst incessant attempts by unpredictable local leaders to drag the United States into war with China, as well as uncertainty about how to contend with Japan's eventual re-emergence as the only major power in Asia. The answer was the power-play—a security design that optimized risk management, trust deficits with local leaders, and defense and deterrence goals. This design played to the US obsession with achieving an unprecedented level of control that reeked of neo-imperialism—anointing one country with the power to determine when another nation could exercise its sovereign right to use force.

This chapter will elaborate on why the United States chose a bilateral rather than multilateral design for Asia. I will argue that a multilateral security structure in Asia offered little value-added in terms of containment and control for three central reasons. First, the United States' military capability was still far superior to that of any of the other countries in Asia, and therefore not significantly enhanced by a collective security arrangement. Second, the United States' commitment to Asia had already been demonstrated by the intervention in the Korean War, and therefore would not be made more credible by a NATO-type arrangement. And third, the United States faced an "entrapment discount" if it went multilateral in Asia—i.e., any appreciable gains in security had to be discounted by the increased likelihood of entrapment by the ally.

A multilateral design had a greater propensity to take alliance decisions out of a bilateral context and put them in the hands of a larger collective body, which would dilute US control.

More Control With Than Without?

Critics might contend that the powerplay argument is based on a rationale for alliance-making that does not exist theoretically or empirically. Theoretically, critics might question whether the fear of entrapment creates a desire to tighten an alliance rather than distance from it. A great deal of literature on the subject—and plain common sense—would lead one to believe that the rational reaction to an ally's erraticism and belligerency is to distance from it.[1] Empirically, the fact that the United States had entrapment fears regarding Korea and Taiwan, but chose to form alliances with them in spite of these fears, critics would argue, does not validate the powerplay argument. Instead, it suggests that US Cold War defense needs (e.g., military bases and operations) dictated the establishment of these alliances, which simply took precedence over any minor entrapment fears.

But this criticism, empirically and theoretically, does not take account of the imperatives that the domino theory put on US action and commitments. As I explained in chapter 2, whether a state chooses "distancing" or "control" strategies in response to entrapment fears depends on how intense those entrapment fears are. These fears will be more intense when ally A *knows* it has no choice but to get dragged into ally B's conflict, however wasteful the conflict might be. In this situation, the costs of employing a control strategy (i.e., expending the resources and assistance to gain B's dependence) are lower than the costs of being entrapped in B's conflict. On the other hand, if state A feels it has a choice—i.e., could intervene on B's behalf, but also might not intervene—then its entrapment fears are, relatively speaking, less intense. In this instance, state A will be more inclined to using passive, distancing strategies to discourage overzealous actions by B and thereby minimize entrapment fears.[2] The US belief that the domino theory was operative in early Cold War Asia heightened entrapment fears. For the United States, the Soviet threat, the 1949 CCP victory, the June 1950 North Korean invasion, the 1954 Quemoy crisis, and the conflict in Indochina constituted a broad-based contest for not just one or two countries, but the entire Asian continent and Pacific. Whether a correct assumption or not, these looked like falling dominoes. Harvard University's Asia scholar John King Fairbank in November 1949 wrote of how Mao's victory had sparked an idealism and energy among not just Chinese but all Asians after decades of repression and colonial rule. For poor, uneducated Asians, the communist victory in China offered the vision of a new world, a path to literacy, better lifestyles, and self-determination: "Communism is accepted as a way to salvation—national salvation quite as much as human salvation in general."[3] A social revolution was taking place first in China that, in Fairbank's words, "can expand to almost any part of Asia that offers conditions similar to those in China, Korea or Indo-China."[4]

The prevalence of domino-theory-thinking compelled the United States to intervene on behalf of Taiwan or the ROK regardless of whether these wasteful wars were provoked by Chiang or Rhee. Though the United States may have stated otherwise in an attempt to discourage Chiang and Rhee from overconfidence, in reality Truman and Eisenhower understood the strategic imperative well. To alleviate these intense entrapment fears merely through a strategy of distancing was suboptimal on two counts. First, the lack of US commitment could have been interpreted as weakness and emboldened the adversary to action. Second, Chiang or Rhee might still have miscalculated, and attacked based on ambiguous US statements. Given the stakes involved, it was more sensible to "double down"—that is, display clarity of commitment (vis-à-vis the adversary) and clarity of control (vis-à-vis the allies) through design of a new bilateral institution.

These alliance institutions and bilateral aid offered the United States many more instruments of control over Taiwan and South Korea than Washington would have had without such ties. In Taipei's case, between 1950 and 1965, the United States provided assistance on an annual average basis that comprised 34 percent of Taiwan's total gross investment, financed some 40 percent of its import bill, and 6.4 percent of its GNP (see table 3.1).[5] The United States provided South Korea with $12.6 billion in economic and military assistance between 1946 and 1976, which amounted to more dollars per capita of aid than that given to any other country except South Vietnam and Israel. Between 1953 and 1962, this aid financed 70 percent of South Korea's imports and comprised some 5 percent of the national GNP (see tables 3.1 and 5.1).[6] The point to be made is that this doubling down gave the United States inordinately more influence than a distancing strategy would have. Indeed, whenever Truman or Eisenhower threatened termination of aid or military assistance in order to rein in Syngman Rhee and Chiang Kai-shek, both truculent leaders were cowed into submission. In November 1953, when Vice

President Nixon told Rhee explicitly that the US Congress would not ratify the mutual defense treaty if Rhee unilaterally attacked the North, the
ROK leader admitted to Nixon, "In my heart I know that Korea cannot
possibly act alone."[7] Similarly, in 1953, Eisenhower withheld deliveries
of jet aircraft to Taiwan until Chiang agreed to defer to US approval on
any decision related to military actions against China.[8] The United States
could not have made similar threats as credibly if it had no preexisting
tie/channel of assistance that was costly enough to the leaders to control
their behavior.

MISSED OPPORTUNITIES FOR ASIAN MULTILATERALISM?

If the powerplay argument is valid, then one must be able to demonstrate that the United States not only sought control through bilateral
alliances, but also purposefully eschewed multilateral institutional designs in Asia. In other words, a "hard test" confirming the powerplay hypothesis requires looking for not only US efforts to consolidate bilateral
alliances, but more important, the calculated and deliberate avoidance
of multilateralism in Asia. There is clear evidence that despite incentives
to pursue multilateralism in Asia, the United States opted against this
because doing so would not afford the same fulfillment of powerplay
objectives.

Saying "No" to the 1949 Pacific Pact Proposal

The first instance of US desires to eschew design of a multilateral security structure for Asia was the 1949 Pacific Pact. The story of this proposal begins in the immediate postwar years when the United States
desperately sought a degree of retrenchment after the long war. In Europe, the United States initially wanted the establishment of a multilateral European Defense Force (EDF), coupled with the rearmament of
Germany that could act as the balance against Soviet power in central
Europe. This would then allow the United States to scale down its own
military presence to a symbolic force (along with Britain and Canada),
while the west European states would contribute the core forces. If this
was the model for Europe, then a similar design should have been seen
as appealing for Asia. In other words, the counterfactual proposition is
that there was much to be gained for US retrenchment to have sought
a regional security institution, with a rearmed and reintegrated Japan

at the core, that would then allow the United States to scale back to a token force presence.

Contrary to this counterfactual, however, the United States showed no interest in the first proposal for a similar institutional design for Asia, which came from three of the region's players. After the formation of NATO, Asian leaders pressed for a "Pacific Pact" along the lines of the Atlantic pact. In the spring of 1949, Philippines President Quirino raised the issue with the State Department, arguing that such a pact would enhance security, economic growth, and development in Asia.[9] Quirino further added that Japan's reemergence in the region could be best managed and directed under the auspices of a US-led regional, multilateral security organization.[10] Quirino referred to Europe, the region in which the United States was concentrating all its multilateral efforts, as "used up—an economic liability." Asia, he noted, "is a virgin region with unmeasured resources and people who are eager to take advantage of the blessings offered by democracy."[11] Manila was not the only supporter of the idea. In the following two months, the South Korean foreign minister and his ambassador to Washington demarched State Department authorities that they concurred with the Philippine proposal.[12] In a May press conference, ROK President Syngman Rhee stated that a Pacific Pact would be "beneficial not only to Asia but to the United States."[13] In July 1949, Quirino, on the occasion of Philippines Independence Day, called for a union of nations in Asia to combat communism: "Our answer to the threat of Red Imperialism and new slavery is a real union of peoples around the Pacific on the basis of common counsel and assistance."[14] Less than a week later, on July 10 and 11, the Philippines president hosted a summit with Taiwan leader Chiang Kai-shek in Baguio. After two days of meetings, the joint statement called on Asian nations "at once to organize themselves into a union" to counter communism, and called for a gathering "at the earliest possible moment to devise concrete measures for its organization."[15] Newspapers in Asia had front-page headlines trumpeting "The Start of the New Pacific Pact."[16]

The minutes of the so-called Baguio Summit have been buried in the remote archives of the Quirino Papers in a museum in the Philippines. The transcript of the discussions between the two leaders provides a fascinating look into the fears, motivations, and goals of the region's indigenous attempt to create a Pacific NATO. Quirino began the first day of discussions emphasizing how a show of unity among Pacific countries will cause "the whole world [to] sit up and take notice of the strength of our people and give us the necessary help to fight Communism, which is a world movement and which must be checked with another world movement."[17] The Philippines president made clear that he wanted US commitments to a multilateral pact in the region:

> We have to strengthen the position of the United States in the Far East; as long as we appear to be weak, disunited, silent, America will not pay attention to us. But the moment she finds us united and determined to band together against a common cause, America will be compelled to adopt a more open attitude in favor of the democracies in this part of the globe.[18]

Chiang Kai-shek wholly agreed with his host's assessment of the geopolitical situation. He drew direct comparisons with the Atlantic Pact, describing a need to design a similar institution based on democracy and "Oriental philosophy" to combat communism and to energize the reluctant Americans to recognize such an effort.[19] Chiang believed that he and Quirino needed to lead, and began to enumerate countries to approach for membership:

> The Generalissimo thinks that certain countries naturally have the same thought as we have, such as Korea, Siam, Burma, the Philippines, and China. . . . The Generalissimo says that we must unite now or else the western countries will say that we have no unity. If we do not unite and begin to show our strength, then the western countries will try to prevent this kind of unity and withhold from us their support.[20]

Chiang told Quirino to use an upcoming visit to Washington to propose a core group of countries—Philippines, Taiwan, and Korea—as the genesis of the Pacific Pact, and to convince the Americans that an American-centered bloc must replace traditional British hegemony in the region. Chiang then talked about bringing the South Koreans into the group, having had conversations with Rhee. Quirino conveyed that his ambassador in Seoul had already heard positive feedback from the ROK president on the idea. The two leaders discussed the possibility of a visit by Rhee to Manila before Quirino's trip to Washington, but both placed an emphasis on getting Quirino to see Truman as soon as possible to "strike while the iron is hot."[21] Quirino boasted to Chiang about his relationship with Truman, saying that he knew the American president well and had a special rapport because they spoke the same language.[22] After two days of talks, Quirino trumpeted the historical importance of the moment in which Asian nations were demonstrating new solidarity.[23] South Korean President Rhee simultaneously issued a press release in Seoul supporting the new collective defense proposal:

> A good start toward organizing the Pacific Peoples in their fight against Communism had been made by President Elpidio Quirino of the Philippine Republic and Generalissimo Chiang Kai-shek of China . . . the Republic of Korea stands ready to join in this movement . . . They see as we see and as all free nations of the world must see, that the common enemy is Communism . . . I sincerely hope that the Generalissimo or President Quirino or both can pay the US a visit at this time and let the US know how we Koreans can best aid our mutual fight against Red terror and totalitarianism.[24]

The following month, on August 7, 1949, Chiang arrived at Chinhae port to begin two days of talks with Rhee to round out the trilateral summitry. Chiang brought a massive entourage of more than thirty advisors to meet with the ROK president and his cabinet.[25] The two issued a joint appeal for a conference of Asian leaders in the Philippines to form a Pacific security pact.[26] Chiang and Rhee then cabled the contents of their discussion to Quirino, who was already in Washington for his state visit, urging the Philippines leader to get Truman's approval.[27]

In Washington, Quirino trumpeted the idea in a speech to the Senate on August 10, 1949:

> No one who realizes the extent of the menace to which Asia is exposed—the threat to Korea, the infiltration into Vietnam, the debacle in China—can afford to rest at ease. Asia, with its vast population—which accounts for more than half that of the world, and with its incalculable resources—cannot and ought not to be lost to Communism. And yet this is bound to happen unless something of the courage and vision that went into the forging of the democratic defences in Europe is applied to the forging of a similar system of defence in Asia. My concern over this problem has led me into taking the first steps towards this end. I fully realize that there are strong reasons why the United States may not too readily welcome the obligations that its active participation in this project would entail.[28]

In a speech to the Commonwealth Club in San Francisco on his way home from Washington, the Philippines leader grew more outspoken in his advocacy, complaining that many in Asia had become "discouraged" with the US fixation on European security when the Pacific faced an "immediate enemy" without any means to protect itself. He implored Americans to watch its "back door" against Communist infiltration in Asia while it guards its front door in Europe.[29]

The enthusiasm evinced by Quirino, Chiang, and Rhee for a Pacific pact spread through the region. Other leaders voiced support and a willingness to join the cause. Among these was Thailand, where the government of Premier Phibun Songgram emerged from a coup attempt in February 1949 reportedly involving Chinese communist supporters. The following month (March 23, 1949), the Siamese Cabinet spokesperson issued a statement to the effect that Siam "was anxious to join any possible Pacific and Asian non-Communist defence bloc similar to the Atlantic Pact group if invited."[30] Rumors abounded in newspapers in the summer of 1949 that a multilateral conference was in the works with Chiang, Quirino, and Park in the lead, and with invitations out to Indochina (Vietnam), Siam (Thailand), Indonesia, India, Pakistan, Australia, and New Zealand.[31]

Given the multilateralism model followed in Europe, one would have expected the United States to embrace this regionally based effort at confronting communism. It was virtually impossible for American policymakers not to view Asian security through the lens of NATO. The Pacific Pact initiatives and shuttle diplomacy involving Chiang, Rhee, and Quirino took place contemporaneously with the Senate's opening debate on ratification of the Atlantic Pact in July 1949. The latter pact passed by an overwhelming majority later that same month, which motivated both Democrat and Republican lawmakers to call on the Truman administration to replicate the tough anti-communist stance in Asia as well. By the summer of 1949, the Nationalist Chinese had lost the war, and as the reality of a mainland communist China set in, US policymakers scrambled to come up with a strategy to check the further advance of the movement in Asia. The administration, moreover, operated in a domestic political environment that was sympathetic to Quirino, Chiang, and Rhee's proposals. Accused of having "lost China," Truman and Acheson faced criticisms from Republicans like William Knowland and Walter Judd who openly supported the July 1949 Baguio Summit's call for a Pacific Pact and called for the authorization of more regionwide funding for collective defense. When Secretary of State Acheson secured $1.45 billion in military assistance largely for Europe, and explicitly stated that

Nationalist China would not receive funding until a thorough review of US policy in Asia had been completed (see chapter 4), Governor Dewey of New York derided Truman for throwing the keys to world peace "into the bottom of the Pacific" and for saving 270 million Europeans at the expense of "losing a billion Asians to the Communists."[32] Congressman Jacob Javits introduced a resolution in August 1949 urging the United States to financially support the creation of a multilateral organization of "Far Eastern and non-European countries."[33] And the criticisms were not just from the opposition. Congressman Walter Huber (D-OH) returned from a trip to Asia in October 1949 calling on the administration to do more to combat the rising tide of communism, and he criticized Acheson for devoting only "one percent" attention to Asia.[34] So, there was real pressure on Truman from the Hill to take a dramatic step as he had done in Europe.

The debate over Asia policy was not just reserved for inside-the-beltway types. The global foreign policy discussion at the time also leaned in the direction of creating an Asian bulwark against communism. Editorial writers strung together a series of major events—the CCP victory (October 1949), the communist insurgencies in Southeast Asia, and the formation of the Communist Federation of Trade Unions (Asian Cominform, December 1949), and wrote that the West needed a response to the new communist multilateral front being formed in Asia.[35] British journalists in the fall of 1949 wrote alarmingly of how the Soviet Union was the only great power to have increased its influence and land holdings in Asia through the end of the Second World War in the form of stealth "Soviet Imperialism."[36] Owen Mortimer Green, a prominent newspaperman at the *London Observer*, wrote of how the Soviets were now augmented by 480 million Chinese communists, and ominously predicted that Korea (quaintly described as "a promontory reaching down from North-east Asia nearly to Japan, about the size of England") could be next to fall.[37] British foreign secretary Philip Noel-Baker cautioned in November 1949 that the hunger of one billion people in Asia feeds the appeal of communism and that there needed to be a strong sign of Western support and allegiance to Asia.[38] In an October 1949 speech, the president of the Royal Central Asiatic Society in London made it clear: "Over an awakening East [Asia] broods the immense figure of Russia with its soulless creed of communism which threatens to affect the lives of all Asia."[39] While there wasn't panic, there was a clear feeling that the communists were consolidating and organizing a multilateral front in Asia and that the United States needed to respond.

The world would be disappointed by Washington's answer. It had no problem with multilateral organizations in Asia for the purpose of economic development like the Economic Commission for Asia and the Far East (ECAFE), but it was not interested in an Asian NATO.[40] Known internally as the Chiang-Quirino-Rhee Pacific Union (or by Kennan as the Philippines-ROC-South Korea entente), the concept was written off as a poorly conceived attempt to copy NATO.[41] Secretary of State Acheson tried to preempt further discussion about the Pacific Pact at press conferences in March and May 1949. On March 23, he stated unambiguously that the United States was not interested in the idea.[42] And on May 18, he responded to Chiang's and Rhee's public endorsements of Quirino's proposal by saying:

> As I have taken the pains to make clear on several occasions, the United States is not currently considering participation in any further specially collective defense arrangements other than the North Atlantic Treaty. Recently there have been a number of public suggestions about a Pacific pact modeled after the North Atlantic Treaty. . . . those who make such suggestions may not have given study to the evolution of the North Atlantic Treaty, which was largely the product of a specific set of circumstances peculiar to Europe.[43]

Acheson argued that NATO was the result of a long, deliberative process; that Western European powers had carefully developed their plan for collective defense before asking for US help; and the United States viewed NATO as a two-way street, but the Pacific Pact would amount to a unilateral security commitment that could only entrap the United States.[44] State Department officials also conveyed messages to this effect individually to Korean and Filipino diplomats.[45] Rhee responded publicly that Acheson was mistaken in his opposition to the pact.[46] Quirino too boldly stated that the pact was the only way for the region to combat "red imperialism."[47]

US disinterest stemmed from concerns that the Koreans and Nationalist Chinese were trying to use the pact to draw more assistance and commitments out of the United States at a time when the Nationalists were losing on the mainland and US forces were drawing down in Korea. Thus, Korea wanted the pact as a way to get arms and assistance from the United States; Chiang wanted the same and both sought to use Quirino, who had better relations with the United States, as the way to pitch the idea. Quirino liked the idea because it portrayed him as an Asian leader, which bolstered his domestic legitimacy.[48]

Washington's negativism toward Asian multilateralism also stemmed from a fundamental distrust that such a framework would increase opportunities for collusion among allies detrimental to US interests. For example, Acheson saw Chiang's inclusion as dangerous because it pulled all potential parties to the pact into Chiang's unwinnable military effort to retake the mainland.[49] There was also concern at the time that the proposed pact would be a propaganda gem for the Soviet Union, looking to expand its influence in the region.[50] There were, moreover, other membership problems. The tripartite pact envisioned the initial inclusion of Taiwan, the Philippines, and South Korea, to be potentially followed by Siam (Thailand), Indochina (Cambodia, Laos, Vietnam), Burma (Myanmar), and Indonesia. Chiang wanted to exclude India, Pakistan, and Australia on the grounds that they were Commonwealth members and had their own anti-communist defense measures. Strategically, this was seen as highly problematic by US government officials. "Nothing would make the Kremlin happier," noted one 1949 State telegram, "than to find its non-Communist Asian opposition divided into American and British blocs."[51]

Key states and US partners too, in and outside of the region, weren't keen on the idea. The Australian and New Zealand governments were reluctant to be drawn into a pact with Nationalist China. Prime Minister Jawaharlal Nehru of India saw the internal conflict of the region as dooming the pact from the start, claiming that "the time was not ripe."[52] Indonesia, mired in a war of independence with the Dutch, not only had more important considerations at hand, but its emerging leadership wanted no part in an organization that would tarnish its Cold War stance of neutrality.[53] The Philippines wanted nothing to do with a Pact that involved "White" Australian governments (represented by politicians like Arthur Calwell) that practiced anti-Filipino, anti-Asian exclusion policies.[54] When the North Atlantic Council of Foreign Ministers met in Washington in September—concerned about keeping the White House's focus on the Marshall Plan—they unsurprisingly rebuffed the idea.[55] And the British foreign office even went as far as to claim that the combination of a discredited Chinese president, an ill-reputed Philippine leader, and the head of a weak, insecure Korean state "reduce[d] the whole thing to absurdity."[56] But perhaps the most important reason for American ambivalence was that the proposed tripartite pact was seen as a strategic liability. Not only would it dilute the effectiveness of the

United States' existing security commitments in the region, but it would hamper the flexibility of US foreign policy in Asia.[57]

US officials therefore sought to kill the idea. The day before Rhee's August 1949 meeting with Chiang in Chinhae, US officials met secretly with the ROK president, counseling him to abstain from committing to any collective defense pacts with Taiwan or the Philippines.[58] In Washington (at the same time as the Chiang-Rhee summit), Quirino was told by State Department officials not to even bring up the topic of the pact during his visit to the White House.[59] Truman was also pre-briefed to tell the Philippine president that a Pacific NATO was impractical. The countries of the region did not possess the militaries to form such a bloc. Moreover, this could force the United States into underwriting a grouping that would have little value-added in terms of deterrence while only heightening US fears of being entrapped into a conflict started by one of the bloc's emboldened members. Instead, the United States, at the summit and in the months preceding it, remained focused on shoring up the bilateral military arrangement and on specific legal issues surrounding the operation of its bases. Truman deflected further discussion of the Pacific Union and pressed Quirino on the bilateral agenda, including Manila's financial situation and the safety of US servicemen at Clark Air Field.[60] Truman administration officials also encouraged Quirino to think about building a multilateral institution closer to home rather than in the vicinity of Beijing. Newspaper accounts noted this American preference explicitly, "American officials were understood to be pleased with the fact that President Quirino of the Philippines had, during the past month, tended to shift the emphasis of his Pacific alliance plan away from China and Oceania into South-East Asia."[61] The message was clear—anything was worthy of discussion except the pact idea. US officials sent similar messages of discouragement to other potential supporters of the idea. Secretary of State Dean Acheson met with the Burmese foreign minister days after the Quirino visit and expressed strong reservations of a regional alliance involving China given Chiang's ambitions to retake the mainland. Channeling Acheson's entrapment fears, the Burmese foreign minister told the press afterward, "We want to be sure that no one power is making use of that grouping for its own interests."[62]

As the central hub in the emerging hub and spokes arrangement, Washington exercised its considerable leverage in squashing the Pacific pact, one partner at a time. As one scholar observed, "[M]ultilateral institutions only undermined the leverage of the United States, which lay precisely in the absence of alternative mediators . . . It was convenient that Asians could not talk with one another very deeply."[63] Furthermore, the opposition to the Pacific pact was not a manifestation of general disinterest or lack of resources. On the contrary, just as the United States was rejecting the idea, it was working hard to shore up bilateral ties, approving $150 million in bilateral assistance to Korea, holding military exercises with the Philippines, providing Marshall Plan funding to Indonesia, and deepening military planning with Australia.[64] A State Department policy planning paper in March 1949 summed up this affinity for bilateralism, advocating that the United States avoid an "area organization" for Asia and instead focusing on "parallel action" among alliance relationships.[65] For Washington, the best design for exercising control and leverage was, even in these early years, the powerplay.

The discussion of the Quirino-Rhee-Chiang proposal suggests two points about the powerplay argument. First, the Quirino-Rhee-Chiang proposal is evidence that there were indeed preferences expressed by regional players for a security design similar to NATO. This discounts the alternative explanation that the emergence of bilateral institutions in Asia occurred because Asian states preferred bilateralism to a multilateral arrangement. Second, there is clear evidence that the United States opposed a multilateral design for Asia even when the United States was constructing NATO in Europe, and it was clear that the communists would win in China (summer of 1949).

Saying "No" to an Asian Front in Korea

US eschewing of multilateral security designs in Asia next became evident during the Korean War. Chiang and Rhee both had revisionist intentions and scores to settle with adversaries, making the prospect of collusion between the two a real, not merely fictional, entrapment scenario for the United States. As noted in chapter 4, just after the US decision to intervene in Korea, Chiang invited MacArthur to Taipei in July 1950 to offer 33,000 of his best equipped troops within five days to help roll back communist aggression.[66] From any number of perspectives, Chiang's offer should have appeared useful to the United States. At the time, Taiwan's military forces constituted 63 percent of all the region's military forces that were potential partners of the United States. Its relative defense spending was ten times greater than that of Japan and second only to Vietnam by the 1960s. In addition, because of US naval superiority in the Western Pacific and in the Straits, defense of the island against a primitive Chinese force would not have been that difficult, leaving a formidable and trained Taiwanese force that could be deployed elsewhere.[67] Chiang's proposal was sanctioned by all US commanders in Korea as helpful to the battlefield situation. MacArthur cabled the Joint Chiefs that "the situation in Korea is critical" and that he needed at least four fully equipped divisions without delay (Chiang's offer would have constituted three divisions).[68] By late 1950 (November-December), after the Chinese intervention shifted the tide of the war, MacArthur reported that without immediate reinforcements of some 50,000–60,000 Nationalist troops, he would soon have to evacuate from Korea.[69] Internal State Department, CIA, and JCS assessments considered utilizing two divisions of Nationalist forces in the war.[70] Moreover, Generals Ridgway and Clark, who succeeded MacArthur in Korea, supported the idea.[71] It was effectively a realization of the US postwar vision—an ally in the region that was willing to contribute to a multilateral security effort and share the burden of beating back communism.

The United States nevertheless consistently rejected the proposal. Truman, Acheson, and Defense Secretary George Marshall saw Chiang's proposal as a not-so-subtle attempt to capitalize on the Korean War to bring the United States back into combat on the Asian mainland with China. When asked once what the utility of his forces would be in Korea, Chiang admitted that they could not decisively affect the war's outcome, but he insisted the training of these battle-hardened Nationalist troops through fighting Chinese communists in Korea would facilitate their eventual "landing" on the mainland.[72]

Truman sent esteemed diplomat and former US Secretary of Commerce Averell Harriman to the region in August 1950 to clamp down on both Chiang and MacArthur.[73] Harriman, a Yale graduate who had also served as Ambassador to the Soviet Union and Great Britain, traveled with Air Force General Lauris Norstad and Army General Matthew Ridgway.[74] His long experience in government and sophisticated understanding of foreign policy and the ways of Washington made him "particularly qualified" in Truman's eyes for such a task.[75] MacArthur met the party on the morning of August 6 at Haneda Airport just outside Tokyo and rode with them back to the US Embassy's guest house where Harriman was to stay.[76] In the first of a series of private meetings with the general, Harriman wasted no time in relaying Truman's message. He pointed out that it was absolutely imperative that Chiang be prevented from starting a war on the mainland, a contingency which threatened to "drag us into a world war."[77] MacArthur obviously had different views. He thought the United States should take on the communists at every opportunity—as he put it, should "fight the communists every place, fight them like hell!"[78] But Harriman stood his ground. In the end, after two days of debate, Harriman left feeling that while MacArthur didn't agree, he was confident that the general would at least obey Truman's wishes.[79] For now, MacArthur and Chiang were on a short leash.

US officials continued to reject the idea when raised by Chiang in subsequent years. A 1952 memo from the top Asia diplomat in the State Department to Secretary-designate John Foster Dulles laid out the entrapment rationale behind US ambivalence:

> The introduction of Chinese Nationalist troops into Korea would immediately throw Korea into the Chinese civil war and would make it much more difficult, if not impossible, for US to maintain the position that we have so far maintained that in any political talks on Korea after an armistice there would be no discussions of any matters outside of Korea.[80]

The key point regarding the powerplay here is not about the US desire to avoid escalation in Korea, but that Washington, because of entrapment fears, purposefully eschewed an opportunity for a collective defense effort. Despite a disadvantageous battlefield situation that could have been helped by the infusion of Nationalist forces, a desire to keep Chiang leashed caused the United States to reject an opportunity for security multilateralism in Asia. Instead, it sought through bilateral channels to exercise even tighter control over Chiang.

American concerns about overzealous allies trying to draw the United States into a larger war under the guise of regional or collective security initiatives were evident in peacetime as well. During a July 1954 summit visit to Washington, Syngman Rhee made national headlines by proposing a collective defense mechanism in Asia. Before a joint session of Congress, Rhee explained that the ROK's capacity to field almost forty divisions of soldiers should be combined with Nationalist China's 630,000 soldiers to fight the communists on land. If the United States, Rhee added, provided the naval and air support for a blockade of China, then they could defeat communism in Asia. The Eisenhower administration was taken by surprise by Rhee's statements and subsequently began deliberations (discussed in chapter 5) on how to restrain Rhee. The *New York Times*, on July 29, 1954, condemned the speech for alarming the free world, providing fresh grist for communist propaganda mills, and risking atomic war.[81]

The failure of Chiang and Rhee's efforts in 1949 to press a Pacific pact did not deter the ROC and ROK from jointly supporting the formation of the Asian Peoples' Anti-Communist League in the years following the Korean War (that eventually floundered). In April 1954, Rhee and Chiang tried to convene a meeting of Asian leaders at Chinhae, South Korea again for the purpose of starting a multilateral security initiative. Government-run South Korean newspapers during the period called for a "Free Asian alliance" or Northeast Asia Treaty Organization featuring Korea and Taiwan as core members.[82]

Again, if US postwar interests were to multilateralize security obligations on the Euro-Asian continent so as to relieve security burdens on the United States, then proposals of this nature should have been welcomed.[83] But each time, the United States rejected the ideas outright because of entrapment concerns. What might have appeared as a multilateral initiative by an ally was perceived in fact to be a parochial attempt to draw the United States into unwanted contingencies that could escalate out of control. While these entrapment concerns related to Northeast Asia, the United States also actively discouraged any parallels drawn between a prospective "PATO" and the Southeast Asian Treaty Organization (SEATO), created in September 1954. The Eisenhower administration created SEATO after the defeat of the French in Indochina as a bulwark against communism, and while multilateral in form, Dulles did not see SEATO as akin to NATO, nor did the members such as Philippines, Thailand, and Pakistan, all of whom would have preferred bilateral security ties with the United States. The power disparities between these small postcolonial nations and the United States were just too vast for all to be considered equals at the multilateral table. The commitment, as Press-Barnathan characterizes, was largely symbolic, and a peculiar outgrowth of US military strategy under Eisenhower's New Look doctrine with mobile strike forces that required flexible regional arrangements in Southeast Asia: "Despite being a regional organization, SEATO was never thought of as a forum for regional cooperation. . . . the forum was perceived as a fig leaf to facilitate American unilateral action."[84] In any event, John Foster Dulles did not want to bring Korea and Taiwan into SEATO (these preferences were lost on Beijing, which became extremely concerned that the United States might fold Chiang into SEATO, thereby "multilateralizing" the Straits dispute).[85] He did not see SEATO as akin to NATO, but because the public (and the Chinese) did, he sought fruitlessly to instruct State Department officials in internal memoranda to avoid the terminology "SEATO" completely in order to delink it from Northeast Asia and from what the United States was doing with NATO.[86]

1951 Dulles's "Dissipating" Pacific Ocean Pact

The last major effort at designing a multilateral security structure in Asia before the creation of the hub and spokes system of bilateral alliances was the Pacific Ocean Pact. Diplomatic historians might point to this 1951 proposal as evidence counter to the powerplay argument. Unlike its earlier twin (1949 Pacific Pact or Pacific Union), the Pacific Ocean Pact was an American concept (rather than one developed by Quirino and Chiang) that emerged in response to the compelling need to define promptly some security institution in the region in the face of the Korean conflict. The United States considered a variety of possible designs such as a unilateral security declaration for the region—something akin to the Monroe Doctrine but for maritime Asia. A second possibility was a series of bilateral agreements with maritime countries. This would have entailed individual bilateral security pacts with the governments of New Zealand, Australia, Japan, and a reaffirmation of the US-Philippine security treaty. A third consideration was a tripartite agreement between the United States, New Zealand, and Australia, and individual bilateral arrangements with Japan and the Philippines. A fourth alternative was a quadripartite pact between the United States, Australia, New Zealand, and the Philippines, and a bilateral alliance between the United States and Japan. A fifth was the idea of a loose association of nations, without firm US defense commitments for the region. And finally, of course, was the consideration of a general multilateral security organization for the region—a Pacific Ocean Pact.[87]

Although the idea of a Pacific Ocean Pact emerged in early 1951, it had percolated in the background since the failure of the Chiang-Rhee-Quirino proposal of 1949. Indeed, even as the United States rejected this 1949 Asian initiative, it was quietly contemplating an institutional design for Asia, but with different players. In late 1949, Deputy Undersecretary of State Dean Rusk sent Ambassador at Large Philip C. Jessup on a three-month, fourteen-country, fact-finding tour of Asia. Jessup's trip followed on the heels of the communist revolution in China and amid real concerns in the United States and in Britain that other Asian countries would align with this victory. Following on bilateral meetings in Washington between Bevin and Acheson, the purpose of Jessup's trip was to research whether a peace treaty with Japan and the transformation of some of Asia's postcolonial regimes into a larger institution with the United States was the best way to deal with the appeal of Chinese communism to the rest of Asia. Upon his return in early 1950, Ambassador Jessup briefed Dean Acheson, Dean Rusk, and George Kennan (among others) on his findings with a presentation tellingly entitled "The Weakness of our 'Friends'."[88] In this briefing, Jessup enumerated a litany of troublesome signs in the region: the non-democratic nature of the states; their lack of adequately trained personnel; their conspicuous corruption and inefficiency; their economic and financial difficulties; their military weakness; and their profound mistrust of the West. On top of all this was the simple fact that there appeared to be very little indigenous support from the majority of states for any sort of union, and the Ambassador therefore concluded that a regional pact was "not a very important subject."[89] In mid-1950 as well, in preparation for a visit by New Zealand Foreign Minister Sir Robert Menzies in which he was expected to bring up the Pacific Ocean Pact (but in the end, didn't), a preparatory memorandum was written up by Assistant Secretary for Far Eastern Affairs John Allison which voiced similar concerns.[90] Allison's memo enumerated mutual suspicion, mistrust of the West, the large disparities of regional political systems and economic development, and a lack of a tradition of cooperation among the reasons for the United States' "rather cautious" approach to the pact. These were followed by a series of rhetorical questions begged by the proposal: Who should be given membership? Would the developed countries not carry an undue load? Would the pact not spur a similar cry in the Middle East? Would the pact not force a majority of the burden on the United States? These were all questions that needed adequate answers before a Pacific Ocean Pact could be supported by the United States.

And yet the idea for a regional security organization refused to die. Part of this initiative came from the British. By 1949, London started to replace their deference to the United States on Asia to an active concern that the communist rise in China might threaten their interests in Hong Kong, Malaya, and Singapore. In August 1949, the British began to entertain the idea of some form of regional military cooperation among countries in the Indian and Pacific Ocean areas. Service chiefs from New Zealand and Australia joined the British in Melbourne to discuss the idea in mid-August 1949. They considered inviting Malaya, India, Pakistan, Ceylon, and Hong Kong to participate. In late August–September 1949, British Foreign Secretary Ernest Bevin started to engage Acheson in discussions about a multilateral grouping in Asia. Among the issues discussed was whether to recognize communism's victory in China (the British did, the

United States did not); how to conclude a peace treaty with Japan; how to increase economic assistance to the region; and how to encourage nationalism among non-communist societies as a check against communist expansion. Given British and US interests in maritime Asia, the two diplomats eventually conceptualized an anti-communist bloc involving only Southeast Asian nations (i.e., specifically excluding China and Korea). In 1951, Dulles and John Allison chose to push for the final and broadest of the arrangements listed above—a regional defense organization involving the United States, Japan, Australia, New Zealand, the Philippines, and Indonesia.[91] The concept was, according to Truman's instructions to Dulles, to create a regional security pact among the six maritime nations in the region—states seen as having a "distinctive community of interests."[92] The core purpose was to defend the island chain in the region that led to Japan, but also to allow Japan to re-arm in a way that was not threatening to the region, along the lines of Germany's reintegration into Europe.[93] In this latter purpose, the pact constituted "collective security" in the sense that it was designed not only to deter attack by external aggressors, but also to reassure and guarantee member states against aggression from any one of the members (particularly with regard to postwar Japan). As Dulles wrote, the concept was to create an international institution in which one could embed Japan's postwar military as part of a regional design rather than as an autonomous national capability.[94]

Even though the Pacific Ocean Pact never came to fruition, the mere fact of US interest in the idea does appear to undermine my argument that Washington was solely committed to bilateral control of its allies. On closer analysis, however, the manner in which the United States thought about the pact, and the story of how the concept eventually devolved to the dustbin of other regional security designs in East Asia, does resonate with certain tenets of the powerplay argument. My rebuttals here are not perfect, but they illustrate how powerplay thinking, on the part of both the United States and key regional players (including Japan), informed the ultimate demise of the pact concept.

First, the defense commitments that were contemplated to undergird the Pacific Ocean Pact were distinctly different from Article V of NATO. Although the Pacific Ocean Pact was nominally a collective security institution, the same "automatic intervention" clause of NATO was omitted. Instead, Article 2 of the draft stated that aggression against members of the pact would be dealt with in accordance with "constitutional processes."[95] Dulles noted in internal memos to Secretary Acheson the desire to avoid a bona fide collective security "automatic intervention" clause. He assured

Acheson that Article 2 of the pact was nominally only a "declaration," and therefore was less binding upon the United States than the "agreement" made in Article V of NATO.[96] This is a conviction that Dulles had held for some time. In an early 1950 meeting, he expressed "grave doubts" about a NATO-type organization for the Pacific, noting that this proliferation of commitments would eventually mean if Soviet aggression took place anywhere in the world, that the United States would inevitably *have* to go to war.[97] Dulles also sought to preserve the informal nature of US commitments by avoiding Senate ratification of the pact:

> In view of the fact that the substantive articles 1 and 2 are merely declarations and not agreements, and since the Council [administrative body of the proposed Pacific Pact] is merely a recommendatory body, it would not seem constitutionally necessary that the pact be submitted to the Senate as a treaty.[98]

Thus, the pact lacked the key distinguishing provision for it to resemble NATO.

Second, the Pacific Ocean Pact proposal was significant for whom it did *not* include—Taiwan and South Korea. The pact had three central defining criteria for its membership. The first was that it should include the major maritime territories in the region. Second, those who were to be included would obviously have to be supportive of the idea of a general security organization for the region. And third, those powers that consented would also have to be persuaded, through the pact, to accept a postwar military capability in Japan. According to these criteria, both Taiwan and South Korea should have been included. They were not, largely for the same reason that the United States balked at including Hong Kong and Indochina, and why the United States would eventually opt for tight bilateral bonds—the anxiety of becoming entrapped. The Pacific Ocean Pact was therefore collective security only in name; it had none of the features normally related to a multilateral institution, amounting at best to a greatly "watered-down version" of NATO.[99]

It is also evident that many of the reasons for the Pact's ultimate failure embody the powerplay logic. Certainly, from the perspective of the United States, the region's wide disparities in culture, language, religion, and levels of economic development were seen as leaving little basis for cooperation. As an early 1951 NSC study on the subject noted, "The lack of affinity among Asian nations means that our policies and programs must be devised and adapted to the situation prevailing in each country."[100]

Further, it was understood that the burden of history—and very recent history at that—weighed heavily on regional relations. But it was more than these preexisting factors that ultimately tipped the scales in favor of bilateralism. First, as capabilities in the region stood, there was not a single state that could contribute militarily in any effective way to what the United States would bring to such a grouping. As Dulles pointed out in a conversation with New Zealand's foreign minister, Frederick Doidge, a general pact would commit the strong, responsible nations in the arrangement (i.e., the United States) to support the irresponsible, highly unstable states they were tied to—regardless of their behavior and conduct.[101] It was essentially a situation in which, for the United States, the costs undoubtedly outweighed the benefits. Rather than diluting the United States' military and political power in the region by tying it to a broad, multilateral organization of militarily underdeveloped states, opting for bilateralism meant that the United States could concentrate its power where and how it wished and allowed it more flexibility to forward its interests in the region.

Second, American desires for greater control in Asia, without outside intervention from other potential members in a Pacific Ocean Pact, also served to undermine the proposal. For Dulles, Allison, and Acheson, the idea was to include "those nations with major Pacific Island territories" (listed above), but disputes arose over whether to include other powers with significant regional interests—Britain, France, Portugal, and the Netherlands. This is significant for the powerplay argument because one of the key reasons that the United States sought not to include the European powers was to minimize the risk of getting pulled into their problems. Dulles was concerned that the inclusion of the UK and France would then tie the United States to commitments in Hong Kong and Indochina.[102] Rusk noted that the Portuguese and Dutch would likely follow suit—having their own interests in Southeast Asia.[103] Not only would this give the pact a distinct "colonial nature," but US policymakers were wary of a potential mushrooming of commitments in the region and the wider world. This fear of entrapment inclined the United States toward dropping the proposal, instead carving out discrete bilateral arrangements.

Finally, the pact ultimately failed because *Japan* did not want to participate and because of opposition by Australia and New Zealand to include Japan. Or, as Secretary Acheson would somewhat snidely put it years later, "most of the applicants for security treaties wanted one with us but no one else."[104] This is perhaps the ultimate irony of Dulles's proposal as it relates to the powerplay argument. The United States wanted Japan's inclusion in the pact. Indeed, the entire purpose of the pact arguably was about reintegrating Japan into the region as a bulwark against communism, and Dulles and Acheson thought that this might best be achieved by embedding Japan in a regional institution—i.e., with military capabilities that were part of a regional security institution rather than as an autonomous capability that would make everyone nervous. But Dulles encountered two obstacles. First, Japan did not want to participate for fear that it might become entrapped in a Korea, Taiwan, or Indochina conflict—despite the best efforts by Dulles to exclude these countries. Second, Australia and New Zealand had little confidence that such a regional institution could be guaranteed to constrain a re-armed Japan. They believed that the best institutional design for Japan's recovery and reintegration was under the tight control of the United States through bilateral alliance ties.[105] For this reason, these two Anglo allies in the Pacific directly opposed the US plan. New Zealand Foreign Minister Doidge stated in February 1951 meetings with Dulles: "[T]he inclusion of Japan, went further than his Government would probably want to go. . . . New Zealand was not yet ready to commit itself to any obligations with respect to Japan."[106] In the same meeting, Australian foreign minister Percy Spender said more bluntly to Dulles that "Australia still feared Japan," and that the inclusion of Japan was a "no-hoper" for the pact.[107] The United States realized that what could be salvaged was a tripartite pact with Australia and New Zealand, and a bilateral pact with Japan. It was at these meetings with Spender and Doidge that Dulles first used the term "spokes on a wheel" (or "hub and spokes") to describe an institutional design for Asia.[108]

Upon Dulles's return to the United States, his speeches use the term "collective security" to describe the institutional design for Asia, but the transformation in his thinking about the bilateral design was clear from his pronouncements and writings that the United States was "working out a series of bilateral pacts."[109] By April 1951, Dulles in press interviews was speaking openly about the new design, centered on the US-Japan treaty, the ANZUS alliance, and a series of bilateral security arrangements, starting with the Philippines.[110] He further begins to characterize the design as a "network" of bilateral treaties and alliances.[111] The following June, when he traveled to London to brief the British Foreign Office on his trip and in television appearances thereafter, Dulles explicitly told the press that the Pacific Ocean Pact concept, a topic of prior conversations with British interlocutors, was no longer being discussed.[112] And when asked about the Pact in Japan in December 1951, Dulles reaffirmed that the concept was dead.[113] However, in a private speech at the Council of Foreign Relations in October 1951, Dulles offered extensive thoughts on his emerging institutional design for Asia. He talked about the four bilateral treaties (Japan, Australia, New Zealand, and Philippines) concluded the previous month as having an "interlocking aspect" with the United States as the common denominator. He talked about a bilateral commitment to Taiwan, though not yet a treaty. The aggregation of these separate arrangements, with the United States as the hub, effectively covered Pacific defense from the Ryukyus to Australia and New Zealand. He underscored to the New York audience that this was the beginning of a security arrangement for Asia that would "Win Japan," use the offshore island chain as a bulwark of defense against communism, and reassure others in the region against Japan's militarist revival.[114] Dulles then rhetorically asked the question as to why he did not advocate a single treaty for these arrangements. His answer was that a pact like NATO no longer made sense for Asia. Fear of Japan among others in the region was still strong, and all preferred that the United States exercise direct control over the former wartime aggressor. Dulles did not rule out a Pacific Ocean Pact in the future, but said the region was not ready for such a superstructure and that the bilateral alliance design provided a good foundation for now.[115]

This sequence of events confirms the powerplay argument. For about eight weeks in 1951, Dulles and Acheson briefly pondered an architectural design very similar to what was practiced in Europe—the postwar reintegration of Japan (as with Germany) in a regional security institution. In the end, however, it was Japanese fears of entrapment and the region's preference and confidence in US bilateral control of Japan that was the only acceptable formula. For the region, a multilateral institution did not instill confidence that it could control Japan. And it was this lack of faith in multilateral controls that was the deal breaker for Australia and New Zealand. As New Zealand Foreign Minister Doidge told Dulles in February 1951:

> Japan has been a nightmare to New Zealand and that the possibility of its resurgence was regarded with horror. Ambassador Dulles' explanation of the [multilateral] controls to which Japan will in any event be subject . . . is highly convincing for the short-run period. But New Zealand must live alongside Japan for a long time to come. Ambassador Dulles' exposition does not seem to cover the long-term possibilities.[116]

In television appearances later in 1951, Dulles continued to talk about bilateralism as the best design. When asked about whether the newly formed ANZUS pact (United States-Australia-New Zealand) was similar to the original concept, Dulles denied it, saying "we don't call it the Pacific pact because it isn't quite as big as that."[117] Very much in line with the powerplay argument, it was the view that control was best exercised over Japan through bilateral controls that inevitably inclined the region away from multilateralism. Thus Dulles, despite a mandate from Truman in January 1951 to devise a Pacific Ocean Pact, returned only four months later to advise the president that one collective institution should instead be divided into three to four bilateral arrangements each with Japan, Philippines, Indonesia, and Australia-New Zealand.[118] In a letter to President Truman drafted by Acheson and then-Defense Secretary George Marshall, they noted that in the wake of Ambassador Dulles's trip, it had become obvious that "the desired results can be better achieved by a *series* of arrangements rather than by a *single* arrangement" (their emphasis).[119] It seemed, as Australian Foreign Minister Spender quipped at the time, that the idea for a general, Pacific Ocean Pact had "dissipated" in the course of Dulles's travels.[120] Multilateralism was out. Bilateralism, in.[121]

———

In sum, Asian multilateralism (at least as it related to Taiwan and Korea) brought the prospect of putting overzealous Asian allies even closer together under a large collective alliance framework. This could only increase the possibilities of conspiracies to embroil the United States into unwanted and parochial revisionist agendas. The increased risk of entrapment would come, moreover, without any additional security benefits by combining the alliances. Again, this is not to deny that the United States sought control objectives in its alliances in Europe as well, but there was an "entrapment discount" regarding multilateralism in Asia that did not exist in Europe. The United States was less worried about smaller allies starting unprovoked wars with communist adversaries in Europe and therefore was more willing to cede some control for the benefits of multilateralization. In Asia, the design that made more sense facilitated control within each bilateral alliance and the avoidance of connections between them.

8

CONCLUSION: US ALLIANCES AND THE COMPLEX PATCHWORK OF ASIA'S ARCHITECTURE

AMERICA'S ACCIDENTAL EMPIRE

The creation of the American alliance system in Asia is a story about accidental and informal empire. When John Foster Dulles traveled through the region in 1951, his intention was to build a multilateral structure for the region, not unlike what was being constructed in Europe. There is little in the archives that reveals a clear American preference for empire-building in this part of the world, in the aftermath of a system-wide war, and where the main priority was the European continent. At most, one could argue that the United States sought imperial-like controls over postwar Japan, the sole great power in the region, but it had little desire for deep involvement with a postcolonial, underdeveloped society in Korea and a regime-in-refuge on Taiwan. The prevalent fear of dominoes falling in Asia to communism, combined with the gnawing anxiety that rogue leaders in these two countries might, through their own machinations to retake territory, set off a wider crisis, forced the United States to construct relationships, but on terms that Washington dictated through direct, bilateral control. The resulting "hub and spokes" system had all of the structural elements of hierarchy—a core power authorizing deep bilateral ties with its satellites, with minimal interaction among the satellite countries.[1] Washington pressed Japan to integrate with the region, but the region's

185

deep distrust of Tokyo remained strong after the war; moreover, the exclusivity of the US-Japan alliance provided little incentive for Tokyo's leaders to reach out and seek reconciliation with the region.

A true mark of informal empire is when imperial control extends to the "micropolitics" of the relationship.[2] Over the years the United States not only shaped the external policies of its allies but also defined the internal legitimacy of its political leaders. The level of American support, both military and economic, made the American stamp of approval critical for domestic leaders to succeed. When they lost that stamp, like Syngman Rhee in 1960, they were robbed of the legitimacy to rule effectively. Sixty years of Liberal Democratic Party rule in Japan was defined in part by the party's symbiotic relationship with the United States. Dictators in Taiwan and Korea used their Cold War ties with Washington as a platform to legitimize their leadership. And when democratization came to these two countries, the legitimacy of that exercise was also associated with the United States.

America's accidental and informal empire in Asia was not without benefits for the satellites. The system undergirded the development and prosperity of all three countries and provided security from the communist threat. But its origins were based as much in *distrust* and *strategic myth* as they were in Cold War security. The distrust came in two forms. Truman and Eisenhower fundamentally did not trust leaders like Chiang and Rhee to refrain from trying to entrap the United States in their civil wars on the Asian mainland. And the region's fundamental distrust of Japan, particularly US allies Australia and New Zealand, undercut any US attempt to design a multilateral mechanism to manage the security challenges. Yet the United States could not remain passive to these challenges because of the strategic obsession with the domino theory. The result for Washington was the powerplay strategy. Truman and Eisenhower were compelled to contemplate deep bilateral ties with each country to manage risk, control uncertainty, and restrain dangerous behavior.

The varied nature of American designs for security institutions in Europe and Asia therefore reflected different priorities and needs. Scholars have looked at the role that trust, reputation, and historical context can play in the rational design of institutions. Depending on what a state needs, it looks for different features, which is why security institutions vary in terms of their scope, membership, centralization, flexibility, and presentation.[3] The powerplay argument advanced in this book shows how two variables, distrust and risk of allied overdependence, shaped the United States' selection of unique design features for its security architecture in Northeast Asia that were different from the features of the European security institutions.

In this sense, the powerplay argument complements our explanations of puzzles about European multilateralism and Asian bilateralism. Realists, for example, cannot explain why the primary conflict that led to multilateralization of security in Europe and coherence of NATO happened in Asia, not Europe (Korean War). They also cannot explain why the Korean War did not lead to a similar type of institutional design for Asia. Liberals cannot explain why efficiency gains from multilateralism, in conjunction with the existence of support among Asian states and the United States for a PATO-type organization, did not result in a multilateral security institution. While constructivists use race and identity variables to explain why the United States favored Europe over Asia in postwar planning, they cannot explain why racial biases would lead to institutional variations in the design of the security structures across the two regions.[4]

The powerplay argument is, I believe, a critical link for each of these explanations. For realism, the Korean War compelled the United States to reinforce security equally in the European and Asian theaters. The reason this took a multilateral format in the former case but not in the latter was because the American commitment to fight the Cold War, enunciated in the Truman Doctrine, created a moral hazard problem in Asia, where the United States had to contend with Asian leaders embroiled in their own civil wars. This posed unique entrapment problems for Truman and Eisenhower such that an added degree of control was necessary to keep potential rogue allies from entrapping the United States. This was best exercised through a tight bilateral relationship. The exclusive nature of this security institution certainly provided benefits to the small ally, but it also amplified the power of the United States so that it could basically call all of the shots in the relationship and keep these unpredictable leaders in Korea and Taiwan in line.

For liberalism, the powerplay rationale helps to explain why the United States thought that a bilateral design for Asia was "efficient." In short, there was an "entrapment discount" in Asia. This caused any perceived efficiency gains from trying European-style multilateralism in Asia to be discounted by the costs associated with giving up control over the allies' actions. In addition, the "soft binding" aspect of the powerplay with Japan set off a secondary dynamic in the region that was inhospitable to multilateralism. As the United States treated Japan as the "favorite son" in Asia in order to ensure its friendly postwar development, this had the unintended consequence of closing off Japan from the region. Anything and everything Japan needed for postwar recovery could be obtained from the United States. The costs of reconciling with neighbors (political and economic, particularly in terms of colonial reparations), on the other hand, were inordinately high. Thus, there were two reinforcing cost-benefit calculations on the US and Japanese sides against multilateralism that emerged from the powerplay rationale.

Finally, for constructivism, the powerplay rationale shows that the reason America put so much more time and effort into building a sophisticated and elaborate security and political architecture in Europe was not because of affect, affinity, or identity. It was a function of rational calculations about risks and benefits in each region, not prejudice. Critics might respond that race still mattered because it was racial stereotypes that caused Americans to think they could "control" Asians better than Europeans.[5] But I would argue that this mentality was not the cause for alliance bilateralism in Asia. It was an effect, not the motivation. The motivation was to avoid entrapment.

THE GENERALIZABILITY OF POWERPLAY

At the core, my argument is about how great powers design bilateral security institutions to manage risk and make their environments more predictable. In the case of postwar Asia, the powerplay took the form of asymmetric bilateral relationships that allowed the great power patron to control the actions of smaller allies. The United States leveraged elements of its alliances to get what it wanted from Japan, Korea, and Taiwan. This dynamic is not unique to this time period, however. Powerplays happen all over the world. The conditions under which we see powerplays in operation are: (1) when the great power seeks an asymmetric bilateral tie to maximize power; (2) this tie is used to control or constrain the behavior of the smaller power (to minimize entrapment); and (3) the resulting bilateral arrangement provides benefits that might otherwise have been harder for the hegemon to accrue in a broader multilateral setting. In this section, I offer some observations of other potential cases of powerplay.

Spain

The United States exercised a powerplay strategy with Spain for about two decades from the early 1950s. The Madrid Pact of 26 September 1953 provided the United States with virtually unlimited discretion over military facilities and bases in Spain in exchange for economic assistance. Moreover, it did so until 1976 without offering a security guarantee in return, thus minimizing any entrapment concerns.

With the onset of the Cold War, the conflict in Korea, and the iron curtain falling across Europe, the United States sought to establish an anti-communist bulwark with access to the Iberian Peninsula and for broader military strategy in Europe. US bases in Spain would allow air and naval forces to access control of the Straits of Gibraltar, the Mediterranean Sea, North Africa, and all of Western Europe.[6] Washington established a deep bilateral tie with Madrid that allowed it to exercise maximum control. The conditions in Spain, moreover, were ripe for the powerplay. Generalissimo Francisco Franco presided over a country that had become isolated from Western institutions because of his fascist rule. Spain had been ousted from the United Nations in 1946. It was poor; had been excluded from the Marshall Plan; was not a member of NATO; and had no access to any external assistance.[7]

The Eisenhower administration used Franco's pariah status to its advantage. It offered some economic assistance ($226 million initially), but more significantly it provided recognition by the United States that could then facilitate Spain's re-entry into the UN (in 1955) and relations with the Vatican (in 1953). These political benefits arguably were as important, if not more so, to Franco's domestic legitimacy than the aid.[8] In return, the United States could write the terms of its military access to the country. In addition to four air and naval bases at Torrejon, Rota, Moron, and Zaragosa, the United States negotiated exclusive criminal jurisdiction for its soldiers, carte blanche in terms of building logistics facilities, as well as secret annexes that granted the United States wide latitude on military operations and nuclear activities to use in countering communist aggression in Europe and anything else deemed "threaten[ing] to the security of the West."[9] Pursuant to the agreement's secret annexes,[10] the United States deployed nuclear weapons to the bases, a practice that became evident to the public with the 1966 Palomares accident when a collision between two nuclear weapons–capable US military aircraft detonated conventional munitions near Spanish population centers.[11] The United States activated the bases for use in Lebanon (1958), Congo (1964), the Cuban missile crisis, and the Yom Kippur war. Sometimes the United States informed the Spanish about the use of the bases, but at other times it did not, like in the case of support for Israel in the 1972 war despite Spain's promise to remain neutral.[12] Internal US communications to the president when the United States contemplated renewal of the base arrangements recorded the privilege: "These bases, with their excellent facilities (they were specifically designed and constructed for strategic operations), ideal weather conditions, and geographic location, together with the complete lack of Spanish restrictions on type of aircraft, or other operational matters, provide the United States with the most flexible foreign base complex we have."[13]

One element of the powerplay is about control. The other element is to use this control to minimize any downside risk. In the case of Spain, the United States executed these agreements, gaining control over bases in the host country while avoiding entrapment. One observer described the relationship not as a full-fledged alliance but as a "quasi-alliance."[14] Another judged it to be one where the hegemon wanted military bases but really nothing else from the client state.[15] Franco wrote directly to Eisenhower in 1953 that the United States was drafting a document of "indenture" with his country rather than a mutual agreement.[16] He complained that

[I]n all the documents other than the basic defense agreement there were stipulations in great detail as to what the Spanish Government would be required to do, even to the extent of naming the locations of the bases, the procedures for entering into contracts, and many other minute details of what the United States required on the part of the Spaniards, but there was no document which provided any indication as to what the United States Government would do with respect to furnishing of arms and equipment to the Spaniards.[17]

NSC 5418/1, which provided guidelines for implementation of the 1953 Pact, stated clearly that, "The United States must endeavor to avoid any identification with the policies of the Spanish Government not required for the effective implementation of these arrangements."[18] This meant no entanglement in issues regarding Spanish territories in Africa; guarding against any efforts by Franco to enlarge the base arrangement to cover Spain's independent defense; and staying out of domestic politics.[19] The Madrid Pact would undergo revisions in 1956, 1963, 1968, and 1970, and in each case, Washington refused to grant Spanish requests for a formal treaty commitment despite Spanish entreaties for a more equitable and "friendly and forthcoming" relationship.[20] Indeed, the Madrid Pact was classified by the United States as an "executive agreement" rather than a formal defense treaty.[21] In this sense, Washington was minimizing its entrapment fears as it was exercising maximum control. Because these ties were established directly with an authoritarian government that was not compelled to reveal details to its public, moreover, the United States was able to maximize control with few complications. Franco agreed to these arrangements over domestic opposition from his own military and from the Catholic Church.

Franco insisted publicly that the Madrid Pact afforded his country great benefits while preserving Spanish sovereignty, but the reality was that the US powerplay established an empire-like arrangement, not unlike what it was doing in Asia. Washington established a deep bilateral tie, created asymmetric dependence in the relationship, and then utilized this to maximize control and set the terms of interaction. As one scholar described, "Compared with other agreements, even others of the early cold war era, the US-Spanish pact was considerably hierarchical and favorable to the United States on many dimensions."[22]

The latitude afforded to the United States in its asymmetric bilateral relations with Madrid was not easy to replicate with European capitals. The United States could not get European leaders to embrace Franco despite the Madrid Pact. And it could not get NATO to admit Spain as a member, as long as Franco was in power. Thus, what the United States could accomplish bilaterally was more than it could do in a multilateral setting. This dynamic also comports with the powerplay theory.

Israel

Jeremy Pressman's study of US-Israeli relations offers useful illustrations of how a great power employed control strategies on a smaller Middle East ally in order to shape behavior. In 2000, Israel Aircraft Industries (IAI) looked to upgrade Chinese hardware with the Phalcon airborne early warning system, a deal worth almost $2 billion. The Clinton administration strongly opposed the sale and Congress threatened to suspend $250 million in assistance with the intention to withhold any new commitments that might come out of an upcoming Israeli-Palestinian summit at Camp David. Prime Minister Ehud Barak canceled the Phalcon sale in July 2000. Five years later Israel planned to sell to China advanced upgrades for the Harpy anti-radar drone. The Bush administration in the spring of 2005 imposed military sanctions against Israel, opposed Israeli participation in the development of the Joint Strike Fighter, withheld night-vision equipment, and suspended certain military development projects in order to exert control over Israeli actions.[23] In June 2005, Prime Minister Ariel Sharon stopped the sale to China.

In each case, the United States assessed that Israel's arms sales to China would impact the delicate balance of forces on the Taiwan Straits, leading potentially to untold consequences. The 2005 sale of anti-radar drone upgrades, for example, could have been used by Beijing to help neutralize Taiwan's ability to offer a credible missile deterrent against a Chinese attack.[24] This could conceivably embolden China into military coercion tactics against Taiwan that would compel US involvement. Israel calculated that in such an eventuality, it would be detrimental for Israel's interests to have their systems implicated in a US-China military conflict. Washington's exercise of control did not occur through some multilateral mechanism, but through a much more direct and efficient mobilization of power resources that leveraged the asymmetrical nature of the alliance tie.[25] Pressman's study of US-Israel interaction shows how entrapment fears by a great power were intense vis-à-vis a smaller ally, and so it exerted control, not through distancing, but through the bilateral exercise of power within the alliance.

Germany

In the context of NATO, the United States leveraged its deep bilateral ties with the Federal Republic of Germany (FRG) to restrain it in ways deemed important to US national interests. Nowhere was this power-play more apparent than in the 1960s when Germany flirted with acquiring a nuclear weapons capability. Germany began talks with France and Italy from November 1957, which eventually led to a trilateral nuclear cooperation agreement in April 1958. FRG Chancellor Adenauer was keen on nuclear cooperation with French President Charles DeGaulle and considered German financing and technical support of French nuclear enrichment facilities as a way to acquire finished nuclear warheads.[26]

The Kennedy and Johnson administrations exercised the powerplay to squash German ambitions. Specifically, both presidents leveraged the extreme reliance of Germany on the alliance militarily and economically to control behavior. The Kennedy administration's top priority became to stop nuclear proliferation in Germany. President Kennedy expressed his concerns to the French about "an independent [nuclear] force unrelated to American responsibility and interest."[27] Secretary of State Dean Rusk underlined these concerns with Adenauer and Foreign Minister Gerhard Schroeder in June 1962. Rusk stated, "We do not believe national nuclear capabilities are the way to solve this problem. . . . The idea that such a force might be used independently of the Alliance is frightening. The indivisibility of the nuclear defense of the West is fundamental. This is a harsh reality."[28] Kennedy thus pressed Germany to become a signatory to the Limited Test Ban Treaty. When the Germans hesitated, National Security Advisor McGeorge Bundy told Foreign Minister Schroeder that it was "unthinkable" for Germany not to comply with the US request.[29] Washington targeted the budding nuclear cooperation with France by telling Germans candidly that any "nuclear-sharing" aspirations of the country would come at the expense of the alliance.[30] In NSC meetings in 1963, Kennedy calculated that he could do little to influence the frosty relationship with DeGaulle, but that he had significant leverage on Germany. Defense Secretary Robert McNamara offered a classic powerplay strategy to distance from France and draw closer to the Germans as a mean of gaining control. Kennedy implemented this strategy by offering assistance to the FRG, but also communicating directly to Adenauer that he was ready to leave Europe if that was the intent of German cooperation with France.[31]

Washington later considered the creation of a Multilateral Force (MLF) of submarine- and ship-based intermediate-range nuclear weapons under US and NATO joint control to assuage Europeans desires for US extended deterrence commitments and shared nuclear control; but in 1965 Lyndon Johnson put the idea aside and sought Germany's accession to the Non-Proliferation Treaty (NPT). Germany reacted negatively to the US proposal as it could effectively cement Germany's inferior position in Europe (while Britain and France had independent nuclear deterrents) and give the Soviet Union some say in Germany's right to nuclear capabilities.[32] They argued that Washington had allowed Moscow to link successfully the shelving of the MLF proposal with the NPT.[33] But the United States was concerned about a classic entrapment scenario—smaller independent nuclear forces that would not alter the strategic balance in the West's favor, but that could ignite nuclear exchanges in Europe not of Washington's choice—as one observer noted, "It would be the Balkan scenario of 1914 replayed in the nuclear age."[34] And so it pressed the Germans hard. In February 1968, Johnson's National Security Advisor Walt Rostow stated that it was a "simple fact" that Berlin would have to join the NPT. He stated in no uncertain terms to legislative leader Rainer Barzel that Germany must sign the treaty and that if it did not, this would "tear apart" the alliance and his country would "face a very difficult period during which you might very well be destroyed. . . . I see no salvation any other way."[35]

German leaders knew that these were very transparent US attempts to get Germany to renounce nuclear weapons, but little could be done to resist this powerplay. The country was deeply reliant on US military and economic assistance, and with an army of only 325,000 soldiers (compared to the Soviet's two million), there was little alternative. As Adenauer stated in 1961, "We cannot allow ourselves to upset the Americans. We need them desperately," and this gave Washington tremendous leverage.[36] One author summed up the powerplay, "Both Kennedy and Johnson understood that West German military dependence gave Washington substantial coercive leverage over its client, and they repeatedly reminded German leaders of their country's military vulnerability."[37]

Asian Allies in Iraq and Afghanistan

Rather than forming a multilateral coalition of countries in Asia for contributions to the wars in Iraq and Afghanistan after September 11, the US powerplay was instead to cut individual deals with each partner in order to maximize support. In Japan's case, the deep bilateral alliance ties allowed the United States to extract the deployment of Japanese naval vessels to the Indian Ocean to provide fresh water and fuel in support of Operation Enduring Freedom.[38] Japan also passed a special measures law that allowed for the dispatch of 600 ground troops to Samawah in Southern Iraq.[39] Both of these were unprecedented acts for Japan, and for the Japanese navy, the first out-of-area deployments since World War II. In the case of South Korea, US entreaties through bilateral alliance channels achieved a no less impressive outcome. In March 2003, President Roh Moo-hyun approved the dispatch of two waves of ground forces to Iraq.[40] The Zaytun Division numbered 3,600 troops, operated in Irbil in Northern Iraq, and constituted the third largest ground contingent in this theater after the United States and UK, composed of engineers, medics, and combat troops. And in the case of Australia, the John Howard government stepped up to be the "tip of the spear" in combat operations in Iraq and Afghanistan, contributing special forces and aircraft.[41]

While Koizumi, Roh, and Howard each justified their decisions as sovereign ones in pursuit of national interests, strong encouragement from the United States was unmistakable. In the counterterrorism campaign after September 11, the US message to allies and others regarding allegiance in this new war was clear—you were either with the United States or against it.[42] Buck-passing the threat was not an option, and Washington made this clear as it leveraged the mutual defense treaties in each bilateral relationship to extract maximum support. And in each case, the results pushed the envelope of what was domestically possible for each leader. Japan's deployment decisions stood in stark contrast to its "checkbook diplomacy" and sitting on the sidelines of the Gulf War ten years earlier.[43] Moreover, even though Koizumi had a close personal relationship with President Bush, his actions ran contrary to his public's mood, as polls showed a precipitous decline in Japan's public trust of the United States following the invasion of Iraq.[44]

The case was even more pronounced in South Korea. Not only was 70 percent of the Korean public opposed to the war in Iraq, only 25 percent supported the dispatch of ROK troops.[45] The national legislature passed a resolution opposing the Iraq war; moreover, the politically progressive South Korean administration, including its president, stood miles apart from the Bush White House on foreign policy. Despite all of these obstacles, the ROK went against its core constituencies to dispatch the two battalions.[46] Like Koizumi, Australian Prime Minister John Howard enjoyed close personal ties with President Bush, but his decision to go into Iraq was terribly controversial at home, where public confidence in the United States declined dramatically with the invasion and eventually resulted in Howard's electoral defeat to opposition leader Kevin Rudd in 2007.[47]

Counterfactuals are hard to prove, but the powerplay argument suggests it is highly unlikely that the United States could have mustered so much support and so quickly if it had tried to organize a multilateral coalition. Indeed, the hub and spokes system in East Asia reinforced the powerplay dynamic because the deeply rooted bilateral ties engendered by this system became the most proximate and efficient means by which to secure support. Again, this is not to say that the allies were unwilling, but the powerplay dynamic led each to do things that were unprecedented, controversial to core constituencies, and politically costly at home.

THE CONTINUED RELEVANCE OF POWERPLAY

What is the role of US alliances in Asia's security architecture today? There is no denying that Asia is vastly more developed institutionally from when the alliance structure was first established.[48] Today, the United States does not command the same power gaps that it held during the Cold War. Moreover, although the powerplay motive of US alliances in East Asia may have been to control and restrain countries during those early years, this is clearly less of an issue today. Democratization, development, and the end of bipolarity render the rationale largely obsolete. South Korea's democratic consolidation, the "march north" doctrine's anachronistic rendering by the sunshine policy of engagement, and the eventual transfer of wartime operational control from the United States to South Korea are just a few manifestations of a vastly different alliance relationship. Japan's postwar direction followed pretty much the path laid out by the United States. Japan did not emerge as the Britain of Asia, but it came pretty close to what Acheson and others had hoped for. And in Taiwan, the declining enthusiasm of pro-independence forces in the country's domestic politics, the growing dependence of Taiwan on the Chinese economy, and the increased political dialogue across the Straits have reduced US fears of entrapment.

If Cold War Asia was defined by the American hub and spokes network, the period since the Cold War's end has seen a proliferation of multilateral groupings indigenous to the region for the purposes of problem-solving (i.e., focused on specific issues like the Six Party talks) and tension-reduction and confidence-building (e.g., EAS, ASEAN). Nevertheless, as much as the region seeks to develop regional-based, inclusive multilateral practices and institutions, I argue that security bilateralism will remain a prominent dynamic in the region. This is because Asia's large powers—a dominant United States and a rising China—are naturally drawn to the powerplay strategy as a way to manage their security environment.

As long as there are hegemons in the system, there will be powerplay dynamics, not just for reasons of avoiding entrapment, but because bilateral control is the best way to manage risk. There are several reasons why hegemons behave this way. The first relates to structure. Great powers like to strike bilateral deals that maximize their power simply because they can. In this sense, the behavior of states like the United States and China are affected by their relative position in the system.[49] The power gaps between great powers and the rest in the region create incentives for them to see such powerplay strategies as not only feasible but desirable. As Michael Mastanduno writes, great powers see it as their "privilege" to exploit their position to their advantage. They are both system-makers and privilege-takers, and have no problem forcing adjustment burdens on others.[50]

The second reason relates to fretting about the future. Whether it is the United States as the lead state in Asia or China as the rising power, each is obsessed with its future position. Indeed, leaders or soon-to-be leaders have a stronger psychological tendency to expect the future to be worse than the present and therefore have a strong inclination to try to shape that future to their advantage. This may mean trying to improve one's position, but more often than not it means trying to keep bad things from happening.[51] Powerplay is therefore appealing because it affords more control over that future than leaving one's fate to committee-wide votes in a multilateral structure.

Bilateralism is also appealing because it allows states like the United States and China to "lock in" legitimacy. Building a hub and spokes network creates certain infrastructures, practices, norms, and rules that continue to legitimize the superior position of the hub.[52] Such a system can work as long as the dominant power is not too hypocritical within its own system, and follows its own rules.[53] If the great power craves legitimacy, then a multilateral system in which the great power follows the rules might offer more legitimacy, but it does not offer the same degree of control.[54] The efficiency gains from multilateralism may be appealing to a great power rather than negotiating and renegotiating agreements with each individual player, but great powers can always afford to pay more to gain control. As Stephen Walt observes, "Instead of favoring highly institutionalized, multilateral arrangements that can tame its power within a web of formal procedures, norms, and rules, the unipole will prefer to operate with ad hoc coalitions of the willing, even if forming each new arrangement involves somewhat greater transaction costs."[55]

We should not underestimate how much great powers are attached to the strategic belief that bilateralism works best. As Jack Snyder argues, grand strategy is often a function of beliefs or myths that dominate the strategic thinking of the day.[56] The international relations arguments that have emerged about the longevity of unipolarity carry tenets that encourage great powers to opt for powerplay. Unipolar theories argue that: (1) maximal power gaps facilitate hegemonic control; (2) maximal power gaps mute counterbalancing behavior by others; and (3) maximal power gaps can encourage not balancing against but bandwagoning with the strong state. These tenets lead to the predominant belief that discrete dyads with smaller powers are the best way to transact business.[57] Finally, it should be noted that smaller powers are often willing participants in the powerplay. They crave the attention of the great power and the benefits that might accrue from an exclusive relationship with it, rather than from an inclusive arrangement with many other partners where they are just one of the crowd. Standing side-by-side with the great power leader also affords domestic legitimacy gains that might be less apparent in a committee of rival smaller powers.

Thus, it should come as no surprise that long after the end of the Cold War, the United States continues not just to maintain, but also to grow its bilateral alliance system in Asia. The spokes, as advanced industrial democracies, are much more independent in their behavior both inside and outside of the alliance. There is infinitely more interaction between the spokes bilaterally and among them with "minilateral" groupings such as the US-Japan-Australia Trilateral Strategic Dialogue (TSD), Trilateral Cooperation Secretariat (Japan-South Korea-China), US-Japan-Korea Trilateral Cooperation Oversight Group (TCOG), US-Japan-India-Australia Quadrilateral Security Dialogue (QSD), Trilateral Commission (US-Japan-EU), among many others. Both the Korea and Japan alliances celebrated their sixtieth anniversaries in 2013 and 2012 respectively with official proclamations emphasizing their robustness and long-term futures (see table 8.1).[58] Under the George W. Bush administration's Asia strategy and the Obama administration's pivot or rebalance to Asia, the United States has negotiated major base realignment agreements with the Republic of Korea and the Government of Japan; signed a free trade agreement with Korea; signed a groundbreaking civil-nuclear agreement with India; reached a Strategic Partnership Dialogue with Singapore; signed new legal protocols with the Philippines on base access; managed a breakthrough in re-establishing political and commercial relations with Myanmar; established a rotation of Marines through Australia;

TABLE 8.1. US MINILATERALS IN ASIA

NAME	FOUNDING DATE
Korean Peninsula Energy Development Organization (KEDO)	1995
U.S.-Japan-Korea Trilateral Coordination and Oversight Group (TCOG)	1999
Six-Party Talks (SPT)	2003
U.S.-India-Japan-Australia Tsunami Core Group (TCG)	2005
5+5 (U.S., Japan, ROK, China, Russia, Indonesia, Australia, New Zealand, Canada and Malaysia)	2006
U.S.-Japan-Australia Trilateral Strategic Dialogue (TSD)	2006
U.S.-Japan-Australia-India Quadrilateral Security Dialogue (QSD)	2007
U.S.-Japan-India Trilateral Ministerial	2015

and renewed the US-Taiwan Section 123 agreement.[59] Washington has supported the growth of other forms of regional architecture, including the East Asia Summit, but this support has not displaced enthusiasm for cultivating deep bilateral relationships in the region.

Similarly, while China has consistently denigrated the US alliance system as Cold War relics and has trumpeted a new era of Asian multilateralism, it too demonstrates a penchant for bilateralism.[60] Over the past decade, China has been quietly building its own China-centered regional architecture (see figure 8.1 and tables 8.2 and 8.3). In the South China Sea, Beijing would much prefer to cut individual deals with each country with which it has territorial disputes rather than negotiate with ASEAN as a group because, as Thomas Christensen argues, "Groups like ASEAN and its ASEAN Regional Forum on security matters were viewed by some nervous Chinese security analysts as opportunities for

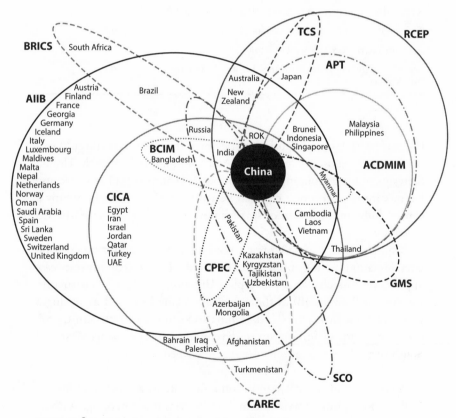

FIGURE 8.1. China-based regional architecture in Asia

TABLE 8.2. CHINA-BASED REGIONAL INSTITUTIONS IN ASIA

NAME	FOUNDING DATE
Greater Mekong Subregion Economic Cooperation Program (GMS)	1992
ASEAN Plus Three (APT)	1997
Central Asia Regional Economic Cooperation Program (CAREC)	1997
Bangladesh–China–India–Myanmar Forum for Regional Cooperation (BCIM)	1999
Conference on Interaction and Confidence-Building Measures in Asia (CICA)	1999
Shanghai Cooperation Organisation (SCO)	2001
Brazil, Russia, India, China and South Africa (BRICS)	2010
Trilateral Cooperation Secretariat (TCS)	2010
Regional Comprehensive Economic Partnership (RCEP)	2012
China—Pakistan Economic Corridor (CPEC)	2013
Asian Infrastructure Investment Bank (AIIB)	2014
ASEAN—China Defense Ministers' Informal Meeting (ACDMIM)	2015

the Southeast Asian Lilliputians to tie down the Chinese Gulliver."[61] Beijing's initial enthusiasm for the East Asia Summit waned once the United States joined the grouping in November 2011 in no small part because China's initial vision of a regional network in which it could occupy a central hub amid a group of smaller powers had been retarded by US ascension.

Beijing's "March West" foreign policy, aimed at cultivating deep bilateral relations with Central Asia, the Middle East, and Southwest Asia, appears very much like a powerplay. Utilizing the Asia Infrastructure Investment Bank (AIIB) as the central financing hub, and espousing a policy of "One Belt, One Road," China seeks to use infrastructure projects as a means of linking up to developing countries to its West and Southwest. The result, as one observer described, is that:

> Asia's political, security, and economic systems are being reshuffled and a Chinese-style hub-and-spoke system is emerging. With its massive economic and military power, China is becoming the

TABLE 8.3. MEMBERSHIP IN CHINA-BASED REGIONAL ARCHITECTURE

	ACDMIM	AIIB	APT	BCIM	BRICS	CAREC	CICA	CPEC	GMS	RCEP	SCO	TCS
AFGHANISTAN						✓	✓					
AUSTRALIA		✓								✓		
AUSTRIA		✓										
AZERBAIJAN		✓				✓	✓					
BAHRAIN							✓					
BANGLADESH		✓		✓			✓					
BRAZIL		✓			✓							
BRUNEI	✓	✓	✓							✓		
CAMBODIA	✓	✓	✓				✓		✓	✓		
EGYPT		✓					✓					
FINLAND		✓										
FRANCE		✓										
GEORGIA		✓										
GERMANY		✓										
ICELAND		✓										
INDIA		✓		✓	✓		✓			✓	✓	
INDONESIA	✓	✓	✓							✓		
IRAN		✓					✓					
IRAQ		✓					✓					
ISRAEL		✓					✓					
ITALY		✓										

(Continued)

TABLE 8.3. (*continued*)

	ACDMIM	AIIB	APT	BCIM	BRICS	CAREC	CICA	CPEC	GMS	RCEP	SCO	TCS
JAPAN		✓	✓							✓		✓
JORDAN		✓					✓				✓	
KAZAKHSTAN		✓				✓	✓				✓	✓
KOREA		✓	✓				✓			✓	✓	
KYRGYZSTAN		✓	✓			✓	✓					
LAOS	✓	✓	✓						✓	✓		
LUXEMBOURG		✓										
MALAYSIA	✓	✓	✓							✓		
MALDIVES		✓										
MALTA		✓										
MONGOLIA		✓	✓			✓	✓					
MYANMAR	✓	✓	✓	✓					✓	✓		
NEPAL		✓										
NETHERLANDS		✓										
NEW ZEALAND		✓								✓		
NORWAY		✓										
OMAN		✓										
PAKISTAN		✓				✓	✓	✓			✓	
PALESTINE			✓				✓					
PHILIPPINES	✓									✓		
PORTUGAL		✓										
QATAR		✓					✓					

RUSSIA	✓			✓		✓
SAUDI ARABIA	✓					
SINGAPORE	✓					✓
SOUTH AFRICA	✓					
SPAIN	✓					
SRI LANKA	✓					
SWEDEN	✓					
SWITZERLAND	✓			✓		
TAJIKISTAN	✓			✓		
THAILAND	✓	✓	✓	✓		✓
TURKEY				✓		
TURKMENISTAN				✓		
UAE	✓			✓	✓	
UK	✓			✓		
UZBEKISTAN	✓			✓	✓	
VIETNAM	✓	✓		✓	✓	✓

Legend

ACDMIM	ASEAN—China Defense Ministers' Informal Meeting	
AIIB	Asian Infrastructure Investment Bank	
APT	ASEAN + 3	
BCIM	Bangladesh—China—India—Myanmar Economic Corridor	
BRICS	Brazil, Russia, India, China, and South Africa	
CAREC	Central Asia Regional Economic Cooperation Program	
CICA	Conference on Interaction and Confidence Building Measures in Asia	
CPEC	China—Pakistan Economic Corridor	
GMS	Greater Mekong Subregion Economic Cooperation Program	
RCEP	Regional Comprehensive Economic Partnership	
SCO	Shanghai Cooperation Organisation	
TCS	Trilateral Cooperation Secretariat	

undisputed hub. While member nations may speak of cooperation to receive various resources from China, they are merely turning into "spoke nations." Accordingly, a hub-and-spoke system is developing where China stands at the center while countries to the west—in Central Asia, the Middle East, and Southwest Asia—are connected to it through bilateral ties.[62]

For the Chinese powerplay to work, it requires not just a strategy from Beijing but the acceptance of such a relationship by the smaller powers. In this vein, attendees at the 2014 CICA summit (except South Korea) did not oppose Chinese president Xi Jinping's denouncement of US alliances as "relics" of the Cold War and his calls for a new "Asia for Asians" security system. Asian counterparts meanwhile "spoke only of bilateral cooperation between their respective countries and China," or between their respective regions with China. This suggests a small power framing of CICA not as a multilateral organization with China as equals; rather, it suggests a semi-hierarchical arrangement with individual states or subregions tied to Beijing as the central hub.[63] As long as the United States and China aspire to hold their positions as leaders in the region, there will be enthusiasm from leaders for cultivating bilateralisms that amplify their power.

THE GEOMETRY OF ASIA

What does powerplay mean for the future of the region's architecture? If the two great powers in the area prefer bilateral designs, then does this retard the evolution of more consensual and broad-based multilateral structures? Does the "lateness" of multilateralism's emergence in Asia stem from the overbearing footprint of American bilateral alliances, which discouraged Asia's neighbors from engaging with one another? And is there "institutional balancing" taking place in the region between the United States and China (see figures 8.1 and 8.2)?

Contrary to most, I do not think US-centered bilateralism and Asia's emerging regional institutions (both ASEAN-centered and China-based as discussed below) operate at odds with one another. This may have been the case in the past. The dominance of the United States as the central hub for five decades of the Cold War certainly delayed the growth of linkages among the spokes.[64] The absence of normalized relations between Japan and Korea for more than a decade after the United States inked defense treaties with each, and the delayed growth of formal

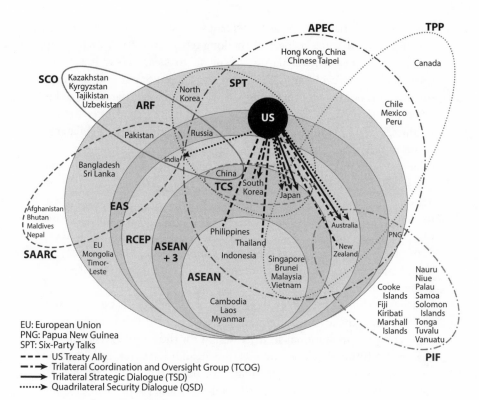

FIGURE 8.2. US and regional architecture in Asia

security ties among these countries, as well as between Australia, India, and Philippines, is a manifestation of the powerplay's success—all got what they needed from the United States, which reduced the incentive to seek ties with others. In this regard, the American powerplay with Japan precipitated a vicious spiral when it came to regional relations. Dulles's 1951 trip to Asia made clear that no party trusted having Japan in a multilateral pact, thus giving the United States sole responsibility for the country's postwar shaping. But this project, however successful, also undercut the motivation for Japan and the region to reconcile and build trust with one another.

The future of the region's architecture, however, is not a battle between two opposing forces. The American-based alliance system is an organic part of Asia's postwar security landscape (see figure 8.2). It is unlikely to dissipate at any time in large part because countries in the region demonstrate a preference for its longevity. Recent polling of strategic elites in the region find that as many as 57 percent see their bilateral relationship with the United States as part of the long-term future, and 79 percent support the American "rebalance" or "pivot" to Asia.[65] There is a definitive architecture evolving in Asia that the United States and its allies support. It is not one dominated by China, nor is it one characterized by US diminution. The picture of the institutions that tie the United States, its allies, and China in the region is much more complex than "bilateral versus multilateral." Instead, it is a "complex patchwork" of line segments (bilaterals), triangles (trilaterals), squares (quadrilaterals), hexagonals (six-sided), and other multilateral configurations that aggregate to include all regional members rather than exclude any. Some of these are designed to solve specific problems in the region, yet others are for the purpose of confidence-building. Some are derivative of the US alliance system. Some are ASEAN-based, and others are China-based. The complexity of this phenomenon is an asset, rather than a flaw, in the geometry of Asian architecture.

This concluding section explains how the US alliance system and the region's emerging architecture mesh together unwittingly in an increasingly complex institutional security design for the region. First, I argue that the US bilateral alliance architecture, in addition to serving the security needs of the allies, has contributed through its "minilateralization" (in the form of trilaterals or quadrilaterals) as a tool for problem-solving in the region. Second, the bilateral and minilateral elements of the US alliance structure operate today alongside ASEAN-based and China-based groupings in increasingly more complex regional architectures, some of which involve the United States (e.g., Transpacific Partnership) and some of which do not (e.g., Asia Infrastructure Investment Bank, CICA). Third, these intertwined and overlapping relationships help to mute security dilemmas, manage relations between great powers, and enhance regional stability. I do not believe there is an evolution in Asia to one overarching regional OSCE-type organization, but that the "messiness" of what has evolved is an imperfect albeit useful substitute.

Asia Is Not Europe

Asia has often been seen as under-institutionalized compared to Europe because there is no single regionwide Asian equivalent of NATO or the EU.[66] However, every region has its own history and identity; what best serves the political, security, and economic interests of one region may not be optimal in another. Asia is less suited to a single regionwide, formal grouping like Europe primarily because practices and norms have evolved differently; moreover, what has emerged there in terms of institutions is more effective than commonly assumed.[67]

Outside of the US alliance system, the history of institution-building in Asia generally suggests that *informal* institutions work better than formal ones. The few attempts at formal European-style security institutions in Northeast Asia have been spectacularly unsuccessful (I define success as tangible and coordinated steps by multilateral partners that advances solutions to substantive problems). As discussed in chapter 7, in the early 1950s, Syngman Rhee, Chiang Kai-shek, and Elpidio Quirino put forward the concept of a PATO that failed to gain support. John Foster Dulles attempted to create a Pacific Ocean Pact conceived with Indonesia, Australia, New Zealand, Philippines, and Japan which also failed.[68] During the Vietnam War, South Korea sought to create a multilateral grouping out of the Vietnam War allies, but this failed as well. In each case, the key similarity was the relative priority placed on the formality of the institution over the functional purpose or task at hand. And, like many institution-building ventures that emphasize structure over purpose, a great deal of attention and energy becomes wasted on the criteria for membership, and the rules of the organization (i.e., in what country should the secretariat be; how should the chairmanship rotate).

Though there has been relative success in Southeast Asia in creating formal institutions with established secretariats, regular meetings, and packed agendas, these are focused more on confidence-building and dialogue, and thus are often criticized for lacking substantive outcomes.[69] Harshest critics rue "talk shop" institutions like the ARF and its "talent show" as an example of the substance-less nature of the meetings in which diplomats discuss and re-discuss issues, and then retire to amateurish performances that may build some goodwill (and lasting photo ops), but do not advance solutions to bilateral or multilateral problems. Many criticize the newest regional initiative, the East Asia Summit, in this fashion. The first meeting of the EAS in December 2005, involving the ASEAN's ten members, the "Plus Three" members (China, Japan, and South Korea), and Australia, New Zealand, and India, was received with much fanfare. Kishore Mahbubani, the former Singaporean foreign ministry official, declared the meeting as marking the official start of the long-touted "Pacific Century."[70] Yet, more energy was expended arguably on the criteria for membership than on substantive issues. It was only after the United States joined EAS in November 2011 and started to shape the organization's agenda to focus on regional security-related public goods (e.g., freedom of navigation, code of conduct) that the organization began to gain traction as a substantive dialogue forum.[71]

Instead of these "feel-good" institutions, ad hoc groupings appear to have been more successful at taking tangible, coordinated steps to solve a substantive problem. In this regard, a significant new addition to the region's architecture since the late 1990s has been the ad hoc "minilateralization" of the different legs of the US alliance system into trilaterals and quadrilaterals (see table 8.1 for a listing). This minilateral pooling of partners serves to solve specific problems, particularly when other regional or international institutions prove unequipped to do so. In December 2004, for example, when the South Asia tsunami killed more than 300,000 people, international actors scrambled to find an appropriate response. I had just begun working on the National Security Council at the time of this crisis, and quickly found that none of the existing institutions like the ASEAN Regional Forum or APEC were capable of responding to the devastation in Indonesia, Sri Lanka, and India. Instead, a makeshift coalition of willing countries—known as the Tsunami Core Group—consisting of the United States, Japan, Australia, and India emerged within the initial forty-eight hours of the crisis to bring relief supplies to the area. The Core Group set up the basing arrangements, provided financial resources, military assets, and 40,000 personnel, and constituted the spearhead of the global response to the problem until other international and UN relief agencies could mobilize on the ground.[72]

If institutions are defined by their capability to address a problem successfully, then the Core Group met that mark. However, if the criterion of success for Asian institutions is the permanence of extant structures and proliferation of flowery joint statements, the Core Group was not successful. It never had any "G-4" type summits, joint communiqués, or secretariats. Consultation consisted initially of phone calls between the US president and the leaders in Tokyo, Canberra, and New Delhi, and then daily 40-minute conference calls, and emails at the deputy foreign minister levels.[73] Moreover, as soon as its mission was accomplished, the Tsunami Core Group disbanded itself, deferring to international disaster response efforts. Then-US Undersecretary of State Marc Grossman put it best: "The Tsunami Core Group was an organization that never met in one of diplomacy's storied cities, never issued a communiqué, never created a secretariat, and took as one of its successes its own demise."[74]

The most striking aspect of Asia's security architecture is the absence of a multilateral security institution for Northeast Asia. As this book has documented, the only formal design for the region has been the US alliance structure. However, functional minilaterals have spun off of the alliance to deal with North Korea. In 1999, the United States, Japan, and Korea formed the Trilateral Coordination and Oversight Group (TCOG) to coordinate in the event of a North Korean contingency. After the 1994 US-DPRK nuclear agreement, the three allies took the lead in creating the Korea Energy Development Organization (KEDO) to address energy issues in North Korea. When North Korea broke the 1994 agreement, the Six-Party Talks was created in 2003 as a multilateral negotiating forum involving six key nations: United States, Republic of Korea, Japan, China, Russia, and North Korea. The ad hoc organization reached interim agreements on denuclearization, and in the process created habits of consultation, greater familiarity, and interaction among the five parties (United States, Japan, ROK, Russia, and China).[75]

Other forms of minilaterals have spun off from the US alliance system (see table 8.1). In the case of the Tsunami Core Group, even though the institution disbanded after the crisis, the experience spawned the growth of other related institutions in Asia including the regional tsunami early warning system (US-Japan); the Trilateral Strategic Dialogue (TSD) involving the United States, Japan, and Australia; and the proposal for a quadrilateral (United States-Japan-Australia-India) based on the original Core Group concept.[76] The Six-Party Talks spawned a secondary body, the Northeast Asia Peace and Security Mechanism (NEAPSM), designed to create a security regime in East Asia. The regularized sessions of the Six-Party Talks, sometimes lasting more than two weeks at a time, also became a staging ground for discussions to create the "A-6" to address climate change (the Asia Pacific Partnership for Climate and Clean Energy Development).[77] In addition, to explain Six-Party diplomacy to other countries in the region, Secretary of State Condoleezza Rice in 2006 created another ad hoc "add-on" institution of the "5+5"—that is, five of the Six-Party countries (without North Korea) plus Indonesia, Australia, Canada, Malaysia, and New Zealand—that met on the sidelines at the ARF or UN General Assembly.[78]

Bilateralism Supports Mini- and Multilateralism

What the concept of minilateralism in Asia demonstrates is that it is wrong to think about bilateralism and multilateralism as operating at odds with one another. On the contrary, they are mutually reinforcing. Conceptually, this would appear to make sense. Any collective effort to address a problem, advance a policy agenda, or build confidence among several players may work best when the players already have preexisting patterns of cooperation, consultation, and a degree of trust.

Again, the 2004 tsunami response is a case of successful regional action where alliance multilateralism and bilateralism are tightly intertwined. The coalition countries pooled resources at unprecedented speed and effectiveness: More than 4,000 Indian first responders arrived in Sri Lanka; the United States supplied more than 12,600 personnel, 21 ships, the USS *Mercy* hospital ship (with 1,000 beds), 14 cargo planes, and more than 90 helicopters (much of it from bases in Japan); Australia and Japan provided more than 1,000 personnel, medical teams, and other material and financial assistance; Singapore and Thailand provided logistics support and bases to move supplies into hardest hit and inaccessible areas in northwest Indonesia.[79] The Core Group showed how a successful multilateral "institution" in Asia effectively grew out of the existing network of bilateral relationships in the region. Based on my own experience in this effort at the NSC, it would have been hard to imagine a similar level of cooperation among countries without such preexisting ties.

There are other noteworthy examples of large, multilateral institutions that are based on core bilateral relationships. The Proliferation Security Initiative (PSI), created in May 2003, is an international coalition of more than one hundred countries dedicated to stop trafficking of weapons of mass destruction and related delivery systems and materials to terrorists and to countries of proliferation concern. PSI is a functionally based institution that relies on voluntary actions by member states to use their existing national and international authorities in joint cooperation to interdict illicit movement of WMD by sea, air, or land.[80] By most accounts, this has been a successful multilateral effort.[81] There have been more than fifty interdiction exercises involving PSI countries.[82] Although specifics have not been publicly released, US officials have asserted that there have been about two dozen cases of successful PSI cooperation to prevent WMD transfer. Current and future US administrations have declared their intentions to strengthen and expand PSI.[83]

The effectiveness of this multilateral institution, however, has rested on strong bilateral relationships. Though the US-led PSI eventually grew to 103 countries, its core and initial formation rested on eleven countries, all of which had already close bilateral relations with the United States (Australia, France, Germany, Italy, Japan, the Netherlands, Poland, Portugal, Spain, and the United Kingdom). This initial group, because of their preexisting ties and common nonproliferation agendas, speedily devised a set of core principles in September 2003. Some of the early flagship exercises that cemented PSI as a real entity were hosted by countries with which the United States already had strong bilateral security relationships: Poland, Singapore, and Australia.

The Trans-Pacific Partnership or TPP is a twelve-member free trade pact negotiation and the most ambitious effort at moving the region to the goal of a free trade area of the Asia-Pacific. TPP countries make up nearly 40 percent of global trade.[84] The pact remains a critical piece of the US administration's Asia policy, and would be potentially the most significant new multilateral institution in the region.[85] However, this multilateral institution's credibility and its potential have rested on the bilateral relationship between the United States and Japan. Without Japan, TPP would have been a useful but minor trade agreement involving the United States and a few smaller Pacific economies. With Japan, TPP has become a new trade agreement that involves the second and third largest economies in the world. The United States worked tirelessly through a separate bilateral negotiation to bring Japan on board with TPP; and Tokyo's decision to join, moreover, was entirely couched in the context of its bilateral relationship with the United States. Indeed, Abe's announcement of Japan's decision to join TPP came during his bilateral summit with Obama on February 22, 2013.[86] Parallel to the multilateral negotiations in TPP, Washington and Tokyo have held separate, bilateral market access negotiations which would basically determine the level of openness of the new agreement for all partners. Thus, bilateralism has empowered TPP to become the premiere multilateral trade institution in Asia, even attracting China's interest as a potential future member.

Non-Zero-Sum

The post–Cold War era witnessed the growth of new regional initiatives like APEC in 1994, and several centered around ASEAN, including the ARF in 1993, ASEAN Plus Three (APT) in 1995, and EAS in 2005 (see table 8.4 for a listing). The Asian financial crisis of 1997 also acted as a spur to regional forms of economic cooperation.[87] Acharya classified these initiatives in terms of "exclusionists" like Malaysia that saw no role for the United States in Asia's institutions, and "inclusionists" like Indonesia and Singapore that disagreed.[88] But this zero-sum thinking also emerged because of negative US reactions. Americans viewed early regional initiatives like Mahathir's East Asia Economic Caucus (EAEC) as deliberately intended to undermine the alliance network.[89] As Press-Barnathan writes, early proposals for a CSCE for Asia (by the Canadians

TABLE 8.4. REGIONAL INSTITUTIONS IN ASIA

NAME	FOUNDING DATE
Association of Southeast Asian Nations (ASEAN)	1967
Pacific Islands Forum (PIF)	1971
South Asian Association for Regional Cooperation (SAARC)	1985
Asia-Pacific Economic Cooperation (APEC)	1989
ASEAN Regional Forum (ARF)	1994
ASEAN Plus Three (APT)	1997
Shanghai Cooperation Organisation (SCO)	2001
Six-Party Talks (SPT)	2003
East Asia Summit (EAS)	2005
Trans-Pacific Partnership (TPP)	2006
Trilateral Cooperation Secretariat (TCS)	2010
Regional Comprehensive Economic Partnership (RCEP)	2012
Asian Infrastructure Investment Bank (AIIB)	2014

and Australians) were opposed by the George H. W. Bush administration, as were proposals by the Japanese for a CSCE-type organization for Asia organized around ASEAN. A debate emerged as to whether to blame the inability to form effective "truly Asian" regional institutions in the post–Cold War directly on the overbearing American alliance system.[90]

Within the last decade, China has become a leading voice espousing the zero-sum nature of Asia's architecture, regularly referring to the US alliance system as "Cold War anachronisms" that are exclusionist, that protect the few at the expense of the many, and that no longer fit with the region's needs.[91] Beijing has embarked on its own campaign to support regional institutions in Asia without the United States (see figure 8.1, table 8.2) such as Regional Comprehensive Economic Partnership (RCEP), "One Belt, One Road," Shanghai Cooperative Organization (SCO), Asean-China Defense Ministers Informal Meeting (ACDMIM), AIIB, and others, that some have described as Beijing's efforts to create its own hub and spokes system (even as it criticizes the US presence). As I noted earlier in this chapter, at the 2014 Conference on Interaction and Confidence Building Measures in Asia (CICA), China highlighted the US alliance system as an obstacle to Asian regional integration and lobbied countries to sign a joint statement calling for a new form of "Asia for Asians" security without the alliances.[92]

The reality is that the US alliance system and Asian regionalism are not locked into a zero-sum death struggle. The alliance system remains strong, and its minilateralization is creating new functionally based trilaterals and quadrilaterals. At the same time, the region is witnessing the proliferation of many new institutions, some of which do not have the US alliance system as its core, as figures 8.1 and 8.2 show. The co-growth of US-alliance-based minilaterals, ASEAN-centered institutions, and China's multilateral institutions may appear like a form of competitive balancing between China and the United States through regional institutions (or "institutional balancing"), but this does not amount to a zero-sum game.[93] These institutions are complementary, at least from the US perspective. The positive-sum view of multilateralism in Asia was first elucidated in the Nye Initiative in 1995 when the United States explicitly supported regional institutions as complementing the US alliance system in Asia.[94] In 2008, Secretary of Defense Bob Gates carried forth this notion when he stated that US policy was to "avoid an approach that treats the quest for a new security architecture as some kind of zero-sum game. . . . The collaborative reality of Asia's security today is to the exclusion of no single country . . . It is instead a continuously developing enterprise undertaken with allies, friends, and partners."[95] Today, if Japan, China, and Korea are improving relations in the context of the Trilateral Cooperation Secretariat (TCS), that has positive ramifications for regional stability, which is, in turn, wholly compatible with US interests. While TPP currently does not have China as a member, the United States has openly called for Beijing to join the institution.[96] During the US-Japan summit of April 2015, the White House stated it was not opposed to China's AIIB (contrary to popular speculation), and that it could complement the efforts of other international financial institutions like the World Bank and Asian Development Bank in building infrastructure in Asia.[97] The Obama administration openly supported independent Korean efforts at promoting an organization based on functional cooperation on nuclear safety, health, climate, and disaster relief in Northeast Asia called NAPCI (Northeast Asian Peace and Cooperation Initiative), and said that it complemented the US policy of "pivot" or "rebalance" to Asia.[98] And at the October 2015 summit with South Korean leader Park Geun-hye, President Obama responded to a question about whether the United States had concerns with the ROK's determined efforts to build bilateral cooperation with China independent of the United States. His response was a classic statement of the positive-sum nature of the issue:

> [S]ometimes there's a perception that if President Park meets with President Xi, that that must cause a problem for us. Well, President Xi was in this room, eating my food. (Laughter.) And we were toasting and having a lengthy conversation. We want South Korea to have a strong relationship with China, just as we want to have a strong relationship with China. . . . So there's no contradiction between the Republic of Korea having good relations with us, being a central part of our alliance, and having a good relationship—good relations with China. . . . So, again, I think there we have a shared interest. And my hope is, is that as a consequence of the outreach that President Park has done, the outreach we do, the interactions that we have with Japan and resolving some of the historical challenges that exist there, that we can create in Northeast Asia the kind of cooperative, forward-looking relationship among all countries that will be good for our children and our grandchildren.[99]

ASIA'S "COMPLEX PATCHWORK"

Business, Not Civilization

Asia's emerging architectural design, replete with US bilaterals and mini-laterals, ASEAN-based organizations, and China-based initiatives, is a "patchwork"—it is made up of an amalgam of groupings, some of which take on a more formal institutional structure, but others don't. Asia's architecture fits with what Karen Alter and Sophie Meunier would define as a "complex international structure" where groups are nested, partially overlapping, and parallel to one another without any clear sense of hierarchy among them.[100] The model for this sort of "regional community" is not civilizational, where a particular "Asia-ness" defines the group (e.g., Hatoyama's East Asia Community concept or Mahathir's EAEC), nor is it based on postwar Western Europe. Instead it is more akin to a business model—where coalitions form among entities with the most direct interests to solve a problem. These meetings are seldom based on ideology, nor are they designed as part of a linear path to formal integration. Instead, entities participate because they seek to secure private goods (i.e., either profits or avoidance of losses), but the aggregation of their atomistic efforts precipitate collective benefits for the region. Asian states gather on a need basis to combat piracy in the Malacca Straits, coordinate anti-terrorism measures, respond to natural disasters, and prevent further destabilization in Asian financial markets. These coalitions are primarily motivated by functional needs and seldom have implications beyond that.

The emphasis on fluidity and complexity in regional cooperation is crucial for Asia in that it lowers barriers to cooperation for states with a deep history of animosity and differences in regime type. States in this region, unlike those of Europe, do not share similar ideas regarding rule of law, human rights, and legal norms. Many states have been colonized by neighbors, have territorial disputes, and have a history of unequal power relations that make nationalism still a salient part of domestic politics. With this in mind, efforts to formalize a single hierarchical institution may repel states rather than attract them. Imagine having the equivalent of a "Copenhagen Criteria" for joining institutions in the Asia-Pacific region—it would never work. Having a patchwork of institutions focused on solving specific substantive issues, however, mitigates the barriers that exist between states in the Asia-Pacific.

As alluded to earlier, these Asia's institutions are more often than not overlapping and interlinked in terms of the memberships. The United States, Japan, and Australia, for example, may discuss UN reform in the TSD, but Japan, China, and Korea will discuss currency swaps at the Chiang Mai Initiative. The United States, Japan, China, and Korea will discuss counterproliferation in the context of the Six-Party Talks, but China, Korea, and Australia will discuss economic development in the context of the Asia Infrastructure Investment Bank. Even ASEAN, one of the more formal institutions in Asia, is fluid in its membership. Depending on the agenda, there will be meetings of just ten ASEAN member states, ASEAN plus three, East Asian Summit, or the ASEAN Regional Forum. Track 2 security forums such as the Council and Security Cooperation in the Asia-Pacific (CSCAP) will exist alongside Track 1 security dialogues. What emerges is not a hub and spokes conception, nor an integrated East Asian Community, but "networks and patchworks" of differently configured and overlapping bilaterals, trilaterals, quadrilaterals, and other multilateral groupings that, stitched together, define the regional architecture.

The Beauty of Complexity

Some may argue that the geometry of regional groupings I describe for Asia is too complex a vision because it has no core, no metrics for coherence, and no single superstructure. The common view is that complexity is suboptimal for multilateral institutions because it decreases efficiency and lacks a preventive capacity. It makes it hard to locate responsibility and thereby reduces accountability. The "hyperactivity" of multiple groupings can also be inefficient where efforts are often duplicative of one another. When groupings are formed in an ad hoc and immediate fashion, this also means that the time horizons of these groups are likely to be short.[101]

Complexity of architecture, however, is an asset to Asia's architecture given the underlying historical animosities, the diversity of regime types, and the shifting balance of power because it solves two problems: security dilemmas and collective action. The addressing of these two dilemmas, moreover, helps the region use its architecture as a tool for better managing relations between the great powers and reducing the potential for destabilizing competition.

The security dilemma in Asia refers to the view that any US-based regional initiative is seen as containing China, and any China-centered regional institution is meant to exclude the United States.[102] This dilemma is exacerbated by the competitive tendencies of the United States and China for institutional control of the region, either with dueling hub and spokes systems (e.g., US alliances in East Asia versus China's "One Belt, One Road" initiative in developing Asia), or through Chinese efforts to discredit the reliability of American alliances.[103] But the nested and parallel nature of Asia's patchwork mutes the security dilemmas between countries distrustful of one another. In particular, the overlapping nature of membership and the absence of hierarchy to the regional institutions are key. The former means that no party can truly be "excluded" or seek to exclude another. And if one party tries to exclude another, the lack of any hierarchy in Asia's institutional design means that there is no constriction of space for formation of more offsetting multilaterals. A quadrilateral among the United States-Japan-Australia-India, as proposed by then-Japanese Prime Minister Shinzo Abe in 2006, or the 2014 US-Japan-South Korea summit at the Hague, for example, might incite insecurities in China, if these were the only regional groupings available, but Beijing would be engaged with Japan in the context of the TCS, with the United States and Japan in the context of a US-Japan-China trilateral, with India in the context of the EAS, and with Korea and Australia in the context of AIIB and ASEAN-plus-six. If one actor does not like the priorities in one grouping, it can "regime-shift" to other available groupings. Or, given the flexibility and absence of hierarchy in institutions, an actor can create altogether new groupings in order to advance an alternate set of rules (arguably this is what China is doing with AIIB and with CICA).[104] Complexity allows great powers of Asia to operate in multiple groupings, sometimes with each other, and sometimes exclusively, which helps to circumvent zero-sum competition. Thus, even if the security dilemma in Asia's architecture is creating, as Kai He observes, "contested regional orders," the region's resulting patchwork ensures that all forms of order can co-exist.[105] The point here is not that insecurities disappear merely with membership in these various groupings, but the complexity and density of these many groupings readily create channels to reduce anxieties associated with exclusion.

Complexity also helps to resolve collective action problems in Asian architecture. States generally harbor stronger inclinations to procure private goods from any multilateral effort rather than providing public goods. This makes it harder to incentivize states to invest in multilateral institutions without a near-term payoff. The fluid nature of nested, partially overlapping, and parallel groupings in Asia facilitates discrete coalitions of actors to deal with a functional issue, whether it is the Tsunami Core Group, TCOG, or AIIB. In such groupings there will be less free-riding because only those with an interest are involved; there will be greater cost-sharing; and there will be an even distribution of risk. The fluid nature of architecture also allows for "forum-shopping" and experimentation in which states can move among a myriad of different groupings to determine which one resonates the most with the issue at hand.[106]

The complexity of Asia's patchwork also helps the region to manage relations between the great powers. This is because of the process of "self-binding regional engineering." That is, in the process of engineering new minilaterals or multilaterals, or engaging in forum-shopping or regime-shifting, great powers through their membership are also allowing themselves to be bound by the myriad of rules in these groupings. By perpetuating and refurbishing the alliance system, for example, the United States is also allowing itself to be bound by desires of alliance partners to resolve disputes peacefully, support the peaceful status quo, remain engaged in the region, and support a liberal trading order. China may be seeking to create its own hub and spokes system with CICA or AIIB, but by sponsoring such organizations with a wide membership stretching from Central Asia to Western Europe, it is also binding itself to a core set of international rules and norms, without which China would lose all credibility.

The sheer "messiness" of Asia's patchwork also can dilute the ability of either great power to leverage the institutions to balance against the other. If one actor wanted to advance a "posse" with an explicit revisionist agenda targeted against another, which organization would it choose among the many? And if the actor sought to round up a coalition of the willing, would it be possible to find partners who were not already connected with the target state through the myriad of other existing institutions? Conversely, should the target state seek a counter-coalition, it would encounter similar obstacles. The messiness of nested and overlapping relationships in the region can mute great power competition.

In addition, smaller powers can use Asia's complexity to their advantage. The myriad of institutions affords the small powers the luxury of not having to choose between a single US- or Chinese-based grouping. They can participate in both, none, or some combination. And as Evelyn Goh argues, small power can utilize a proactive strategy of "enmeshment." Smaller powers, concerned about the future impact of the United States and China on the region's stability, can aggressively "enmesh" the two great powers into their own Lilliputian patchwork of institutions to ensure they comply with the rules and norms.[107] "Enmeshment" on the part of smaller powers, and "self-binding regional engineering" ensure two things regarding regional architecture. It generates enduring demand by the region for the patchwork of institutions. And it ensures that the region places a positive value on the complexity of the architecture.

Finally, the American bilateral alliance system works as a "thread" that keeps the patchwork architecture together. While certainly not wholly constitutive of the architecture, the alliance system still plays a very important role. It is already providing much of the public goods in the Asia-Pacific regarding security, as well as an open market. This creates an environment for states to adjust and coordinate remaining divergences without worrying about upsetting much of existing regional dynamics. Many of the minilateral groupings in Asia "spin off" of the bilateral alliances, and in some cases, like TPP, the bilateral alliance cooperation is critical to the future success of arguably Asia's most important new multilateral institution. By expanding existing consultation procedures, the alliance framework is also creating new partnerships among Asian states. Americans should take pride in a non-zero-sum approach to its bilateral alliances and support for multilateralism for Asia. The hub and spokes alliance system reinforces Asia's regional institutions.

Final Thoughts

As we sat on the Secretary's plane approaching Sydney, the debate over whether the United States should join EAS became heated. Some said we should not join EAS because it was not Asia's answer to the European

Union, and because it would detract from the power of our alliances. Something about that statement, as authoritative as the voice was, struck me as wrongheaded. US alliances, I thought to myself, having been so deeply ingrained in the region and having provided such critical public goods like security and stability, could not possibly be at odds with the growth of new, more inclusive and broad-based regional institutions. The prescriptive point to be made in this book is not an opposition to regionwide groupings, but merely that the expectation of the "answer" to Asian regional architecture equating with a single institution may be misplaced. Heaping such expectations on efforts such as the East Asia Summit is unfair. It not only creates a standard that is impossible for the institution to meet given the history and diversity of the region, but also creates competition on design and hierarchy of institutions that can only exacerbate security dilemmas in the region. Moreover, it leads to false judgments regarding the failure of the US alliance system to help create regional architecture in Asia.[108]

When Truman and Eisenhower contemplated the creation of a bilateral alliance network in the early 1950s in Asia, they probably gave little forethought to how this network would nest in the complex patchwork of Asia's architecture that would emerge years later. Today's institutional design for the region is neither a single umbrella institution like EAS, nor solely a US hub and spokes alliance system. Instead, the geometry of Asia is a complex collection of different shapes—triangles, quadrilaterals, hexagonals—that are functional, fluid, and overlapping. Each of these shapes serves a distinct purpose contributing to an Asia-Pacific region that is more cooperative, transparent, and peaceful.

NOTES

Chapter 1

1. Prior to the Barack Obama administration, the United States could not accede to signing the Treaty of Amity and Cooperation, which was a prerequisite for EAS signatories. This treaty contained a clause about noninterference in the internal affairs of member states, which was a problem for the United States, given human rights violations in Burma. Full text of "Treaty of Amity and Cooperation in Southeast Asia" (1976, February 24) in Bali, Indonesia, available here: http://www.asean.org/news/item.treaty -of-amity-and-cooperation-in-southeast-asia-indonesia-24-february-1976-3 (accessed November 11, 2015).

2. Thomas Donilon, "The United States and the Asia-Pacific in 2013," *Asiasociety.org* (March 11, 2013), http://asiasociety.org/new-york/complete-transcript -thomas-donilon-asia-society-new-york (accessed March 22, 2013).

3. On alliances, multilateralism, and hegemonic controls of power, see Paul Schroeder, "Alliances, 1815–1945: Weapons of Power and Tools of Management," in Klaus Knorr, ed., *Historical Dimensions of National Security Problems* (Lawrence: University Press of Kansas, 1976), 227–62; Joseph Grieco, "Understanding the Problem of International Cooperation: The Limits of Neoliberal Institutionalism and the Future of Realist Theory," in David R. Baldwin, ed., *Neorealism and Neoliberalism: The Contemporary Debate* (New York: Columbia University Press, 1993), 301–38; G. John Ikenberry, "Is American Multilateralism in Decline?" *Perspectives on Politics*, 1, no. 3 (September 2003), 533–50; Joseph Nye, *The Paradox of American Power* (New York: Oxford University Press, 2002); Ethan Kapstein and Michael Mastanduno, eds., *Unipolar Politics: Realism and State Strategies after the Cold War* (New York: Columbia University Press, 1999); William C. Wohlforth, "The Stability of a Unipolar World," *International Security*, 24, no. 1 (Summer 1999), 5–41; Steve Weber, *Multilateralism in NATO: Shaping the postwar Balance, 1945–1961* (Berkeley: University of California Press, 1991); G. John Ikenberry, "America's Imperial Ambition," *Foreign Affairs*, 81, no. 5 (September/October 2002), 44–60; and Charles Krauthammer, "The Unipolar Moment Revisited," *National Interest*, no. 70 (Winter 2002–03), 5–17; other works cited below.

4. For power-based hierarchy arguments, see Robert Gilpin, *War and Change in World Politics* (Cambridge, UK: Cambridge University Press, 1981); Gilpin, *Political Economy of International Relations* (Princeton, NJ: Princeton University Press, 1987); Stephen D. Krasner, "State Power and the Structure of International Trade," *World Politics*, 28, no. 3 (April 1976), 317–47. For

the classic work on international "order" see Hedley Bull, *The Anarchical Society: A Study of Order in World Politics*, 3rd ed. (New York: Columbia University Press, 2002). For order-related hierarchy arguments, see G. John Ikenberry, *After Victory: Institutions, Strategic Restraint, and the Rebuilding of Order After Major Wars* (Princeton, NJ: Princeton University Press, 2001). For arguments of a consensual, legitimated hierarchy, see David Lake, *Hierarchy in International Relations* (Ithaca, NY: Cornell University Press, 2009); John M. Hobson and J. C. Sharman, "The Enduring Place of Hierarchy in World Politics: Tracing the Social Logics of Hierarchy and Political Change," *European Journal of International Relations*, 11, no. 1 (2005), 63–98. For arguments about "informal empire," see Daniel H. Nexon and Thomas Wright, "What's at Stake in the American Empire Debate," *American Political Science Review*, 101, no. 2 (May 2007), 253–71; Alexander Wendt and Daniel Friedheim, "Hierarchy Under Anarchy: Informal Empire and the East German State," *International Organization*, 49, no. 4 (Autumn 1995), 689–721.

5. The Cold War itself, of course, inhibited counterbalancing tendencies within the US alliance system as well. On power differentials rendering balancing irrelevant, see Stephen G. Brooks and William C. Wohlforth, *World Out of Balance: International Relations and the Challenge of American Primacy* (Princeton, NJ: Princeton University Press, 2008), ch. 2.

6. For recent works in network theory, see R. Charli Carpenter, "Vetting the Advocacy Agenda: Network Centrality and the Paradox of Weapons Norms," *International Organization*, 65, no. 1 (Winter 2011), 69–102; Emilie M. Hafner-Burton, Miles Kahler, and Alexander H. Montgomery, "Network Analysis for International Relations," *International Organization*, 63, no. 3 (Summer 2009), 559–92; Miles Kahler, ed., *Networked Politics: Agency, Power, and Governance* (Ithaca, NY: Cornell University Press, 2009); and Nexon and Wright, "What's at Stake in the American Empire Debate."

7. Miles Kahler, "Networked Politics: Agency, Power and Governance," in Kahler, ed., *Networked Politics*, 13.

8. "States that are the sole link between clusters of highly connected states might gain influence as brokers within the network." Miles Kahler, "Networked Politics: Agency, Power, and Governance," 12. See also David A. Lake and Wendy H. Wong, "The Politics of Networks: Interests, Power, and Human Rights Norms," in Kahler, ed., *Networked Politics*, 127–50; and Hafner-Burton, Kahler, and Montgomery, "Network Analysis for International Relations," 571–72.

9. Seminal works in this field are by Michael Mandelbaum, *The Nuclear Revolution: International Politics Before and After Hiroshima* (New York: Cambridge University Press, 1981); Glenn H. Snyder, "The Security Dilemma in Alliance Politics," *World Politics*, 36, no. 4 (July 1984), 461–95; Thomas J. Christensen and Jack Snyder, "Chain Gangs and Passed Bucks: Predicting Alliance Patterns in Multipolarity," *International Organization*, 44, no. 2 (Spring 1990), 137–68; and Randall L. Schweller, "Tripolarity and the Second World War," *International Studies Quarterly*, 37, no. 1 (March 1993), 73–103.

10. John Duffield, "Why Is There No APTO? Why Is There No OSCAP?: Asia-Pacific Security Institutions in Comparative Perspective," *Contemporary Security Policy*, 22, no. 2 (August 2001), 70.

11. Robert Blum, *Drawing the Line: The Origin of the American Containment Policy in East Asia* (New York: W.W. Norton, 1982), 3–4.

12. John Gerard Ruggie, "The Past as Prologue?: Interests, Identity, and American Foreign Policy," *International Security*, 21, no. 4 (Spring 1997), 105, n.62; Ralph Braibanti, "The Southeast Asia Collective Defense Treaty," *Pacific Affairs*, 30, no. 4 (December 1957), 321–41 (esp. 327–28). Moreover, US official statements at the time explicitly stated that SEATO was not NATO. State department officials even considered changing the organization's name to avoid public confusion.

13. Duffield, "Why is there no APTO?" 72–73.

14. For a prominent realist argument incorporating power, threats, and geography, see Stephen Walt, *The Origins of Alliances* (Ithaca, NY: Cornell University Press, 1987); Stephen Walt, "Testing Theories of Alliance Formation: the Case of Southwest Asia," *International Organization*, 42, no. 2 (March 1988), 275–316. Geography also plays a central role in Robert Jervis, "Cooperation under the Security Dilemma," *World Politics*, 30, no. 2 (January 1978), 167–214; and John J. Mearsheimer, *The Tragedy of Great Power Politics* (New York: W.W. Norton, 2001). For a prominent realist argument, which includes relative cost concerns, see Gilpin, *War and Change*. On relative costs, see also Stephen G. Brooks, "Dueling Realisms," *International Organization*, 51, no. 3 (June 1997), 445–77.

15. Paul Bracken, *Fire in the East* (New York: HarperCollins, 1999), 26; and Duffield, "Why is there no APTO?" 79.

16. For realist arguments focusing on hegemony, see Gilpin, *War and Change*; Krasner, "State Power and the Structure of International Trade." On regional hegemony in particular, see Mearsheimer, *The Tragedy of Great Power Politics*.

17. For prominent realist arguments focusing on nuclear weapons, see Robert Jervis, *The Meaning of the Nuclear Revolution: Statecraft and the Prospect of Armageddon* (Ithaca, NY: Cornell University Press, 1989); and Kenneth N. Waltz, "Nuclear Myths and Political Realities," *American Political Science Review*, 84, no. 3 (September 1990), 731–45. For realist examination of military doctrine, see Barry Posen, *The Sources of Military Doctrine: France, Britain, and Germany Between the World Wars* (Ithaca, NY: Cornell University Press, 1984); and Jack Snyder, *The Ideology of the Offensive: Military Decision Making and the Disasters of 1914* (Ithaca, NY: Cornell University Press, 1984).

18. See Christopher M. Hemmer and Peter J. Katzenstein, "Why Is There No NATO in Asia?: Collective Identity, Regionalism, and the Origins of Multilateralism," *International Organization*, 56, no. 3 (Summer 2002), 582.

19. Mark Beeson, "Rethinking Regionalism: Europe and East Asia in Comparative Historical Perspective," *Journal of European Public Policy*, 12, no. 6 (2005), 969–85.

20. Adlai Stevenson, "Korea in Perspective," *Foreign Affairs*, 30, no. 3 (April 1952), 349–60.

21. *Statistical Abstract of the United States, 1954* (Washington, DC: US Department of Commerce, 1954), sec. 32, no. 1074, 899 (Europe), 901 (Asia).
22. On economic development and interdependence, see Robert O. Keohane and Joseph S. Nye, Jr., *Power and Interdependence*, 4th ed. (New York: Pearson, 2012). For regime type arguments, see Mike E. Brown, Sean M. Lynn-Jones, and Steven E. Miller, eds., *Debating the Democratic Peace* (Cambridge, MA: MIT Press, 1996). Shared interests tie into liberal discussions of "absolute gains" concerns. On this, see Robert Axelrod, *The Evolution of Cooperation*, Revised ed. (New York: Basic Books, 2006); Robert O. Keohane, *After Hegemony: Cooperation and Discord in the World Political Economy*, 2nd ed. (Princeton, NJ: Princeton University Press, 2005); Kenneth Oye, ed., *Cooperation Under Anarchy* (Princeton, NJ: Princeton University Press, 1986).
23. These 12 countries include: Austria, Belgium, Denmark, Finland, France, West Germany, Italy, the Netherlands, Norway, Sweden, Switzerland, and the United Kingdom. Figures in 1990 US dollars.
24. These allies and partners include: Japan, the Philippines, South Korea, Thailand, and Taiwan. Figures in 1990 US dollars. GDP figures from Europe and Asia from Angus Maddison, "Statistics on World Population, GDP, and Per Capita GDP, 1–2008 AD," *Maddison Project* (2008), http://www.ggdc.net/maddison/oriindex.htm (accessed March 26, 2013).
25. This excludes 1949 data (unavailable).
26. US-Japan, US-Taiwan, and US-Korea trade figures and percentages derived from United Nations, *Yearbook of International Trade Statistics, 1955* (New York: United Nations, 1956); *Yearbook of International Trade Statistics, 1958* (New York: United Nations, 1959); *Yearbook of International Trade Statistics, 1960* (New York: United Nations, 1962).
27. Here "Asia" refers to: Japan, China (Taiwan), Cambodia, Laos, Vietnam, Indonesia, the Republic of Korea, the Philippines, Thailand, Portuguese India (various locations in modern India), Portuguese Timor (modern East Timor), Netherlands New Guinea (modern Papua province of Indonesia), and the Ryukyu Islands (modern Japan).
28. This excludes 1949. Actual figures of cumulative trade volume from 1948–1960 are: Western Europe, $201,310 million; Asia, $8,602 million. Europe vs. Asian regional trade figures from United Nations (1962); *Statistical Yearbook, 1960* (New York: United Nations, 1961).
29. See Javed Maswood, "The Rise of the Asia-Pacific," in Anthony McGrew and Christopher Brook, eds., *Asia-Pacific in the New World Order* (London: Routledge, 1998), 57.
30. Variations in individual regime types can be seen at Monty G. Marshall and Keith Jaggers, "Polity IV Project: Political Regime Characteristics and Transitions, 1900–2011" (2013), http://www.systemicpeace.org/polity/polity4.htm (accessed March 25, 2013).
31. Aaron Friedberg, "Ripe for Rivalry: Prospects for Peace in a Multipolar Asia," *International Security*, 18, no. 3 (Winter 1993/94), 13–14.
32. Duffield, "Why is there no APTO?" 80–81.
33. Quoted in Guy de Carmoy, *The Foreign Policies of France, 1944–1968*, trans. Elaine P. Halperin (Chicago: University of Chicago Press, 1970), 27.

34. Hugh Dalton quoted in Saki Dockrill, *Britain's Policy for West German Rearmament, 1950–1955* (Cambridge, UK: Cambridge University Press, 1991), 6–7.

35. Thomas U. Berger, *Cultures of Antimilitarism: National Security in Germany and Japan* (Baltimore: Johns Hopkins University Press, 1998).

36. Germany trailed only France, which averaged about 650,000 troops between 1955 and 1990, and Italy, which averaged 460,000 (Germany's average was 430,000). "National Military Capabilities (v4.0)," The Correlates of War Project (2013), www.correlatesofwar.org/COW2 Data/Capabilities/nmc4 .htm (accessed March 27, 2013).

37. Victor Cha, *Alignment Despite Antagonism* (Stanford, CA: Stanford University Press, 1999), ch. 3; and Miles Kahler, "Institution-Building in the Asia-Pacific," in Andrew Mack and Mark Ravenhill, eds., *Pacific Cooperation: Building Economic and Security Regimes in the Asia-Pacific Region* (Australia: Allen & Unwin, 1994), 16–39.

38. Charles Kindleberger, "Dominance and Leadership in the International Economy: Exploitation, Public Goods, and Free Rides," *International Studies Quarterly*, 25, no. 2 (June 1981), 242–54; and Robert Keohane, "The Theory of Hegemonic Stability and Changes in International Economic Regimes, 1967–1977," in Ole Holsti, Randolph Siverson, and Alexander George, eds., *Change in the International System* (Boulder, CO: Westview, 1980), 131–62.

39. Donald Crone, "Does Hegemony Matter?: The Reorganization of the Pacific Political Economy," *World Politics*, 45, no. 4 (July 1993), 501–25; and David H. Capie, "Power, Identity, and Multilateralism: The United States and Regional Institutionalization in the Asia-Pacific," Ottawa: National Library of Canada, 2003 (York University, PhD dissertation, 2002).

40. For a good study on strategic choice and institutional forms of cooperation, see Galia Press-Barnathan, *Organizing the World: The United States and Regional Cooperation in Asia and Europe* (New York: Routledge, 2003),

41. Ruggie, "The Past as Prologue," 105; and John Gerard Ruggie, "Multilateralism: The Anatomy of an Institution," in John Ruggie, ed., *Multilateralism Matters: The Theory and Praxis of an Institutional Form* (New York: Columbia University Press, 1993), 3–48. Also see Crone, "Does Hegemony Matter?"

42. Robert Gilpin, "International Politics and the Pacific Rim Era," in *Annals of the American Academy of Political and Social Sciences: The Pacific Region* (Newbury, CA: Sage, 1989), 66–67.

43. Lisa Martin, "The Rational State Choice of Multilateralism," in John Ruggie ed., *Multilateralism Matters: The Theory and Praxis of an Institutional Form* (New York: Columbia University Press, 1993); David Lake, *Entangling Relations—American Foreign Policy in Its Century* (Princeton, NJ: Princeton University Press, 1999); David Lake and Patrick Morgan eds., *Regional Orders: Building Security in a New World* (University Park: Pennsylvania State University Press, 1997); Press-Barnathan, *Organizing the World*, 17–19; Barbara Koremenos, Charles Lipson, and Duncan Snidal, "The Rational Design of Institutions," *International Organization*, 55, no. 4 (Autumn 2001), 761–99; and Etel Solingen, *Regional Orders at Century's Dawn: Global and Domestic Influences on Grand Strategy* (Princeton, NJ: Princeton University Press, 1998).

44. Ikenberry, "Is American Multilateralism in Decline?" 536.
45. On the centrality of identity to constructivist thought, see John Gerard Ruggie, "What Makes the World Hang Together?: Neo-Utilitarianism and the Social Constructivist Challenge," *International Organization*, 52, no. 4 (Autumn 1998), 855–85; and Alexander Wendt, *Social Theory of International Politics* (Cambridge, UK: Cambridge University Press, 1999).
46. Duffield, "Why is there no APTO?"; Franziska Seraphim and Gerrit W. Gong, "Memory and History in East and Southeast Asia: Issues of Identity in International Relations," *Journal of Asian Studies*, 62, no. 2 (2003), 560–62; and Nicholas Kristof, "The Problem of Memory," *Foreign Affairs*, 77, no. 6 (November/December 1998), 37–49.
47. John Foster Dulles, "Security in the Pacific," *Foreign Affairs*, 30, no. 2 (January 1952), 72.
48. Beeson, "Rethinking Regionalism, 969–85.
49. Kahler, "Institution-Building in the Asia-Pacific; Peter Katzenstein, "Regionalism in Comparative Perspective," *Cooperation and Conflict*, 31, no. 2 (June 1996), 123–59. US officials resisted even the hint of a "PATO"-type organization in Asia. Jacob Javits (R-NY) in 1950 introduced legislation for an East Asian NATO that got nowhere. Acheson consciously tried to make the point that security institutions in Asia and Europe were two different things. This is discussed in greater detail in chapter 7.
50. Hemmer and Katzenstein summarize the nature of this security transaction: "Europeans could be trusted with the additional power a multilateral institution would give them and that the Europeans deserved this increased influence." ("Why is there no NATO in Asia?" 588); also see Beeson, "Rethinking Regionalism," 977.
51. Coral Bell states the Asians were diplomatically unskilled compared with Europeans and therefore could not get a better deal from the United States besides bilateral arrangements. See Coral Bell, "The Future of American Policy in the Pacific," in Gary Klintworth, ed., *Asia-Pacific Security: Less Uncertainty, New Opportunities* (New York: St. Martin's Press, 1996).
52. Cited in Blum, *Drawing the Line*, 5.
53. "Memorandum by the Regional Planning Advisor (Ogburn), Bureau of Far Eastern Affairs to the Assistant Secretary of State for Far Eastern Affairs (Allison), 21 January 1953," in *Foreign Relations of the United States, 1952–1954, East Asia and the Pacific*, vol. 12, 260–62 (hereafter *FRUS*). Dulles once stated in a letter to Acheson in late 1950 that the only two dependable countries in the Pacific were Australia and New Zealand (cited in Capie, "Power, Identity, and Multilateralism," 127).
54. Cited in Hemmer and Katzenstein, "Why is there no NATO in Asia?" 593.
55. Bruce Cumings, *The Origins of the Korean War: The Roaring Cataract, 1947–1950, Volume II* (Princeton, NJ: Princeton University Press, 1990), 93; Capie, "Power, Identity, and Multilateralism."
56. "The Situation in the Far East," Testimony of Dean Acheson, Senate Foreign Relations Committee, 12 October 1949, *Executive Sessions of the Senate Foreign Relations Committee 1950* (Washington, DC: US Government Printing Office, 1976), 87. MacArthur also testified in 1951 that his rule of thumb

during his command of the occupation in Japan was to treat the Japanese like twelve-year-olds. See John Dower, *War without Mercy: Race and Power in the Pacific War* (New York: Pantheon, 1986), 303.

57. Hemmer and Katzenstein, "Why is there no NATO in Asia?" 588; also Capie, "Power, Identity, and Multilateralism," 68.

58. The fact that even today, the United States has intelligence-sharing programs such as "Five Eyes" suggests the point about race and trust.

59. Hemmer and Katzenstein, "Why is there no NATO in Asia?" 588.

60. Ibid., 600.

61. Barbara F. Walter, *Reputation and Civil War: Why Separatist Conflicts Are So Violent* (Cambridge: Cambridge University Press, 2009).

62. I am indebted to Tom Christensen for raising this point.

63. Rudra Sil and Peter Katzenstein, *Beyond Paradigms: Analytic Eclecticism in the Study of World Politics* (New York: Palgrave MacMillan, 2010).

Chapter 2

1. On state choice and design of institutions, see Barbara Koremenos, Charles Lipson, and Duncan Snidal, "The Rational Design of International Institutions," *International Organization*, 55, no. 4 (Autumn 2001), 761–99; Lisa Martin, "The Rational State Choice of Multilateralism," in John Ruggie, ed., *Multilateralism Matters: The Theory and Praxis of an Institutional Form* (New York: Columbia University Press, 1993), 91–122; Michaela Mattes, "Democratic Reliability: Precommitment of Successor Governments, and the Choice of Alliance Commitment," *International Organization*, 66, no. 1 (Winter 2012), 153–72; Lisa Martin and Beth Simmons, "Theories and Empirical Studies of International Institutions," *International Organization*, 52, no. 4 (Autumn 1998), 729–57; Kenneth Abbott and Duncan Snidal, "Why States Act through Formal Organization," *Journal of Conflict Resolution*, 42, no. 1 (February 1998), 3–32; Katja Weber, "Hierarchy Amidst Anarchy: A Transaction Costs Approach to International Security Cooperation," *International Studies Quarterly*, 41, no. 2 (1997), 321–40; David Lake and Robert Powell, eds., *International Relations: A Strategic-Choice Approach* (Princeton, NJ: Princeton University Press, 1999); Robert Keohane, *After Hegemony: Cooperation and Discord in the World Political Economy* (Princeton, NJ: Princeton University Press, 1984); and Kenneth Oye, *Cooperation Under Anarchy* (Princeton, NJ: Princeton University Press, 1986).

2. Schroeder first used this term in 1976 to describe how alliances serve as tools of management in addition to deterrence ("Alliances as Tools of Management," in Klaus Knorr, ed., *Economic Issues and National Security* (Lawrence: Regent's Press of Kansas, 1977), 230; also see Schroeder, "Alliances, 1815–1914: 1815–1945: Weapons of Power and Tools of Management," in Klaus Knorr, ed., *Historical Dimensions of National Security Problems* (Lawrence: University of Kansas Press, 1976)). I attempt to delineate more specifically some of the conditions and causal mechanisms by which alliances are used as instruments of control.

3. Mike Brown first suggested to me the use of the term, "rogue allies."

4. For concurrent views on alliances as institutions, not just capability-aggregators, see the volume, Haftendorn, Keohane, and Wallander, eds., *Imperfect Unions: Security Institutions over Time and Space* (New York: Oxford University Press, 1999). For empirical studies on the variations in alliance contracts, see Brett Ashley Leeds, Jeffrey Ritter, Sara McLaughlin Mitchell, and Andrew Long, "Alliance Treaty Obligations and Provisions, 1815–1944," *International Interactions*, 28, no. 3 (2002), 237–60; Brett Ashley Leeds and Michaela Mattes, "Alliance Politics during the Cold War: Aberration, New World Order, or Continuation of History?" *Conflict Management and Peace Science*, 24, no. 3 (2007), 183–99; Katja Weber, "Hierarchy Amidst Anarchy: A Transaction Costs Approach to International Security Cooperation," *International Studies Quarterly*, 41, no. 2 (1997), 321–40; Michaela Mattes, "Reputation, Symmetry, and Alliance Design, *International Organization*, 66, no. 4 (Fall 2012), 679–708; and Mattes, "Democratic Reliability, Precommitment of Successor Governments, and the Choice of Alliance Commitment," *International Organization*, 66, no.1 (Winter 2012), 153–72.

5. Nation-states balance against threats through internal and external means. Internal balancing refers to the bolstering of sovereign capabilities. External balancing refers to the use of outside actors to aggregate one's capabilities. The primary means of external balancing is through the formation of alliances or security bargains with other entities to contend with a threat. Alliances are therefore, as Glenn Snyder wrote, a form of power accretion or capability aggregation. For the classic statements, see George Liska, *Nations in Alliance: The Limits of Interdependence* (Baltimore: Johns Hopkins University Press, 1962); and Glenn Snyder, *Alliance Politics* (Ithaca, NY: Cornell University Press, 1997); Stephen Walt, *The Origins of Alliances* (Ithaca, NY: Cornell University Press, 1987). For studies of alliances as effective capability-aggregation institutions in deterring or winning wars, see Alastair Smith, "Alliance Formation and War," *International Studies Quarterly*, 39, no. 4 (December 1995), 405–26; James Morrow, "Alliance and Asymmetry: An Alternative to the Capability Aggregation Model," *American Journal of Political Science*, 35, no. 4 (November 1991), 904–34; Scott Gartner and Randolph Siverson, "War Expansion and War Outcomes," *Journal of Conflict Resolution*, no. 40 (March 1996), 4–15; Douglas Gibler, "The Costs of Reneging: Reputation and Alliance Formation," *Journal of Conflict Resolution*, 52, no. 3 (June 2008), 426–54; Tongfi Kim, "Why Alliances Entangle but Seldom Entrap States," *Security Studies*, 20, no. 3 (July 2011), 350–77; David Bearce, Kristen Flanagan, and Katharine Floros, "Alliances, Internal Information, and Military Conflict among Member States," *International Organization*, 60, no. 3 (July 2006), 595–625; Brett Benson, *Constructing International Security: Alliances, Deterrence, and Moral Hazard* (Cambridge: Cambridge University Press, 2012); Patricia Weitsman, *Dangerous Alliances: Proponents of Peace, Weapons of War* (Stanford, CA: Stanford University Press, 2004); and Scott Bennett and Allan Stam, "How Long Has This Been Going On: The Duration of Interstate Wars, 1816–1985," *American Political Science Review*, no. 90 (June 1996), 239–57.

6. I use the term "pathology" because it generally connotes compulsive and undesirable behavior by the ally beyond what might be considered normal expectations.

7. "The Security Dilemma in Alliance Politics," *World Politics*, 36, no. 4 (July 1984), 461–95.

8. On signaling and alliances, see James Fearon, "Signaling Versus the Balance of Power and Interests: An Empirical Test of a Crisis Bargaining Model," *Journal of Conflict Resolution*, 38, no. 2 (June 1994), 236–70; Peter Cowhey, "Domestic Institutions and the Credibility of International Commitments: Japan and the United States," *International Organization*, 47, no. 2 (April 1993), 299–326; Kurt Gaubatz, "Democratic States and Commitment in International Relations," *International Organization*, 50, no. 1 (December 1996),109–39; Brett Ashley Leeds, Michaela Mattes, and Jeremy Vogel, "Interest, Institutions, and the Reliability of International Commitments," *American Journal of Political Science*, 53, no. 2 (April 2009), 461–76; and Michaela Mattes, "Democratic Reliability: Precommitment of Successor Governments, and the Choice of Alliance Commitment," *International Organization*, 66, no. 1 (Winter 2012), 153–72.

9. For strategies to deal with abandonment, see Mattes, "Reputation, Symmetry, and Alliance Design"; Kenneth Abbott and Duncan Snidal, "Hard and Soft Law in International Governance," *International Organization*, 54, no. 3 (August 2000), 421–56; Barbara Koremenos, Charles Lipson, and Duncan Snidal, "The Rational Design of Institutions," *International Organization*, 55, no. 4 (February 2003), 761–99; Snyder, "The Security Dilemma in Alliance Politics"; Brett Ashley Leeds and Burgu Savun, "Terminating Alliances: Why do States Abrogate Agreements?" *Journal of Politics*, 69, no. 4 (November 2007), 1118–32; and Cha, "Abandonment, Entrapment, and Neoclassical Realism."

10. Fearon, "Signaling Versus the Balance of Power and Interests."

11. Keohane, "The Big Influence of Small Allies," 171.

12. Ibid., 172–74.

13. On the role of emotion in US decision-making in response to the 1950 North Korean invasion, and the trepidations among some European powers of US overextension, see Jonathan Mercer, "Emotion and Strategy in the Korean War," *International Organization*, vol. 67, no. 2 (Spring 2013), 235–39.

14. Keohane, "The Big Influence of Small Allies," 176–79; John J. Mearsheimer and Stephen M. Walt, *The Israel Lobby and U.S. Foreign Policy* (New York: Farrar, Straus, and Giroux, 2007).

15. Yaacov-Bar-Siman Tov, "Alliance Strategy: US-Small Allies Relationship," *Journal of Strategic Studies*, 3, no. 2 (1980), 202–16; Peter M. Baehr, "Small States: A Tool for Analysis," *World Politics*, 28, no. 3 (April 1975); and Klaus Knorr, *On the Uses of Military Power in the Nuclear Age* (Princeton, NJ: Princeton University Press, 1966).

16. For classic statements in this vein, see Robert Rothstein, *Alliances and Small Powers* (New York: Columbia University Press, 1968); George Liska, *Nations in Alliance: The Limits of Interdependence* (Baltimore: Johns Hopkins

University Press, 1962); Ole Holsti, P. Terrence Hopmann, and John D. Sullivan, *Unity and Disintegration in International Alliances: Comparative Studies* (New York: John Wiley & Sons, 1973); Annette Baker Fox, *The Power of Small States: Diplomacy in World War II* (Chicago: University of Chicago Press, 1959).

17. Small allies may have some worries about overdependence creating undesired equities in a larger patron's broader agenda, but in general, the small ally's marginal contribution to such a cause is not significant enough to register demands by the patron state.

18. Keohane, "The Big Influence of Small Allies," 171.

19. Hans Morgenthau, "Alliances in Theory and Practice," in Arnold Wolfers, ed., *Alliance Policy in the Cold War* (Baltimore: Johns Hopkins Press, 1959), 211.

20. Bar-Siman-Tov, "US-Small Allies Relationship," p, 204; Alexander George and Richard Smoke, *Deterrence in American Foreign Policy: Theory and Practice* (New York: Columbia University Press, 1974), 553; Thomas Schelling, *Arms and Influence* (New Haven, CT: Yale University Press, 1966), 55–60; and Franklin Weinstein, "The Concept of a Commitment in International Relations," *Journal of Conflict Resolution*, 13, no. 3 (March 1969), 38–56.

21. Loyalty can lead to undercommitment by the ally, however, if one's loyalty is taken for granted by the ally regardless of how irresponsibly the ally behaves.

22. On attribution errors in alliance politics, also see Jonathan Mercer, *Reputation in International Politics* (Ithaca, NY: Cornell University Press, 1996).

23. For the classic statement, see Mancur Olson, Jr., and Richard Zeckhauser, "An Economic Theory of Alliances," *Review of Economics and Statistics*, 48, no. 3 (August 1966), 266–79.

24. Snyder, "The Security Dilemma in Alliance Politics"; Thomas Christensen and Jack Snyder, "Chain Gangs and Passed Bucks: Predicting Alliance Patterns in Multipolarity," *International Organization*, 44, no. 2 (Spring 1990), 137–68.

25. Brett V. Benson, Patrick Bentley, and James Lee Ray, "Ally Provocateur: Why Allies Do Not Always Behave," *Journal of Peace Research*, 50, no. 1 (January 2013), 47–58.

26. Benjamin Friedman, Eugene Gholz, Daryl Press, and Harvey Sapolsky, "Restraining Order: For Strategic Modesty," *World Affairs*, 172, no. 2 (Fall 2009), 84–94.

27. James Morrow, "Alliances: Why Write Them Down?" *Annual Review of Political Science*, 3, no. 1 (June 2000), 63–83; and Keohane, "The Big Influence of Small Allies." For a similar typology of entrapment, see Michael Beckley, "The Myth of Entangling Alliances," *International Security*, 39, no. 4 (Spring 2015), 7–48, esp. 13.

28. Beckley, "The Myth of Entangling Alliances"; Tongfi Kim, "Why Alliances Entangle but Seldom Entrap"; Robert Art, *A Grand Strategy for America* (Ithaca, NY: Cornell University Press, 2003); Michael Mandelbaum, *The Case for Goliath: How America Acts as the World's Government in the Twenty-First Century* (New York: Public Affairs 2005); Stephen Brooks, G. John

Ikenberry, and William Wohlforth, "Don't Come Home, America: The Case Against Retrenchment," *International Security*, 37, no. 3 (Winter 2012/13), 7–51; and Jesse Johnson and Brett Ashley Leeds, "Defense Pacts: A Prescription for Peace?" *Foreign Policy Analysis*, 7, no. 1 (January 2011), 45–65.

29. Nikolas Gvosdev and Travis Tanner, "Wagging the Dog," *National Interest*, no. 77 (October 2004), 5–10; Christopher Layne, *The Peace of Illusions: American Grand Strategy from 1940 to the Present* (Ithaca, NY: Cornell University Press, 2006), 163–72; Eugene Gholz, Daryl Press, and Harvey Sapolsky, "Come Home, America: The Strategy of Restraint in the Face of Temptation," *International Security*, 21, no. 4 (Spring 1997), 5–48; Robert Jervis, *Perception and Misperception in International Politics* (Princeton, NJ: Princeton University Press, 1976), ch. 3.

30. On loopholes, see Beckley, "The Myth of Entangling Alliances," 18–19. Also see Leeds, "Do Alliances Deter Aggression?" On escape clauses, see Kim, "Why Alliances Entangle but Seldom Entrap," 359; and Benson, *Constructing International Security*.

31. On side-stepping, see Beckley, "The Myth of Entangling Alliances," 19–20. Also see Snyder, *Alliance Politics*, ch. 1; and Mattes, "Reputation, Symmetry, and Alliance Design."

32. For more on all of these responses, see Victor Cha, "Abandonment, Entrapment, and Neoclassical Realism in Asia," *International Studies Quarterly*, 44, no. 2 (June 2000), 261–91.

33. Schroeder, "Alliances, 1815–1945"; Robert Osgood, *Alliances in American Foreign Policy* (Baltimore: Johns Hopkins University Press, 1968); Patricia Weitsman, *Dangerous Alliances: Proponents of Peace, Weapons of War* (Stanford, CA: Stanford University Press, 2004); Yaacov-Bar-Siman Tov, "Alliance Strategy: US-Small Allies Relationship," *Journal of Strategic Studies*, 3, no. 2 (1980), 202–16; Chris Gelpi, "Alliances as Instruments of Intra-Allied Control or Restraint," in Helga Haftendorn, Robert Keohane, and Celeste Wallander, eds., *Imperfect Unions: Security Institutions over Time and Space* (New York: Oxford University Press, 1999); Jeremy Pressman, *Warring Friends: Alliance Restraint in International Politics* (Ithaca, NY: Cornell University Press, 2008); Christopher Gelpi, "Alliances as Instruments of Intra-Allied Control," in *Imperfect Unions: Security Institutions over Time and Space*, 107–39; Douglas Gibler, "Alliances That Never Balance: The Territorial Settlement Treaty," *Conflict Management and Peace Science*, 15, no. 1 (1996), 75–97; Mattes, "Democratic Reliability," 153–72; and Galia Press-Barnathan, *Organizing the World: The United States and Regional Cooperation in Asia and Europe* (New York: Routledge, 2003).

34. Morrow, "Alliances and Asymmetry."

35. Keohane, "The Big Influence of Small Allies"; and Chang-jin Park, "The Influence of Small States on the Superpowers," *World Politics*, 28, no. 1 (October 1975), 97–117; Stephen David, "Explaining Third World Alignment," *World Politics*, 43, no. 2 (1991); Alvin Rubenstein, *Red Star on the Nile: The Soviet-Egyptian Influence Relationship since the June War* (Princeton, NJ: Princeton University Press, 1977); Warren Bass, *Support any Friend:*

Kennedy's Middle East Policy and the Making of the US-Israeli Alliance (New York: Oxford University Press, 2003); Stephen Walt, "Alliances in a Unipolar World," in Ikenberry, Mastanduno, and Wohlforth, *International Relations Theory and the Consequences of Unipolarity*, 112–13; Bar-Siman-Tov, "Alliance Strategy: U.S-Small Allies Relationships"; Stanley Hoffmann, "Notes on the Effectiveness of Modern Power," *International Journal*, 30 (Spring 1975); and Arthur Lall, *Modern International Negotiation* (New York: Columbia University Press, 1966).

36. G. John Ikenberry, *After Victory: Institutions, Strategic Restraint, and the Rebuilding of Order after Major Wars* (Princeton, NJ: Princeton University Press, 2001); David Lake, *Entangling Relations: American Foreign Policy in its Century* (Princeton, NJ: Princeton University Press, 1999); Patricia Weitsman, *Dangerous Alliances: Proponents of Peace, Weapons of War* (Stanford, CA: Stanford University Press, 2004); Jeremy Pressman, *Warring Friends: Alliance Restraint in International Politics* (Ithaca, NY: Cornell University Press, 2008); Press-Barnathan, *Organizing the World*. For classics that observed this phenomenon but did not delve deeply, see Schroeder, "Alliances, 1815–1945"; George Liska, *Nations in Alliance* (Baltimore: Johns Hopkins University Press, 1962), 116; Robert Osgood, *Alliances and American Foreign Policy* (Baltimore: Johns Hopkins University Press, 1968), 22, 28; and Randall Schweller, *Deadly Imbalances: Tripolarity and Hitler's Strategy of World Conquest* (New York: Columbia University Press, 1998), 70–71.

37. Beckley, "The Myth of Entangling Alliances."

38. For example, see Gelpi, "Alliances as Instruments of Intra-Allied Control," 107–39; Songying Fang, Jesse C. Johnson, and Brett Ashley Leeds, "To Concede or to Resist? The Restraining Effect of Military Alliances," *International Organization*, 68, no. 4 (Fall 2014), 775–810; and Beckley, "The Myth of Entangling Alliances."

39. "Minutes of Discussion, President Eisenhower and President Rhee, July 27, 1954," in *FRUS, 1952–1954, Korea*, vol. 15, part 2, 1839–1847.

40. Morrow, "Alliances and Asymmetry," 904–33; Morrow, "Arms versus Allies: Trade-Offs in the Search for Security," *International Organization*, 47, no. 2 (Spring 1993), 207–33; Michael Altfeld, "The Decision to Ally: A Theory and Test," *Western Political Science Quarterly*, 37, no. 4 (December 1984), 523–44; Clifton Morgan, "A Spatial Model of Crisis Bargaining," *International Studies Quarterly*, 28, no. 4 (December 1984), 407–26; and Paul Schroeder, "Alliances, 1815–1945: Weapons of Power and Tools of Management," in *Historical Dimensions of National Security Problems*, ed. Klaus Knorr (Lawrence: University Press of Kansas, 1976).

41. "The cost of forming a new alliance or increasing the commitment in an existing alliance increases with the conflicting interests between the parties. Either or both parties must modify their positions on those conflicts to make the alliance credible" (Morrow, "Arms Versus Allies," 215).

42. Schroeder, "Alliances, 1815–1945," 242.

43. For a concurring argument that wide power asymmetries affect the choice of bilateral versus regional or multilateral cooperation, see Press-Barnathan, *Organizing the World*, 29–31. Also see Morrow, "Alliances and Asymmetry."

44. The work on alliances as instruments of control is quite undertheorized. Initial efforts were made by Schroeder, "Alliances, 1815–1945"; Liska, *Nations in Alliance*; and Schweller, *Deadly Imbalances*; and James Morrow, "Alliances: Why Write Them Down?" *Annual Review of Political Science*, 3, no.1 (2000), 63–83. These works note the restraint aspect of alliances, but do not deduce specific propositions about (1) when control is most likely to be a critical rationale of alliance formation; and (2) whether such control is best exercised through bilateral or multilateral alliances.

45. Snyder, *Alliance Politics*; and Gene Gerzhoy, "Alliance Coercion and Nuclear Restraint: How the United States Thwarted West Germany's Nuclear Ambitions," *International Security*, 39, no. 4 (Spring 2015), 95.

46. William Wohlforth, "The Stability of a Unipolar World," *International Security*, 24, no. 1 (Summer 1999), 5–41; and Wohlforth, "Unipolarity, Status Competition, and Great Power War," in G. John Ikenberry, Michael Mastanduno, and William Wohlforth, eds., *International Relations Theory and the Consequences of Unipolarity* (New York: Cambridge University Press, 2011), 33–66.

47. On soft balancing, see Stephen Walt, *Taming American Power*; Kai He and Huiyun Feng, "If no Soft Balancing, then What? Reconsidering Soft Balancing and US Policy toward China," *Security Studies* 17, no. 2 (April-June 2008), 363–95; ThazhaVarkey Paul, "Soft Balancing in an Age of US Primacy," *International Security*, 30, no. 1 (July 2005); and Robert Pape, "Soft Balancing against the United States," *International Security*, 30, no. 1 (July 2005), 7–45.

48. G. John Ikenberry, "Is American Multilateralism in Decline?" *Perspectives on Politics*, 1, no. 3 (September 2003), 534–35; Robert Kagan, "Power and Weakness," *Policy Review*, 111 (June/July 2002), 3–28; Joseph Nye, *The Paradox of American Power: Why the World's Only Superpower Can't Go It Alone* (New York: Oxford University Press, 2002); Fareed Zakaria, "Our Way: The Trouble with Being the World's Only Superpower," *New Yorker*, 14 (October 2002), 72–81; Daniel Deudney and Ikenberry, "Realism, Structural Liberalism, and the Western Order," in Ethan Kapstein and Michael Mastanduno, eds., *Unipolar Politics: Realism and State Strategies after the Cold War* (New York: Columbia University Press, 1999); John Van Oudenaren, "What Is 'Multilateral'?" *Policy Review*, 117 (February 2003); John Van Oudenaren, "Unipolar versus Unilateral," *Policy Review*, 124 (April 2004); Charles Krauthammer, "The Bush Doctrine: ABM, Kyoto, and the New American Unilateralism," *Weekly Standard*, 4 (June 2001); John Mearsheimer, *The Tragedy of Great Power Politics* (New York: W.W. Norton, 2001); Charles Kupchan, *The End of the American Era: US Foreign Policy and the Geopolitics of the Twenty-First Century* (New York: Knopf, 2002); John Bolton, "Should We Take Global Governance Seriously?" *Chicago Journal of International Law*, 1, no. 2, 205–22; Lisa Martin, "The Rational State Choice of Multilateralism," in John Ruggie, ed., *Multilateralism Matters: The Theory and Praxis of an Institutional Form* (New York: Columbia University Press, 1993), 91–122; Koremenos, Lipson, and Snidal, "The Rational Design of Institutions"; and Jack Snyder, "Imperial Temptations," *National Interest* (Spring 2003), 29–40.

49. G. John Ikenberry, "Is American Multilateralism in Decline?," 534–35; and Joseph Grieco, "Understanding the Problem of International Cooperation: The Limits of Neoliberal Institutionalism and the Future of Realist Theory," in Robert Baldwin, ed., *Neorealism and Neoliberalism* (New York: Columbia University Press, 1993), 301–38.

50. G. John Ikenberry, "Institutions, Strategic Restraint and the Persistence of the American Order," *International Security*, 23, no. 3. (Winter, 1998–1999), 43–78; Alastair Iain Johnston and Robert Ross, eds., *Engaging China: The Management of an Emerging Power* (London: Routledge, 1999).

51. Grieco, "Understanding the Problem of International Cooperation," 331; Ikenberry, "Is American Multilateralism in Decline?" 535; and Albert O. Hirschman, *Exit, Voice and Loyalty: Responses to Decline in Firms, Organizations, and States* (Cambridge, MA: Harvard University Press, 1970).

52. Pressman, *Warring Friends*, 36–40. After the Arab summit framework unwound in 1965, Egypt attempted to contro! Syria through a direct bilateral alliance which ultimately failed to prevent conflict with Israel.

53. Wohlforth, "The Stability of a Unipolar World"; Steve Weber, *Multilateralism in NATO, Shaping the Postwar Balance 1945–1961* (Berkeley: University of California Press, 1991); Crone, "Does Hegemony Matter?"; Miles Kahler, "Institution-Building in the Pacific," in *Pacific Cooperation: Building Economic and Security Regimes in the Asia-Pacific Region* (Boulder, CO: Westview, 1996); Davis Bobrow, "Hegemony Management: The US in the Asia-Pacific," *Pacific Review*, 12, no. 2 (1999), 173–97; and Mattes, "Reputation, Symmetry, and Alliance Design," 689–90.

54. Robert Kagan, "Power and Weakness," *Policy Review*, 113 (June 2002), 3–28.

55. Kent Calder, *Pacific Defense: Arms, Energy, and America's Future in Asia* (New York: Morrow, 1996), 194.

56. For further elaboration on these cases, see Schroeder, "Alliances, 1815–1945," 233, 236–37, 241.

57. This has been China's position particularly after the financial crisis in 2008, seeking to avoid being tied down by ASEAN and EAS.

58. Kagan, "Power and Weakness"; Kurt Campbell, "America's Asia Strategy During the Bush Administration," in Michael Armacost and Dan Okimoto, eds., *The Future of America's Alliances in Northeast Asia* (Stanford, CA: APARC, 2004), 6; Robert Jervis, "Explaining the Bush Doctrine," *Political Science Quarterly*, 118, no. 3 (Fall 2003), 365–88; and Ikenberry, "Is American Multilateralism in Decline."

59. The follow-on question here of what alliance regime types are most conducive to control is beyond the scope of this study. The findings from a number of large-N studies of alliance formation and commitment suggest that alliances between large and small states where both are democracies are likely to be ones where control is most effectively exercised, particularly if the controls are embedded in the alliance contract. This proposition rests largely on the notion advanced in this literature that democracies tend to make credible alliance commitments and are less likely to break them. See Kurt Gaubatz, "Democratic States and Commitment in International Relations," *International Organization*, 50, no. 1 (Winter 1996), 109–39; James

Fearon, "Domestic Political Audiences and the Escalation of International Disputes," *American Political Science Review*, 88, no. 3 (1994), 577–92; Brett Ashley Leeds, "Domestic Political Institutions, Credible Commitments, and International Cooperation," *American Journal of Political Science*, 43, no. 4, 979–1002; Brian Lai and Dan Reiter, "Democracy, Political Similarity, and International Alliances, 1816–1992," *Journal of Conflict Resolution*, 44, no. 2 (April 2000), 203–27; Randolph Siverson and Juliann Emmons, "Birds of a Feather: Democratic Political Systems and Alliance Choices," *Journal of Conflict Resolution*, 35, no. 2 (June 1991), 285–306; Brett Ashley Leeds, "Alliance Reliability in Times of War: Explaining State Decisions to Violate Treaties" *International Organization*, 57, no. 4 (Fall 2003), 801–28; and D. Scott Bennett, "Testing Alternative Models of Alliance Duration, 1816–1984," *American Journal of Political Science*, 41, no. 3 (July 1997), 846–78.

60. Stephen David, "Explaining Third World Alignment," *World Politics*, 43, no. 2 (January 1991).

61. The objective of seeking access to strategic resources is substantively different as a control objective of alliances than seeking security through a defense commitment from the other (smaller) ally.

62. For this and the previous Metternich example, see Schroeder, "Alliances, 1815–1945," 232, 234.

63. Ibid., 243.

64. This strategy does not necessarily eliminate entrapment fears of the larger power. It merely represents a more effective means of minimizing entrapment fears by increasing control. There is no denying that once the larger power chooses this strategy, an ensuing battle of bargaining leverages is likely to take place. The smaller power, knowing the larger one is even more committed than before, may seek to manipulate the larger power. On the other hand, the larger power's leverage has also been enhanced by the additional commitments the smaller party now enjoys (and could lose). On leverage in patron-client relations, see Douglas J. MacDonald, *Adventures in Chaos: American Intervention for Reform in the Third World* (Cambridge, MA: Harvard University Press, 1992). Thanks to Bob Jervis for this cite and for discussions on these points.

65. Koremenos, Lipson, and Snidal, "The Rational Design of International Institutions." Also see Peter Rosendorff and Helen Milner, "The Optimal Design of International Trade Institutions: Uncertainty and Escape," *International Organization*, 55, no. 4 (November 2001), 829–57; Brian Rathbun, "Before Hegemony: Generalized Trust and the Creation and Design of International Security Organizations," *International Organization*, 65, no. 2 (Spring 2011), 243–76; and Mark Copelovitch and Tonya Putnam, "Design in Context: Existing International Agreements and New Cooperation," *International Organization*, 68, no. 2 (Spring 2014), 471–93.

66. Complicated bargaining leverage factors deserve mention here. If patron A makes these additional commitments and B knows that patron A is "locked in" (obligated to intervene on B's behalf), then bargaining leverage may go to B and control by A may be harder to implement. But if patron A makes

the additional commitment, but still leaves ambiguous to B that it is obligated to intervene on B's behalf (i.e., it hedges conditional commitments to the ally and unconditional ones to the adversary), then A's leverage and control over B could be enhanced through the additional commitments.

67. The exception of a small power with intense entrapment fears but without the resources to employ a control strategy is depicted in quadrant IV.

68. See Pressman, *Warring Friends*, 116; and Wade Boese, "Israel Halts Chinese Phalcon Deal," *Arms Control Today* (September 1, 2000), https://www.armscontrol.org/act/2000_09/israelsept00 (accessed January 20, 2016). This case is discussed further in chapter 8.

69. Snyder, "The Security Dilemma in Alliance Politics."

70. For an excellent and innovative theoretical study of the impact of alliance and adversary signaling during the early Cold War in Asia and the effectiveness of deterrence, see Thomas Christensen, *Worse than a Monolith: Alliance Politics and Problems of Coercive Diplomacy in Asia* (Princeton, NJ: Princeton University Press, 2011). On alliances and war expansion, also see Randolph Siverson and Joel King, "Alliances and the Expansion of War," in J. David Singer and Michael D. Wallace, eds., *To Augur Well: Early Warning Indicators in World Politics* (Beverly Hills, CA: Sage, 1979), 37–49.

71. Gelpi, "Alliances as Instruments of Intra-Allied Control."

72. The data are drawn from the International Crisis Behavior (ICB) dataset. For how Gelpi derives the set, see ibid., 121–23.

73. Gelpi finds that a state with equal ties to the two disputants and no alliance with others is successful at mediating behavior 31 percent of the time. But if the state shares a defense pact with one of those disputants, then it is successful 81 percent of the time (ibid., 132).

74. Ibid., 132–34.

75. Mattes, "Reputation, Symmetry, and Alliance Design," 690–92.

76. Ibid., 701: In her words, "Thus, while military institutionalization in symmetric alliances is at least in part the result of an attempt to mitigate enforcement problems, in asymmetric alliances it likely reflects the major power's attempt to control the minor power."

77. Songying Fang, Jesse C. Johnson, and Brett Ashley Leeds, "To Concede or to Resist? The Restraining Effect of Military Alliances," *International Organization*, 68, no. 4 (Fall 2014), 775–810.

78. Fang, Johnson, and Leeds, "To Concede or to Resist?" 792–800.

79. Beckley, "The Myth of Entangling Alliances."

80. Celeste Wallander and Robert O. Keohane, "Risk, Threat, and Security Institutions," in Haftendorn, Keohane, and Wallander, *Imperfect Unions: Security Institutions over Time and Space* (New York: Oxford University Press, 1999), 21–46.

81. Daniel Nexon and Thomas Wright, "What's at Stake in the American Empire Debate," *American Political Science Review*, 101, no. 2 (May 2007), 253–71; G. John Ikenberry, Michael Mastanduno, and William C. Wohlforth, eds., *International Relations Theory and the Consequences of Unipolarity* (New York: Cambridge University Press, 2011); Peter Katzenstein, *A World of Regions: Asia and Europe in the American Imperium* (Ithaca, NY: Cornell

University Press, 2006); Samuel Huntington, "The Lonely Superpower," *Foreign Affairs*, 78, no. 2 (March/April 1999), 35–49; Charles Maier, *Among Empires: American Ascendancy and its Predecessors* (Cambridge, MA: Harvard University Press, 2006); Niall Ferguson, *Colossus: The Price of America's Empires* (New York: Penguin, 2004); and Chalmers Johnson, *The Sorrows of Empire: Militarism, Secrecy, and the End of the Republic* (New York: Metropolitan Books, 2004).

82. William Wohlforth, "The Stability of a Unipolar World," *International Security*, 24, no. 1 (Summer 1999), 5–41.

83. Miles Kahler, ed., *Networked Politics: Agency, Power and Governance* (Ithaca, NY: Cornell University Press, 2009); Emilie Hafner-Burton, Miles Kahler, and Alexander H. Montgomery, "Network Analysis for International Relations," *International Organization*, 63, no. 3 (Summer 2009), 559–92; Stephen Borgatti and Daniel S. Halgin, "On Network Theory," *Organization Science*, 22, no. 5 (2011), 1168–81; Charles Kadushin, *Understanding Social Networks: Theories, Concepts, and Findings* (New York: Oxford University Press, 2012); Barry Wellman and S. D. Berkowitz, eds., *Social Structures: A Network Approach* (New York: Cambridge University Press, 1998); Charli Carpenter, "Vetting the Advocacy Agenda: Network Centrality and the Paradox of Weapons Norms," *International Organization*, 65, no. 1 (Winter 2011), 69–102; Stacie Goddard, "Brokering Change: Networks and Entrepreneurs in International Politics," *International Theory*, 1, no. 2 (July 2009), 249–81; and Ruth Oldenziel, "Islands: The United States as a Networked Empire," in Gabrielle Hecht, ed., *Entangled Geographies: Empire and Technopolitics in the Global Cold War* (Cambridge, MA: MIT Press, 2011), 13–42.

84. Ikenberry, "Liberal Sources of American Unipolarity," in Ikenberry, Mastanduno, and Wohlforth, eds., *International Relations Theory and the Consequences of Unipolarity*," 219.

85. The Grand Central Station reference is Ikenberry's (217).

86. Ikenberry, "Liberal Sources of American Unipolarity," in Ikenberry, Mastanduno, and Wohlforth, eds., *International Relations Theory and the Consequences of Unipolarity*, 222.

Chapter 3

1. A. Whitney Griswold, *The Far Eastern Policy of the United States* (New York: Harcourt Brace and Company, 1938), 7.

2. Robert Jervis, "The Impact of the Korean War on the Cold War," *Journal of Conflict Resolution*, 24, no. 4 (December 1980), 563–92.

3. For a concise description of Truman's transformation into a "cold warrior," see Thomas J. Christensen, *Useful Adversaries: Grand Strategy, Domestic Mobilization, and Sino-American Conflict, 1947–1958* (Princeton, NJ: Princeton University Press, 1996), 33–36.

4. Jervis, "The Impact of the Korean War on the Cold War," 568.

5. For a view on how US security policies in Europe were characterized by a mix of uncertainty and incoherence in the 1947 to 1950 period, see Jervis, "The Impact of the Korean War on the Cold War."

6. Christensen, *Useful Adversaries*, 36.

7. Philip Zelikow, "American Engagement in Asia," in Robert D. Blackwill and Paul Dibb, eds., *America's Asian Alliances* (Cambridge, MA: MIT Press, 2000), 23.

8. Quoted in Melvyn Leffler, *A Preponderance of Power: National Security, the Truman Administration, and the Cold War* (Stanford, CA: Stanford University Press, 1992), 277.

9. Waldo Heinrichs, "American China Policy and the Cold War in Asia: A New Look," in Dorothy Borg and Waldo Heinrichs, eds., *Uncertain Years: Chinese-American Relations, 1947–1950* (New York: Columbia University Press, 1980), 282.

10. Ibid.

11. Warren I. Cohen, "Acheson, His Advisors, and China 1949–1950," in Dorothy Borg and Waldo Heinrichs, eds., *Uncertain Years: Chinese-American Relations, 1947–1950* (New York: Columbia University Press, 1980), 16–17.

12. Dean Acheson, *Present at Creation* (New York: W.W. Norton, 1969), 305–7.

13. The story is recounted in Robert Blum, *Drawing the Line: The Origin of the American Containment Policy in East Asia* (New York: Norton, 1982), 41.

14. Warren I. Cohen, "Acheson, His Advisors, and China 1949–1950," in Dorothy Borg and Waldo Heinrichs, eds., *Uncertain Years: Chinese-American Relations, 1947–1950* (New York: Columbia University Press, 1980), 16–17.

15. Blum, *Drawing the Line*, 66.

16. Dean Acheson, "Crisis in Asia—an Examination of United States Policy," *Department of State Bulletin*, 22 (January 23, 1950), 116. The speech was delivered at the National Press Club in Washington, DC, on January 12, 1950.

17. Or, as General Matthew Ridgway—who would succeed Douglas MacArthur in the war effort on the peninsula—explained in his memoirs, "[I]t is a gross and misleading simplification to lay the blame for the outbreak of the Korean War upon Dean Acheson's 'writing off' of Korea as beyond our defense perimeter. He was merely voicing an already accepted United States policy. Korea had always been outside our defense perimeter and we had written her off several times in the history of our dealings with her." See Matthew Ridgway, *The Korean War: How We Met the Challenge. How All-Out Asian War Was Avoided. Why MacArthur Was Dismissed. Why Today's War Objectives Must Be Limited* (New York: Doubleday, 1967), 10.

18. Marshall especially relied on Kennan. Acheson generally consulted with the policy planning staff less than his predecessor, held some substantively different views than Kennan (e.g., on Germany), and therefore did not anoint Kennan the way Marshall did, but Kennan's early postwar views on Asia remained influential in the formulation of US strategy. See Paul Heer, "George F. Kennan and US Foreign Policy in East Asia," PhD dissertation, George Washington University, May 14, 1995, 63–69.

19. X (George F. Kennan), "The Sources of Soviet Conduct," *Foreign Affairs*, 25, no. 4 (July 1947), 575.

20. Heer, "George F. Kennan and US Foreign Policy in East Asia," ch. 1; Blum, *Drawing the Line*, 15–16.

21. "George Kennan to Secretary of State Marshall, March 14, 1948," in *FRUS, 1948, General; the United Nations*, vol. 1, part 1, 531.

22. John Lewis Gaddis, "Was the Truman Doctrine a Real Turning Point?" *Foreign Affairs*, 52, no. 1 (January 1974), 391–92; and Gaddis, "The Strategic Perspective: The Rise and Fall of the Defense Perimeter Concept, 1947–1951," in Borg and Heinrichs, eds., *Uncertain Years: Chinese-American Relations, 1947–1950* (New York: Columbia University Press, 1980), 67.

23. Though I talk about Formosa in a historical context, from here I shall refer to it as "Taiwan."

24. Capie, "Power, Identity, and Multilateralism," 100.

25. Kennan Naval War College Lecture, October 11, 1948 as cited in Gaddis, "The Strategic Perspective," 68.

26. George Kennan, *Memoirs, 1925–1950* (New York: Pantheon, 1967), 374.

27. Ibid., 374–75.

28. *Kennan Papers*, 16 November 29, 1948, Box 23 as cited in Heer, "George F. Kennan," 48–49.

29. Gaddis, "The Strategic Perspective," 72–73.

30. JSPC 877/72, "The Impact of Current Far Eastern Developments on Emergency War Planning," September 14, 1949, Army Staff Records, P&O 1949–50 381 TS, sec. 3 case 56 as cited in Gaddis, "The Strategic Perspective," 74.

31. Blum, *Drawing the Line*, 71.

32. "A Report to the President by the National Security Council, NSC 48/2, 30 December 1949," in *FRUS, 1949, The Far East and Australasia*, vol. 7, 1219–20.

33. Gaddis, "The Strategic Perspective," 65–66.

34. Deborah Larsen, *Origins of Containment: A Psychological Explanation* (Princeton, NJ: Princeton University Press, 1985), 227.

35. Poll results cited in Christensen, *Useful Adversaries*, 122–23.

36. Leffler, *A Preponderance of Power*, 304.

37. Ridgeway, *The Korean War*, 11.

38. Thomas Christensen, *Useful Adversaries: Grand Strategy, Domestic Mobilization, and Sino-American Conflict 1947–1958* (Princeton, NJ: Princeton University Press, 1996), 8; Jervis, "The Impact of the Korean War on the Cold War," 568; and Leffler, *A Preponderance of Power*, 260–63.

39. Christensen, *Worse than a Monolith*, 29.

40. Kennan, *Memoirs*, 381.

41. "Joint Chiefs of Staff to Forrestal, 2 November 1948, in NSC 35, 'Existing Commitments Involving the Possible Use of Armed Forces,' November 17, 1948," in *FRUS, 1948, General; the United Nations*, vol. 1, 661.

42. Ridgway, *The Korean War*, 13.

43. Ibid., 34.

44. Joint Chiefs of Staff to Forrestal, November 2, 1948, as cited in NSC 35, "Existing Commitments Involving the Possible use of Armed Forces, 17 November 1948," in *FRUS, 1948, General; the United Nations*, vol. 1, 661.

45. See Blum, *Drawing the Line*, 147.

46. Heer, "George F. Kennan," 304–5; and Andrew Rotter, *The Path to Vietnam: The Origins of the American Commitment to Southeast Asia* (Ithaca, NY: Cornell University Press 1987).

47. "Memorandum by Mr. Charlton Ogburn, Jr. to the Assistant Secretary of State for Far Eastern Affairs (Rusk), 18 August 1950," in *FRUS, 1950, East Asia and the Pacific*, vol. 6, 863.

48. Kennan, *Memoirs*, 368. It should be noted that these resource constraints also permeated the discussion of NATO. Gaining support for it in Congress was no small feat as both John Foster Dulles and Senator Vandenberg advised Secretary Marshall in 1948 (see "Memorandum of Conversation by the Undersecretary of State (Lovett), 27 April 1948," in *FRUS, 1948, Western Europe*, vol. 3, 104–8).

49. NSC 48/1, December 23, 1949, Pentagon Papers, vol. 8, 256–37, as cited in Gaddis, "The Strategic Perspective," 73–77.

50. Christensen goes on to show how these perceptions created bizarrely different conclusions by Mao and Stalin about US resolve that eventually allowed Kim Il-sung to manipulate agreement from both to go to war. See Christensen, *Worse than a Monolith*, 45, 86–88.

51. Gaddis, "The Strategic Perspective," 75–76.

52. Quoted in Christensen, *Worse than a Monolith*, 89.

53. Cited in Gaddis, "The Strategic Perspective," 113–14, n.150.

54. Quoted in Blum, *Drawing the Line*, 168.

55. "Memorandum by Mr. Charlton Ogburn, Jr. to the Assistant Secretary of State for Far Eastern Affairs (Rusk), 18 August 18, 1950," in *FRUS, 1950, East Asia and the Pacific*, vol. 6, 863.

56. See Christensen, *Useful Adversaries*, 183.

57. Jervis, "The Impact of the Korean War on the Cold War," 572.

58. US Central Intelligence Agency, *Consequences of US Troop Withdrawal from Korea in Spring 1949*, 28 February 1949. http://www.foia.cia.gov/Korean War /EstimatesMisc/NIEEstmates/1949–02.28.pdf, cited in Jonathan Mercer, "Emotion and Strategy in the Korean War," *International Organization*, 67, no. 2 (Spring 2013), 231.

59. Gaddis, "The Strategic Perspective," 102–3.

60. Heer, "George F. Kennan," 233–34.

61. These views initially were incorporated into NSC-8 (April 1948) which called for the handing over of the Korean problem to the UN. See Heer, "George F. Kennan," 236.

62. The United States initially placed forces in Korea at the end of World War II under General John Hodge largely to prevent the Soviets from occupying the entire peninsula after the Japanese surrender, but had no intention to keep them there when there were severe manpower shortages in Europe. See John Lewis Gaddis, "Korea in American Politics, Strategy, and Diplomacy, 1945–50," in Nagai and Iriye, eds., *Origins of the Cold War in Asia*, 277–78.

63. America's Wars, Department of Veteran Affairs, http://www.va.gov/opa /publications/factsheets/fs_americas_wars.pdf. Stephen Daggett, "Costs of Major US Wars," *Congressional Research Service*, June 29, 2010, http://fas.org /sgp/crs/natsec/RS22926.pdf.

64. William Stueck, *The Road to Confrontation: American Policy Toward Korea and China, 1947–1950* (Chapel Hill: University of North Carolina Press,

1981); and William Stueck, *The Korean War: An International History* (Princeton, NJ: Princeton University Press, 1997).

65. Robert Beisner, *Dean Acheson: A Life in the Cold War* (Oxford, UK: Oxford University Press, 2006), 340. On the emotive nature of the US reaction to the North Korean invasion, see Mercer, "Emotion and Strategy in the Korean War," 232–39.

66. Joint War Planning Committee 476/1, June 16, 1947, JCS Records, 381 USSR (3–2-46) cited in Gaddis, "Korea in American Politics, Strategy, and Diplomacy, 1945–50," 103.

67. Beverly Smith, "The White House Story: Why We Went to War in Korea," *Saturday Evening Post*, November 10, 1951, 83.

68. Philip C. Jessup, *The Birth of Nations* (New York: Columbia University Press, 1974), 10.

69. *Department of State Bulletin*, October 2, 1950, 544.

70. Elsey Papers, Telegram Extract, John Foster Dulles and John Allison to the Secretary of State and Assistant Secretary Rusk, Tokyo, June 25, 1950, at http://www.trumanlibrary.org/whistlestop/study_collections/koreanwar/documents/index.php?documentdate=1950–06–25&documentid=ki-1–6&pagenumber=1 (accessed May 13, 2013).

71. Paige, *The Korean Decision*, 177.

72. Smith, "Why We Went to War in Korea," 82.

73. "Extracts of Memorandum of Conversations, Mr. W. Averell Harriman, Special Assistant to the President with General MacArthur, Tokyo 6 and 8 August 1950," in *FRUS, 1950, East Asia and the Pacific*, vol. 6, 544.

74. Smith, "Why We Went to War in Korea," 82.

75. Elsey Papers, Notes Regarding Meeting with Congressional Leaders, 27 June 1950, at http://www.trumanlibrary.org/whistlestop/study_collections/koreanwar/documents/index.php?documentdate=1950–06–27&documentid=ki-2–40&pagenumber=1, 4 (accessed May 13, 2013).

76. John K. Fairbank, "The Problem of Revolutionary Asia," *Foreign Affairs*, 29, no. 1 (October 1950), 106; and Fairbank, "Toward a Dynamic Far Eastern Policy," *Far Eastern Survey*, 18, no. 18 (September 7, 1949), 209–12.

77. "Kennan memorandum to Acheson, 'Possible Further Communist Initiatives in the Light of the Korean Situation, June 26, 1950,'" *Kennan Papers*, Box 24 as cited in Gaddis, "Korea in American Politics, Strategy, and Diplomacy, 1945–50," 12.

78. "Memorandum by the Joint Chiefs of Staff to the Secretary of Defense (Marshall) 28 November 1950," in *FRUS, 1950, East Asia and the Pacific*, vol. 6, 946.

79. Smith, "Why We Went to War in Korea," 77.

80. James Schnabel and Robert Watson, *The History of the Joint Chiefs of Staff: The Korean War*, vol. 3, part 1 (Wilmington, DE: Scholarly Resources, 1979), 71–72.

81. Gaddis, "The Strategic Perspective," 107.

82. "Dulles to Walter Lippmann, July 13, 1950," *Dulles Papers*, Box 48 cited in Gaddis, "The Strategic Perspective," 107–8.

83. Seung-Young Kim, "American Elites' Strategic Thinking Towards Korea: From Kennan to Brzezinski," *Diplomacy and Statecraft*, 12, no. 1 (March

2001); 193–95; and Paul Nitze, *From Hiroshima to Glasnost: At the Centre of Decision, A Memoir* (New York: Weidenfeld & Nicolson, 1989), 107.

84. Walter L. Hixson, *George F. Kennan: Cold War Iconoclast* (New York: Columbia University Press, 1989), 106; and Kim, "American Elites' Strategic Thinking Towards Korea," 185–212.

85. Leffler, *A Preponderance of Power*, 361–62.

86. Stephen E. Ambrose, *Rise to Globalism: American Foreign Policy since 1938* (Baltimore: Penguin, 1971), 194–95.

87. Gaddis, "Korea in American Politics, Strategy, and Diplomacy, 1945–50," 12.

88. Quoted from Christensen, *Useful Adversaries*, 190–91; also see David Kepley, *The Collapse of the Middle Way: Senate Republicans and Bipartisan Foreign Policy, 1948–52* (New York: Greenwood Press, 1988).

89. In a speech before the Ohio County Women's Republican Club in Wheeling, West Virginia in February 1951, junior senator McCarthy charged the State Department with harboring communist "pink cells" who were influencing America's China policy. See Blum, *Drawing the Line*, 181–84.

90. Tucker, "Nationalist China's Decline," 165–67; and Keohane, "The Big Influence," 179.

91. Though most advisors had shifted to support of rollback after the Incheon landing, Kennan, though he was no longer in the government, expressed grave concerns about the rollback views being supported by the State Department and told Dean Acheson of his frustration about the strategic risks of what he deemed a highly emotional and moralistic decision. See Heer, "George F. Kennan," 106–7. Kennan's views on Korea later shifted. After the Chinese intervention, he opposed those who called for US withdrawal on the grounds that American credibility was at stake. After the battlefield stalemate became apparent in 1951, he shifted to calling for US withdrawal. These shifts, however, underscore a consistency in Kennan's view that the United States should be minimally engaged on the peninsula to avoid sapping US resources.

92. Christopher Twomey, *The Military Lens: Doctrinal Difference and Deterrence Failure in Sino-American Relations* (Ithaca, NY: Cornell University Press, 2010), ch. 4.

93. Cumings, *Origins*, volume 2, 710.

94. Leffler, *A Preponderance of Power*, 396.

95. "Memorandum by the Joint Chiefs of Staff to the Secretary of Defense (Marshall), 28 November 1950," in *FRUS, 1950, East Asia and the Pacific*, vol. 6, 946.

96. Leading among the strategists calling for such change when the battlefield situation had stalemated was John Foster Dulles, who initially pressed for rollback during the Truman administration but switched under President Eisenhower to advocating containment over rollback (Cumings, *Origins*, vol. 2, 708; and Heer, "George F. Kennan," 273–74).

97. See the discussion in Christensen, *Useful Adversaries*, 181–93.

98. Harry Truman, "Address to the Nation, 11 April 1951," [Speech Text] in *Dulles Papers*, "Duplicate Correspondence," Box 56, 5 pages.

Chapter 4

1. See Heer, "George F. Kennan," ch. 1; Christensen, *Useful Adversaries*, 59–66; and Gaddis, *Strategies of Containment*, 41–52.
2. Department of State, *United States Relations with China, With Special Reference to the Period 1944–1949*, Publication no. 3573, Far Eastern Series, 30 (Washington, DC: Government Printing Office, 1949); also see Nancy Bernkopf Tucker, *Taiwan, Hong Kong, and the United States, 1945–1992* (New York: Twayne Publishers, 1994), 24. For the negative reactions by Congress and the public, see Christensen, *Useful Adversaries*, 96–97, and Blum, *Drawing the Line*, 94–95.
3. See Heer, "George F. Kennan," ch. 1; and Blum, *Drawing the Line*, 39–41.
4. Warren Cohen, "Acheson, His Advisors, and China, 1949–1950," in Dorothy Borg and Waldo Heinrichs, eds., *Uncertain Years: Chinese-American Relations, 1947–1950* (New York: Columbia University Press, 1980), 13–14; and Goldstein, *The United States and the Republic of China*, 6.
5. Christensen, *Useful Adversaries*, 82.
6. Ibid., 138.
7. The CIA memo of 19 October 1949 was titled, "Survival Potential of Residual Non-Communist Regimes in China," as cited in Blum, *Drawing the Line*, 173.
8. See discussion in Christensen, *Useful Adversaries*, 100–5. US interest undeniably was dampened by the hard line taken by Mao through 1949, which was the requirement of a complete break in relations with the KMT and no additional concessions (as suggested by Stalin). See Christensen, *Worse than a Monolith*, 44.
9. Some in the US government argued that the strategic value of Taiwan increased after the Sino-Soviet treaty of 1950, but Christensen states that there is little evidence of this in the archives, at least until after the Korean War. See Christensen, *Worse than a Monolith*, 33; also see Blum, *Drawing the Line*, 192.
10. Quoted in Blum, *Drawing the Line*, 191 and 40, respectively.
11. Cited in Christensen, *Useful Adversaries*, 121.
12. Blum, *Drawing the Line*, 9.
13. Heer, "George F. Kennan," 10; and Cohen, "Acheson, His Advisors, and China," 15.
14. Policy planning paper, "Review of Current Trends: US Foreign Policy," as quoted in Heer, "George F. Kennan," 34. Kennan's views on Taiwan changed in mid-1949 to one of considering a commitment, which many historians see as a strange twist in his thinking likely related to the CCP victory, the ambiguity of the US position, and his own impending departure from policy planning. See Heer, "George F. Kennan," 80–84.
15. "Transcript of Presentation" by Kennan at "Q" Building, 14 October 1949, *Kennan Papers*, Box 17, as cited in Heer, "George F. Kennan," 87.
16. Cohen, "Acheson, His Advisors, and China," 49.
17. See Christensen, *Useful Adversaries*, 109 for the quote. Also see A. Doak Barnett, *China and the Major Powers in East Asia* (Washington, DC: Brookings

Institution, 1977), 176; Clough, *Island China*, 7; and Peter Van Ness, "Taiwan and Sino-American Relations," in Michel Oksenberg and Robert Oxnam, eds., *Dragon and Eagle* (New York: Basic, 1973), 264; and Tucker, *Taiwan, Hong Kong and the United States*, 30. On MacArthur's leaking of the State Department memo, see Blum, *Drawing the Line*, 179.

18. *Presidential Papers of the United States: Harry S. Truman, 1950* (Washington, DC: Government Printing Office, 1965), 11–12; and Gaddis, "The Strategic Perspective," 83–84.

19. "Memorandum of Conversation, by the Secretary of State, January 5, 1950," in *FRUS, 1950, East Asia and the Pacific*, vol. 6, 258–63; and Cohen, "Acheson, His Advisors, and China," 30.

20. Tucker, *Taiwan, Hong Kong and the United States*, 32.

21. Blum, *Drawing the Line*, 215.

22. "NSC 48/5 United States Objectives, Policy and Courses of Action in Asia, May 17, 1951," in *FRUS, 1951, East Asia and the Pacific*, vol. 6, part 1, 41. These internal US government assessments did not surface before the North Korean invasion, which spoke volumes to the high-level policy ambivalence on deeply engaging in Asia prior to June 1950.

23. For the argument of how the Korean conflict made Taiwan strategically more valuable to the United States, see David Finkelstein, *Washington's Taiwan Dilemma, 1949–1950: From Abandonment to Salvation* (Fairfax, VA: George Mason University Press, 1993). For the novel view that Korea made Taiwan important in an instrumental rather than strategic sense, see Christensen, *Useful Adversaries*, 133–37. Christensen argues that the administration's continued ambivalence regarding support for Taiwan in the face of the 1949 revolution and the 1950 Korean communist invasion would have severely hampered Truman's efforts to garner congressional and public backing of massive increases in military support for Korea and most importantly for Europe. Thus, the issue was not that Korea changed US policy on Taiwan, but that support for Taiwan became necessary to expand defense commitments to Korea (and Europe) in the face of the North Korean invasion.

24. "NSC 48/5 United States Objectives, Policy and Courses of Action in Asia, May 17, 1951," *in FRUS, 1951, East Asia and the Pacific*, vol. 6, part 1, 55–56; and Gaddis, "The Strategic Perspective," 93.

25. "US Action to Counter Chinese Communist Aggression, Washington, January 17, 1951," in *FRUS, 1951, Korea and China*, vol. 7, part 2, 1515–17; and "The Secretary of State to the Embassy in the Republic of China, Washington, January 20, 1951," in *FRUS, 1951, Korea and China*, vol. 2, part 2, 1521–522.

26. "NSC 48/5 United States Objectives, Policy and Courses of Action in Asia, May 17, 1951," in *FRUS, 1951, East Asia and the Pacific*, vol. 6, part 1, 38–39.

27. See Clough, *Island China*, 10 and Goldstein, "The United States and the Republic of China," 6.

28. See minutes of June 26, 1950 Blair House meeting chaired by President Truman in "Memorandum of Conversation, by the Ambassador at Large (Jessup), Washington, June 26, 1950," in *FRUS, 1950, Korea*, vol. 7, 180; and Glenn D. Paige, *The Korean Decision* (New York: Free Press, 1968), 140.

29. Tucker, *Taiwan, Hong Kong and the United States*, 33.
30. John Garver, *The Sino-American Alliance: Nationalist China and American Cold War Strategy in Asia* (New York: M.E. Sharpe, 1997), 52–53.
31. Ibid., 54–55. A discussion of "unleashing Chiang" under Eisenhower and the purported differences from Truman are discussed later in this chapter.
32. The shelling commenced shortly after the 1954 Geneva conference on Indochina. This was the first international conference attended by the PRC. Although a compromise was reached regarding the temporary division of Vietnam until national elections were held, the Chinese Premier Chou En-lai was offended by US behavior, in particular, Secretary Dulles's unwillingness to shake hands with Chou let alone sign any agreements with the communist regime. See Clough, *Island China*, 10.
33. Goldstein, "The United States and the Republic of China," 12.
34. Ibid., 12, and Tucker, *Taiwan, Hong Kong and the United States*, 54.
35. Blum, *Drawing the Line*, 194.
36. For US discussion of Chiang's offer (and eventual rejection), see "Memorandum by the Deputy Assistant Secretary of State for Far Eastern Affairs (Merchant) to the Secretary of State, June 29, 1950," in *FRUS, 1950, Korea*, vol. 7, 239; "Memorandum of Conversation, by the Acting Deputy Director of the Office of Chinese Affairs, June 30, 1950," in *FRUS, 1950, Korea*, vol. 7, 262–63; and "Secretary of State to the Chinese Ambassador, July 1, 1950," in *FRUS, 1950, Korea*, vol. 7, 276–77.
37. Chiang moreover said he could do this at one-third the cost of US operations in Korea. See "Charge in Republic of China (Jones) to the Department of State, 22 July 1952," in *FRUS, 1952–1954, China and Japan*, vol. 14, 76–77.
38. For example, see "Memorandum Richard E. Johnson of the Office of Chinese Affairs to the Director of That Office (Clubb), 4 June 1951," in *FRUS, 1951, Korea and China*, vol. 7, 1699–1700.
39. Nancy Bernkopf Tucker, "Nationalist China's Decline and Its Impact on Sino-American Relations, 1949–1950," in Dorothy Borg and Waldo Heinrichs, eds., *Uncertain Years: Chinese-American Relations, 1947–1950* (New York: Columbia University Press, 1980), 154–55; and Christensen, *Useful Adversaries*, 119.
40. "Charge in the Republic of China (Jones) to the Department of State, 27 May 1953," in *FRUS, 1952–1954, China and Japan*, vol. 14, 197; and Tucker, *Taiwan, Hong Kong and the United States*, 71.
41. Tucker, *Taiwan, Hong Kong and the United States*, 42.
42. Garver, The *Sino-American Alliance*, 90.
43. Goldstein, "The United States and the Republic of China," 16.
44. Tucker, *Taiwan, Hong Kong, and the United States*, 64. The CIA operated under the cover of a company called Western Enterprises, which provided training, logistics, and materials to carry out flights, dropping leaflets and radio broadcasting into China (ibid.).
45. Ross Y. Koen, *The China Lobby in American Politics* (New York: Macmillan, 1960); and Stanley Bachrack, *The Committee of One Million: "China Lobby" Politics, 1953–1971* (New York: Columbia University Press, 1976).

46. Tucker, "Nationalist China's Decline and its Impact on Sino-American Relations, 1949–1950," 151.
47. For this discussion, see Blum, *Drawing the Line*, 18–23.
48. See Robert P. Newman, "Clandestine Chinese Nationalist Efforts to Punish Their American Detractors," *Diplomatic History*, 7, no. 3 (1983), 205–22; and Tucker, *Taiwan, Hong Kong, and the United States*, 75.
49. Robert Jervis, "What Do We Want to Deter and How Do We Deter it?" in L. Benjamin Ederington and Michael Mazarr, eds., *Turning Point: The Gulf War and US Military Strategy* (Boulder, CO: Westview Press, 1994). Also see Timothy Crawford, *Pivotal Deterrence: Third Party Statecraft and the Pursuit of Peace* (Ithaca, NY: Cornell University Press, 2003).
50. Cohen, "Acheson, His Advisors, and China, 1949–1950," 14; and May, *Truman and China*, 30–32.
51. See Blum, *Drawing the Line*, 28–29.
52. By May 1949, Merchant reported that such an idea was not possible. See NSC 37/2, "The Current Position of the United States with Respect to Formosa, February 3, 1949," in *FRUS, 1949, The Far East: China*, vol. 9, 288–89; and "The Secretary of State to the Ambassador in China (Stuart), February 14, 1949," in *FRUS, 1949, The Far East: China*, vol. 9, 287–88.
53. Blum, *Drawing the Line*, 194.
54. Cohen, "Acheson, His Advisors, and China, 1949–1950," 32.
55. As cited in Cohen, "Acheson, His Advisors, and China, 1949–1950," 48.
56. "The Secretary of State to the Embassy in China, June 27, 1950," in *FRUS, 1950, Korea*, vol. 7, 188.
57. Truman said this in June 26, 1950 Blair House meetings regarding US intervention in Korea (as cited in Paige, *The Korean Decision*, 167–68).
58. *Department of State Bulletin*, July 3, 1950, 5. Also see Truman's statement to Congress on the Korea situation (July 19, 1950) in which he reiterates the point (*Public Papers of the Presidents of the United States: Harry S. Truman, 1950*, 527).
59. "Memorandum of Conversation, Leonard Price of the Office of the Special Assistant for Mutual Security Affairs, 20 February 1952," in *FRUS, 1952–1954, China and Japan*, vol. 14, 13.
60. "Memorandum of Discussion at the 139th Meeting of the National Security Council, Washington, 8 April 1953," in *FRUS, 1952–1954, China and Japan*, vol. 14, 181–82; also see "Charge in the Republic of China (Jones) to the Department of State, 23 April 1953," for the text of the agreement; and "The Chief of the Military Assistance Advisory Group, Formosa (Chase) to the Chief of General Staff, Republic of China (Chow), 5 February 1953," in *FRUS, 1952–1954, China and Japan*, vol. 14, 193, 144–45.
61. "The Joint Chiefs of Staff to the Commander in Chief, Far East (MacArthur), 29 June 1950," in *FRUS, 1950, Korea*, vol. 7, 240–41.
62. Conveyed as an Aide-Memoire through the Chinese embassy to the State Department, the offer was for "[O]ne army [*sic*] of troops of approximately 33,000 men suitable for operations in plains or hilly terrain." Chiang promised these troops would be well-equipped and would provide C-46 transport planes to deliver them within five days. See "The Chinese Embassy to

the Department of State, 20 June 1950," in *FRUS, 1950, Korea*, vol. 7, 262–63. Paige's account argues that Truman was initially supportive of the KMT troop offer, but the unanimous dissent of his advisors at a June 30, 1950 meeting changed the president's mind (Paige, *The Korean Decision*, 249–50, 258–59).

63. Paige, *The Korean Decision*, 249.
64. Bertil Lintner, "The CIA's First Secret War: Americans Helped Stage Raids into China from Burma," *Far Eastern Economic Review*, September 16, 1993, 56.
65. "Memorandum Assistant Secretary of State for Far Eastern Affairs (Allison) to John Foster Dulles, 24 December 1952," in *FRUS, 1952–1954, China and Japan*, vol. 12, 119.
66. "The Secretary of State to the Chinese Ambassador (Koo), 1 July 1950," in *FRUS, 1950, Korea*, vol. 7, 276–77.
67. See July 3, 1950 discussions between Rusk and Wellington Koo in "Memorandum of Conversation, by the Assistant Secretary of State for Far Eastern Affairs (Rusk), 3 July 1950," in *FRUS, 1950, Korea*, vol. 7, 285–86; and Paige, *The Korean Decision*, 259.
68. "Acheson to Louis Johnson, 31 July 1950," in *FRUS, 1950, East Asia and the Pacific*, vol. 6, 404, 478–80. US policy in the first half of 1950 took a more supportive tone for Taiwan after the appointment of Republican John Foster Dulles as an advisor and the appointment of Dean Rusk as assistant secretary of state for the Far East, both in April. Dulles and Rusk looked for opportunities to work with Defense Secretary Johnson and MacArthur to shore up Taiwan support, but each was acutely aware of the overdependence dangers posed by Chiang.
69. *Public Papers of the Presidents of the United States: Harry S. Truman, 1950*, 527.
70. Cohen, "Acheson, His Advisors, and China, 1949–1950," 42–43; and Gaddis, "The Strategic Perspective," 90.
71. "Extracts of Memorandum of Conversations, Mr. W. Averell Harriman, Special Assistant to the President with General MacArthur, Tokyo 6 and 8 August 1950," in *FRUS, 1950, East Asia and the Pacific*, vol. 6, 427–30; Garver, *The Sino-American Alliance*, 38–39; and Tucker, *Taiwan, Hong Kong and the United States*, 32–33, 64.
72. Cohen, "Acheson, His Advisors, and China, 1949–1950," 45–48.
73. "The Acting Secretary of State to the Embassy in India, 4 October 1950," in *FRUS, 1950 Korea*, vol. 7, 875–76.
74. Bertil Lintner, "The CIA's First Secret War: Americans Helped Stage Raids into China from Burma," *Far Eastern Economic Review*, September 13, 1993, 56–58; Garver, *The Sino-American Alliance*, 148–49; Richard Gibson and Wenhua Chen, *The Secret Army: Chiang Kai-shek and the Drug Warlords of the Golden Triangle* (Singapore: John Wiley & Sons, 2011); and Bertil Lintner, *Burma in Revolt: Opium and Insurgency Since 1948* (Boulder, CO: Westview, 1994). The CIA operated initially through deliveries of ammunition and weapons from Okinawa and Thailand, but later directly supplied Li's forces in Burma as well as provided technical and communications support. Li was also paid a monthly wage of $9,000 USD.

75. Lintner, "The CIA's First Secret War," 57.

76. Garver, *The Sino-American Alliance*, 151–52.

77. The US ambassador in Rangoon, David Key, who had not been read into the CIA's operation, resigned because of the damage the covert operation had done to US-Burma relations. See Garver, *The Sino-American Alliance*, 152–54, and Lintner, "The CIA's First Secret War," 57.

78. For examples of these instructions to US diplomats, see "Secretary of State to US Embassy in Burma, 22 August 1951," in *FRUS 1951, Asia and the Pacific*, vol. 6, part 1, 289–90; "Ambassador in Burma (Key) to the Secretary of State, 24 September 1951," in *FRUS 1951, Asia and the Pacific*, vol. 6, part 1, 296–97; and "Charge in China (Rankin) to the Secretary of State, 3 October 1951," in *FRUS 1951, Asia and the Pacific*, vol. 6, part 1, 300–301.

79. "Secretary of State to the Embassy in the Republic of China, 19 February 1953," in *FRUS 1952–1954, East Asia and the Pacific*, vol. 12, part 2, 53. Also see "Acting Secretary of State (Dulles) to the Embassy in the Republic of China, 30 January 1953," in *FRUS 1952–1954, East Asia and the Pacific*, vol. 12, part 2, 48–49.

80. For these delicate negotiations, see Karl Rankin, *China Assignment* (Seattle: University of Washington Press, 1964); and Garver, *The Sino-American Alliance*, 155–60.

81. See meeting between ROC Ambassador Koo and Secretary Dulles, "Memorandum of Conversation by the Assistant Secretary of State for Far Eastern Affairs (Allison), March 19, 1953," in *FRUS 1952–1954, China and Japan*, vol. 14, part 1, 159. Also see Tucker, *Taiwan, Hong Kong and the United States*, 64–66. Chiang eventually withdrew the 4,000 troops eight years later in 1961 under strong US pressure (Garver, *The Sino-American Alliance*, ch. 8).

82. Quoted in "Secretary of State to the Embassy in the Republic of China, 4 April 1953," in *FRUS, 1952–1954, East Asia and the Pacific*, vol. 12, part 2, 92–93; also see "Secretary of State to the Embassy in the Republic of China, 28 July 1953," in *FRUS, 1952–1954, East Asia and the Pacific*, vol. 12, part 2, 121–22.

83. "President Eisenhower to President Chiang Kai-shek, 28 September 1953," in *FRUS, 1952–1954, East Asia and the Pacific*, vol. 12, part 2, 152–53; "Secretary of State to the Embassy in the Republic of China," in *FRUS, 1952–1954, East Asia and the Pacific*, vol. 12, part 2, 154–58.

84. Garver, *The Sino-American Alliance*, 160–61.

85. Christensen, *Worse than a Monolith*, 141.

86. "Memorandum of Discussion at the 221st Meeting of the National Security Council, Washington, November 2, 1954," in *FRUS, 1952–1954, China and Japan*, vol. 14, 835. Also see Dulles's remarks in "Memorandum of Discussion at the 214th Meeting of the National Security Council, Denver, September 12, 1954," in *FRUS, 1952–1954, China and Japan*, vol. 14, 613–24.

87. "Memorandum of Discussion at the 221st Meeting of the National Security Council, Washington, November 2, 1954," in *FRUS, 1952–1954, China and Japan*, vol. 14, 831.

88. Or, as Eisenhower recalled some of the letters saying, "Letters to him constantly say what do we care what happens to those yellow people out there?"

See "Memorandum of Discussion at the 214th Meeting of the National Security Council, Denver, September 12, 1954," in *FRUS, 1952–1954, China and Japan*, vol. 14, 621–22.

89. "Memorandum Prepared by the Secretary of State, September 12, 1954," in *FRUS, 1952–1954, China and Japan*, vol. 14, part 1, 611–13; and Garver, *The Sino-American Alliance*, 123–24.

90. Garver, *Sino-American Alliance*, 134–35; and Beckley, "The Myth of Entangling Alliances," 28.

91. For the 1958 crisis, see Allen Whiting, "New Light on Mao; Quemoy 1958: Mao's Miscalculations," *China Quarterly*, 62 (June 1975); and Gordon Chang, *Friends and Enemies: The United States, China, and the Soviet Union, 1948–1972* (Stanford, CA: Stanford University Press, 1990).

92. For example, see "Memorandum by the Regional Planning Adviser in the Bureau of Far Eastern Affairs (Green), 18 September 1958," in *FRUS, 1958–1960 China*, vol. 19, 222.

93. Quoted in Garver, *The Sino-American Alliance*, 139.

94. Republican Party Platforms: "Republican Party Platform of 1952," July 7, 1952. Online by Gerhard Peters and John T. Woolley, *The American Presidency Project*. http://www.presidency.ucsb.edu/ws/?pid=25837

95. Michael S. Mayer, *The Eisenhower Years* (New York: Facts on File, 2009), vii.

96. http://www.eisenhower.archives.gov/all_about_ike/speeches/1953_state_of_the_union.pdf

97. Handcuffs quote comes from *New York Daily News*, "Will Live up to Pledges," June 24, 1953, and second quote comes from *New York Journal American*, "First Energetic Step," February 3, 1953, from "Excerpts From Editorial Comment on President's State of the Union Message," *New York Times* (1923–current file); February 3, 1953; *ProQuest Historical Newspapers: The New York Times (1851–2010)*, 17. The president's announcement on Taiwan headlined most news stories of the speech and became the topic of much commentary and analysis. See, for example, Edward T. Folliard, "Democrats Voice Concern about New Policy toward Formosa: Ike's First Message Praised," *Washington Post*, February 3, 1953; C. P. Trussell, "Congress praises Eisenhower talk: But 7th Fleet Decision Brings Fear of War Extension and Deeper U. S. Involvement," Special to the *New York Times* (1923–current file); February 3, 1953, 1; and William S. White, "Senate Democrats hit Formosa plan: Admiral Radford is urging Eisenhower to blockade Red China," Special to the *New York Times* (1923–current file); February 7, 1953, 1.

98. "Taipeh hails Formosa Policy; Europe, India press unhappy," *Washington Post (1923–1954)*, February 4, 1953, 3; (U) Msg, CINCFE C 56410 to DA for JCS, 29 May 50, CM IN 4359,4444, cited in James F. Schnabel and Robert J. Watson, *The Joint Chiefs of Staff and National Policy, Volume III 1950–1951* (Washington, DC: Office of the Joint History, 1998), p. 18.

99. John D. Caute, *The Great Fear: The Anti-Communist Purge Under Truman and Eisenhower* (London: Secker & Warburg, 1978); and Robert Griffith, *The Politics of Fear: Joseph R. McCarthy and the Senate* (Lexington: University Press of Kentucky, 1970).

100. Robert Accinelli, *Crisis and Commitment: United States Policy toward Taiwan 1950–1955* (Chapel Hill and London: University of North Carolina Press, 1996), ch. 6.
101. "Memorandum of Discussion at the 338th Meeting of the National Security Council, October 2, 1957," in *FRUS, 1955–1957, China*, vol. 3, 614.
102. "Memorandum of Conversation, Assistant Secretary of State for Far Eastern Affairs (Allison) and Ambassador Koo, Chinese Embassy, 2 February 1953," in *FRUS, 1952–1954, China and Japan*, vol. 14, 137–38. For Eisenhower's statement, see "Message From the President to the Congress [Extract], February 2, 1953," in ibid., 140.
103. "Memorandum by the Deputy Under Secretary of State (Matthews) to the Secretary of State, 31 March 1953," in *FRUS, 1952–1954, China and Japan*, vol. 14, 170; and "139th meeting, NSC, 8 April 1953," in *FRUS 1952–1954, China and Japan*, vol. 14, 181.
104. "Secretary of State to the Embassy in the Republic of China, 24 June 1953," in *FRUS, 1952–1954, China and Japan*, vol. 14, 214.
105. Tucker, "John Foster Dulles and the Taiwan Roots of the Two Chinas Policy," in Richard Immerman, ed., *John Foster Dulles and the Diplomacy of the Cold War* (Princeton, NJ: Princeton University Press, 1989), 235–63; and Accinelli, *Crisis and Commitment*, 169–70.
106. "Talking Paper Prepared by Secretary of State Dulles, 21 October 1958," in *FRUS, 1958–1960, China*, vol. 19, 413–17.
107. "Memorandum of Conversation, Secretary of State and Chinese Ambassador-designate George Yeh, 13 September 1958," in *FRUS, 1958–1960, China*, vol. 19, 179–83; and "Memorandum of Conversation Chiang Kai-shek and John Foster Dulles, 21 October 1958," in *FRUS, 1958–1960, China*, vol. 19, 418–19; and "Memorandum of Conversation Secretary's Trip to Rome, England, Alaska, and Taiwan, 22 October 1958," in *FRUS, 1958–1960, China*, vol. 19, 421–23. For the interesting argument that China never intended to escalate the 1958 crisis, seeking instead to manipulate an external crisis short of all-out war as a way to garner domestic support for prosecuting the Great Leap Forward, see Christensen, *Useful Adversaries*, ch. 6.
108. "Telegram From the Department of State (Dulles) to the Embassy in the Republic of China (Drumright), 1 October 1958," in *FRUS, 1958–1960, China*, vol. 19, 315–16.
109. "Memorandum of Conversation [Between Chiang Kai-shek and Ambassador Alan Kirk], September 6, 1962," in *FRUS, 1961–1963, Northeast Asia*, vol. 22, 311.
110. Goldstein, "The United States and the Republic of China," 11. Or, as Garver wrote, "US leaders feared that once the United States was obligated by treaty to come to Taiwan's assistance, Taipei might provoke a conflict with the PRC by initiating large-scale offensive operations against the mainland or by stationing large concentrations on Jinmen and Mazu thereby triggering a Communist attack against those islands. To prevent this, US representatives insisted that Taipei agree that all Nationalist military actions against the mainland be initiated only after joint consultations and US consent." See Garver, *The Sino-American Alliance*, 57.

111. For NSC 146/2, see "United States Objectives and Courses of Action with Respect to Formosa and the Chinese Nationalist Government, 6 November 1953," in *FRUS, 1952–1954, China and Japan*, vol. 14, 307–11, especially p. 309. Also see the attached NSC Staff study in support of NSC 146/2, in ibid., 311–30. Additional internal NSC documents stated more directly, "Conclude a Mutual Defense Treaty with the Republic of China covering Formosa and the Pescadores , together with appropriate safeguards against Chinese nationalist offensive action . . . refrain from assisting or encouraging offensive actions against Communist China, and restrain the Chinese nationalists from such actions" ("Draft Statement of Policy, Prepared by the NSC Planning Board/NSC 5429/3, 19 November 1954," in *FRUS 1952–54, China and Japan*, vol. 14, 913).

112. Though Robertson played the heavy in the negotiations, he personally favored bolstering Taiwan's capabilities. For the treaty negotiations see "Memorandum of Conversation by the Director of the Office of Chinese Affairs (McConaughy), 16 November 1954," in *FRUS, 1952–1954, China and Japan*, vol. 14, 906; "Memorandum of Conversation by the Director of the Office of Chinese Affairs (McConaughy), 22 November 1954," in *FRUS, 1952–1954, China and Japan*, vol. 14, 921–22; and "Memorandum of Conversation by the Director of the Office of Chinese Affairs (McConaughy), 23 November 1954," in *FRUS, 1952–1954, China and Japan*, vol. 14, 927–28.

113. *United States Treaties and Other International Agreements*, vol. 6, part 1 (Washington, DC: USGPO, 1956), 454.

114. Christensen, *Worse than a Monolith*, 143.

115. Dulles's exchange with Senator Fulbright during his February 1955 testimony on the treaty is indicative. See *Executive Sessions of the Senate Foreign Relations Committee (Historical Series). Vol. VII, 309–380, Hearings before the United States Senate Committee on Foreign Relations, and Senate Committee on Armed Services, Eighty-Fourth Congress, first session* (Washington, DC: USGPO, 1978), 321–26.

116. A. Doak Barnett, *China and the Major Powers in East Asia* (Washington, DC: Brookings Institution, 1977), 185; Clough, *Island China*, 12.

117. "Memorandum by the Secretary of State to the President, 23 November 1954," in *FRUS, 1952–1954, China and Japan*, vol. 14, 929.

118. John Foster Dulles, "Statement before Senate Foreign Relations Committee, 7 February 1955," in *State Department Bulletin*, February 21, 1955, 289.

119. Goldstein, "The United States and the Republic of China," 10.

120. Ibid., 13.

121. These numbers refer to the period from 1954 to 1963; see David Chang, "US Aid and Economic Progress in Taiwan," *Asian Survey*, 5, no. 3 (March 1965), 152–53; and Tucker, *Taiwan, Hong Kong and the United States, 1945–1992*, 57–60.

122. For internal US communications between US Pacific Command and the Military Assistance Advisory Group in Taiwan on the specific guidelines and restrictions on Taiwanese military actions (e.g., no attacking PRC vessels in port, civilians; and no actions beyond neutralization of mainland artillery attacks), see "Memorandum by Gerald Stryker of the Office of

Chinese Affairs to the Deputy Director of That Office (Martin), September 22, 1954," in *FRUS, 1952–1954, China and Japan*, vol. 14, 655–58.

123. See, for example, "Telegram from the Embassy in the Republic of China to the Department of State, 12 October 1958," in *FRUS 1958–1960, China*, vol. 19, 374; and "Memorandum for the Record [Presidential Conference on Taiwan], May 29, 1962," in *FRUS 1961–1963, Northeast Asia*, vol. 22, 239–40.

124. Goldstein, "The United States and the Republic of China," 14; and Garver, *The Sino-American Alliance*, 68.

125. For example, see "Memorandum to the Chief of the Central Intelligence Agency Station in Taipei, March 31, 1962," in *FRUS, 1961–1963, Northeast Asia*, vol. 22, 206–7; and "Memorandum of Conversation, 13 September 1958," in *FRUS 1958–1960, China*, vol. 19, 179–83.

126. Goldstein, "The United States and the Republic of China," 15; and "Memorandum of Discussion at the 139th Meeting of the National Security Council, 8 April 1953," in *FRUS 1952–1954, China and Japan*, vol. 14, 180–81.

127. "In any event, in view of the fact that use of force by either party affects the other, we would expect that regardless of the gravity and emergency nature of the situation, the GRC would consult the United States to the maximum extent feasibly before taking retaliatory action against CHICOM positions or forces on the mainland." Dwight D. Eisenhower: office files 1953–1961 Pent 2, International series: Formosa 1952–57 (1) "The Taiwan Straits Situation, 1 September 1958" Appendix section 4a, 4b.

128. The offshore islands were identified as Jinmen, Jieyu, Mazu, Beigantang, Koo-Teng Hsu, Xiquan Dao, and Dongyin Shan of Mazu Group. Dwight D. Eisenhower: Office files 1953–1961 Pent 2 International series Formosa 1952–57 (1) "The Taiwan Straits Situation, 1 September 1958" Appendix section 4d, 6b.

129. Tucker, *Taiwan, Hong Kong, and the United States*, 4.

130. "Letter from President Chiang Kai-shek to President Eisenhower, December 11, 1956," in *FRUS, 1955–1957, China*, vol. 3, 446–48.

131. "Memorandum of Conversation between President Eisenhower and Secretary of State Dulles, September 11, 1958 in *FRUS, 1958–1960, China*, vol. 19, 161–63; and "376th Meeting of the National Security Council, August 14, 1958," in *FRUS, 1958–1960, China*, vol. 19, 51–53.

132. "Memorandum of Meeting, Summary of Meeting at the White House on the Taiwan Straits Situation, August 29, 1958," in *FRUS, 1958–1960, China*, vol. 19, 98–99.

133. "The Taiwan Straits Situation, 1 September 1958," Dwight D. Eisenhower: Office files 1953–1961, Pent 2, International series: Formosa 1952–57 (1) Appendix section 3. Eisenhower made the same point directly to Chiang in October 1958. See "Memorandum of Conference with President Eisenhower, October 13, 1958," in *FRUS, 1958–1960, China*, vol. 19, 381–82; "Letter, Eisenhower to Chiang Kai-shek, May 17, 1956," *FRUS, 1955–57, China*, vol. 3, 361; Tucker, *Taiwan, Hong Kong and the United States*, 42; Clough, *Island China*, 20; and Christensen, *Useful Adversaries*, 196–97. Dulles made an agreement with Chiang to reduce these garrisons by 15,000 men in exchange for enhanced military equipment.

134. For example, see "Memorandum of Conversation [President Chiang Kai-shek and Ambassador Alan G. Kirk], September 6, 1962," in *FRUS, 1961–1963 Northeast Asia*, vol. 22, 306–12.
135. *Public Papers of the Presidents: John F. Kennedy, 1962* (USGPO, 1963), 276–77, 508–9; Clough, *Island China*, 21; Tucker, *Taiwan, Hong Kong, and the United States*, 45; and Garver, *The Sino-American Alliance*, 91. A full discussion of the Kennedy administration's policy toward Taiwan is beyond the scope of this chapter. The policy of restraining Chiang was similar to that of his predecessors, only Kennedy was more wary of getting into another ground war in Asia. He put more pressure on the regime to withdraw its forces from the offshore islands as well as from Burma. Kennedy conveyed to the Chinese his desire to maintain ambassadorial contacts through Warsaw to ensure that Chiang could not provoke a US-China conflict. See Goldstein, "The United States and the Republic of China," 89. For representative examples of internal instructions to block Chiang's requests, see "Telegram from the Embassy in the Republic of China to the Department of State, March 6, 1962," 189–90; "Message from the President's Special Assistant for National Security Affairs (Bundy) to the Chief of the Central Intelligence Agency Station in Taipei (Cline), March 6, 1962," 191–92; and "Draft Message from President Kennedy to Assistant Secretary of State for Far Eastern Affairs (Harriman), March 9, 1962," 191–92, all in *FRUS, 1961–1963, Northeast Asia*, vol. 22.
136. For example, see "Memorandum of Conversation (President Chiang Kai-shek and Ambassador Alan G. Kirk), September 6, 1962," in *FRUS, 1961–1963, Northeast Asia*, vol. 22, 309.
137. "Memorandum of Discussion at the 338th Meeting of the National Security Council, October 2, 1957," in *FRUS, 1955–1957, China*, vol. 3, 614.
138. "Memorandum of Conversation (President Kennedy and General Chiang Ching-kuo), September 11, 1963," in *FRUS 1961–1963, Northeast Asia*, vol. 22, p. 392.

Chapter 5

1. Byung-chul Koh, *The Foreign Policy Systems of South and North Korea* (Berkeley: University of California Press, 1984); Young-Whan Kihl, ed., *Korea and the World* (Boulder, CO: Westview, 1994); Victor Cha, "National Unification: The Long and Winding Road," *In Depth*, 4, no. 2 (Spring 1994), 89–123.
2. Quote from *New York Times*, June 25, 1953.
3. Jerry Hess, "Oral History Interview with John J. Muccio," Washington, DC, February 10, 1971; available at http://www.trumanlibrary.org/oralhist/muccio1.htm.
4. Mark W. Clark, *From the Danube to the Yalu* (New York: Harper and Brothers, 1954), 142–43.
5. Robert Oliver, *Syngman Rhee and American Involvement in Korea, 1942–1960* (Seoul, Korea: Panmun, 1978), 48.
6. "Royall memorandum of conversation with Rhee, February 8, 1949," in *FRUS, 1949, The Far East and Australasia*, vol. 7, 957.

7. Ridgway, *The Korean War*, 156, 171.

8. "The Ambassador in Korea (Muccio) to the Secretary of State, Seoul, May 9, 1949," in *FRUS, 1949, The Far East and Australasia*, vol. 7, 1013.

9. "Korean Claim," *Straits Times*, October 1, 1949, 6; http://newspapers.nl .sg/Digitised/Page/straitstimes19491001.1.6.aspx; and "S. Korea Accused Before UN," *Straits Times*, October 3, 1949, 2; http://newspapers.nl.sg /Digitised/Page/straitstimes19491003.1.2.aspx; National Library Board Archives of Singapore (accessed 13 February 2012).

10. "South Korea's Hopes," *Straits Times*, November 3, 1949, 6. http://newspapers .nl.sg/Digitised/Page/straitstimes19491103.1.6.aspx; National Library Board Archives of Singapore (accessed 13 March 2012).

11. Jerry Hess, "Oral History Interview with John J. Muccio," Washington, DC, February 10, 1971; available at http://www.trumanlibrary.org/oralhist /muccio1.htm.

12. Christensen, *Worse than a Monolith*, chs. 2–3.

13. For histories of the war, see Blair Clay, *The Forgotten War: America in Korea, 1950–1953* (New York: Times Books, 1987); Bruce Cumings, *The Korean War: A History* (New York: Modern Library, 2010); T. R. Fehrenbach, *This Kind of War: The Classic Korean War History* (Washington, DC and London: Brassey, 1994); Rosemary Foot, *A Substitute for Victory: The Politics of Peacemaking at the Korean Armistice Talks* (Ithaca, NY: Cornell University Press, 1990); David Halberstam, *The Coldest Winter: America and the Korean War* (New York: Hyperion, 2007); Max Hastings, *The Korean War* (London: M. Joseph, 1987); Matthew Ridgway, *The Korean War: How We Met the Challenge, How All-Out Asian War Was Averted, Why MacArthur Was Dismissed, Why Today's War Objectives Must Be Limited* (Garden City, NY: Doubleday, 1967); Martin Russ, *Breakout: The Chosin Reservoir Campaign, Korea 1950* (New York: Fromm International, 1999); and William Stueck, *The Korean War: An International History* (Princeton, NJ: Princeton University Press, 1997).

14. Acheson, *Present at Creation*, 451.

15. Chang-jin Park, "The Influence of Small States Upon the Superpowers," *World Politics*, 28, no. 1 (October 1975), 101; Ronald Caridi, *The Korean War and American Politics: The Republican Party as a Case Study* (Philadelphia: University of Pennsylvania Press, 1968).

16. Caridi, *The Korean War and American Politics*.

17. Rhee's remarks in this regard were first reported to the American public in a July 13, 1950 CBS "World News Round-Up" broadcast. This led to a flurry of internal US government communications about Rhee's efforts to corner the United States publicly into a rollback strategy. See "Memorandum by the Director of the Office of Northeast Asian Affairs (Allison) to the Assistant Secretary of State for Far Eastern Affairs (Rusk), 13 July 1950" (pp. 373–74); "Memorandum by Mr. John Foster Dulles, Consultant to the Secretary of State, to the Director of the Policy Planning Staff (Nitze), 14 July 1950" (pp. 386–87); "The Secretary of State to the Embassy in Korea, 14 July 1950" (p. 387); and "Memorandum by the Director of the Office of Northeast Asian Affairs (Allison) to the Assistant Secretary of State for Far

Eastern Affairs (Rusk), 15 July 1950" (pp. 393–5), all in *FRUS, 1950, Korea*, vol. 7.

18. "The President of the Republic of Korea (Rhee) to President Truman, 19 July 1950," in *FRUS, 1950, Korea*, vol. 7, 428–30.

19. Quoted in Clark, *From the Danube to the Yalu*, 270.

20. Clark, *From the Danube to the Yalu*, 271; and Tae Gyun Park, *An Ally and Empire: Two Myths of South Korea-United States Relations, 1945–1980* (Seoul, Korea: Academy of Korean Studies Press, 2012), 119.

21. Clark, *From the Danube to the Yalu*, 147.

22. Park, *An Ally and Empire*, 113–15.

23. See discussion in ibid., 129–30.

24. Clark, *From the Danube to the Yalu*, 170.

25. Park, *An Ally and Empire*, 133.

26. Clark, *From the Danube to the Yalu*, 150–51.

27. Ibid., 160–61.

28. John Foster Dulles, "The Evolution of Foreign Policy," Before the Council of Foreign Relations, New York, NY, *Department of State, Press Release*, no. 81 (January 12, 1954).

29. Jerry Hess, "Oral History Interview with John J. Muccio," Washington, DC, February 18, 1971, available at http://www.trumanlibrary.org/oralhist /muccio2.htm. Ambassador Muccio recalled that Rhee "didn't like *anything* about [the truce]" (emphasis in original).

30. Taehan Min'guk Kongbusil, *Syngman Rhee Through Western Eyes* (Seoul, Korea: Office of Public Information, 1954), 2.

31. Robert Oliver, *Syngman Rhee and the American Involvement in Korea, 1942–1960*, 446; and Park, "The Influence of Small States Upon the Superpowers," 115.

32. Dwight D. Eisenhower, *Mandate for Change, 1953–1956: The White House Years* (New York: Doubleday, 1963), 182.

33. Ibid., 181; and Park, "The Influence of Small States Upon the Superpowers," 109.

34. Clark, *From the Danube to the Yalu*, 261.

35. Ibid., 273.

36. Park, "The Influence of Small States Upon the Superpowers," 112.

37. Eisenhower, *Mandate for Change*, 183.

38. Ibid., 185.

39. Clark, *From the Danube to the Yalu*, 279–83; and Sheila Miyoshi Jager, *Brothers at War* (New York: W.W. Norton, 2013), 279.

40. Eisenhower, *Mandate for Change*, 185. For details of this event, see Foot, *A Substitute for Victory*, 184.

41. Park, "The Influence of Small Powers," 98; Eisenhower, *Mandate for Change*, 185.

42. Eisenhower, *Mandate for Change*, 187 (emphasis added).

43. Jager, *Brothers at War*, 284.

44. Quoted in Bruce Cumings, "The Structural Basis of 'Anti-Americanism' in the Republic of Korea," in David Steinberg, ed., *Korean Attitudes toward the United States: Changing Dynamics* (Armonk, NY: M.E. Sharpe, 2005).

45. State Department 895.00 file, box 946, Muccio to Butterworth, November 1, 1949: Truman Library, Muccio oral history interview no. 177, December 27, 1973, cited in Cumings, "The Structural Basis of 'Anti-Americanism,'" n.33.
46. Park, "The Influence of Small States Upon the Superpowers," 97.
47. Clark, *From the Danube to the Yalu*, 272.
48. Richard McKinzie, "Oral History Interview with John J. Muccio," Washington, DC, December 27, 1973, available at http://www.trumanlibrary.org /oralhist/muccio3.htm.
49. Stephen Jin-Woo Kim, *Master of Manipulation: Syngman Rhee and the Seoul-Washington Alliance 1953–1960* (Seoul, Korea: Yonsei University Press, 2001), 177.
50. Ibid., 175–76.
51. "Paper Submitted by the Commanding General of the United States Eighth Army (Taylor), Seoul, May 4, 1953," in *FRUS, 1952–1954, Korea*, vol. 15, 965–68.
52. Ibid. Also see Park, *An Ally and Empire*, 117–19.
53. For examples of these deliberations, see "Memorandum of the Substance of Discussion at a Department of State-Joint Chiefs of Staff Meeting, Washington, May 29, 1953," in *FRUS, 1952–1954, Korea*, vol. 15, 1114–19; "The Commander in Chief, Far East (Clark) to the Joint Chiefs of Staff, Tokyo, May 30, 1953," in *FRUS, 1952–1954, Korea*, vol. 15, 1120–21; "The Ambassador in Korea (Briggs) to the Department of State, Seoul, May 30, 1953," in *FRUS, 1952–1954, Korea*, vol. 15, 1121–22; "The Chief of Staff, United States Army (Collins) to the Commander in Chief, Far East (Clark), Washington, May 30, 1953," in *FRUS, 1952–1954, Korea*, vol. 15, 1122–23.
54. Kim, *Master of Manipulation*, 141.
55. Excerpted from "Memorandum of the Substance of Discussion at a Department of State-Joint Chiefs of Staff Meeting, Washington, May 29, 1953," in *FRUS, 1952–1954, Korea*, vol. 15, 1114–19.
56. Cumings, "The Structural Basis of 'Anti-Americanism,'" n.33.
57. Kim, *Master of Manipulation*, 181.
58. Meeting of the Military Subcommittee, 7/28/54. Folder: Minutes of Meetings, July 1954, United States and Republic of Korea, Box 11 Correspondence File, 1953–54. Far East Command, cited in Kim, *Master of Manipulation*, 179.
59. Oliver, *Syngman Rhee*, 260.
60. Clark, *From the Danube to the Yalu*, 274.
61. "The Chief of Staff, United States Army (Collins) to the Commander in Chief, Far East (Clark), Washington, May 30, 1953," in *FRUS, 1952–1954, Korea*, vol. 15, 1122–23.
62. Eisenhower, *Mandate for Change*, 183 (emphasis added).
63. See "Robertson, Walter Spencer (1893–1970)," in Spencer C. Tucker, ed., *US Leadership in Wartime: Clashes, Controversy, and Compromise* (Santa Barbara, CA: ABC-CLIO, 2009), 729–30.
64. "The Assistant Secretary of State for Far Eastern Affairs (Robertson) to the Secretary of State, Seoul, June 27, 1953," in *FRUS, 1952–1954, Korea*, vol. 15, 1278.

65. "Memorandum of a Discussion Held at Tokyo on the Korean Situation, June 24–25, 1953," in *FRUS, 1952–1954, Korea*, vol. 15, 1266.

66. "The Assistant Secretary of State for Far Eastern Affairs (Robertson) to the Secretary of State, Seoul, June 27, 1953," in *FRUS, 1952–1954, Korea*, vol. 15, 1279.

67. The pertinent draft language of the memorandum of understanding was: "The above assurances from the Government of the US are dependent upon agreement of the Government of the ROK: (a) To accept the authority of the UNC to conduct and conclude the hostilities, (b) To support the armistice entered into between CINCUNC and the commanders of the Communist forces, and to pledge its full support and collaboration in carrying out the terms thereof, and, (c) That the armed forces of the ROK will remain under operational control of CINCUNC until Governments of the US and ROK mutually agree that such arrangements are no longer necessary." "The Assistant Secretary of State for Far Eastern Affairs (Robertson) to the Department of State, Seoul, June 27, 1953," in *FRUS, 1952–1954. Korea*, vol. 15, 1280. Also see Clark, *From the Danube to the Yalu*, 285–88.

68. "The Assistant Secretary for Far Eastern Affairs (Robertson) to the Department of State, Seoul, July 1, 1953," in *FRUS, 1952–1954, Korea*, vol. 15, 1291.

69. "Aide-Memoire From the President of the Republic of Korea (Rhee) to the Assistant Secretary of State for Far Eastern Affairs (Robertson), Seoul, June 28, 1953," in *FRUS, 1952–1954, Korea*, vol. 15, 1282.

70. "The Secretary of State to the Embassy in Korea, Washington, July 1, 1953," in *FRUS, 1952–1954, Korea*, vol. 15, 1296.

71. "Memorandum of Conversation, by the Assistant Secretary of State for Far Eastern Affairs, Seoul, July 4, 1953," in *FRUS, 1952–1954, Korea*, vol. 15, 1326–29.

72. "The Secretary of State to the Embassy in Korea, Washington, July 6, 1953," in *FRUS, 1952–1954, Korea*, Vol. XV, 1340.

73. "The Secretary of State to the Embassy in Korea, Washington, July 8, 1953," in *FRUS, 1952–1954, Korea*, vol. 15, 1354.

74. "The President of the Republic of Korea (Rhee) to President Eisenhower, Seoul, July 11, 1953," in *FRUS, 1952–1954, Korea*, vol. 15, 1368–69; "The President of the Republic of Korea (Rhee) to the Assistant Secretary of State for Far Eastern Affairs (Robertson), Seoul, July 9, 1953," in *FRUS, 1952–1954, Korea*, vol. 15, 1357–60; and "The Secretary of State to the President of the Republic of Korea (Rhee), Washington, July 24, 1953," in *FRUS, 1952–1954, Korea*, vol. 15, 1430.

75. "The President of the Republic of Korea (Rhee) to the Assistant Secretary of State for Far Eastern Affairs (Robertson), Seoul, July 11, 1953," in *FRUS, 1952–1954, Korea*, vol. 15, 1375.

76. "Memorandum of Conversation by the Assistant Secretary of State for Far Eastern Affairs (Robertson), Seoul, July 11, 1953," in *FRUS, 1952–1954, Korea*, vol. 15, 1374.

77. "The Secretary of State to the President of Korea (Rhee), Washington, July 24, 1953," in *FRUS, 1952–1954, Korea*, vol. 15, 1430–31; and "The President of the Republic of Korea (Rhee) to the Secretary of State, Seoul, July 25,

1953," in *FRUS, 1952–1954, Korea*, vol. 15, 1436–38; and "The President of the Republic of Korea (Rhee) to the Secretary of State, Seoul, July 26, 1953," in *FRUS, 1952–1954, Korea*, vol. 15, 1440–41.

78. There were five official meetings and one confidential one-on-one meeting between Rhee and Dulles, see "Draft Memorandum of Conversation, by the Secretary of State, Seoul, August 5, 1953," in *FRUS, 1952–1954, Korea*, vol. 15, 1474–75.

79. "Memorandum of Conversation by the Assistant Secretary of State for Far Eastern Affairs (Robertson), Seoul, August 7, 1953," in *FRUS, 1952–1954, Korea*, vol. 15, 1488–89. Chinese troops would not leave the peninsula until 1958.

80. See "President Eisenhower to the President of the Republic of Korea (Rhee), Washington, July 27, 1953," in *FRUS, 1952–1954, Korea*, 1445; Eisenhower, *Mandate for Change*, 187; and "The Assistant Secretary of State for Far Eastern Affairs (Robertson) to the President of the Republic of Korea (Rhee), Washington, July 21, 1953," in *FRUS, 1952–1954, Korea*, vol. 15, 1411–12.

81. Richard McKinzie, "Oral History Interview with John J. Muccio," Washington, DC, December 7, 1973, available at http://www.trumanlibrary.org /oralhist/muccio3.htm.

82. "The Assistant Secretary of State for Far Eastern Affairs (Robertson) to the Department of State, Tokyo, July 9, 2013," in *FRUS, 1952–1954, Korea*, vol. 15, 1355.

83. "The Commander in Chief, United Nations Command (Clark) to the Joint Chiefs of Staff, Tokyo, July 15, 1953," in *FRUS, 1952–1954, Korea*, vol. 15, 1380–81. Also see talking points guidance from the JCS to Clark on this point for use with the communists which stated explicitly: "You are assured that UNC which includes ROK forces is prepared to carry out terms of armistice. Although it is entirely internal matter for our side, I told you that we had received suitable assurances from ROK that will enable us to carry out this obligation. Form and contents of such assurances as have been received from ROK Govt [*sic*] are not properly matters for concern by ur [*sic*] side. However, I again assure you we have received from ROK Govt [*sic*] necessary assurances that it will not obstruct in any manner the implementation of terms of draft armistice agreement. I will have nothing further to say on this." "The Joint Chiefs of Staff to the Commander in Chief, Far East (Clark), Washington, July 15, 1953," in *FRUS, 1952–1954, Korea*, vol. 15, 1382.

84. Full text available at "Mutual Defense Treaty between the Republic of Korea and the United States of America, October 1 1953," United States Forces Korea, http://www.usfk.mil/usfk/sofa.1953.mutual.defense.treaty.76 (accessed August 2, 2013).

85. "Memorandum of Discussion at the 156th Meeting of the National Security Council, Thursday, July 23, 1953," in *FRUS, 1952–1954, Korea*, vol. 15, 1420–28.

86. "Report by the National Security Council Planning Board to the National Security Council, Washington, July 17, 1953," *FRUS, 1952–1954, Korea*, vol. 15, 1385–86.

87. "The Ambassador in Korea (Briggs) to the Department of State, Seoul, July 23, 1953," *FRUS, 1952–1954, Korea*, vol. 15, 1419.

88. For example, see on this point, "The Representative for the Korean Political Conference (Dean) to the Department of State, Seoul, October 24, 1953," in *FRUS, 1952–1954, Korea*, vol. 15, 1558–60.

89. "Memorandum by the Director of the Executive Secretariat (Scott) to the Secretary of State, Washington, October 28, 1953," in *FRUS, 1952–1954, Korea*, vol. 15, 1570.

90. "Memorandum of Discussion at the 168th meeting of the National Security Council, Thursday, October 29, 1953," in *FRUS, 1952–1954, Korea*, vol. 15, 1573.

91. The text of NSC 167/2, "US Course of Action in Korea in the Absence of an Acceptable Political Settlement," is found in "Report by the Executive Secretary (Lay) to the National Security Council, Washington, November 6, 1953," in *FRUS, 1952–1954, Korea*, vol. 15, 1598–60. For the text of NSC 170/1, "US Objectives and Courses of Action in Korea," see "Report by the Executive Secretary (Lay) to the National Security Council, Washington, November 20, 1953," in *FRUS, 1952–1954, Korea*, vol. 15, 1620–24.

92. "President Eisenhower to the President of the Republic of Korea (Rhee), Washington, November 4, 1953," in *FRUS, 1952–1954, Korea*, vol. 15, 1591–92 (emphasis in original).

93. "Draft Telegram from the Vice-President to the Secretary of State, Seoul, November 13, 1953," in *FRUS, 1952–1954, Korea*, vol. 15, 1609–10.

94. Dulles to Nixon, November 4, 1953. Folder John Foster Dulles, Chronological, November 1953 (5), Box 5 JFD Chronological Series, Dulles Papers; Eisenhower to Rhee, November 4, 1953. Folder: Rhee, Syngman 1953–57 (4), Box 37 International Series Anne Whitman Files/Dwight Eisenhower Presidential Library; and "The Vice-President to the Secretary of State, Tokyo, November 19, 1953," in *FRUS, 1952–1954, Korea*, vol. 15, 1615–16.

95. "Memorandum of Discussion at the 172nd Meeting of the National Security Council, Monday, November 23, 1953," in *FRUS, 1952–1954, Korea*, vol. 15, 1625. Also see *FRUS, 1952–1954, Korea*, vol. 15, 1615, fn.2.

96. Kim, *Master of Manipulation*, 144–45.

97. This section is based on American archival documents declassified from the Eisenhower administration. Although these archives have been available for some time, I believe this is the first analysis of the "restraint" aspect of the US-ROK alliance that utilizes these materials about US contingency plans on South Korean governments.

98. This letter constituted the sole legal basis of operational command throughout the Korean War. Quoted in Clark, *From the Danube to the Yalu*, 169.

99. Cossa, "The Future of US Forces," 120.

100. NSC 5817 "Statement of US Policy Toward Korea, August 11, 1958," in *FRUS, 1958–1960, Japan, Korea*, vol. 18, 485.

101. "Memorandum of Discussion at the 411th Meeting of the National Security Council, Washington June 25, 1959," in *FRUS, 1958–1960, Japan, Korea*, vol. 18, 569.

102. See NSC 170/1 "US Objectives and Courses of Action in Korea, November 20, 1953," in *FRUS, 1952–1954, Korea*, vol. 15, 1620–24.

103. These measures referred to the earlier 1953 revision of the plan "Memorandum by the Director of the Executive Secretariat (Scott) to the

Secretary of State, Washington, October 28, 1953," in *FRUS, 1952–1954, Korea*, vol. 15, 1570.

104. "Memorandum from the Acting Executive Secretary of the National Security Council (Gleason) to the Secretary of State, February 18, 1955," in *FRUS, 1955–1957, Southeast Asia*, vol. 22, 37–38.

105. See NSC 5907 July 1, 1959 "Statement of US Policy Toward Korea," *FRUS, 1958–1960, Japan, Korea*, vol. 18, 571–79. Also see superseding policy document NSC 6018, November 28, 1960, which carried the same provisions (*FRUS, 1958–1960, Japan, Korea*, vol. 18, 699–707).

106. One State Department–JCS meeting on Korea in 1958 highlighted the criticality of command authority in this context: "we retain operational control of the Republic of Korea armed forces so as to preclude any possibility of unilateral action on the part of the Republic of Korea Government in attacking North Korea." "Memorandum on the Substance of Discussion at a Department of State-Joint Chiefs of Staff Meeting, Washington, February 28, 1958," in *FRUS, 1958–1950, Japan, Korea*, vol. 18, 443.

107. Clark, *From the Danube to the Yalu*, 157.

108. Ibid., 167.

Chapter 6

1. This was known as the Pacific Ocean Pact and will be the subject of the next chapter.

2. George Kennan, *Memoirs 1950–1963* (New York: Pantheon, 1972), 41.

3. William R. Nester, *Power Across the Pacific: A Diplomatic History of American Relations with Japan* (London: MacMillan Press, 1996), 196.

4. Michael Schaller, *Altered States: The United States and Japan Since the Occupation* (New York: Oxford University Press, 1997), 8.

5. Douglas MacArthur, *Reminiscences* (New York: McGraw-Hill, 1964), 283–84.

6. Kenneth B. Pyle, *Japan Rising: The Resurgence of Japanese Power and Purpose* (New York: PublicAffairs, 2007), 218.

7. "Class A" war criminals were those who planned, prepared, and/or initiated the waging of aggressive war. "Class B" included those who violated the laws and conventions of conduct during the war. And "Class C" war criminals were those who committed inhumane acts against civilian populations such as murder, extermination, enslavement, deportation, and rape. For exact definitions, see *Far Eastern Commission Policy Decision FEC 007/3, April 3, 1946*, "Policy in Regard to the Apprehension, Trial and Punishment of War Criminals in the Far East," in *FRUS, 1946, The Far East*, vol. 8, 424–27.

8. Schaller, *Altered States*, 10.

9. Douglas MacArthur quoted in Nester, *Power Across the Pacific*, 209–10.

10. "The Constitution of the Empire of Japan (1889)," *Hanover.edu* (2010), http://history.hanover.edu/texts/1889con.html (accessed July 31, 2011).

11. "The Constitution of Japan," *Kantei.go.jp* (2010), http://www.kantei.go.jp/foreign/constitution_and_government_of_japan/constitution_e.html (accessed July 31, 2011).

12. David John Lu, *Sources of Japanese History*, vol. 2 (New York: McGraw-Hill, 1974), 191.

13. JCS 1380/15, "Basic Initial Post Surrender Directive to Supreme Commander for the Allied Powers for the Occupation and Control of Japan" (November 3, 1945), http://www.ndl.go.jp/constitution/e/shiryo/01/036/036tx.html (accessed July 31, 2011), part 2, A, 13.

14. Nester, *Power Across the Pacific*, 215–16; 238–40.

15. Walter LaFeber, *The Clash: A History of US-Japan Relations* (New York: W.W. Norton, 1998), 260.

16. Nester, *Power Across the Pacific*, 216; Schaller, *Altered States*, 12.

17. Nester, *Power Across the Pacific*, 217–18.

18. Ibid., 219.

19. William H. Draper quoted in Schaller, *Altered States*, 14; *Fortune* magazine quote in Roger Buckley, *US-Japan Alliance Diplomacy, 1945–1990* (Cambridge, UK: Cambridge University Press, 1997), 24; also see Heer, "George F. Kennan," 132–33.

20. See PPS/10, "Results of Planning Staff Study of Questions Involved in the Japanese Peace Settlement (14 October 1947)," in *FRUS, 1947, The Far East*, vol. 6, 537–43.

21. SWNCC 384 cited in Howard B. Schonberger, *Aftermath of War: Americans and the Remaking of Japan, 1945–1952* (Kent, OH: Kent State University Press, 1989), 166–67. For a response agreeing with Draper's sentiment, see *FRUS, 1947, The Far East*, vol. 6, 313–14.

22. Cumings, *Origins of the Korean War*, volume 2, 96.

23. Herbert Hoover, for example, wrote to SCAP General MacArthur (in 1947) even before the Nationalists' defeat in China that Japan was the only area in the world where the United States is in "dominant action" and therefore should give high priority to cultivating this relationship.

24. Kennan, *Memoirs*, 374.

25. Ibid., 369.

26. Ibid., 368.

27. See George F. Kennan, *Realities of American Foreign Policy* (Princeton, NJ: Princeton University Press, 1954), 63–65; John Lewis Gaddis, *Strategies of Containment: A Critical Appraisal of American National Security Policy During the Cold War*, Revised ed. (New York: Oxford University Press, 2005), 29–30; Kennan, *Memoirs*, 359.

28. Dean Acheson, "The Requirements of Reconstruction," *Department of State Bulletin*, 16, no. 411 (May 8, 1947), 991–94.

29. Clark, *From the Danube to the Yalu*, 118.

30. Kennan, *Memoirs*, 382.

31. Ibid., 383.

32. For Kennan's earlier views, see PPS/10, "Memorandum by the Director of the Policy Planning Staff (Kennan), October 14, 1947," in *FRUS, 1947, The Far East*, vol. 6, 542; For Kennan's views during the visit, see "Conversation between General of the Army MacArthur, Undersecretary of the Army Draper, and Mr. George F. Kennan (21 March 1948)," in *FRUS, 1948, The Far East*, vol. 6, 714–17; Kennan, *Memoirs*, 389; and Heer, "George F. Kennan."

33. "The Acting Political Adviser in Japan (Sebald) to the Secretary of State (23 March 1948)," in *FRUS, 1948, The Far East*, vol. 6, 689–90; and Heer, "George F. Kennan," 162–63.

34. "Explanatory Notes by Mr. George F. Kennan, March 25, 1948," in *FRUS, 1948, The Far East*, vol. 6, 718.

35. Kennan, *Memoirs*, 388.

36. PPS/28, "Report by the Director of the Policy Planning Staff (Kennan) (25 March 1948)," in *FRUS, 1948, The Far East*, vol. 6, 699–700.

37. "Memorandum of Conversation by Mr. Marshall of the Division of Northeast Asian Affairs (28 May 1948)," in *FRUS, 1948, The Far East*, vol. 6, 793.

38. "PPS/28, "Report by the Director of Policy Planning Staff (Kennan) (25 March 1948)," in *FRUS, 1948, The Far East*, vol. 6, 691–96.

39. Heer, "George F. Kennan," 122–23.

40. Full NSC report can be seen in NSC 13/2, "Report by the National Security Council on Recommendations with Respect to the United States Policy Toward Japan (07 October 1948)," in *FRUS, 1948, The Far East and Australasia*, vol. 6, 858–62; "Memorandum by the Director of the Office of Far Eastern Affairs (Butterworth) to the Acting Secretary of State (27 October 1948)," in *FRUS, 1948, The Far East*, vol. 6, 878.

41. Kennan, *Memoirs: 1925–1950*, 393.

42. George Kennan, *The Cloud of Danger: Current Realities of American Foreign Policy* (Boston: Little, Brown, 1977), 108–09 cited in Kim, "American Elites' Strategic Thinking Towards Korea," 185–212.

43. As Acheson instructed MacArthur in March 1948, "[T]he objectives of the Potsdam Declaration . . . made provision for the security of the Allies from Japanese aggression . . . [I]n view of the developing world situation the keynote of occupation policy, from here on out, should lie in the achievement of maximum stability of Japanese society, in order that Japan may be best able to stand on her own feet when the protecting hand is withdrawn." "Conversation between General of the Army MacArthur and Mr. George F. Kennan, March 5, 1948," in *FRUS, 1948, The Far East*, vol. 6, 699.

44. "Position of the Department of State on United States Policy Toward a Japanese Peace and Security Settlement (09 March 1950)," in *FRUS, 1950, East Asia and the Pacific*, vol. 6, 1140.

45. http://www.ioc.u-tokyo.ac.jp/~worldjpn/documents/texts/JPUS/19480106.S1E.html

46. "Statement of the United States Government, Economic Stabilization of Japan (10 December 1948)," in *FRUS, 1948, The Far East*, vol. 6, 1059–60.

47. "Report by the National Security Council on Recommendations with Respect to United States Policy Toward Japan, October 7, 1948 [NSC 13/2]," in *FRUS, 1948, The Far East*, vol. 6, 858–59.

48. Nester, *Power Across the Pacific*, 224.

49. "Department of State Comments on NSC 49 (June 15, 1949)," in *FRUS, 1949, The Far East and Australasia*, vol. 7, 872.

50. Acheson, *Present at the Creation*, 428.

51. "Report by the National Security Council on Recommendations With Respect to United States Policy Toward Japan, 06 May 1949 (NSC 13/3)," in *FRUS, 1949, The Far East and Australasia*, vol. 7, 730–36.

52. Heer, "George F. Kennan," 123–24.

53. For reaction to the Korean War in this regard, see "Unsigned Memorandum by the Policy Planning Staff, 26 July 1950, Assumption of Japan for a Greater Measure of Responsibility for its own Security, Both Internal and External," in *FRUS, 1950, East Asia and the Pacific*, vol. 6, 1255–57.

54. During a September 1947 Policy Planning Staff meeting, it was noted that "A major shift in US policy toward Japan is being talked about under cover. Idea of eliminating Japan as a military power for all time is changing." See Nester, *Power Across the Pacific*, p. 249; See 1948 document in *FRUS, 1948, The Far East and Australasia*, vol. 6, 706.

55. See JCS memorandum in "Memorandum by the Joint Chiefs of Staffs for the Secretary of Defense (Forrestal), 1 March 1949," in *FRUS, 1949, The Far East and Australasia*, vol. 7, 672. For more on 1949 draft peace treaty, see Schaller, *Altered States*, 24.

56. "Memorandum by Robert A. Feary of the Office of Northeast Asian Affairs, 16 February 1951," in *FRUS, 1951, Asia and the Pacific*, vol. 6, 160.

57. See Yoshida Shigeru, "Japan and the Crisis in Asia," *Foreign Affairs*, 29, no. 2 (January 1951), 174. Kennan, in particular, made the argument about a moral obligation to defend the defeated adversary. See Kennan, *The Cloud of Danger*, 108–9.

58. Welfield, *An Empire in Eclipse*, 28.

59. "Outline of Far Eastern and Asian Policy for Review with the President, 14 November 1949," in *FRUS, 1949, The Far East and Australia*, vol. 7, 1213.

60. Kennan, *The Cloud of Danger*, 108–9.

61. See "Potsdam Declaration," National Diet Library (26 July 1945), http://www.ndl.go.jp/constitution/e/etc/c06.html (accessed 11 November 2015).

62. "Conversation between General of the Army MacArthur, Undersecretary of the Army Draper, and Mr. George F. Kennan, March 21, 1948 (amended March 23, 1948)," in *FRUS, 1948, The Far East and Australasia*, vol. 6, 712.

63. The Chinese foreign minister Wang Shih-chieh conveyed this view to John Foster Dulles in September 1948 ("Memorandum by Mr. John Foster Dulles, United States Delegation at the United Nations General Meeting Assembly to the Secretary of State, October 1, 1948"), in *FRUS, 1948, The Far East and Australasia*, vol. 6, 856.

64. "Conversation between General of the Army MacArthur, Under Secretary of the Army Draper, and Mr. George F. Kennan, March 21, 1948 (Amended March 23, 1948)," in *FRUS, 1948, The Far East and Australasia*, vol. 6, 712–13.

65. See Kennan's consultations with Canadian ambassador in "Memorandum of a Conversation with Mr. George F. Kennan, Chief of the Division of Planning and Policy in the United States State Department, attended by Mr. R. Atherton, Mr. E. Reid, Mr. R. G. Riddell, Mr. D. Johnson, Mr. R. E. Collins and Mr. A. R. Menzies, June 1, 1948, Ottawa," in *FRUS, 1948, The Far East and Australasia*, vol. 6, 806.

66. Dulles's views shifted over time. He was not in favor of a militarily neutered Japan, and at times moved in the direction of the gamma option. But after being appointed as Truman's special envoy in 1950, his views hewed toward the middle option.

67. Another option considered by an internal working group at the State Department in the early 1950s was known as the "halfway house" strategy. This entailed restoration of Japanese political and economic autonomy, but continuing the military occupation. While this option was favored by the working group, it was rejected by Acheson and Rusk. See "Memorandum by the Assistant Secretary of State for Far Eastern Affairs (Butterworth) to the Secretary of State, 18 January 1950," in *FRUS, 1950, East Asia and the Pacific*, vol. 6, 1117–28; and David W. Mabon, "Elusive Agreements: The Pacific Pact Proposals of 1949–1951," *Pacific Historical Review*, 57, no. 2 (May 1988), 158–59.

68. See "Conversation between General of the Army MacArthur, Under Secretary of the Army Draper, and Mr. George F. Kennan, March 21, 1948 (Amended March 23, 1948)," in *FRUS, 1948, The Far East and Australasia*, vol. 6, 713; and "Memorandum by the Assistant Secretary of State for Occupied Areas (Saltzman) to the Director of the Office of Far Eastern Affairs (Butterworth), April 9, 1948," in *FRUS, 1948, The Far East and Australasia*, vol. 6, 728.

69. "Report by the National Security Council on Recommendations with Respect to United States Policy toward Japan, October 7, 1948," in *FRUS, 1948, The Far East and Australasia*, vol. 6, 877–78.

70. LaFeber, *The Clash*, 297–98.

71. Eisenhower's comments were made to the pro-Taiwan Senate members in 1954 in the context of debates about how much the United States should stifle Japan's relations with China. Stifling Japan was characteristic of an "alpha strategy" strain of thought that the best way to deal with Japan's postwar status was to keep it down and isolated. Eisenhower quote comes from LaFeber, *The Clash*, 305–6.

72. These exchanges were with Treasury Secretary Humphrey and with NSC advisor Robert Cutler, cited in ibid.

73. Pyle, *Japan Rising*, 223.

74. In the spring of 1950, Acheson made personnel changes in Asia policy at State to deflect Republican criticism. The maligned Butterworth, who was seen as too sympathetic to China, was replaced by Dean Rusk. Acheson also appointed former senator John Sherman Cooper, a Republican from Kentucky, as a consultant to the Department. Vandenberg wanted Dulles to be appointed to such a position, but Truman was hesitant for reasons stated above. Truman agreed to bring Dulles aboard (but did not want him to have the title of ambassador at large). Acheson then negotiated with Dulles for two days because Dulles wanted to ensure he had a prestigious title with his appointment (named as a "top advisor"). See Blum, *Drawing the Line*, 189. For Dulles's views of Truman's Fair Deal program which the senator criticized as creating too much central government authority, see *Cornell Daily Sun*, 21 September 1949, http://cdsun.library.cornell.edu/cgi -bin/cornell?a=d&d=CDS19490921-01.2.2&e=01.0.0&e= (accessed August 14, 2015).

75. See "Memorandum of Conversation, by the Charge in Japan (Huston), 16 July 1949," in *FRUS, 1949, The Far East and Australasia*, vol. 7, 805–7;

"Memorandum of Conversation, by Mr. Robert A. Fearey of the Office of Northeast Asian Affairs, 02 November 1949," in *FRUS, 1949, The Far East and Australasia*, vol. 7, 890–94; and see "Strategic Evaluation of United States Security Needs in Japan, 09 June 1949," in *FRUS, 1949, The Far East and Australasia*, vol. 7, 774–77.

76. See, for example, "Memorandum of Conversation, by the Special Assistant to the Secretary (Howard), 24 April 1950," in *FRUS, 1950, East Asia and the Pacific*, vol. 6, 1176.

77. Acheson quoted from "Informal Memorandum by the Secretary of State to the British Ambassador (Franks), 24 December 1949," in *FRUS, 1949, The Far East and Australasia*," vol. 7, 928; Dulles quoted in "Memorandum of Conversation, by the Special Assistant to the Secretary (Howard), 07 April 1950," in *FRUS, 1950, East Asia and the Pacific*, vol. 6, 1161–62.

78. See Ronald W. Pruessen, *John Foster Dulles: The Road to Power* (New York: Free Press, 1982), 454.

79. See, for example, "Memorandum by the Special Assistant to the Secretary (Howard) to the Assistant Secretary of State for Far Eastern Affairs (Rusk), 26 July 1950," in *FRUS, 1950, East Asia and the Pacific*, vol. 6, 1258.

80. For an excellent encapsulation of the State-JCS divide, see "Memorandum of Conversation, by the Special Assistant to the Secretary (Howard), 24 April 1950," in *FRUS, 1950, East Asia and the Pacific*, vol. 6, 1175–82.

81. Presidential approval noted in footnote 5, in "Memorandum for the President, 07 September 1950," in *FRUS, 1950, East Asia and the Pacific*, vol. 6, 1293–96.

82. See "Document 38: Letter to: John Foster Dulles, From: Harry S. Truman (10 January 1951)," in Dennis Merrill, ed., *Documentary History of the Truman Presidency: The Emergence of an Asian Pacific Rim in American Foreign Policy*, vol. 22 (Bethesda, MD: University Publications of America, 1998), 193–94.

83. Dulles, "Security in the Pacific," 175.

84. Dulles referred to this formative experience numerous times with his Japanese interlocutors to assure them of his genuine desire for peaceful reconciliation. See "Informal Remarks Made by John Foster Dulles to the Women Members of the National Diet who called upon him on Tuesday, February 6, 1951 at 3:15 p.m.," *Dulles Papers* (January-April 1951), Box 303.

85. John Foster Dulles, "Japanese Peace Treaty in Retrospect," Governor's Conference, Gatlinburg, Tennessee (01 October 1951), *Dulles Papers*, Box 305, 3–4.

86. John Foster Dulles, "Statement: Upon Arrival in Japan," Tokyo, Japan, January 25, 1951, Dulles Papers, Box 303, 1.

87. John Foster Dulles, "Press Conference: Trip to the Far East," Washington, DC, February 28, 1951, *Dulles Papers*, Box 303, 3.

88. John Foster Dulles, "Statement: Upon Departure from Japan," Tokyo, Japan, February 11, 1951, *Dulles Papers*, Box 303, 2.

89. John Foster Dulles, "The Informal Remarks of John Foster Dulles at a Luncheon Tendered Him by the Institute of Pacific Relations, Manila, Philippines, February 12, 1951," *Dulles Papers* (January-April 1951), Box 303, 5–10.

90. John Foster Dulles, "Remarks Upon Departure from Australia," *Dulles Paper* (January-April 1951), Box 303, 1–13.

91. "Memorandum, Notes on Conversation among Ambassador Dulles, Australian and New Zealand Ministers for External Affairs, and Staffs, 16 February 1951," in *FRUS, 1951, Asia and the Pacific*, vol. 6, 160.

92. John Foster Dulles, "The Cooperation of Sovereign Equals," American Chamber of Commerce in Japan and the Japanese Chamber of Commerce and Industry, Tokyo, Japan, December 14, 1951, *Dulles Papers* (January–April 1951), Box 305, 2.

93. LaFeber, *The Clash*, 192.

94. Welfield, *An Empire in Eclipse*, 25.

95. See "Memorandum of Conversation, by the Officer in Charge of Korean Affairs in the Office of Northeast Asian Affairs (Emmons), 09 July 1951," in *FRUS, 1951, Asia and the Pacific*, vol. 6, 1182–84; "Memorandum of Conversation, by the Officer in Charge of Korean Affairs in the Office of Northeast Asian Affairs (Emmons), 19 July 1951," in *FRUS, 1951, Asia and the Pacific*, vol. 6, 1202–6; See also Sung-hwa Cheong, *The Politics of Anti-Japanese Sentiment* (New York: Greenwood Press, 1991).

96. John Foster Dulles, "Peace in the Pacific," Whittier College Dinner, Los Angeles, California (31 March 1951), *Dulles Papers* (January-April 1951), Box 303, 6.

97. John Foster Dulles, "Laying the Foundations for Peace in the Pacific," CBS Broadcast (March 1, 1951), *Dulles Papers* (January-April 1951), Box 303, 5.

98. Cited from "Japan's Future: Interview with John Foster Dulles," *Newsweek*, September 10, 1951.

99. "Extracts from the Digest of the Sixth and Final of the Study Group on Japanese Peace Treaty Problems (May 25, 1951)," in Michael A. Guhin, *John Foster Dulles: A Statesman and his Times* (New York: Columbia University Press, 1972), 315–18 (appendix A).

100. "Document 38," in Merrill, *Documentary History of the Truman Presidency*, 194.

101. "Memorandum by Mr. Robert A. Fearey of the Office of Northeast Asian Affairs (16 February 1951), "Notes on Conversation Among Ambassador Dulles, Australian and New Zealand Ministers for External Affairs, and Staffs," in *FRUS, 1951, Asia and the Pacific*, vol. 6, 157.

102. Dulles, "Security in the Pacific," 182.

103. "The Acting Political Adviser in Japan (Sebald) to the Secretary of State (20 August 1949)," in *FRUS, 1949, The Far East and Australasia*, vol. 7, 836. Also see John Foster Dulles, "Letter to President Truman, 3 October 1951," *Dulles Papers* Box 56 MC #016, 1 page.

104. Heer, "George F. Kennan," 151–52.

105. The US defense of SCAP's approval of allowing travel abroad for Japanese nationals was particularly revealing of US disdain for cumbersome multilateral structures. The State Department maintained that it submitted these issues to the FEC, but that the lack of a decision compelled the United States to act bilaterally and work out individual arrangements with countries seeking to receive visits by Japanese nationals. Regarding fishing

expeditions, the United States maintained that it was simply too cumbersome to require every request for extension of authorized fishing areas for Japan be run through the FEC.

106. "The Department of State to the Australian Embassy, Aide-Memoire, June 12, 1948," in *FRUS, 1948, The Far East and Australasia*, vol. 6, 813.

107. "Agreed State-Army Draft for Incorporation in NSC 13/2," in *FRUS, 1948, The Far East and Australasia*, vol. 6, 880. President Truman approved these provisions as part of NSC 13/2 on November 22, 1948.

108. "Report by the National Security Council on Recommendations with Respect to United States Policy toward Japan, October 7, 1948 (NSC 13/2)," in *FRUS, 1948, The Far East and Australasia*, vol. 6, 877–78.

109. "Memorandum by the Assistant Secretary of State for Occupied Areas (Saltzman) to the United States Representative on the Far Eastern Commission (McCoy), December 3, 1948," in *FRUS, 1948, The Far East and Australasia*, vol. 6, 913–14.

110. "Press and Radio News Conference, Wednesday, February 28, 1951, Department of State," *Dulles Papers* (Writings About or Relating to John Foster Dulles, 1949–1951), Box 399, 1–2.

111. Indeed, Prime Minister Yoshida wanted this arrangement negotiated at an executive level so that it would not be held up in controversy in the Japanese legislature.

112. LaFeber, *The Clash*, 316.

113. Quoted in Leffler, *A Preponderance of Power*, 392.

114. LaFeber, *The Clash*, 335.

115. Ibid., 299, 304; and Leffler, *A Preponderance of Power*, 391.

116. Roger Dingman, "The Dagger and the Gift: The Impact of the Korean War Upon Japan," *Journal of American-East Asian Relations*, no. 2 (Spring 1993), 30–31; and John W. Dower, *Empire and Aftermath: Yoshida Shigeru and the Japanese Experience, 1878–1954* (Cambridge, MA: Harvard Asia Center, 1988), 389–91.

117. Tim Weiner, "CIA Spent Millions to Support Japanese Right in 50's and 60's," *New York Times*, October 9, 1994. The newspaper report came out just after the collapse of LDP one-party rule in Japan, and was based on interviews of former US officials, declassified CIA documents, and interviews of former operations officers. The "Dooman operation" entailed the smuggling of tons of tungsten from Japanese military supplies to the Pentagon between 1950 and 1953 for $10 million. The CIA provided US$2.8 million to finance the operations according to the news report. The article details how these and other monies were covertly provided to conservative Japanese politicians until the early 1970s. Also see Chalmers Johnson, "The 1955 System and the American Connection," *Japan Policy Research Institute Working Paper*, 11 (July 1995).

118. LaFeber, *The Clash*, 318; and Weiner, "CIA Spent Millions."

119. Michael Schaller, "America's Favorite War Criminal: Kishi Nobusuke and the Transformation of US-Japan Relations," *Japan Policy Research Institute Working Paper*, 11 (July 1995), http://www.jpri.org/publications/workingpapers/wp11.html (accessed 4 March 2009).

120. LaFeber, *The Clash*, 335–36.

121. "Memorandum, Notes on Conversation among Ambassador Dulles, Australian and New Zealand Ministers for External Affairs, and Staffs, 16 February 1951," in *FRUS, 1951, Asia and the Pacific*, vol. 6, 160.

122. Edwin O. Reischauer, *The United States and Japan*, 3rd ed. (Cambridge, MA: Harvard University Press, 1965), 50.

123. Dulles, "Security in the Pacific."

124. LaFeber, *The Clash*, 293.

125. Kennan said that such a formula was preferable to "Korean mismanagement, Chinese interference, or Russian bureaucracy." See Michael Schaller, *The American Occupation of Japan: The Origins of the Cold War in Asia* (New York: Oxford, 1985); and Welfield, *An Empire in Eclipse*, 91.

126. "The Koreans cannot really maintain their own independence in the face of both Russian and Japanese pressures. From the standpoint of our own interests it is preferable that Japan should dominate Korea than that Russia should do so. But Japan, at the moment, is too weak to compete. We must hope that with the revival of her normal strength and prestige, Japan will regain her influence there." ("Memorandum by the Counselor [Kennan] to the Secretary of State, 21 August 1950," in *FRUS, 1950, Korea*, vol. 7, 627–29.)

127. John Foster Dulles, "Japanese Peace Treaty, Meeting of Washington Representatives of National Organizations," Washington, DC, August 23, 1951, *Dulles Papers*, Box, 304, 41.

128. The treaty entered into force with an exchange of ratifications starting August 27, 1952.

129. The treaty entered into force with the completion of all three ratifications on April 29, 1952.

130. Full text of speech available at Harry S. Truman, "Address in San Francisco at the Opening of the Conference on the Japanese Peace Treaty," *UCSB.edu* (04 September 1951), http://www.presidency.ucsb.edu/ws/index.php?pid=13906#axzz1VE2n6VTg (accessed 16 August 2011).

131. For Soviet complaints about the unilateral manner in which the United States was cutting communist China and the Soviet Union out of treaty preparations for Japan, see "Remarks of Govt of USSR on Matter of USA Draft Peace Treaty with Japan, 7 May 1951," *Dulles Papers* (Japan to Korea, 1951), Box 55, 1–3. Also see exchange of correspondence dated 17 August 1951 between Mr. Reston of the *New York Times* and Dulles in *Dulles Papers* (Japan to Korea, 1951)," Box 55, 9 pages.

132. See "Memorandum of Conversation, by the United States Political Adviser to SCAP (Sebald), 03 September 1951," in *FRUS, 1951, Asia and the Pacific*, vol. 6, 1315–17.

133. Nester, *Power Across the Pacific*, 211.

134. Michael Yoshitsu, *Japan and the San Francisco Peace Settlement* (New York: Columbia University Press, 1983).

135. Miyazawa Kiichi quoted in Pyle, *Japan Rising*, 230.

136. "Statement by Prime Minister Yoshida, January 25, 1951," *Dulles Papers* (Writings About or Relating to John Foster Dulles, 1949–1951), Box 399; and Schaller, *The American Occupation of Japan*, 7.

137. "Memorandum of Conversation, by the Counselor of the Mission in Japan (Huston), 08 April 1950," in *FRUS, 1950, Korea*, vol. 6, 1166.

138. John Foster Dulles, "Japanese Peace Settlement Mission," Australian Institute of International Affairs, Sydney, Australia, February 19, 1951 in *Dulles Papers*, Box 303, 8.

139. Chalmers A. Johnson, *Blowback* (New York: Metropolitan Books, 2000), 177.

140. Leffler, *A Preponderance of Power*, 467.

141. Schaller, *The American Occupation of Japan*, 53; and Leffler, *A Preponderance of Power*, 393, 467.

142. Nester, *Power Across the Pacific*, 241, 276.

143. Andrew Rotter, *The Path to Vietnam* (Ithaca, NY: Cornell University Press, 1987), 127.

144. Yoshida quoted in Nester, *Power Across the Pacific*, 244.

145. Response by Senator Sparkmen to a question by Kyodo News reporter in transcript of Joint Press Conference by John Foster Dulles and Senators Smith and Sparkman, 10 December 1951, in *Dulles Papers* (Writings about or Relating to John Foster Dulles, 1949–1951), Box 399, 10–11. Also see Shimizu Sayuri, "Perennial Anxiety: Japan-US Controversy over Recognition of the PRC, 1952–58," *Journal of American-East Asian Relations*, 4, no. 3 (Fall 1995); and Michael Yoshitsu, *Japan and the San Francisco Peace Settlement* (New York: Columbia University Press, 1983).

146. LaFeber, *The Clash*, 293; and Leffler, *A Preponderance of Power*, 464.

147. William Borden, *The Pacific Alliance: United States Foreign Economic Policy and Japanese Trade Recovery, 1947–1955* (Madison: University of Wisconsin Press, 1984), 210–12.

148. Ibid., 212–14.

149. LaFeber, *The Clash*, 305. Also see Sadako Ogata, "The Business Community and Japanese Foreign Policy: Normalization of Relations with the People's Republic of China," in Robert Scalapino, ed., *The Foreign Policy of Modern Japan* (Berkeley: University of California Press, 1977). The United States ultimately chose a middle path on this issue, allowing the private trade agreements and Japanese trade with China in some goods that were on the restricted CHINCOM lists. The rationale behind this was that it was important to grant the Japanese some interaction with China for its economic growth, but also that the increments of trade might be able to lure China away from the Soviet bloc, as well as reduce any Japanese pique that might endear them to initiatives Khrushchev was making in the region at the time.

150. NSC 125/2, "Statement of Policy Proposed by the National Security Council on United States Objectives and Courses of Action with Respect to Japan, 07 August 1952," in *FRUS, 1952–1954, China and Japan*, vol. 14, 1307.

151. Rotter, *The Path to Vietnam*, ch. 6; and Nester, *Power Across the Pacific*, 243.

152. Rotter, *The Path to Vietnam*, 128–29.

153. Ibid., 129–31.

154. Quoted in Borden, *The Pacific Alliance*, 214.

155. These are the countries referred to as "Sterling Asia" or "Other Asia" according to UN statistics: Burma (Myanmar), Ceylon (Sri Lanka), India,

Pakistan, Malaya (Malaysia), Singapore, Sarawak (part of Malaysia), Brunei, North Borneo (part of Malaysia), Hong Kong, Taiwan, Cambodia, Laos, Republic of Vietnam (South), Indonesia, Republic of Korea (South), Philippines, Thailand, Portuguese India (part of India) and Portuguese Timor (East Timor), Netherlands New Guinea (Irian Jaya in Indonesia).

156. These are the countries referred to as "China (Mainland) according to UN statistics: the People's Republic of China, Mongolian People's Republic, the Democratic People's Republic of Korea, and the Democratic Republic of Vietnam."

157. *United Nations Statistics Yearbook: 1960* (New York: United Nations, 1960); *United Nations Statistics Yearbook: 1961* (New York: United Nations, 1961).

158. I do not deny that after the Cultural Revolution and through the 1970s, bilateral trade, first informal memorandum trade, and then formal trade, between China and Japan increased substantially. In part, this was a willingness on the part of the United States to allow some of this activity to "fly under the radar," but this trade was also informally condoned by the United States as the Sino-Soviet split grew worse and Washington grew interested in making diplomatic inroads with Beijing.

159. NSC 125/2 states "the entry to Japanese goods into the United States market should be facilitated" and recommends "the reestablishment of mutually beneficial business relationships between United States and Japanese nationals through the development of trade and investment opportunities." See "United States Objectives and Courses of Action with Respect to Japan, 7 August 1952 (NSC 125/2)," in *FRUS, 1952–1954, China and Japan*, vol. 14, 1307–08.

160. Nester, *Power Across the Pacific*, 275–76.

161. *United Nations* (1960, 1961).

162. Marius B. Jansen, *The Making of Modern Japan* (Cambridge, MA: Harvard University Press, 2000), 703.

163. *Statistics Bureau—Ministry of International Affairs and Communications* (Japan), (2011), http://www.stat.go.jp/english/ (accessed 16 August 2011); "Japan," *World Bank Data* (2011), http://data.worldbank.org/country/japan (accessed 16 August 2011).

164. "National Economic Accounts," *Bureau of Economic Analysis, Department of Commerce* (2011), http://www.bea.gov/national/index.htm (accessed 16 August 2011).

165. See "United States Objectives and Courses of Action with Respect to Japan, 7 August 1952 (NSC 125/2)," in *FRUS, 1952–1954, China and Japan*, vol. 14, 1307–08.

166. Ibid., 1307.

167. *Ministry of International Affairs and Communications* (Japan) (2011); *World Bank Data* (2011).

168. See "The Charge in Japan (Huston) to the Secretary of State, 21 July 1949," in *FRUS, 1949, The Far East and Australasia*, vol. 7, 803–5.

169. Other frequent members are Argentina (8), Columbia (7), India (7), Canada (6), Italy (6), Belgium (5), Germany (5), the Netherlands (5), Panama (5), and Poland (5). See "UN Security Council—Members," *UN.org* (2011), http://www.un.org/sc/members.asp (accessed 17 August 2011).

170. For 55 other initial members, see "Member States of the IAEA," IAEA.org (2011), http://www.iaea.org/About/Policy/MemberStates/ (accessed 17 August 2011).

171. See "United States Objectives and Courses of Action with Respect to Japan, 7 August 1952 (NSC 125/2)," in *FRUS, 1952–1954, China and Japan*, vol. 14, 1305–06.

172. Tim Kane, "Global US Troop Deployment, 1950–2005," *Heritage.org* (2006), http://www.heritage.org/research/reports/2006/05/global-us-troop -deployment-1950–2005 (accessed 17 August 2011).

173. Nester, *Power Across the Pacific*, 270.

174. Leffler, *A Preponderance of Power*, 464–65.

175. Ibid. Also see Hans Kristensen, "Japan Under the US Nuclear Umbrella," *Nautilus Institute Report* (June 2015), http://www.nautilus.org/wp-content /uploads/2015/06/Japan-Under-the-US-Nuclear-Umbrella.pdf (accessed 6 February 2016).

176. LaFeber, *The Clash*, 311 and 316.

177. Ibid., 313.

178. Ibid., 299.

179. For the seminal work, see George R. Packard, *Protest in Tokyo: The Security Treaty Crisis of 1960* (Princeton, NJ: Princeton University Press, 1966).

180. Kristensen, "Japan Under the US Nuclear Umbrella."

181. LaFeber, *The Clash*, 320.

182. Full text can be seen at "Administrative Agreement under Article III of the Security Treaty between the United States of America and Japan," (28 February 1952), http://www.ioc.u-tokyo.ac.jp/~worldjpn/documents/texts/docs /19520228.T1E.html (accessed 17 August 2011).

183. Max Weber, "The Profession and Vocation of Politics," in Peter Lassman and Ronald Speirs, eds., *Weber: Political Writings* (Cambridge, UK: Cambridge University Press, 1994), 309–69.

184. Full text available at "Treaty of Mutual Cooperation and Security between Japan and the United States of America," (19 January 1960), http://www .ioc.u-tokyo.ac.jp/~worldjpn/documents/texts/docs/19600119.T1E.html (accessed 17 August 2011).

185. The "cork in the bottle" analogy was coined by Lt. General Henry Stackpole, who commanded the third Marine division in Okinawa, in a March 1990 interview with the *Washington Post*. See Thomas Berger, *Redefining Japan & the US-Japan Alliance* (New York: Japan Society, 2004), 46; and Stuart Harris and Richard Cooper, "The US-Japan Alliance," in Blackwill and Dibb, *America's Asian Alliances* (Cambridge, MA: MIT Press, 2000), 31.

186. Johnson, *Blowback*, 60.

Chapter 7

1. See, for instance, Thomas Christensen and Jack Snyder, "Chain Gangs and Passed Bucks: Predicting Alliance Patterns in Multipolarity," *International Organization*, 44, no. 2 (Spring 1990), 137–68; Randall Schweller, "Tripolarity and the Second World War," *International Studies Quarterly*, 37, no. 1 (March 1993), 84, 87–92.

2. The costs associated with a proactive control strategy in this instance are inordinately high. For the determinants of when entrapment fears are intense enough to warrant control over distancing strategies, see chapter 2.

3. John K. Fairbank, "The Problem of Revolutionary Asia," *Foreign Affairs*, 29, no. 1 (October 1950), 106.

4. Fairbank, "The Problem of Revolutionary Asia," 106; and Fairbank, "Toward a Dynamic Far Eastern Policy," *Far Eastern Survey*, 18, no. 18 (September 7, 1949), 209–12.

5. Tucker, *Taiwan, Hong Kong, and the United States*, 54.

6. Carter Eckert, Ki-baik Lee, Young Ick Lew, Michael Robinson, and Edward Wagner, *Korea Old and New* (Seoul, Korea: Ilchokak Publishers, 1990), 396.

7. Kim, *Master of Manipulation*, 145.

8. Tucker, *Taiwan, Hong Kong, and the United States*, 36.

9. "Telegram, Charge in the Philippines (Lockett) to the Secretary of State, 22 March 1949"; "Telegram, Secretary of State (Acheson) to Charge in the Philippines (Lockett), 23 March 1949"; and "Telegram, Charge in the Philippines (Lockett) to the Secretary of State, 24 March 1949," in *FRUS, 1949, The Far East and Australasia*, vol. 7, 1125–27. Quirino's motives for the pact ranged from domestic political capital (as he faced an impending election) to the desire to secure US military aid in peacetime.

10. "The Secretary of State to the Charge in the Philippines (Lockett), 23 March 1949," in *FRUS, 1949, The Far East and Australasia*, vol. 7, 1126.

11. See "The Charge in the Philippines (Lockett) to the Secretary of State, 21 March 1949," in *FRUS, 1949, The Far East and Australasia*, vol. 7, 1124.

12. "Memorandum of Conversation, Director of the Office for Far Eastern Affairs (Butterworth) with Dr. John M. Chang, Ambassador of the Republic of Korea, Mr. Niles W. Bond, Assistant Chief, Division of Northeast Asian Affairs, 8 April 1949"; "Memorandum of Conversation, Counselor of the Embassy in Korea (Drumright), 28 May 1949," in *FRUS, 1949, The Far East and Australasia*, vol. 7, 1141–42; 1145–46.

13. Syngman Rhee quoted in "The Ambassador in Korea (Muccio) to the Secretary of State, 20 May 1949," in *FRUS, 1949, The Far East and Australasia*, vol. 7, 1144.

14. "'Pacific Union'—President Quirino," *Straits Times*, 5 July 1949, 1. http://newspapers.nl.sg/Digitised/Page/straitstimes19490705.1.1.aspx, National Library Board of Singapore Archives (accessed 26 November 2011).

15. Quoted in Roger Dingman, "Forgotten Summit: The Quirino-Chiang Kai-shek Conversations, July, 1949," *American Historical Collection*, 19, no. 3 (July-September 1991), n.37.

16. "Chiang-Quirino United Front: Starting a Pacific Pact," *Straits Times*, 12 July 1949, 1 http://newspapers.nl.sg/Digitised/Page/straitstimes19490712.1.1.aspx; and "Chiang Flies to Manila for Anti-Red Talks," *Straits Times*, 11 July 1949, http://newspapers.nl.sg/Digitised/Page/straitstimes19490711.1.1.aspx, National Library Board Archives of Singapore (both accessed 21 November 2011).

17. Dingman, "Forgotten Summit," 43.

18. Ibid.

19. Chiang said: "The Generalissimo agrees wholeheartedly with Mr. President as regards the unity of the Asiatic countries, not only for the purpose of checking the spread of Communism in this area but also to show to the leading powers in the democratic group that these countries in the Far East are united and determined to fight against this threat. But the Generalissimo feels that at this particular moment if the Asiatic countries do not show their determination for unity, it will be difficult to make the United States to take a firm attitude against Communism in the Far East. . . . That is why we must think in terms of Oriental philosophy and reflect what we can do for ourselves to show other peoples of the earth that we believe in democracy and have the determination to achieve something in order to change the attitude of the United States and realize the strength of the Asiatic peoples." See Dingman, "Forgotten Summit," 44.

20. Other countries Chiang mentioned were Indonesia, Australia, and New Zealand.

21. Dingman, "Forgotten Summit," 47.

22. There was a domestic political angle to Quirino's enthusiasm for the Pacific Pact. The Philippines president was up for re-election and did not want his summit with Truman to be interpreted as a blatant campaign ploy. Having a substantive issue like the Pacific Pact proposal gave Quirino political cover and also displayed statesmanship as a representative of the other Asian nations.

23. Dingman, "The Forgotten Summit," 53.

24. "Telegram, Ambassador in Korea (Muccio) to Secretary of State, 12 July 1949"; "Telegram, Charge in the Philippines (Lockett) to Secretary of State, 12 July 1949," in *FRUS, 1949, The Far East and Australasia*, vol. 7, 1152–55.

25. "Anti-Red Talks in US," *Straits Times* 8 August 1949, 1, http://newspapers .nl.sg/Digitised/Page/straits, National Library Board of Singapore Archives (accessed 13 December 2011).

26. "Telegram, Ambassador in Korea (Muccio) to Secretary of State, 8 August 1949," in *FRUS, 1949, The Far East and Australasia*, vol. 7, 1184; "Chiang-Rhee Anti-Red Pact Plea," *Straits Times*, 9 August 1949, 1, http://newspapers.nl .sg/Digitised/Page/straitstimes19490809.1.1.aspx, National Library Board Archives of Singapore (accessed 21 November 2011); and Donald S. Mac-Donald, *US-Korea Relations from Liberation to Self-Reliance* (Boulder, CO: Westview, 1992), 139.

27. "Appeal Cabled to Quirino," *Straits Times*, 9 August 1949, 3, http:// newspapers.nl.sg/Digitised/Page/straitstimes19490810.1.3.aspx, National Library Board of Singapore Archives (accessed 12 December 2011).

28. "Quirino Will Not Go Home with Nothing," *Straits Times*, 11 August 1949, 1, http://newspapers.nl.sg/Digitised/Page/straitstimes19490811.1.1.aspx, National Library Board of Singapore Archives (accessed 9 January 2012).

29. "US Told Watch the Back Door," *Straits Times*, 17 August 1949, 2, http:// newspapers.nl.sg/Digitised/Page/straitstimes19490817.1.1.aspx, National Library Board of Singapore Archives (accessed 31 January 2012).

30. "'Interested' in Pact," *Straits Times*, 23 March 1949, http://newspapers.nl .sg/Digitised/Page/straitstimes19490323.1.1.aspx, National Library Board

of Singapore Archives (accessed 27 November 2011); and "Reds Won't Hold Asia," ibid. 24 March 1949 http://newspapers.nl.sg/Digitised/Page /straitstimes19490324.1.1.aspx, National Library Board of Singapore Archives (accessed 27 November 2011).

31. For example, see "Pacific Union Pact Talks," *Straits Times*, 19 July 1949, http://newspapers.nl.sg/Digitised/Page/straitstimes19490719.1.1.aspx, National Library Board of Singapore Archives (accessed 28 November 2011).

32. "Key Thrown in Pacific," *Straits Times*, 29 July 1949, 1, http://newspapers.nl .sg/Digitised/Page/straitstimes19490729.1.1.aspx, National Library Board of Singapore Archives (accessed 11 December 2011); and "No More US Aid for Chiang," *Straits Times*, 30 July 1949, 3, http://newspapers.nl.sg/Digitised /Page/straitstimes19490730.1.3.aspx, National Library Board of Singapore Archives (accessed 12 December 2011).

33. "US Aid Proposal for Far Eastern Union," *Straits Times*, 15 August 1949, 1, http://newspapers.nl.sg/Digitised/Page/straitstimes19490815.1.1.aspx National Library Board of Singapore Archives (accessed 30 January 2012).

34. "US Told 'Keep Reds Out of Asia,'" *Straits Times*, 12 October 1949, 1 http:// newspapers.nl.sg/Digitised/Page/straitstimes19491012.1.1.aspx National Library Board Archives of Singapore (accessed 13 February 2012).

35. "Asian Cominform to be Set Up," *Straits Times*, 3 December 1949, 1, http:// newspapers.nl.sg/Digitised/Page/straitstimes19491203.1.1.aspx, National Library Board Archives of Singapore (accessed 22 June 2012).

36. O. M. Green, "Soviet Imperialism in Asia," *Straits Times*, 21 November 1949, 4, http://newspapers.nl.sg/Digitised/Page/straitstimes19491121.1.4.aspx, National Library Board Archives of Singapore (accessed 14 June 2012).

37. Ibid.

38. "T.U.C. of Asian Countries," *Straits Times*, 3 November 1949, 1, http:// newspapers.nl.sg/Digitised/Page/straitstimes19491103.1.1.aspx National Library Board Archives of Singapore (accessed 15 March 2012); "Hunger Feeds Communism," *Straits Times*, 4 November 1949, 1, http://newspapers .nl.sg/Digitised/Page/straitstimes19491104.1.1.aspx, National Library Board Archives of Singapore (accessed 16 May 2012).

39. "'Threat to Asia' Warns Wavell,' *Straits Times*, 21 October 1949, 3, http:// newspapers.nl.sg/Digitised/Page/straitstimes19491021.1.3.aspx, National Library Board Archives of Singapore (accessed 18 February 2012).

40. ECAFE was created in 1947 and had thirteen participants (Australia, Burma, China, France, India, Netherlands, New Zealand, Pakistan, Philippines, Thailand, USSR, UK, and US), and associate members (Malay and British Borneo, Cambodia, Ceylon, Hong Kong, Indonesia, Nepal, and Laos) to promote economic interaction (largely over raw material exports to the industrialized world), but had no political or military identity. The meetings were far from cordial and manifested the emerging Cold War tensions as the USSR delegation opposed US economic agenda items as exploitative and capitalist. See "US Accused, Advertising at ECAFE," *Straits Times*, 18 October 1949, http://newspapers.nl.sg/Digitised/Page/straitstimes19491018.1.1.aspx, National Library Board Archives of Singapore (accessed 13 February 2012).

41. "Memorandum by Policy Information Office of the Office of Far Eastern Affairs (Fisher) to the Director of the Office (Butterworth), 15 July 1949," in

FRUS, 1949, The Far East and Australasia, vol. 7, 1162; and "Memorandum by Policy Information Office of the Office of Far Eastern Affairs (Fisher) to the Director of the Office (Butterworth), 15 July 1949," in *FRUS, 1949, The Far East and Australasia*, vol. 7, 1162.

42. See "Telegram, Secretary of State (Acheson) to the Charge in the Philippines (Lockett), 23 March 1949"; "Charge in the Philippines (Lockett) to the Secretary of State (Acheson), 28 March 1949," in *FRUS, 1949, The Far East and Australasia*, vol. 7, 1126–28; and David W. Mabon, "Elusive Agreements," 151.

43. *Department of State Bulletin*, 20 (January-June 1949), 696.

44. Mabon, "Elusive Agreements," 147–78, especially 151.

45. For example, "Memorandum of Conversation, Director of the Office for Far Eastern Affairs (Butterworth) and Ambassador of the Republic of Korea (Chang), 8 April 1949"; "Telegram. Secretary of State to the Charge in the Philippines (Lockett), 23 March 1949," in *FRUS, 1949, The Far East and Australasia*, vol. 7, 1141, 1126.

46. *New York Times*, 5 July 1949, 3.

47. *New York Times*, 24 May 1949, 4.

48. "Memorandum by the Policy Information Officer of the Office of Far Eastern Affairs (Fisher) to the Director of the Office (Butterworth), 15 July 1949," in *FRUS, 1949, The Far East and Australasia*, vol. 7, 1161.

49. As a State Department memo put it, "Chiang's inclusion saddles the embryonic union with a military problem it can't hope to solve" (see "Memorandum by the Policy Information Officer of the Office of Far Eastern Affairs [Fisher] to the Director of the Office [Butterworth], 15 July 1949,") in *FRUS, 1949, The Far East and Australasia*, vol. 7, 1162; and "The Secretary of State to the Embassy in Korea, 29 July 1949," in *FRUS, 1949, The Far East and Australasia*, vol. 7, 1177–78; "The Secretary of State to Certain Diplomatic and Consular Offices, 20 July 1949, in *FRUS, 1949, The Far East and Australasia*, Vol. VII, 1170–1171; "The Secretary of State to the Embassy in Thailand, 25 July 1949," in *FRUS, 1949, The Far East and Australasia*, vol. 7, 1174–75; and "Telegram, Secretary of State to the Embassy in Korea, 29 July 1949," in *FRUS, 1949, The Far East and Australasia*, vol. 7, 1177–78).

50. As then-US Ambassador to the Soviet Union Admiral Allan Kirk noted, US involvement in the Chiang-Quirino proposal would "play squarely into Soviet hands." See "The Ambassador in the Soviet Union (Kirk) to the Secretary of State, 22 July 1949," in *FRUS, 1949, The Far East and Australasia*, vol. 7, 1172.

51. Ibid.

52. Nehru quoted in Dean Acheson, "Pacific Pact Corresponding to North Atlantic Treaty Untimely (18 May 1949)," *Department of State Bulletin*, 20 (April–June 1949), 696.

53. Mabon, "Elusive Agreements, 151.

54. "Manila Cool on Pact Plan," *Straits Times*, October 10, 1949, 3 http://newspapers.nl.sg/Digitised/Page/straitstimes19491010.1.3.aspx National Library Board Archives of Singapore (accessed 13 February 2012).

55. Spencer C. Tucker, ed., *Encyclopedia of the Korean War: A Political, Social, and Military History* (Santa Barbara, CA: ABC-CLIO, Inc., 2000), 504.

56. "The Ambassador in the United Kingdom (Douglas) to the Secretary of State, 26 July 1949," in *FRUS, 1949, The Far East and Australasia*, vol. 7, 1176.

57. "Memorandum by the Assistant Secretary of State for Far Eastern Affairs (Butterworth) to the Secretary of State, 18 November 1949," in *FRUS, 1949, The Far East and Australasia*, vol. 7, 901–2.

58. "Rhee stated he understood US position regarding Nationalist China; . . . that he will not enter into any hard and fast commitments as result of talks with Chiang." See "Telegram, Ambassador in Korea (Muccio) to the Secretary of State, 3 August 1949," in *FRUS, 1949, The Far East and Australia*, vol. 7, 1181–82.

59. Dobbs, "The Pact that Never Was," 34.

60. "Memorandum of Conversation by the Chief of the Division of Philippine Affairs (Ely), 9 August 1949"; also see "Charge in the Philippines (Lockett) to the Secretary of State, 8 August 1949," both in *FRUS, 1949, The Far East and Australia*, vol. 7, 596–99. For US bilateral base agreement negotiations with Manila in the months preceding the summit, see "Secretary of Defense (Johnson) to the Secretary of State, 19 April 1949"; "The Secretary of State to the Embassy in the Philippines, 5 May 1949"; "The Ambassador in the Philippines (Cowen) to the Secretary of State, 23 May 1949"; and "The Secretary of State to the Embassy in the Philippines, 28 June 1949," all in *FRUS, 1949, The Far East and Australia*, vol. 7, 592–96.

61. "US May Aid Alliance," *Straits Times*, 13 August 1949, 1, http://newspapers .nl.sg/Digitised/Page/straitstimes19490813.1.1.aspx, National Library Board of Singapore Archives (accessed 30 January 2012).

62. "US Told Watch the Back Door," *Straits Times*, 17 August 1949, 2, http:// newspapers.nl.sg/Digitised/Page/straitstimes19490727.1.1.aspx, National Library Board of Singapore Archives (accessed 31 January 2012).

63. Calder, *Pacific Defense*, 194.

64. The military assistance was part of a $1.45 billion package under the Truman administration. Korea and the Philippines were the only Asian countries proposed in the plan which included Greece, Turkey, Iran in addition to Western Europe. "Far East's Share of US Arms Aid," *Straits Times*, 27 July 1949, 1, http://newspapers.nl.sg/Digitised/Page/straitstimes19490727.1.1 .aspx, National Library Board of Singapore Archives (accessed 11 December 2011); "Biggest Pacific Naval Exercises This Month," *Straits Times*, 4 October 1949, 3, http://newspapers.nl.sg/Digitised/Page/straitstimes19491004.1.3 .aspx, National Library Board Archives of Singapore (accessed 13 February 2012); and US resumes Marshall Aid to Indonesia," *Straits Times*, 9 November 1949, 3, http://newspapers.nl.sg/Digitised/Page/straitstimes19491109.1.3 .aspx National Library Board of Singapore Archives (accessed 18 May 2012).

65. "Policy Planning Staff Paper on United States Policy Toward Southeast Asia, 29 March 1949, PPS 51," in *FRUS, 1949, The Far East and Australia*, vol. 7, 1130.

66. "Memorandum of Conversation, Acting Deputy Director of the Office of Chinese Affairs (Freeman), 30 June 1950"; "Aide-Memoire. The Chinese Embassy to the Department of State, 30 June 1950," in *FRUS, 1950, Korea*, vol. 7, 262–63; "Memorandum by the Deputy Assistant Secretary of State

for Far Eastern Affairs (Merchant) to the Secretary of State, 29 June 1950," in *FRUS, 1950, Korea*, vol. 7, 239; Garver, *The Sino-American Alliance*, 42; Tucker, *Taiwan, Hong Kong, and the United States*, 32–33, 63–64.

67. Garver, *The Sino-American Alliance*, 64–65; and "Memorandum of Conversation by the Assistant Secretary of State for Far Eastern Affairs (Rusk) and Chinese Ambassador (Koo), 3 July 1950," in *FRUS, 1950, Korea*, vol. 7, 285–86.

68. "Telegram, Commander in Chief Far East (MacArthur) to the Joint Chiefs of Staff, 9 July 1950," in *FRUS, 1950, Korea*, vol. 7, 336.

69. "United States Delegation Minutes of the Sixth Meeting of President Truman and Prime Minister Attlee," in *FRUS, 1950, Korea*, vol. 7, 1469, n.3. After his dismissal by Truman, MacArthur testified before Congress that had he been able to use Chiang's forces, the outcome in Korea could have been radically different (see Leffler, *A Preponderance of Power*, 405).

70. For example, see "Memorandum by the Acting Office in Charge of Korean Affairs (Emmons) to the Deputy Director of the Office of Northeast Asian Affairs (Johnson), 28 November 1950," in *FRUS, 1950, Korea*, vol. 7, 1239–40.

71. See, for example, "Recommendations by Major General Chase, Chief of Military Assistance Advisory Group in Formosa," in "Memorandum of Conversation, Leonard Price of the Office of the Special Assistant for Mutual Security Affairs, 20 February 1952," in *FRUS, 1952–1954, China and Japan*, vol. 14, 13–14; also see Garver, *The Sino-American Alliance*, 47–48.

72. "Telegram, Charge in the Republic of China (Rankin) to the Department of State, 27 October 1952," in *FRUS, 1952–1954, China and Japan*, vol. 14, 113.

73. "Extracts of Memorandum of Conversations, Mr. W. Averell Harriman, Special Assistant to the President with General MacArthur, Tokyo, 6 and 8 August 1950," in *FRUS, 1950, East Asia and the Pacific*, vol. 6, 427–30; Garver, *The Sino-American Alliance*, 38–39; Tucker, *Taiwan, Hong Kong and the United States*, 32–33, and 64.

74. "Memorandum of Conversation, by Lieutenant General Matthew B. Ridgway, Deputy Chief of Staff for Administration, United States Army," in *FRUS, 1950, Korea*, vol. 7, 540.

75. Harry S. Truman, *Memoirs: Volume II, Years of Trial and Hope* (Garden City, NY: Doubleday, 1956), 354.

76. Ibid., 349.

77. Ibid., 351; "Extracts of a Memorandum of Conversation, by Mr. W. Averell Harriman, Special Assistant to the President, With General MacArthur in Tokyo on August 6 and 8, 1950," in *FRUS, 1950, East Asia and the Pacific*, vol. 6, 427–30.

78. Truman, *Memoirs*, 353; "Extracts of a Memorandum of Conversation, by Mr. W. Averell Harriman, Special Assistant to the President, With General MacArthur in Tokyo on August 6 and 8, 1950," in *FRUS, 1950, East Asia and the Pacific*, vol. 6, 427–28.

79. "Extracts of a Memorandum of Conversation, by Mr. W. Averell Harriman, Special Assistant to the President, With General MacArthur in Tokyo on August 6 and 8, 1950," in *FRUS, 1950, East Asia and the Pacific*, vol. 6, 428.

80. "Memorandum, Assistant Secretary of State for Far Eastern Affairs (Allison) to John Foster Dulles, 24 December 1952," in *FRUS, 1952–1954, China and Japan*, vol. 14, 119.

81. *New York Times*, July 29, 1954, 22.

82. See Donald MacDonald, *US-Korea Relations from Liberation to Self-Reliance: The Twenty Year Record* (Boulder, CO: Westview, 1992), 139–40.

83. Tucker, *Taiwan, Hong Kong, and the United States*, 21, 66–67.

84. Galia Press-Barnathan, "The Impact of Regional Dynamics on US Policy Towards Regional Security Arrangements in East Asia," *International Relations of the Asia-Pacific*, 14, no. 3 (2014), 367; and John L. Gaddis, *Strategies of Containment* (Oxford: Oxford University Press, 1982).

85. See discussion in Christensen, *Worse than a Monolith*, 136–44.

86. "In accordance with your suggestion some weeks ago, we have attempted to get away from the designation 'SEATO' so as to avoid fostering the idea that an organization is envisioned for SEA [Southeast Asia] and the Pacific similar to NATO with all its connotations of elaborate military machinery and large standing forces in the area equipped and maintained principally by US military aid. In spite of our efforts, the designation 'SEATO' has stuck, mainly because the press has been using it for many months. Furthermore, the other prospective members of the Pact seem to prefer 'SEATO' to any other name we have suggested. *I suggest that we accept that 'SEATO' is here to stay and that we continue to make clear in our substantive discussions that so far as the US is concerned, the SEA Pact is not conceived as a parallel to NATO* (emphasis in original)." "Memorandum by the Assistant Secretary for European Affairs (Merchant) to the Secretary of State, 18 August 1954, Washington," in *FRUS, 1952–1954, East Asia and the Pacific*, vol. 12, 740.

87. For discussions of these options see "The Secretary of State to the United States Political Adviser to SCAP (Sebald), 8 February 1951," in *FRUS, 1951, Asia and the Pacific*, vol. 6, 150–51; "Memorandum by Mr. Robert A. Fearey of the Office of Northeast Asian Affairs, 16 February 1951," in *FRUS, 1951, Asia and the Pacific*, vol. 6, 162; "Memorandum on the Substance of Discussions at a Department of State-Joint Chiefs of Staff Meeting, 11 April 1951," in *FRUS, 1951, Asia and the Pacific*, vol. 6, 195.

88. "Memorandum of Conversation, by Mr. Charlton Ogburn, Policy Information Officer, Bureau of Far Eastern Affairs, 3 April 1950"; "Oral Report from the Ambassador-at-Large Philip C. Jessup upon his Return from the East," in *FRUS, 1950, East Asia and the Pacific*, vol. 6, 68–76.

89. Ibid., 71.

90. "Memorandum by the Assistant Secretary of State for European Affairs (Perkins) to the Secretary of State, 27 July 1950," in *FRUS, 1950, East Asia and the Pacific*, vol. 6, 121–23.

91. Dulles was appointed in January 1951 by Truman as a special assistant to consider potential defense arrangements for the Pacific and Japan (see "Memorandum, Special Assistant (Allison) to the Ambassador at Large (Jessup), 4 January 1951," in *FRUS, 1951, Asia and the Pacific*, vol. 6, 132–34; Charles Dobbs, "The Pact That Never Was: The Pacific Pact of 1949," *Journal*

of Northeast Asian Studies, 3, no. 4 (Winter 1984), 29–42; and Mabon, "Elusive Agreements."

92. See the January 10, 1951 letter from Truman to Dulles appointing him as Special Representative to the President prior to Dulles' trip to Asia in *Dulles Papers* (Japan to Korea, 1951), Box 53, 2; also see "Memorandum by the Special Assistant to the Consultant (Allison) to the Ambassador at Large (Jessup)," in *FRUS, 1951, Asia and the Pacific*, vol. 6, 133.

93. For excerpts of Truman's appointment letter to Dulles, see "Memorandum, Secretary of State (Acheson) to Secretary of Defense (Marshall), 9 January 1951, Enclosure 2, 'Draft Letter to Mr. Dulles,'" in *FRUS, 1951, Asia and the Pacific*, vol. 6, 787–89.

94. "Memorandum, John Foster Dulles, the Consultant to the Secretary, to the Ambassador at Large (Jessup), 4 January 1951," in *FRUS, 1951, Asia and the Pacific*, vol. 6, 135. Also see "Address of Ambassador John Foster Dulles At the Luncheon held at the Industry Club of Japan on February 2, 1951," *Dulles Papers* (January-April 1951), Box 303.

95. "Draft of a Possible Pacific Ocean Pact, 3 January 1951," in *FRUS, 1951, Asia and the Pacific*, vol. 6, 133; E.D.L. Killen, "The ANZUS Pact and Pacific Security," *Far Eastern Survey*, 21, no. 14 (October 1962), 138.

96. "Memorandum by John Foster Dulles, the Consultant to the Secretary, to the Ambassador at Large (Jessup), 4 January 1951," in *FRUS, 1951, Asia and the Pacific*, vol. 6, 135.

97. "Memorandum of Conversation, by the Special Assistant to the Secretary (Howard), 7 April 1950," in *FRUS, 1950, East Asia and the Pacific*, vol. 6, 1162–63.

98. Ibid., 136.

99. Killen, "The Anzus Pact," 138.

100. "Report to the National Security Council by the Executive Secretary (Lay), 17 May 1951, NSC Staff Study on United States Objectives, Policies and Courses of Action in Asia," in *FRUS, 1951, Asia and the Pacific*, vol. 6, 43.

101. "Memorandum of Conversation, by Colonel Stanton Babcock of the Department of Defense, 19 October 1950," in *FRUS, 1950, East Asia and the Pacific*, vol. 6, 1323.

102. As Dulles wrote, "The 'major 'island' formula excludes the UK. This is desirable to avoid possible complication with Hongkong [*sic*], which the JCS feel must be excluded. Also, if the UK is included it would be difficult not to include France, with possible complications in relation to Indo-China." See "Comment on Draft (1/3/51) of Pacific Ocean Pact, (Dulles to Jessup), 4 January 1951," in *FRUS, 1951, Asia and the Pacific*, vol. 6, 135. In presentations to the British Foreign Office, Undersecretary of State Rusk stated that the inclusion of these European powers might give the Pact a neocolonial quality, but the primary US concerns centered on entrapment. See "Memorandum of Conversation, Burton Kitain (Office of British Commonwealth and Northern European Affairs) with Dean Rusk, 8 February 1951," in *FRUS, 1951, Asia and the Pacific*, vol. 6, 148.

103. "The Secretary of State to the United States Political Adviser to SCAP (Sebald), 8 February 1951," in *FRUS, 1951, Asia and the Pacific*, vol. 6, 150–51.

104. Acheson, *Present at the Creation*, 540.
105. "Address by the Honorable John Foster Dulles over the Columbia Broadcasting System Network, Thursday, March 1, 1951," *Dulles Papers* (Writing About or Relating to John Foster Dulles, 1949–1951), Box 399, 5.
106. "Memorandum of Conversation among Ambassador Dulles, Australian and New Zealand Ministers for External Affairs, and Staffs, 17 February 1951," in *FRUS, 1951, Asia and the Pacific*, vol. 6, 164.
107. "Memorandum of Conversation Among Ambassador Dulles, Ministers of External Affairs of Australia and New Zealand, 17 February 1951," in ibid., 170; and Sir Percy Spender, *Exercises in Diplomacy: The ANZUS Treaty and the Colombo Plan* (Sydney, Australia: Sydney University Press, 1969), 90.
108. Mabon, "Elusive Agreements," 164.
109. "Chance to End Cold War—Mr. Foster Dulles," *Reuters*, 1 April 1951 in *Dulles Papers* (Japan to Korea, 1951), Box 53.
110. For example, see "Verbatim Transcript—Press Conference Questions, Radio Tokyo Building, 19 April 1951, *Dulles Papers* (Writings about or Relating to John Foster Dulles, 1949–1951), Box 399, 6.
111. See, for example, "Interview with John Foster Dulles on Japanese Peace Treaty Conference to be held in San Francisco, 16 August 1951," in *Dulles Papers* (Writings about or Relating to John Foster Dulles, 1949–1951), Box 399, 5.
112. "Transcript of Notes Taken by Leonard Greenup during Press Conference by John Foster Dulles at Dorchester Hotel, June 5, 1951," *Dulles Papers* (Japan to Korea, 1951), Box 55, 2.
113. Joint Press Conference by John Foster Dulles and Senators Smith and Sparkman, 10 December 1951, in *Dulles Papers* (Writings about or Relating to John Foster Dulles, 1949–1951), Box 399, 18–19; also see "Transcript of Recording for Voice of America Mr. Dulles interviewed by Mr. Hogan," n.d., *Dulles Papers* (Writings about or Relating to John Foster Dulles, 1949–1951), Box 399, 3. Dulles in the latter transcript explicitly answers a question about the Pacific Ocean Pact by saying "We do not have anything in mind at the present time which you can properly call a Pacific Pact."
114. In Dulles's words, "One thing about this Treaty, which is worth mentioning, but which does not appear in the terms of the Treaty itself; it is the reassurance which is given to other countries against a revival of aggression by Japan. . . . Japan's security would not be just a charge upon Japan alone, but would be a joint responsibility of Japan and the US." "Speech Before the Council on Foreign Relations, October 31, 1951," *Dulles Papers* (Writings about or Relating to John Foster Dulles, 1949–1951), Box 399, 16–17, and 21–23.
115. Ibid., 24–26.
116. "Memorandum of Conversation Among Ambassador Dulles, Ministers for External Affairs of Australia and New Zealand, 17 February 1951," in *FRUS, 1951, Asia and the Pacific*, vol. 6, 171.
117. Transcript of interview of John Foster Dulles with CBS, 15 May 1951 in the Capitol Cloak Room, *Dulles Papers* (Acheson, Dean to Illinois Bankers Association, 1951), Box 52, 8.

118. "Draft Memorandum for the President attachment, Secretary of State to Secretary of Defense (Marshall), 5 April 1951," in *FRUS, 1951, Asia and the Pacific*, vol. 6, 183–85. "It is believed that the three arrangements contemplated, one with Japan, one with the Philippines, one with Australia and New Zealand, and possibly one with Indonesia, will in fact achieve what your letter of January 10, 1951 described as the 'dual purpose of assuring combined action as between the members to resist aggression from without and also to resist attack by one of the members, e.g., Japan, if Japan should again become aggressive" (p. 185). Also see "Letter to the President Truman, 3 October 1951," *Dulles Papers*, Box 56, 1 page.

119. Ibid., 184.

120. "Memorandum by Mr. Robert A. Fearey of the Office of Northeast Asian Affairs, 16 February 1951, Notes on Conversation Among Ambassador Dulles, Australian and New Zealand Ministers for External Affairs, and Staffs," in *FRUS, 1951, Asia and the Pacific*, vol. 6, 157.

121. After the Korean War and the realization of the bilateral alliance structure in 1954, the United States considered again the concept of a multilateral security organization for Northeast Asia (NEATO) amalgamating the alliances with Japan, Taiwan, and South Korea, but this ran into the same problems as the 1951 effort. Japan was content with its bilateral arrangement with the United States and saw no need for a broader arrangement. South Korea preferred tight bilateralism with the United States and did not want Japan involved in Korean security in any way. And once Japan was hard to integrate into a NEATO concept, Washington saw little interest in an arrangement involving just Korea and Taiwan because of concerns about entrapment. See "New Asian Line-up Studied by Dulles," *New York Times*, August 4, 1954; and Sakata Yasuyo, "The Western Pacific Collective Security Concept and Korea in the Eisenhower Years: The US-ROK Alliance as an Asia-Pacific Alliance," *Journal of Kanda University of International Studies*, no. 20 (March 2008), 1–30.

Chapter 8

1. Daniel Nexon, "What's This, Then? 'Romanes Eunt Domus?'" *International Studies Perspective*, 9, no. 3 (August 2008), 304–5; Alexander J. Motyl, *Imperial Ends: The Decay, Collapse, and Revival of Empires* (New York: Columbia University Press, 2001); Motyl, "Empire Falls," *Foreign Affairs*, 85, no. 4 (July 2006), 190–94; Charles Tilly, "How Empires End," in K. Barkey and M. Von Hagen, eds., *After Empire: Multiethnic Societies and Nation-Building* (Boulder, CO: Westview, 1997).

2. Nexon, "What's This, Then? 'Romanes Eunt Domus?'"; and Ji-Young Lee, "Hegemonic Authority and Domestic Legitimation: Japan and Korea Under the Chinese Hegemonic Order in Early Modern East Asia," unpublished paper presented at the American Political Science Association meeting, Washington, DC, August 28–31, 2014.

3. On trust, see Barbara Koremenos, Charles Lipson, Duncan Snidal, eds., *The Rational Design of International Institutions* (New York: Cambridge

2004); Andrew Kydd, *Trust and Mistrust International Relations* (Princeton, NJ: Princeton University Press, 2004); Charles Lipson, "Why Are Some International Agreements Informal?" *International Organization*, 45, no. 4 (Autumn 1991), 495–538; Koremenos, "Contracting Around International Uncertainty," *American Political Science Review*, 99, no. 4 (November 2005), 549–65; and Brian Rathbun, "Before Hegemony: Generalized Trust and the Creation and Design of International Security Organizations," *International Organization*, 65, no. 2 (Spring 2011), 243–76. On reputation and institutional design, see Michaela Mattes, "Reputation, Symmetry, and Alliance Design, *International Organization*, 66, no. 4 (Fall 2012), 679–708. On historical context, see Mark Copelovitch and Tonya Putnam, "Design in Context: Existing International Agreements and New Cooperation," *International Organization*, 68, no. 2 (Spring 2014), 471–93. Also see Lisa Martin, "The Rational State Choice of Multilateralism," in John Ruggie, ed., *Multilateralism Matters: The Theory and Praxis of an Institutional Form* (New York: Columbia University Press, 1993); David Lake, *Entangling Relations— American Foreign Policy in Its Century* (Princeton, NJ: Princeton University Press, 1999); David Lake and Patrick Morgan, eds., *Regional Orders: Building Security in a New World* (University Park: Pennsylvania State University Press, 1997); Galia Press-Barnathan, *Organizing the World: The United States and Regional Cooperation in Asia and Europe* (New York: Routledge, 2003), 17–19; and Etel Solingen, *Regional Orders at Century's Dawn: Global and Domestic Influences on Grand Strategy* (Princeton, NJ: Princeton University Press, 1998).

4. See literature review in chapter 1 for elaboration.

5. Cumings's characterization of MacArthur is representative—"[MacArthur] prided himself on his command of "oriental psychology,' which reflected nineteenth-century renderings of Asians as obedient, dutiful, child-like, and quick to follow resolute leadership." Cumings, *Origins of the Korean War*, volume 2, 97.

6. "Statement of Policy by the National Security Council, NSC 5418/1, 10 June 1954, Washington, D.C.," in *FRUS, 1952–1954, Western Europe and Canada*, vol. 6, part 2, 1980–1981.

7. Alexander Cooley, *Base Politics: Democratic Change and the US Military Overseas* (Ithaca, NY: Cornell University Press, 2008), 57–58.

8. As an internal NSC document in 1954 stated, "Spain (nominally a monarchy but without king or regent) is an authoritarian state with the strength and stability of the regime due in large part to General Franco's dominant position. . . . Its prestige will be further strengthened by the US aid and base programs." "Statement of Policy by the National Security Council, NSC 5418/1, 10 June 1954, Washington, D.C.," in *FRUS, 1952–1954, Western Europe and Canada*, vol. 6, part 2, 1981.

9. Cooley, *Base Politics*, 14; and Tongfi Kim, "Why Alliances Entangle but Seldom Entrap States," *Security Studies*, 20, no. 3 (2011), 371.

10. For discussion of the annexes (otherwise known as "Technical Agreements"), see "The Charge in Spain (Jones) to the Spanish Minister of Foreign Affairs (Artajo), 16 March 1953," in *FRUS, 1952–1954, Western Europe and Canada*,

vol. 6, part 2, 1920. For discussion of Spanish consent on US nuclear weapons, see Boris Nikolaj Liedtke, "International Relations Between the U.S. and Spain 1945–1953: Economics, Ideology and Compromise" PhD dissertation, London School of Economics and Political Sciences, 2014, 339.

11. David Stiles, "A Fusion Bomb over Andalucia: US Information Policy and the 1966 Palomares Incident," *Journal of Cold War Studies*, 8, no. 1 (Winter 2006), 49–67; and Randall Maydew, *America's Lost H-Bomb: Palomares, Spain, 1966* (Manhattan, KS: Sunflower University Press, 1997).

12. Kim, "Why Alliances Entangle but Seldom Entrap States."

13. "Report on US Policy Toward Spain, undated, Washington, DC," in *FRUS, 1961–1963 Western Europe and Canada*, vol. 13, 1013.

14. Preston Whitaker, *Spain and Defense of the West; Ally and Liability* (New York: Harper, 1961), 45.

15. Kim, "Why Alliances Entangle but Seldom Entrap States," 369.

16. "Letter from Generalissimo Franco to President Eisenhower, 22 August 1953, San Sebastian," in *FRUS, 1952–1954, Western Europe and Canada*, vol. 6, part 2, 1950.

17. "Memorandum by the Ambassador to Spain (Dunn) to the Secretary of State," 31 August 1953," in *FRUS, 1952–1954, Western Europe and Canada*, vol. 6, part 2, 1952–53.

18. "Statement of Policy by the National Security Council NSC 5418/1, 10 June 1954, Washington, D.C., in *FRUS, 1952–1954, Western Europe and Canada*, vol. 6, part 2, 1982–83.

19. For example, see Memorandum by the Deputy Assistant Secretary of State for European Affairs (Bonbright) to the Secretary of State, 14 September 1953, Washington, DC, in *FRUS, 1952–1954, Western Europe and Canada*, vol. 6, part 2, pp. 905–6; and "Report on US Policy Toward Spain, undated, Washington, DC," in *FRUS, 1961–1963 Western Europe and Canada*, vol. 13, 1017.

20. See "Memorandum of Conversation between the President and the Spanish Ambassador, 3 May 1963, Washington, D.C.," in *FRUS, 1961–1963, Western Europe and Canada*, vol. 13, 1007; and Daniel Druckman, "Stages, Turning Points, and Crises: Negotiating Military Base Rights: Spain and the United States," *Journal of Conflict Resolution*, 30, no. 2 (June 1986), 327–60.

21. Cooley, *Base Politics*, 61. It would not be until 1976 that the United States would offer a security guarantee in renegotiations with the post-Franco government.

22. Ibid., 60.

23. Pressman, *Warring Friends*, 116.

24. Ibid.

25. Pressman's work uses the term "mobilization of power resources" to explain situations in which the United States used material capabilities to exert control versus merely rhetorical measures. Unlike this study, Pressman considers not just sanctions but also inducements in an ally's control strategy portfolio.

26. See Marc Trachtenberg, *A Constructed Peace*, 246; and T.V. Paul, *Power Versus Prudence: Why Nations Forgo Nuclear Weapons* (Montreal and Kingston: McGill-Queen's University Press, 2000), 39–40; Catherine Kelleher,

Germany and the Politics of Nuclear Weapons (New York: Columbia University Press, 1975); and Wolfgang Krieger, "The Germans and the Nuclear Question," German Historical Institute Occasional Paper No. 14, Fifth Alois Mertes Memorial Lecture, Washington, DC, 1995.

27. "Memorandum of Conversation between the President and Ambassador Alphand, M. Malraux, 11 May 1962, Washington, D.C.," in *FRUS, 1961– 1963, Western Europe and Canada*, vol. 13, 697.

28. "Memorandum of Conversation between the Secretary of State and the German Chancellor, 22 June 1962, Bonn, Germany," in *FRUS, 1961–1963, Western Europe and Canada*, vol. 13, 419–22.

29. Krieger, "The Germans and the Nuclear Question," p. 18, and Gene Gerzhoy, "Alliance Coercion and Nuclear Restraint: How the United States Thwarted West Germany's Nuclear Ambitions," *International Security*, 39, no. 4 (Spring 2015), 117.

30. Gerzhoy, "Alliance Coercion and Nuclear Restraint," 114.

31. "Summary Record of NSC Executive Committee Meeting, 25 January 1963, Washington, D.C.," in *FRUS, 1961–1963, Western Europe and Canada*, vol. 13, 486–91.

32. Krieger, "The Germans and the Nuclear Question," 16–17.

33. T.V. Paul, *Power Versus Prudence*, 40–41.

34. Krieger, "The Germans and the Nuclear Question," 17–18.

35. "Memorandum of Conversation between Walt Rostow and Rainer Barzel at the White House, 23 February 1968," in *FRUS, 1964–1968, Germany and Berlin*, vol. 15, 637.

36. Quoted in Gerzhoy, "Alliance Coercion and Nuclear Restraint," 107

37. Gerzhoy, "Alliance Coercion and Nuclear Restraint," 107 and 125. Germany eventually signed the NPT in 1970 under the Willy Brandt government.

38. Richard Tanter, "Japan's Indian Ocean Naval Deployment: Blue Water Militarization in a 'Normal Country,'" *Japan Focus*, May 15, 2006, http://japanfocus .org/-Richard-Tanter/1700/article.html (accessed 1 November 2015).

39. Prime Minister of Japan and his Cabinet, "The Outline of the Basic Plan regarding Response Measures Based on the Law Concerning the Special Measures on Humanitarian and Reconstruction Assistance in Iraq," December 9, 2003, http://japan.kantei.go.jp/policy/2003/031209housin_e.html (accessed 1 November 2015).

40. Howard French, "South Korea Agrees to Send Troops to Iraq," *New York Times*, April 3, 2003, http://www.nytimes.com/2003/04/03/international /worldspecial/03KORE.html (accessed 1 November 2015).

41. Michael Green, "The Iraq War and Asia: Assessing the Legacy," *Washington Quarterly*, 31, no. 2 (Spring 2008), 181–200, especially 187.

42. President George W. Bush, "Address to a Joint Session of Congress and the American People," *The White House*, September 20, 2001, http:// georgewbush-whitehouse.archives.gov/news/releases/2001/09/20010920–8 .html (Accessed 1 November 2015).

43. Jim Mann, "Baker Tells Japan: Take Global Role: Policy: Move beyond 'checkbook diplomacy,' he advises in policy speech," *Los Angeles Times*, http://articles.latimes.com/1991–11–11/news/mn-996_1_foreign-policy (accessed 1 November 2015).

44. Green, "The Iraq War and Asia: Assessing the Legacy," 181–200, especially 183–84; and "53% of Japanese Do Not Trust the US: Dissatisfaction on Iraq," *Yomiuri Shimbun*, December 16, 2004, 1.

45. Gerald Geunwook Lee, "South Korea's Faustian Attitude: The Republic of Korea's Decision to Send Troops to Iraq Revisited," *Cambridge Review of International Affairs*, 19, no. 3 (September 2006), 481–93; especially 482; and Phillip Saunders, "The United States and East Asia After Iraq," *Survival*, 49, no. 1 (2007), 141–52.

46. S. T. Sim, "Opposition Mounts against Dispatching Combat Troops," *Korea Herald*, 18 September 2003; and S. T. Sim, "Foreign Ministry's US Policy Bureau Faces Major Reshuffle," *Korea Herald*, 16 January 2004. J. Y. Shim, "Roh Says NK Nuke Talks Big Factor in Troop Dispatch," *Korea Times*, 1 October 2003.

47. Tim Johnston, "Ally of Bush Is Defeated in Australia," *New York Times*, November 25, 2007, http://www.nytimes.com/2007/11/25/world/asia /25australia.html?_r=1 (accessed 1 November 2015); Rohan Sullivan, "Bush Ally Howard Defeated in Australia; Next Prime Minister Promises New Course on Iraq, Warming," *Washington Post*, November 25, 2007, A17; and Green, "The Iraq War and Asia," 187.

48. For good overviews, see Dick Nanto, *East Asian Regional Architecture* (Congressional Research Service, April 15, 2010), accessible at: http://fpc.state .gov/documents/organization/142760.pdf (accessed 1 November 2015), p. 5. Kent Calder and Francis Fukuyama, eds., *East Asian Multilateralism: Prospects for Regional Stability*. (Baltimore: Johns Hopkins University Press, 2008); Bates Gill and Michael J. Green, eds., *Asia's New Multilateralism: Cooperation, Competition, and the Search for Community* (New York: Columbia University Press, 2009); and Mark Beeson and Richard Stubbs, eds., *Routledge Handbook of Asian Regionalism* (New York: Routledge, 2012).

49. Jervis, "Unipolarity: A Structural Perspective," in Ikenberry, Mastanduno, and Wohlforth eds., *International Relations Theory and the Consequences of Unipolarity*, 269.

50. Michael Mastanduno, "System Maker and Privilege Taker: US Power and the International Political Economy," in Ikenberry, Mastanduno, and Wohlforth, eds., *International Relations Theory and the Consequences of Unipolarity*, 141.

51. Jervis, "Unipolarity: A Structural Perspective," 266.

52. Ruth Oldenziel, "Islands: The United States as a Networked Empire," in Gabrielle Hecht, ed., *Entangled Geographies: Empire and Technopolitics in the Global Cold War* (Cambridge, MA: MIT Press, 2011), 13–42.

53. Finnemore, "Legitimacy, Hypocrisy and Unipolarity," in Ikenberry, Mastanduno and Wohlforth, eds., *International Relations Theory and the Consequences of Unipolarity*, 87–89; David Lake, "Legitimating Power: The Domestic Politics of US International Hierarchy," *International Security*, 38, no. 2 (Fall 2013), 74–111.

54. Walt, "Alliances in a Unipolar World," in Ikenberry, Mastanduno, and Wohlforth, eds., *International Relations Theory and the Consequences of Unipolarity*, 134–35.

55. Ibid.

56. See Jack Snyder, *Myths of Empire: Domestic Politics and International Ambition* (Ithaca, NY: Cornell University Press, 1993) and Snyder, "Imperial Temptations."

57. Wohlforth, "The Stability of a Unipolar World"; Walt, "Alliances in a Unipolar World," in Ikenberry, Mastanduno, and Wohlforth, eds., *International Relations Theory and the Consequences of Unipolarity*, pp. 134–5; and Ethan Kapstein and Michael Mastanduno, eds., *Unipolar Politics: Realism and State Strategies after the Cold War* (New York: Columbia University Press, 1999).

58. For Korea, see "Joint Vision for the Alliance of the United States of America and the Republic of Korea," The White House, 16 June 2009, http://www.whitehouse.gov/the_press_office/Joint-vision-for-the-alliance-of-the-the-United-States-of-America-and-the-Republic-of-Korea; "Joint Declaration in Commemoration of the 60th Anniversary of the Alliance between the Republic of Korea and the United States of America," The White House, 7 May 2013, accessible here: http://www.whitehouse.gov/the-press-office/2013/05/07/joint-declaration-commemoration-60th-anniversary-alliance-between-republ. Accessed 1 November 2015. For Japan, see "United States-Japan Joint Statement: A Shared Vision for the Future," The White House, 30 April 2012, accessible here: http://www.whitehouse.gov/the-press-office/2012/04/30/united-states-japan-joint-statement-shared-vision-future (accessed 1 November 2015).

59. For India, see full text of the "United States-India Nuclear Cooperation Approval and Nonproliferation Enhancement Act." Accessible at: https://www.govtrack.us/congress/bills/110/hr7081/text (accessed 1 November 2015); The White House, "President Bush Signs H.R. 7081, the United States-India Nuclear Cooperation Approval and Nonproliferation Enhancement Act," 8 October 2008, accessible here: http://georgewbush-whitehouse.archives.gov/news/releases/2008/10/20081008–4.html (accessed 1 November 2015). For Singapore, see US Department of State, "Joint Statement of the United States-Singapore Strategic Partners Dialogue," 18 January 2012, accessible here: http://www.state.gov/r/pa/prs/ps/2012/01/181488.htm (accessed 1 November 2015). For the Philippines, see The White House, "Remarks by President Obama and President Benigno Aquino III of the Philippines in Joint Press Conference," 28 April 2014, accessible here: http://www.whitehouse.gov/the-press-office/2014/04/28/remarks-president-obama-and-president-benigno-aquino-iii-philippines-joi (accessed 1 November 2015). For Myanmar, see The White House, "Remarks by President Obama at the University of Yangon," 19 November 2012, accessible here: http://www.whitehouse.gov/the-press-office/2012/11/19/remarks-president-obama-university-yangon (accessed 1 November 2015). For Australia, see The White House, "Remarks by President Obama and Prime Gillard of Australia in Joint Press Conference," 16 November 2011, accessible here: http://www.whitehouse.gov/the-press-office/2011/11/16/remarks-president-obama-and-prime-minister-gillard-australia-joint-press (accessed 1 November 2015). For Taiwan, see The White House, "Message to the Congress—Agreement for Cooperation between the American Institute in Taiwan and the Taipei Economic and Cultural Representative Office Concerning Peaceful Uses of Nuclear Energy," 7 January 2014, accessible here: http://www.whitehouse

.gov/the-press-office/2014/01/07/message-congress-agreement-cooperation -between-american-institute-taiwan (accessed 1 November 2015). Also see Jeffrey Bader, *Obama and China's Rise: An Insider's Account of America's Asia Strategy* (Washington, DC: Brookings Institution, 2012); and Victor Cha, "Winning Asia: Washington's Untold Success Story," *Foreign Affairs*, 86, no. 6 (November/December 2007).

60. David Shambaugh, "China Engages Asia: Reshaping the Regional Order," *International Security*, 29, no. 3 (2004/5), 64–99.

61. Thomas Christensen, *The China Challenge: Shaping the Choices of a Rising Power* (New York: W.W. Norton, 2015), 11.

62. Lee Jae-hyon, "China is Recreating the American 'Hub-and-Spoke' System in Asia," *Diplomat*, September 11, 2015 http://thediplomat.com/2015/09 /china-is-recreating-the-american-hub-and-spoke-system-in-asia/ (accessed 18 October 2015).

63. Quotes in this paragraph are from Lee, "China is Recreating the American 'Hub-and-Spoke' System in Asia."

64. Mark Beeson, "Rethinking Regionalism: Europe and East Asia in Comparative Historical Perspective," *Journal of European Public Policy*, 12, no. 6 (2005), 977.

65. Michael Green and Nicholas Szechenyi, "Power and Order in Asia: A Survey of Regional Expectations," (Washington, DC: CSIS, July 2014), http:// csis.org/files/publication/140605_Green_PowerandOrder_WEB.pdf (accessed 1 November 2015).

66. Parts of this section are derived from an earlier and different publication of mine, "Complex Patchworks: US Alliances as a Part of Asia's Regional Architecture," *Asia Policy*, 11 (January 2011).

67. For arguments that Asia is bereft of working regional institutions, see Paul Bracken, *Fire in the East* (New York: HarperCollins, 1999), 26; Gerrit Gong, ed., *Memory and History in East and Southeast Asia* (Washington, DC: CSIS, 2001); Nicholas Kristof, "The Problem of Memory," *Foreign Affairs*, 77, no. 6 (November/December 1998), 37–49; Hemmer and Katzenstein, "Why is There no NATO in Asia?, 58; Anthony McGrew and Christopher Brook, eds., *Asia-Pacific in the New World Order* (London: Routledge, 1998), 57; and Aaron Friedberg, "Ripe for Rivalry: Prospects for Peace in a Multipolar Asia," *International Security*, 18, no. 3 (Winter 1993/94), 13–14.

68. Cha, "Powerplay: Origins of the US Alliance System in Asia."

69. Amitav Acharya, *Constructing a Security Community in Southeast Asia: ASEAN and the Problem of Regional Order* (London: Routledge, 2000), especially ch. 6.

70. "Rising Unity in East Test for Global Trade," *New Zealand Herald*, November 19, 2005 cited in Bruce Vaughn, "East Asia Summit (EAS): Issues for Congress" (Congressional Research Service: January 11, 2006), 4.

71. Vaughn, "East Asia Summit (EAS): Issues for Congress," p. 4; and "Pivot to the Pacific? The Obama Administration's "Rebalancing" Toward Asia," March 28, 2012, http://fas.org/sgp/crs/natsec/R42448.pdf.

72. Daniel Twining, "America's Grand Design in Asia," *Washington Quarterly*, 30, no. 3 (Summer 2007), 79–94; and Ralph Cossa, "South Asian Tsunami:

US Military Provides Logistical Backbone for Relief Operation," *eJournal USA: Foreign Policy Agenda* (March 4, 2005), http://www.america.gov/st /washfile-english/2005/March/20050304112100dmslahrellek0.5331537.html #ixzz0a5F8S6oo (accessed December 18, 2009).

73. "Bush Announces Tsunami Aid Coalition," *CNN.com*, 29 December 2004, http://www.cnn.com/2004/US/12/29/bush.quake/index.html (accessed December 30, 2009).

74. Marc Grossman, "The Tsunami Core Group: A Step toward a Transformed Diplomacy in Asia and Beyond," *Security Challenges*, 1, no. 1 (2005), 11.

75. For the Joint Statement, see http://www.state.gov/p/eap/regional/c15455 .htm (accessed 31 August 2009).

76. The TSD was not a direct result of the Core Group experience, but disaster response became a core element of the TSD agenda (to carry on the cooperation experienced among the three). See William Tow, "Assessing the Trilateral Strategic Dialogue," *East Asia Forum*, no. 12 (February 2009), http://www .eastasiaforum.org/2009/02/12/assessing-the-trilateral-strategic-dialogue/ (accessed 30 August 2009). The Quad concept was pushed by the Abe government in Japan. See Brahama Chellaney, "Quad Initiative: An Inharmonious Concert of Democracies," *Japan Times*, 19 July 2007, http://search.japantimes .co.jp/cgi-bin/eo20070719bc.html (accessed 30 August 2009).

77. The AP-6 (US, Japan, South Korea, China, India, Australia) was officially inaugurated in January 2006 in Sydney, Australia, but key discussions on concept and membership occurred on the sidelines of the Six-Party Talks. See "US Agrees Climate Deal with Asia," *BBC News*, 28 July 2005. http://news .bbc.co.uk/2/hi/science/nature/4723305.stm (accessed 30 August 2009).

78. "Asia, US hold talks without Defiant North Korea," *Agence France Presse*, 28 July 2006, available at http://www.aseanregionalforum.org/News/tabid/59 /newsid399/36/Default.aspx (accessed 31 August 2009).

79. Grossman, "The Tsunami Core Group: A Step toward a Transformed Diplomacy in Asia and Beyond," and Cossa, "South Asian Tsunami."

80. The principles call on PSI participants, as well as other countries, to not engage in WMD-related trade with countries of proliferation concern and to permit their own vessels and aircraft to be searched if suspected of transporting such goods. The principles further urge that information on suspicious activities be shared quickly to enable possible interdictions and that all vessels "reasonably suspected" of carrying dangerous cargo be inspected when passing through national airports, ports, and other transshipment points. See "Proliferation Security Initiative," US Department of State available at http://www.state.gov/t/isn/c10390.htm.

81. China, Indonesia, Malaysia and Iran oppose PSI, disputing the legality of its efforts.

82. Opening Remarks by Acting Deputy Assistant Secretary of State Tony Foley at the PSI Regional Operational Experts Group Meeting (June 22, 2009), Sopot, Poland, 5, http://dtirp.dtra.mil/TIC/treatyinfo/psi/psi_remarks.pdf (accessed December 30, 2009); and Arms Control Association, " The Proliferation Security Initiative (PSI) At a Glance," accessible here: https://www .armscontrol.org/factsheets/PSI

83. "Remarks by President Barack Obama," Hradcany Square, Prague, Czech Republic (April 5, 2009) http://www.whitehouse.gov/the_press_office /Remarks-By-President-Barack-Obama-In-Prague-As-Delivered/ (accessed December 30, 2009).

84. Office of the United States Trade Representative, "Overview of the Trans Pacific Partnership," http://www.ustr.gov/tpp/overview-of-the-TPP (accessed 3 February 2016). For an overview of TPP, see "The Trans-Pacific Partnership (TPP) Negotiations and Issues for Congress," Congressional Research Service, 13 December 2013, http://fas.org/sgp/crs/row/R42694 .pdf (accessed 3 February 2016); C. L. Lim, Deborah Kay Elms, and Patrick Low, eds., *The Trans-Pacific Partnership: A Quest for a Twenty-first Century Trade Agreement* (Cambridge, UK: Cambridge University Press, 2013). Mark Beeson and Richard Stubbs, eds., *Routledge Handbook of Asian Regionalism* (New York: Routledge, 2012).

85. Bernard Gordon, "Trading Up in Asia," *Foreign Affairs*, 91, no. 4 (July/ August 2012).

86. The White House, "Joint Statement by the United States and Japan," 22 February 2013 http://www.whitehouse.gov/the-press-office/2013/02/22 /joint-statement-united-states-and-japan. (accessed 3 February 2016). For an overview of RCEP, see "Shujiro Urata, "Constructing and Multilateralizing the Regional Comprehensive Economic Partnership: An Asian Perspective," ADBI Working Paper 449, December 2013, http://www.adbi.org/files /2013.12.02.wp449.regional.economic.partnership.asia.pdf (accessed 3 February 2016).

87. Stephen Haggard, *The Political Economy of the Asian Financial Crisis* (Washington, DC: Institute for International Economics, 2000); Amitav Acharya, "Regional Institutions and Asian Security Order: Norms, Power, and Prospects for Peaceful Change," in Muthiah Alagappa, ed., *Asian Security Order: Instrumental and Normative Features* (Stanford, CA: Stanford University Press, 2003), 210–40; and D. Webber, "Two Funerals and a Wedding? The Ups and Downs of Regionalism in East Asia and Asia-Pacific after the Asian Crisis," *Pacific Review*, 14, no. 3 (2001), 339–72.

88. Amitav Acharya, "The Strong in the World of the Weak: Southeast Asia in Asia's Regional Architecture," in Michael Green and Bates Gill, eds., *Asia's New Multilateralism: Cooperation, Competition, and the Search for Community* (New York: Columbia University Press, 2009), 172–92.

89. In November 1990, Secretary of State James Baker criticized as inappropriate the notion of regional security dialogues replacing the American hub and spokes network of bilateral alliances in Asia which had been at the center of Asian security and prosperity for four decades. See *Australian Financial Review*, 2 May 1991 ("Security, in Letter and Spirit"). Statements by then-assistant secretary for East Asia Richard Solomon in October 1990 typified the attitude: "the nature of the security challenges we anticipate in the years ahead—do not easily lend themselves to region-wide solutions. When we look at the key determinants of stability in Asia . . . it is difficult to see how a Helsinki-type institution would be an appropriate forum for enhancing security or promoting conflict resolution." Cited in Paul Midford,

"Japan's Leadership Role in East Asian Security Multilateralism," *Pacific Review*, 13, no. 3 (2000), 372.

90. See Press-Barnathan, "The Impact of Regional Dynamics on US Policy Toward Regional Security Arrangements in East Asia," 369–71; Beeson, "Rethinking Regionalism: Europe and East Asia"; Midford, "Japan's Leadership Role in East Asian Security Multilateralism," 367–97; Joseph Nye, "East Asian Security: The Case for Deep Engagement," *Foreign Affairs*, 74, no. 4 (1995), 90–102; Chalmers Johnson and E. B. Keehn, "East Asian Security: The Pentagon's Ossified Strategy," *Foreign Affairs*, 74, no. 4, 103–14; Richard Stubbs, "ASEAN Plus Three: Emerging East Asian Regionalism?" *Asian Survey*, 42, no. 3 (2002), 440–55; T. Terada, "Constructing an 'East Asia' Concept and Growing Regional Identity: From EAEC to ASEAN+3," *Pacific Review*, 16, no. 2 (2003), 251–77; Robert Wade, "The US Role in the Long Asian Crisis of 1990–2000," in A. Lukanskas and F. Rivera-Batiz, eds., *The Political Economy of the East Asian Crisis and Its Aftermath: Tigers in Distress* (Cheltenham, UK: Edward Elgar, 2001), 195–226; David Lake and Patrick Morgan, "The New Regionalism in Security Affairs," in David Lake and Patrick Morgan, eds., *Regional Orders: Building Security in a New World* (University Park: Pennsylvania State University Press, 1997), 3–19; G. Hook, "The East Asian Economic Caucus: A Case of Reactive Subregionalism?," in G. Hook and I. Kearns, eds., *Subregionalism and World Order* (Basingstoke, UK: Macmillan, 1999), 223–45; Mark Beeson, "US Hegemony and Southeast Asia: The Impact of, and Limits to, American Power and Influence," *Critical Asian Studies*, 36, no. 3 (2004), 323–54 and Yoichi Funabashi, "The Asianisation of Asia," *Foreign Affairs*, 72, no. 5 (1993), 75–85.

91. For example, see David Shambaugh, "China Engages Asia: Reshaping the Regional Order," *International Security*, 29, no. 3 (2004/5), 64–99.

92. Mu Chunshan, "What is CICA (and Why Does China Care about it?)," *The Diplomat*, May 17, 2014, http://thediplomat.com/2014/05/what-is-cica-and-why-does-china-care-about-it/ (accessed 18 October 2015); and Lee, "China is Recreating the American Hub and Spoke System in Asia,"; also on Chinese visions of hierarchy and international order, see David C. Kang, "Getting Asia Wrong: The Need for New Analytical Frameworks," *International Security*, 27, no. 4 (2003), 57–85; and M. Vatikiotis and Murray Hiebert, "How China is Building an Empire," *Far Eastern Economic Review*, November 20, 2003.

93. On "institutional balancing," see Kai He "Contested Regional Orders and Institutional Balancing in the Asia-Pacific," *International Politics*, 52, no. 2, 208–22; and on competitive regionalism see Press-Barnathan, "The Impact of Regional Dynamics on US Policy," 369–71.

94. Press-Barnathan, "The Impact of Regional Dynamics on US Policy," 375; and Joseph Nye, "The 'Nye Report': Six Years Later," *International Relations of Asia-Pacific*, 1, no. 1 (2001), 95–103.

95. Robert M. Gates, "Speech Delivered at the International Institute for Strategic Studies, (Singapore)." Washington: US Department of Defense, 2008, http://www. defense.gov/speeches/speech.aspx?speechid=1253 (accessed 18 October 2015).

96. "America's Future in Asia: Remarks As Prepared for Delivery by National Security Advisor Susan E. Rice at Georgetown University, Gaston Hall, Washington, D.C., Wednesday November 20, 2013." https://www.whitehouse.gov/the-press-office/2013/11/21/remarks-prepared-delivery-national-security-advisor-susan-e-rice (accessed 3 February 2016).

97. "Remarks by President Obama and Prime Minister Abe of Japan in Joint Press Conference, 28 April 2015." https://www.whitehouse.gov/the-press-office/2015/04/28/remarks-president-obama-and-prime-minister-abe-japan-joint-press-confere (accessed 17 October 2015).

98. Scott Snyder and Jung-yeop Woo, "The US Rebalance and the Seoul Process: How to Align US and ROK Visions for Cooperation in East Asia," Occasional Paper, Council on Foreign Relations, New York, January 2015, http://www.cfr.org/asia-and-pacific/us-rebalance-seoul-process-align-us-rok-visions-cooperation-east-asia/p35926 (accessed 18 October 2015).

99. "Remarks by President Obama and President Park of the Republic of Korea in Joint Press Conference, 16 October 2015." https://www.whitehouse.gov/the-press-office/2015/10/16/remarks-president-obama-and-president-park-republic-korea-joint-press (accessed 17 October 2015).

100. Karen J. Alter and Sophie Meunier, "The Politics of International Regime Complexity," *Perspectives on Politics*, 7, no. 1 (March 2009), 13–24.

101. "The business reality of the humanitarian endeavor is this: organizations are obliged to fulfill the requirements of the donor grants that fuel them, most of which are no longer than eighteen months old, as a means to survive. As such, institutions become focused on bankrolling their efforts with short-term outputs and are, hence, inherently discouraged from developing a coordinated longer-terms strategic vision." See Stacey White, "Disaster Management in Asia: The Promise of Regional Architecture." in *Asia's Response to Climate Change and Natural Disasters: Implications for an Evolving Regional Architecture* (Washington, DC: Center for Strategic and International Studies, 2010), 61.

102. For elaboration of this dilemma, see Cha, "Complex Patchworks." This is sometimes referred to as "institutional balancing." See Kai He, *Institutional Balancing in the Asia-Pacific: Economic Interdependence and China's Rise* (London: Routledge, 2009).

103. Lee, "China is Recreating the American Hub and Spoke System in Asia." Also see Randall Schweller and Xiaoyu Pu, "After Unipolarity: China's Visions of International Order in an Era of US Decline," *International Security*, 36, no. 1 (Summer 2011), 41–72.

104. On regime-shifting, see Alter and Meunier, "The Politics of International Regime Complexity," 16–17; Laurence Helfer, "Regime Shifting in the International Intellectual Property System," 39–44; and Alexander Betts, "Institutional Proliferation and the Global Refugee Regime," 53–58 in ibid.

105. On the virtues of overlapping membership, also see, Kai He "Contested Regional Orders and Institutional Balancing in the Asia-Pacific," *International Politics*, 52, no. 2, 208–22.

106. See Alter and Meunier, "The Politics of International Regime Complexity"; Christina Davis, "Overlapping Institutions in Trade Policy," 25–31;

and Judith Kelley, "The More the Merrier? The Effects of Having Multiple International Election Monitoring Organizations," 59–64, all in ibid.; and Marc L. Busch, "Overlapping Institutions, Forum Shopping, and Dispute Settlement in International Trade," *International Organization*, 61, no. 4 (Winter 2007), 735–61.

107. Evelyn Goh, "Hierarchy and the Role of the United States in the East Asian Security Order," *International Relations of the Asia-Pacific*, 8, no. 3 (2008), 353–77; and Alastair Iain Johnston, "The Myth of the ASEAN Way? Explaining the Evolution of the ASEAN Regional Forum," in Haftendorn, Keohane, and Wallander, eds., *Imperfect Unions: Security Institutions over Time and Space* (Oxford: Oxford University Press, 1999), 287–324.

108. Amitav Acharya, "Ideas, Identity, and Institution-Building: From the ASEAN way to the 'Asia-Pacific Way'? *Pacific Review*, 10, no. 4 (1997), 319–46; Richard Higgot, "Ideas, Identity and Policy Coordination in the Asia-Pacific," *Pacific Review*, 7, no. 4 (1994), 367–79; Muthiah Alagappa ed., *Asian Security Order: Instrumental and Normative Features* (Stanford, CA: Stanford University Press, 2003); and Capie, "Power, Identity, and Multilateralism."

BIBLIOGRAPHY

Abbott, Kenneth W., and Duncan Snidal. "Why States Act Through Formal International Organizations." *Journal of Conflict Resolution* 42 (February 1998): 3–32.

Abbott, Kenneth W., and Duncan Snidal. "Hard and Soft Law in International Governance." *International Organization* 54, no. 3 (Summer 2000): 421–56.

Accinelli, Robert. *Crisis and Commitment: United States Policy toward Taiwan 1950–1955.* Chapel Hill & London: University of North Carolina Press, 1996.

Acharya, Amitav. "Ideas, Identity, and Institution-building: From the 'ASEAN Way' To the 'Asia-Pacific Way'?" *Pacific Review* 10, no. 4 (1997): 319–46.

Acharya, Amitav. *Constructing a Security Community in Southeast Asia: ASEAN and the Problem of Regional Order.* London: Routledge, 2003.

Acharya, Amitav. "Regional Institutions and Asian Security Order: Norms, Power, and Prospects for Peaceful Change." In *Asian Security Order: Instrumental and Normative Features*, edited by Muthiah Alagappa, 210–40. Stanford, CA: Stanford University Press, 2003.

Acharya, Amitav. "The Strong in the World of the Weak: Southeast Asia in Asia's Regional Architecture." In *Asia's New Multilateralism: Cooperation, Competition, and the Search for Community*, edited by Michael J. Green and Bates Gill, 172–92. New York: Columbia University Press, 2009.

Acheson, Dean. "The Requirements of Reconstruction," *Department of State Bulletin* 16, no. 411 (May 8, 1947): 991–94.

Acheson, Dean. "Pacific Pact Corresponding to North Atlantic Treaty Untimely." May 28, 1949. *Department of State Bulletin* 20 (April–June 1949): 696.

Acheson, Dean. "Crisis in Asia—an Examination of United States Policy." *Department of State Bulletin* 22 (January 23, 1950): 110–16.

Acheson, Dean. *Present at the Creation: My Years in the State Department.* New York: Norton, 1969.

Administrative Agreement under Article III of the Security Treaty between the United States of America and Japan. February 28, 1952. Accessed August 17, 2011. http://www.ioc.u-tokyo.ac.jp/~worldjpn/documents/texts/docs/19520228.T1E.html

Agence France Presse. "Asia, US hold talks without Defiant North Korea." July 28, 2006. Accessed August 31, 2009. http://www.aseanregionalforum.org/News/tabid/59/newsid399/36/Default.aspx

Alagappa, Muthiah, ed. *Asian Security Order: Instrumental and Normative Features.* Stanford, CA: Stanford University Press, 2003.

Alter, Karen J., and Sophie Meunier. "The Politics of International Regime Complexity." *Perspectives on Politics* 7, no. 1 (March 2009): 13–24.

Altfeld, Michael F. "The Decision to Ally: A Theory and Test." *Political Research Quarterly* 37, no. 4 (December 1984): 523–44.

Ambrose, Stephen E. *Rise to Globalism: American Foreign Policy since 1938*. Baltimore: Penguin Books, 1971.

Arms Control Association. "The Proliferation Security Initiative (PSI) At a Glance." June 2013. Accessed October 11, 2014. http://www.armscontrol.org/factsheets/PSI

Art, Robert J. *A Grand Strategy for America*. Ithaca, NY: Cornell University Press, 2003.

ASEAN. "Treaty of Amity and Cooperation in Southeast Asia." February 24, 1976. Accessed November 4, 2015. http://www.asean.org/news/item/treaty-of-amity-and-cooperation-in-southeast-asia-indonesia-24-february-1976-3

Axelrod, Robert M. *The Evolution of Cooperation*. Revised ed. New York: Basic Books, 2006.

Bachrack, Stanley. *The Committee of One Million: 'China Lobby' Politics, 1953–1971*. New York: Columbia University Press, 1976.

Bader, Jeffrey A. *Obama and China's Rise: An Insider's Account of America's Asia Strategy*. Washington, DC: Brookings Institution Press, 2012.

Baehr, Peter R. "Small States: A Tool for Analysis?" *World Politics* 28, no. 3 (April 1975): 456–66.

Bank of Korea. The Bank of Korea Economic Statistics System (2013). Accessed August 2, 2013. http://ecos.bok.or.kr/EIndex_en.jsp

Barnett, Doak A. *China and the Major Powers in East Asia*. Washington, DC: Brookings Institution Press, 1977.

Bar-Siman-Tov, Yaacov. "Alliance Strategy: U.S.–Small Allies Relationships." *Journal of Strategic Studies* 3, no. 2 (1980): 202–16.

Bass, Warren. *Support Any Friend: Kennedy's Middle East and the Making of the U.S.-Israel Alliance*. Oxford: Oxford University Press, 2003.

BBC News. "US Agrees Climate Deal with Asia." July 28, 2005. Accessed August 30, 2009. http://news.bbc.co.uk/2/hi/science/nature/4723305.stm

Bearce, David H., Kristen M. Flanagan, and Katharine M. Floros. "Alliances, International Information and Military Conflict among Member States." *International Organization* 60, no. 3 (July 2006): 595–625.

Beckley, Michael. "The Myth of Entangling Alliances." *International Security* 39, no. 4 (Spring 2015): 7–48.

Beeson, Mark. "US Hegemony and Southeast Asia: The Impact of, and Limits to, American Power and Influence." *Critical Asian Studies* 36, no. 3 (2004): 323–54.

Beeson, Mark. "Rethinking Regionalism: Europe and East Asia in Comparative Historical Perspective." *Journal of European Public Policy* 12, no. 6 (2005): 969–85.

Beeson, Mark, and Richard Stubbs, eds. *Routledge Handbook of Asian Regionalism*. New York: Routledge, 2012.

Beisner, Robert L. *Dean Acheson: A Life in the Cold War*. Oxford: Oxford University Press, 2006.

Bell, Coral. "The Future of American Policy in the Pacific." In *Asia-Pacific Security: Less Uncertainty, New Opportunities*, edited by Gary Klintworth. New York: St. Martin's Press, 1996.

Bennett, D. Scott. "Testing Alternative Models of Alliance Duration, 1816–1984." *American Journal of Political Science* 41, no. 3 (1997): 846–78.

Bennett, D. Scott, and Allan Stam. "How Long Has This Been Going On: The Duration of Interstate Wars, 1816–1985." *American Political Science Review* 90 (June 1996): 239–57.

Benson, Brett V. *Constructing International Security: Alliances, Deterrence, and Moral Hazard.* Cambridge, UK: Cambridge University Press, 2012.

Benson, Brett V., Patrick R. Bentley, and James L. Ray. "Ally Provocateur: Why Allies Do Not Always Behave." *Journal of Peace Research* 50, no. 1 (January 2013): 47–58.

Berger, Thomas U. *Cultures of Antimilitarism: National Security in Germany and Japan.* Baltimore: Johns Hopkins University Press, 1998.

Berger, Thomas U. *Redefining Japan and the U.S.-Japan Alliance.* New York: Japan Society, 2004.

Betts, Alexander. "Institutional Proliferation and the Global Refugee Regime." *Perspectives on Politics* 7, no. 1 (March 2009): 53–58.

Blum, Robert. *Drawing the Line: The Origin of the American Containment Policy in East Asia.* New York: W.W. Norton, 1982.

Bobrow, Davis B. "Hegemony Management: The US in the Asia-Pacific." *Pacific Review* 12, no. 2 (1999): 173–97.

Boese, Wade. "Israel Halts Chinese Phalcon Deal." *Arms Control Today.* September 1, 2000. https://www.armscontrol.org/act/2000_09/israelsept00

Bolton, John. "Should We Take Global Governance Seriously?" *Chicago Journal of International Law* 1, no. 2 (2001): 205–22.

Borden, William. *The Pacific Alliance: United States Foreign Economic Policy and Japanese Trade Recovery, 1947–1955.* Madison: University of Wisconsin Press, 1984.

Borgatti, Stephen P., and Daniel S. Halgin. "On Network Theory." *Organization Science* 22, no. 5 (April 2011): 1161–81.

Bracken, Paul. *Fire in the East.* New York: Harper Collins, 1999.

Braibanti, Ralph. "The Southeast Asia Collective Defense Treaty." *Pacific Affairs* 30, no. 4 (December 1957): 321–41.

Brooks, Stephen G. "Dueling Realisms." *International Organization* 51, no. 3 (Summer 1997): 445–77.

Brooks, Stephen G., G. John Ikenberry, and William C. Wohlforth. "Don't Come Home, America: The Case against Retrenchment." *International Security* 37, no. 3 (Winter 2012/13): 7–51.

Brooks, Stephen G., and William C. Wohlforth. *World Out of Balance: International Relations and the Challenge of American Primacy.* Princeton, NJ: Princeton University Press, 2008.

Brown, Michael E., Sean M. Lynn-Jones, and Steven E. Miller, eds. *Debating the Democratic Peace.* Cambridge, MA: MIT Press, 1996.

Buckley, Roger. *US-Japan Alliance Diplomacy, 1945–1990.* Cambridge, UK: Cambridge University Press, 1997.

Bull, Hedley. *The Anarchical Society: A Study of Order in World Politics.* 3rd ed. New York: Columbia University Press, 2002.

Busch, Marc L. "Overlapping Institutions, Forum Shopping, and Dispute Settlement in International Trade." *International Organization* 61, no. 4 (Winter 2007): 735–61.

Calder, Kent E. *Pacific Defense: Arms, Energy, and America's Future in Asia.* New York: W. Morrow, 1996.

Calder, Kent E., and Francis Fukuyama, eds. *East Asian Multilateralism: Prospects for Regional Stability*. Baltimore: Johns Hopkins University Press, 2008.

Campbell, Kurt. "America's Asia Strategy during the Bush Administration." In *The Future of America's Alliances in Northeast Asia*, edited by Michael Armacost and Dan Okimoto, 25–34. Stanford, CA: APARC, 2004.

Capie, David H. *Power, Identity and Multilateralism the United States and Regional Institutionalization in the Asia-Pacific*. Ottawa: National Library of Canada, 2003.

Caridi, Ronald. *The Korean War and American Politics: The Republican Party as a Case Study*. Philadelphia: University of Pennsylvania Press, 1968.

Carmoy, Guy De. *The Foreign Policies of France, 1944–1968*. Chicago: University of Chicago Press, 1970.

Carpenter, R. Charli. "Vetting the Advocacy Agenda: Network Centrality and the Paradox of Weapons Norms." *International Organization* 65, no. 1 (January 2011): 69–102.

Caute, John D. *The Great Fear: The Anti-Communist Purge Under Truman and Eisenhower*. London: Secker & Warburg, 1978.

Cha, Victor D. "National Unification: The Long and Winding Road." *In Depth* 4, no. 2 (1994): 89–123.

Cha, Victor D. *Alignment Despite Antagonism: The United States-Korea-Japan Security Triangle*. Stanford, CA: Stanford University Press, 1999.

Cha, Victor D. "Abandonment, Entrapment, and Neoclassical Realism in Asia: The United States, Japan, and Korea." *International Studies Quarterly* 44, no. 2 (June 2000): 261–91.

Cha, Victor D. "Winning Asia: Washington's Untold Success Story." *Foreign Affairs* 86, no. 6 (2007): 98–113.

Cha, Victor D. "Powerplay: Origins of the U.S. Alliance System in Asia." *International Security* 34, no. 3 (Winter 2009/10): 158–96.

Cha, Victor D. "Complex Patchworks: U.S. Alliances as Part of Asia's Regional Architecture." *Asia Policy* 11 (January 2011): 27–50.

Chang, David. "US Aid and Economic Progress in Taiwan." *Asian Survey* 5, no. 3 (1965): 152–53.

Chang, Gordon H. *Friends and Enemies: The United States, China, and the Soviet Union, 1948–1972*. Stanford, CA: Stanford University Press, 1990.

Chellaney, Brahama. "Quad Initiative: An Inharmonious Concert of Democracies." *Japan Times*, July 19, 2007. Accessed August 30, 2009. http://www.japantimes.co.jp/opinion/2007/07/19/commentary/quad-initiative-an-inharmonious-concert-of-democracies/#.VKcHiWTF83I

Cheong, Sung-hwa. *The Politics of Anti-Japanese Sentiment in Korea: Japanese-South Korean Relations under American Occupation, 1945–1952*. New York: Greenwood Press, 1991.

Christensen, Thomas J. *Useful Adversaries: Grand Strategy, Domestic Mobilization, and Sino-American Conflict, 1947–1958*. Princeton, NJ: Princeton University Press, 1996.

Christensen, Thomas J. *Worse than a Monolith: Alliance Politics and Problems of Coercive Diplomacy in Asia*. Princeton, NJ: Princeton University Press, 2011.

Christensen, Thomas J. *The China Challenge: Shaping the Choices of a Rising Power*. New York: W.W. Norton, 2015.

Christensen, Thomas J., and Jack Snyder. "Chain Gangs and Passed Bucks: Predicting Alliance Patterns in Multipolarity." *International Organization* 44, no. 2 (Spring 1990): 137–68.

Clark, Mark W. *From the Danube to the Yalu*. New York: Harper and Brothers, 1954.

Clay, Blair. *The Forgotten War: America in Korea, 1950–1953*. New York: Times Books, 1987.

Clough, Ralph N. *Island China*. Cambridge, MA: Harvard University Press, 1978.

CNN. "Bush Announces Tsunami Aid Coalition." December 29, 2004. Accessed December 30, 2009. http://www.cnn.com/2004/US/12/29/bush.quake/

Cohen, Warren I. "Acheson, His Advisors, and China 1949–1950." In *Uncertain Years: Chinese-American Relations, 1947–1950*, edited by Dorothy Borg and Waldo Heinrichs, 15–52. New York: Columbia University Press, 1990.

Cooley, Alexander. *Base Politics: Democratic Change and the U.S. Military Overseas*. Ithaca, NY: Cornell University Press, 2008.

Copelovitch, Mark, and Tonya Putnam. "Design in Context: Existing International Agreements and New Cooperation." *International Organization* 68, no. 2 (2014): 471–93.

Cossa, Ralph A. "South Asian Tsunami: U.S. Military Provides 'Logistical Backbone' for Tsunami Relief." *eJournal USA: Foreign Policy Agenda*. March 4, 2005. Accessed December 18, 2009. http://www.america.gov/st/washfile-english /2005/March/20050304112100dmslahrellek0.5331537.html#ixzz0a5F8S6oo

Cowhey, Peter F. "Domestic Institutions and the Credibility of International Commitment: Japan and the United States." *International Organization* 47, no. 2 (Spring 1993): 299–326.

Crawford. Timothy. *Pivotal Deterrence: Third Party Statecraft and the Pursuit of Peace*. Ithaca, NY: Cornell University Press, 2003.

Crone, Donald. "Does Hegemony Matter? The Reorganization of the Pacific Political Economy." *World Politics* 45, no. 4 (July 1993): 501–25.

Cumings, Bruce. *The Origins of the Korean War: The Roaring Cataract, 1947–1950*. Vol. 2. Princeton, NJ: Princeton University Press, 1990.

Cumings, Bruce. "The Structural Basis of 'Anti-Americanism' in the Republic of Korea." In *Korean Attitudes toward the United States: Changing Dynamics*, edited by David Steinberg, 91–115. Armonk, NY: M.E. Sharpe, 2005.

Cumings, Bruce. *The Korean War: A History*. New York: Modern Library, 2010.

Daggett, Stephen. "Costs of Major U.S. Wars." Congressional Research Service Report for Congress. June 29, 2010. Accessed March 9, 2014. http://fas.org/sgp /crs/natsec/RS22926.pdf

David, Steven R. "Explaining Third World Alignment." *World Politics* 43, no. 2 (January 1991): 233–56.

Davis, Christina L. "Overlapping Institutions in Trade Policy." *Perspectives on Politics* 7, no. 1 (March 2009): 25–31.

Deudney, Daniel, and G. John Ikenberry. "Realism, Structural Liberalism, and the Western Order." In *Unipolar Politics: Realism and State Strategies after the Cold War*, edited by Ethan B. Kapstein and Michael Mastanduno, 103–37. New York: Columbia University Press, 1999.

Dingman, Roger. "Forgotten Summit: The Quirino-Chiang Kai-shek Conversations." In *Quirino-Chiang Kai-shek Conversations*, 40–57. Vol. 19. Bulletin of the American Historical Collection, 1991.

Dingman, Roger. "The Dagger and the Gift: The Impact of the Korean War on Japan." *Journal of American-East Asian Relations* 2, no. 1 (Spring 1993): 29–55.

Dobbs, Charles. "The Pact That Never Was: The Pacific Fleet of 1949." *Journal of Northeast Asian Studies* 3, no. 4 (1984): 29–42.

Dockrill, Saki. *Britain's Policy for West German Rearmament, 1950–1955.* Cambridge, UK: Cambridge University Press, 1991.

Donilon, Thomas. "The United States and the Asia-Pacific in 2013." Asia Society. March 11, 2013. Accessed December 9, 2014. http://asiasociety.org/new-york /complete-transcript-thomas-donilon-asia-society-new-york

Dower, John W. *War without Mercy: Race and Power in the Pacific War.* New York: Pantheon Books, 1986.

Dower, John W. *Empire and Aftermath: Yoshida Shigeru and the Japanese Experience, 1878–1954.* Cambridge, MA: Harvard Asia Center, 1988.

Druckman, Daniel. "Stages, Turning Points, and Crises: Negotiating Military Base Rights: Spain and the United States." *Journal of Conflict Resolution* 30, no. 2 (June 1986): 327–60.

Duffield, John. "Why Is There No APTO? Why Is There No OSCAP?: Asia-Pacific Security Institutions in Comparative Perspective." *Contemporary Security Policy* 22, no. 2 (2001): 69–95.

Dulles, John Foster. "Security in the Pacific." *Foreign Affairs* 30, no. 2 (January 1952): 175–87.

Dulles, John Foster. "The Evolution of Foreign Policy." Lecture, Council of Foreign Relations, New York, NY, January 12, 1954.

Eckert, Carter J., Ki-baik Lee, Young Ick Lew, Michael Robinson, and Edward Wagner. *Korea, Old and New: A History.* Seoul, Korea: Ilchokak Publishers, 1990.

Eisenhower, Dwight D. "Annual Message to the Congress on the State of the Union." February 2, 1953. Accessed October 21, 2011. http://www.eisenhower .archives.gov/all_about_ike/speeches/1953_state_of_the_union.pdf

Eisenhower, Dwight D. *Mandate for Change, 1953–1956: The White House Years.* Garden City, NY: Doubleday, 1963.

Elsey Papers. Telegram Extract, John Foster Dulles and John Allison to the Secretary of State and Assistant Secretary Rusk, Tokyo. June 25, 1950. Accessed May 13, 2013. http://www.trumanlibrary.org/whistlestop/study_collections /koreanwar/documents/index.php?documentdate=1050–06–25&documentid =ki-1–6&pagenumber=1

Executive Sessions of the Senate Foreign Relations Committee (Historical Series). Vol. VII. Hearings before the United States Senate Committee on Foreign Relations, and Senate Committee on Armed Services, Eighty-Fourth Congress, first session. Washington, DC: Government Printing Office, 1978.

"Extracts from the Digest of the Sixth and Final of the Study Group on Japanese Peace Treaty Problems." In *John Foster Dulles: A Statesman and His Times,* edited by Michael A. Guhin, 315–18. New York: Columbia University Press, 1972.

Fairbank, John K. "Toward a Dynamic Far Eastern Policy." *Far Eastern Survey* 18, no. 18 (1949): 209–12.

Fairbank, John K. "The Problem of Revolutionary Asia." *Foreign Affairs* 29, no. 1 (1950): 106–7.

Fang, Songying, Jesse C. Johnson, and Brett A. Leeds. "To Concede or to Resist? The Restraining Effect of Military Alliances." *International Organization* 68, no. 5 (2014): 775–810.

Fearon, James D. "Signaling Versus the Balance of Power and Interests: An Empirical Test of a Crisis Bargaining Model." *Journal of Conflict Resolution* 38 (June 1994, Special Issue): 236–69.

Fearon, James D. "Domestic Political Audiences and the Escalation of International Disputes." *American Political Science Review* 88, no. 3 (September 1994): 577–92.

Fehrenbach, T. R. *This Kind of War: The Classic Korean War History.* Washington and London: Brassey, 1994.

Ferguson, Niall. *Colossus: The Price of America's Empire.* New York: Penguin Press, 2004.

Fergusson, Ian F., Mark A. McMinimy, and Brock R. Williams. "The Trans-Pacific Partnership (TPP) Negotiations and Issues for Congress." *Congressional Research Service*, March 20, 2015. Accessed November 9, 2015. https://www.fas.org/sgp/crs/row/R42694.pdf

Finkelstein, David. *Washington's Taiwan Dilemma, 1949–1950: From Abandonment to Salvation.* Fairfax, VA: George Mason University Press, 1993.

Finnemore, Martha. "Legitimacy, Hypocrisy and Unipolarity." In *International Relations Theory and the Consequences of Unipolarity*, edited by G. John Ikenberry, Michael Mastanduno, and William Wohlforth, 67–98. Cambridge, UK: Cambridge University Press, 2011.

Foley, Tony. "Opening Remarks by Acting, Deputy Assistant Secretary of State Tony Foley." Lecture, PSI Regional Operational Experts Group Meeting, Sopot, Poland, June 22, 2009. Accessed November 9, 2015. http://dtirp.dtra.mil/pdfs/psi_remarks.pdf

Folliard, Edward T. "Democrats Voice Concern about New Policy toward Formosa: Ike's First Message Praised." *Washington Post.* February 3, 1953.

Foot, Rosemary. *A Substitute for Victory: The Politics of Peacemaking at the Korean Armistice Talks.* Ithaca, NY: Cornell University Press, 1990.

Fox, Annette Baker. *The Power of Small States: Diplomacy in World War II.* Chicago: University of Chicago Press, 1959.

French, Howard. "South Korea Agrees to Send Troops to Iraq." *New York Times.* April 3, 2003. Accessed November 1, 2015. http://www.nytimes.com/2003/04/03/international/worldspecial/03KORE.html

Friedberg, Aaron L. "Ripe for Rivalry: Prospects for Peace in a Multipolar Asia." *International Security* 18, no. 3 (1993): 13–14.

Friedman, Benjamin, Eugene Gholz, Daryl G. Press, and Harvey M. Sapolsky. "Restraining Order: For Strategic Modesty." *World Affairs* (Fall 2009): 84–94.

Funabashi, Yoichi. "The Asianisation of Asia." *Foreign Affairs* 72, no. 5 (November/December 1995): 75–85.

Gaddis, John Lewis. "Was the Truman Doctrine a Real Turning Point?" *Foreign Affairs* 52, no. 2 (January 1974): 391–92.

Gaddis, John Lewis. "Korea in American Politics, Strategy, and Diplomacy, 1945–50." In *Origins of the Cold War in Asia*, edited by Yonosuke Nagai and Akira Iriye, 277–80. Tokyo: University of Tokyo Press, 1977.

Gaddis, John Lewis. "The Strategic Perspective: The Rise and Fall of the Defense Perimeter Concept, 1947–1951." In *Uncertain Years: Chinese-American Relations, 1947–1950*, edited by Dorothy Borg and Waldo Heinrichs. New York: Columbia University Press, 1980.

Gaddis, John Lewis. *Strategies of Containment: A Critical Appraisal of Postwar American National Security Policy*. Revised ed. New York: Oxford University Press, 2005.

Gartner, Scott S., and Randolph M. Siverson. "War Expansion and War Outcome." *Journal of Conflict Resolution* 40, no. 1 (March 1996): 4–15.

Garver, John W. *The Sino-American Alliance: Nationalist China and American Cold War Strategy in Asia*. Armonk, NY: M.E. Sharpe, 1997.

Gates, Robert M. "Speech Delivered at the International Institute for Strategic Studies (Singapore)." May 31, 2008. Accessed October 18, 2015. http://www. defense.gov/speeches/speech.aspx?speechid=1253

Gaubatz, Kurt T. "Democratic States and Commitment in International Relations." *International Organization* 50, no. 1 (1996): 109–39.

Gelpi, Christopher. "Alliances as Instruments of Intra-Allied Control or Restraint." In *Imperfect Unions: Security Institutions over Time and Space*, edited by Helga Haftendorn, Robert Keohane, and Celeste Wallender. Oxford: Oxford University Press, 1999.

George, Alexander L., and Richard Smoke. *Deterrence in American Foreign Policy: Theory and Practice*. New York: Columbia University Press, 1974.

Gerzhoy, Gene. "Alliance Coercion and Nuclear Restraint: How the United States Thwarted West Germany's Nuclear Ambitions." *International Security* 39, no. 4 (Spring 2015): 91–129.

Gholz, Eugene, Daryl G. Press, and Harvey M. Sapolsky. "Come Home, America: The Strategy of Restraint in the Face of Temptation." *International Security* 21, no. 4 (Spring 1997): 5–48.

Gibler, Douglas M. "Alliances That Never Balance: The Territorial Settlement Treaty." *Conflict Management and Peace Science* 15, no. 1 (Spring 1996): 75–97.

Gibler, Douglas M. "The Costs of Reneging: Reputation and Alliance Formation." *Journal of Conflict Resolution* 52, no. 3 (June 2008): 426–54.

Gibson, Richard, and Wenhua Chen. *The Secret Army: Chiang Kai-shek and the Drug Warlords of the Golden Triangle*. Singapore: John Wiley & Sons, 2011.

Gill, Bates, and Michael J. Green, eds. *Asia's New Multilateralism: Cooperation, Competition, and the Search for Community*. New York: Columbia University Press, 2009.

Gilpin, Robert. "International Politics in the Pacific Rim Era." *Annals of the American Academy of Political and Social Science* 505 (September 1989): 56–67.

Gilpin, Robert. *War and Change in International Politics*. Cambridge, UK: Cambridge University Press, 1981.

Gilpin, Robert. *The Political Economy of International Relations*. Princeton, NJ: Princeton University Press, 1987.

Goddard, Stacie E. "Brokering Change: Networks and Entrepreneurs in International Politics." *International Theory* 1, no. 2 (2009): 249–81.

Goh, Evelyn. "Hierarchy and the Role of the United States in the East Asian Security Order." *International Relations of the Asia-Pacific* 8, no. 3 (2008): 353–77.

Goldstein, Steven M. "The United States and the Republic of China, 1949–1979: Suspicious Allies." APARC Working Paper, Stanford University (February 2000).

Gordon, Bernard K. "Trading Up in Asia." *Foreign Affairs* 91, no. 4 (2012): 17–22.

Graham, Chad, and Arnold Heidenheimer. "Dulles Attacks Fair Deal, Meets Local GOP Heads." *Cornell Daily Sun* 67, no. 3 (September 21, 1949). Accessed August 14, 2015. http://cdsun.library.cornell.edu/cgi-bin/cornell?a=d&d=CDS19490921–01.2.2&e=–––––20–1–––all––

Green, Michael J. "The Iraq War and Asia: Assessing the Legacy." *Washington Quarterly* 31, no. 2 (Spring 2008): 181–200.

Green, Michael J., and Nicholas Szechenyi. "Power and Order in Asia: A Survey of Regional Expectations." CSIS. July 1, 2014. Accessed October 1, 2014. http://csis.org/files/publication/140605_Green_PowerandOrder_WEB.pdf

Green, O. M. "Soviet Imperialism in Asia." *Straits Times*, November 21, 1949. Accessed June 14, 2012. http://newspapers.nl.sg/Digitised/Page /straitstimes19491121.1.1.aspx

Grieco, Joseph. "Understanding the Problem of International Cooperation: The Limits of Neoliberal Institutionalism and the Future of Realist Theory." In *Neorealism and Neoliberalism: The Contemporary Debate*, edited by Robert Baldwin, 301–38. New York: Columbia University Press, 1993.

Griffith, Robert. *The Politics of Fear: Joseph R. McCarthy and the Senate*. Lexington: University Press of Kentucky, 1970.

Griswold, A. Whitney. *The Far Eastern Policy of the United States*. New York: Harcourt Brace and Company, 1938.

Grossman, Marc. "The Tsunami Core Group: A Step toward a Transformed Diplomacy in Asia and Beyond." *Security Challenges* 1, no. 1 (2005): 11–14.

Guhin, Michael A. *John Foster Dulles: A Statesman and His Times*. New York: Columbia University Press, 1972.

Gvosdev, Nikolas, and Travis Tanner. "Wagging the Dog." *National Interest* 77 (October 2004): 5–10.

Hafner-Burton, Emilie M., Miles Kahler, and Alexander H. Montgomery. "Network Analysis for International Relations." *International Organization* 63, no. 6 (July 2009): 559–92.

Haftendorn, Helga, Robert Keohane, and Celeste Wallender, eds. *Imperfect Unions: Security Institutions over Time and Space*. Oxford: Oxford University Press, 1999.

Haggard, Stephen. *The Political Economy of the Asian Financial Crisis*. Washington, DC: Institute for International Economics, 2000.

Halberstam, David. *The Coldest Winter: America and the Korean War*. New York: Hyperion, 2007.

Harris, Stuart, and Richard N. Cooper. "The U.S.-Japan Alliance." In *America's Asian Alliances*, edited by Robert D. Blackwill and Paul Dibbs, 31–60. Cambridge, MA: MIT Press, 2000.

Hastings, Max. *The Korean War*. London: M. Joseph, 1987.

He, Kai. "Contested Regional Orders and Institutional Balancing in the Asia-Pacific." *International Politics* 52, no. 2 (2015): 208–22.

He, Kai, and Huiyun Feng. "If Not Soft Balancing, Then What? Reconsidering Soft Balancing and U.S. Policy toward China." *Security Studies* 17, no. 2 (April/June 2008): 363–95.

Heer, Paul. "George F. Kennan and US Foreign Policy in East Asia." PhD dissertation, George Washington University, May 14, 1994.

Heinrichs, Waldo. "American China Policy and the Cold War in Asia: A New Look." In *Uncertain Years: Chinese-American Relations*, edited by Dorothy Borg and Waldo Heinrichs, 281–92. New York: Columbia University Press, 1980.

Helfer, Laurence. "Regime Shifting in the International Intellectual Property System." *Perspective on Politics* 7, no. 1 (2009): 39–44.

Hemmer, Christopher, and Peter J. Katzenstein. "Why Is There No NATO in Asia? Collective Identity, Regionalism, and the Origins of Multilateralism." *International Organization* 56, no. 3 (Summer 2002): 575–607.

Hess, Jerry. "Oral History Interview with John J. Muccio." February 10, 1971, Washington DC. Accessed October 1, 2015. http://www.trumanlibrary.org/oralhist/muccio1.htm

Higgott, Richard. "Ideas, Identity and Policy Coordination in the Asia-Pacific." *Pacific Review* 7, no. 4 (1994): 367–79.

Hirschman, Albert O. *Exit, Voice, and Loyalty; Responses to Decline in Firms, Organizations, and States*. Cambridge, MA: Harvard University Press, 1970.

Hixon, Walter L. *George F. Kennan: Cold War Iconoclast*. New York: Columbia University Press, 1989.

Hobson, John M., and Jason C. Sharman. "The Enduring Place of Hierarchy in World Politics: Tracing the Social Logics of Hierarchy and Political Change." *European Journal of International Relations* 11, no. 1 (2005): 63–98.

Hoffman, Stanley. "Notes on the Effectiveness of Modern Power." *International Journal* 30 (1975): 183–206.

Holsti, Ole R., P. Terrence Hopmann, and John D. Sullivan. *Unity and Disintegration in International Alliances: Comparative Studies*. New York: John Wiley & Sons, 1973.

Hook, Glenn. "The East Asian Economic Caucus: A Case of Reactive Subregionalism?" In *Subregionalism and World Order*, edited by Glenn Hook and Ian Kearns, 223–45. London: MacMillan, 1999.

Huntington, Samuel P. "The Lonely Superpower." *Foreign Affairs* 78, no. 2 (1999): 35–49.

IAEA. "Member States of the IAEA." January 1, 2011. Accessed August 17, 2011. http://www.iaea.org/About/Policy/MemberStates/

Ikenberry, G. John. "Institutions, Strategic Restraint, and the Persistence of American Postwar Order." *International Security* 23, no. 3 (Winter 1998/1999): 43–78.

Ikenberry, G. John. *After Victory: Institutions, Strategic Restraint, and the Rebuilding of Order after Major Wars*. Princeton, NJ: Princeton University Press, 2001.

Ikenberry, G. John. "America's Imperial Ambition." *Foreign Affairs* 81, no. 5 (September 2002): 44–60.

Ikenberry, G. John. "Is American Multilateralism in Decline?" *Perspectives on Politics* 1 (September 2003): 533–50.

Ikenberry, G. John. "Liberal Sources of American Unipolarity." In *International Relations Theory and the Consequences of Unipolarity*, edited by G. John Ikenberry, Michael Mastanduno, and William C. Wohlforth, 216–51. Cambridge, UK: Cambridge University Press, 2011.

Jager, Sheila Miyoshi. *Brothers at War: The Unending Conflict in Korea*. New York: W.W. Norton, 2013.

Jansen, Marius B. *The Making of Modern Japan*. Cambridge, MA: Harvard University Press, 2000.

JCS1380–15. "Basic Initial Post Surrender Directive to Supreme Commander for the Allied Powers for the Occupation and Control of Japan." *Joint Chiefs of Staff*. November 3, 1945. Accessed July 31, 2011. http://www.ndl.go.jp /constitution/e/shiryo/01/036/036tx.html

Jervis, Robert. *Perception and Misperception in International Politics*. Princeton, NJ: Princeton University Press, 1976.

Jervis, Robert. "Cooperation under the Security Dilemma." *World Politics* 30, no. 2 (January 1978): 167–214.

Jervis, Robert. "The Impact of the Korean War on the Cold War." *Journal of Conflict Resolution* 24, no. 4 (December 1980): 563–92.

Jervis, Robert. *The Meaning of the Nuclear Revolution: Statecraft and the Prospect of Armageddon*. Ithaca, NY: Cornell University Press, 1989.

Jervis, Robert. "What Do We Want to Deter and How Do We Deter It?" In *Turning Point: The Gulf War and U.S. Military Strategy*, edited by L. Benjamin Ederington and Michael J. Mazarr, 122–24. Boulder, CO: Westview Press, 1994.

Jervis, Robert. "Explaining the Bush Doctrine." *Political Science Quarterly* 118, no. 3 (2003): 365–88.

Jervis, Robert. "Unipolarity: A Structural Perspective." In *International Relations Theory and the Consequences of Unipolarity*, edited by G. John Ikenberry, Michael Mastanduno, and William Wohlforth, 252–81. Cambridge, UK: Cambridge University Press, 2011.

Jessup, Phillip C. *The Birth of Nations*. New York: Columbia University Press, 1974.

John Foster Dulles Papers; 1860–1988 (mostly 1945–1960), Public Policy Papers, Department of Rare Books and Special Collections, Princeton University Library.

Johnson, Chalmers A. "The 1955 System and the American Connection: A Bibliographic Introduction." *Japan Policy Research Institute*. Working Paper 11 (July 1995).

Johnson, Chalmers A. *Blowback: The Costs and Consequences of American Empire*. New York: Metropolitan Books, 2000.

Johnson, Chalmers A. *The Sorrows of Empire: Militarism, Secrecy, and the End of the Republic*. New York: Metropolitan Books, 2004.

Johnson, Chalmers A., and E. B. Keehn. "East Asian Security: The Pentagon's Ossified Strategy." *Foreign Affairs* 74, no. 4 (July/August 1995): 103–14.

Johnson, Jesse C., and Brett Ashley Leeds. "Defense Pacts: A Prescription for Peace?" *Foreign Policy Analysis* 7, no. 1 (January 2011): 45–65.

Johnston, Alastair I. "The Myth of the ASEAN Way? Explaining the Evolution of the ASEAN Regional Forum." In *Imperfect Unions: Security Institutions over*

Time and Space, edited by Helga Haftendorn, Robert O. Keohane, and Celeste A. Wallander, 287–324. Oxford: Oxford University Press, 1999.

Johnston, Alastair I., and Robert Ross, eds. *Engaging China: The Management of an Emerging Power*. London: Routledge, 1999.

Johnston, Tim. "Ally of Bush Is Defeated in Australia." *New York Times*. November 25, 2007. Accessed November 1, 2015. http://www.nytimes.com/2007/11/25/world/asia/25australia.html?_r=1

Kadushin, Charles. *Understanding Social Networks: Theories, Concepts, and Findings*. New York: Oxford University Press, 2012.

Kagan, Robert. "Power and Weakness." *Policy Review* 111 (June/July 2002): 3–28.

Kahler, Miles. "Institution-Building in the Asia-Pacific." In *Pacific Cooperation: Building Economic and Security Regimes in the Asia-Pacific Region*, edited by Andrew Mack and Mark Ravenhill, 16–39. Australia: Allen & Unwin, 1994.

Kahler, Miles, ed. *Networked Politics: Agency, Power, and Governance*. Ithaca, NY: Cornell University Press, 2009.

Kane, Tim. "Global U.S. Troop Deployment, 1950–2005." Heritage Foundation. May 24, 2006. Accessed August 17, 2011. http://www.heritage.org/research/reports/2006/05/global-us-troop-deployment-1950–2005

Kang, David C. "Getting Asia Wrong: The Need for New Analytical Frameworks." *International Security* 27, no. 4 (2003): 57–85.

Kantei. "The Constitution of Japan." n.d. Accessed July 31, 2011. http://www.kantei.go.jp/foreign/constitution_and_government_of_japan/constitution_e.html

Kapstein, Ethan B., and Michael Mastanduno, eds. *Unipolar Politics: Realism and State Strategies after the Cold War*. New York: Columbia University Press, 1999.

Katzenstein, Peter J. "Regionalism in Comparative Perspective." *Cooperation and Conflict* 31, no. 2 (1996): 123–59.

Katzenstein, Peter J. *A World of Regions: Asia and Europe in the American Imperium*. Ithaca, NY: Cornell University Press, 2006.

Kelleher, Catherine. *Germany and the Politics of Nuclear Weapons*. New York: Columbia University Press, 1975.

Kelley, Judith. "The More the Merrier? The Effects of Having Multiple International Election Monitoring Organizations." *Perspective on Politics* 7, no. 1 (March 2009): 59–64.

Kennan, George F. "The Sources of Soviet Conduct." *Foreign Affairs* 25, no. 4 (July 1947).

Kennan, George F. "U.S. Foreign Policy." Lecture conducted from Naval War College, Newport, RI, October 11, 1948.

Kennan, George F. *Realities of American Foreign Policy*. Princeton, NJ: Princeton University Press, 1954.

Kennan, George F. *Memoirs, 1925–1950*. Boston: Little, Brown & Company, 1967.

Kennan, George F. *The Cloud of Danger: Current Realities of American Foreign Policy*. Boston: Little, Brown & Company, 1977.

Kennedy, John F. *Public Papers of the Presidents: John F. Kennedy, 1962*. Washington, DC: Government Printing Office, 1963.

Keohane, Robert O. "The Big Influence of Small Allies." *Foreign Policy* no. 2 (Spring 1971): 161–82.

Keohane, Robert O. "The Theory of Hegemonic Stability and Changes in International Economic Regimes." In *Change in the International System*, edited by Ole Holsti, Randolph Siverson, and Alexander George, 131–62. Boulder, CO: Westview Press, 1980.

Keohane, Robert O. *After Hegemony: Cooperation and Discord in the World Political Economy*. 2nd ed. Princeton, NJ: Princeton University Press, 2005.

Keohane, Robert O., and Joseph S. Nye. *Power and Interdependence: World Politics in Transition*. 4th ed. New York: Pearson, 2012.

Keohane, Robert O., and Celeste Wallander. "Risk, Threat, and Security Institutions." In *Imperfect Unions: Security Institutions over Time and Space*, edited by Helga Haftendorn, Robert Keohane, and Celeste Wallander, 21–46. Oxford: Oxford University Press, 1999.

Kepley, David. *The Collapse of the Middle Way: Senate Republicans and Bipartisan Foreign Policy, 1948–1952*. New York: Greenwood Press, 1988.

Kihl, Young-Whan, ed. *Korea and the World*. Boulder, CO: Westview Press, 1994.

Killen, E.D.L. "The Anzus Pact and Pacific Security." *Far Eastern Survey* 21, no. 14 (1952): 137–41.

Kim, Seung-Young. "American Elites' Strategic Thinking Towards Korea: From Kennan to Brzezinski." *Diplomacy and Statecraft* 12, no. 1 (March 2001): 185–92.

Kim, Stephen Jin-woo. *Master of Manipulation: Syngman Rhee and the Seoul-Washington Alliance, 1953–1960*. Seoul, Korea: Yonsei University Press, 2001.

Kim, Tongfi. "Why Alliances Entangle but Seldom Entrap States." *Security Studies* 20, no. 3 (July 2011): 350–77.

Kindleberger, Charles P. "Dominance and Leadership in the International Economy: Exploitation, Public Goods, and Free Rides." *International Studies Quarterly* 25, no. 2 (1981): 242–54.

Knorr, Klaus. *On the Uses of Military Power in the Nuclear Age*. Princeton, NJ: Princeton University Press, 1966.

Koen, Ross Y. *The China Lobby in American Politics*. New York: Macmillan, 1960.

Koh, Byung Chul. *The Foreign Policy Systems of North and South Korea*. Berkeley: University of California Press, 1984.

Koremenos, Barbara. "Contracting Around International Organization." *American Political Science Review* 99, no. 4 (2005): 549–65.

Koremenos, Barbara, Charles Lipson, and Duncan Snidal. "The Rational Design of International Institutions." *International Organization* 55, no. 4 (2001): 761–99.

Krasner, Stephen D. "State Power and the Structure of International Trade." *World Politics* 28, no. 3 (1976): 317–47.

Krauthammer, Charles. "The Bush Doctrine: ABM, Kyoto, and the New American Unilateralism." *Weekly Standard* 4 (June 2001): 21–25.

Krauthammer, Charles. "The Unipolar Moment Revisited." *National Interest* 70 (Winter 2002): 5–17.

Krieger, Wolfgang. "The Germans and the Nuclear Question." *German Historical Institute Occasional Paper* 14, Fifth Alois Mertes Memorial Lecture, Washington, DC, 1995.

Kristensen, Hans. "Japan Under the US Nuclear Umbrella." *Nautilus Institute Report*. June 2015. http://www.nautilus.org/wp-content/uploads/2015/06/Japan-Under-the-US-Nuclear-Umbrella.pdf

Kristof, Nicholas. "The Problem of Memory." *Foreign Affairs* 77, no. 6 (November/December 1998): 37–49.

Kupchan, Charles. *The End of the American Era: U.S. Foreign Policy and the Geopolitics of the Twenty-first Century.* New York: Alfred A. Knopf, 2002.

Kydd, Andrew H. *Trust and Mistrust in International Relations.* Princeton, NJ: Princeton University Press, 2005.

LaFeber, Walter. *The Clash: A History of U.S.-Japan Relations.* New York: W.W. Norton, 1998.

Lai, Brian, and Dan Reiter. "Democracy, Political Similarity, and International Alliances, 1816–1992." *Journal of Conflict Resolution* 44, no. 2 (2000): 203–27.

Lake, David A. *Entangling Relations: American Foreign Policy in Its Century.* Princeton, NJ: Princeton University Press, 1999.

Lake, David A. *Hierarchy in International Relations.* Ithaca, NY: Cornell University Press, 2009.

Lake, David A. "Legitimating Power: The Domestic Politics of U.S. International Hierarchy." *International Security* 38, no. 2 (Fall 2013): 74–111.

Lake, David A., and Patrick Morgan. "The New Regionalism in Security Affairs." In *Regional Orders: Building Security in a New World*, edited by David A. Lake and Patrick Morgan, 3–19 (University Park: Pennsylvania State University Press, 1997).

Lake, David A., and Patrick Morgan, eds. *Regional Orders: Building Security in a New World.* University Park: Pennsylvania State University Press, 1997.

Lake, David A., and Robert Powell, eds. *International Relations: A Strategic-Choice Approach.* Princeton, NJ: Princeton University Press, 1999.

Lake, David A., and Wendy H. Wong. "The Politics of Networks: Interests, Power and Human Rights Norms." In *Networked Politics: Interests, Power and Human Rights*, edited by Miles Kahler, 127–50. Ithaca, NY: Cornell University Press, 2009.

Lall, Arthur S. *Modern International Negotiation; Principles and Practice.* New York: Columbia University Press, 1966.

Larsen, Deborah. *Origins of Containment: A Psychological Explanation.* Princeton, NJ: Princeton University Press, 1985.

Layne, Christopher. *The Peace of Illusions: American Grand Strategy from 1940 to the Present.* Ithaca, NY: Cornell University Press, 2006.

Lee, Gerald Geunwook. "South Korea's Faustian Attitude: The Republic of Korea's Decision to Send Troops to Iraq Revisited." *Cambridge Review of International Affairs* 19, no. 3 (September 2006): 481–93.

Lee, Jae-hyon. "China Is Recreating the American 'Hub-and-Spoke' System in Asia." *Diplomat.* September 11, 2015. Accessed October 18, 2015. http://thediplomat.com/2015/09/china-is-recreating-the-american-hub-and-spoke-system-in-asia/

Lee, Ji-Young. "Hegemonic Authority and Domestic Legitimation: Japan and Korea under the Chinese Hegemonic Order in Early Modern East Asia." Presented at the American Political Science Association Meeting, Washington, DC, August 28, 2014.

Leeds, Brett Ashley. "Domestic Political Institutions, Credible Commitments, and International Cooperation." *American Journal of Political Science* 43, no. 4 (October 1999): 979–1002.

Leeds, Brett Ashley. "Do Alliances Deter Aggression? The Influence of Military Alliances on the Initiation of Militarized Interstate Disputes." *American Journal of Political Science* 47, no. 3 (July 2003): 427–39.

Leeds, Brett Ashley. "Alliance Reliability in Times of War: Explaining State Decisions to Violate Treaties." *International Organization* 57, no. 4 (Autumn 2003): 801–27.

Leeds, Brett Ashley, and Michaela Mattes. "Alliance Politics during the Cold War: Aberration, New World Order, or Continuation of History?" *Conflict Management and Peace Science* 24, no. 3 (2007): 183–99.

Leeds, Brett Ashley, Michaela Mattes, and Jeremy Vogel. "Interest, Institutions, and the Reliability of International Commitments." *American Journal of Political Science* 53, no. 2 (2009): 461–76.

Leeds, Brett Ashley, Jeffrey Ritter, Sara Mitchell, and Andrew Long. "Alliance Treaty Obligations and Provisions, 1815–1944." *International Interactions* 28, no. 3 (2002): 237–60.

Leeds, Brett Ashley, and Burcu Savun. "Terminating Alliances: Why Do States Abrogate Agreements?" *Journal of Politics* 69, no. 4 (2007): 1118–32.

Leffler, Melvyn P. *A Preponderance of Power: National Security, the Truman Administration, and the Cold War*. Stanford, CA: Stanford University Press, 1992.

Liedtke, Boris Nikolaj. "International Relations Between the U.S. and Spain 1945 – 1953: Economics, Ideology and Compromise." PhD dissertation, London School of Economics and Political Sciences, 2014.

Lim, Chin Leng, Deborah K. Elms, and Patrick Low, eds. *The Trans-Pacific Partnership: A Quest for a Twenty-first Century Trade Agreement*. Cambridge, UK: Cambridge University Press, 2013.

Lintner, Bertil. "The CIA's First Secret War: Americans Helped Stage Raid into China from Burma." *Far Eastern Economic Review* (September 1993): 56–58.

Lintner, Bertil. *Burma in Revolt: Opium and Insurgency since 1948*. Boulder, CO: Westview Press, 1994.

Lipson, Charles. "Why Are Some International Agreements Informal?" *International Organization* 45, no. 4 (1991): 495–538.

Liska, George. *Nations in Alliance: The Limits of Interdependence*. Baltimore: Johns Hopkins University Press, 1962.

Lu, David John. *Sources of Japanese History*. Vol. 2. New York: McGraw-Hill, 1974.

Mabon, David W. "Elusive Agreements: The Pacific Pact Proposals of 1949–1951." *Pacific Historical Review* 57, no. 2 (May 1988): 147–77.

MacArthur, Douglas. *Reminiscences: Douglas MacArthur, General of the Army*. New York: McGraw-Hill, 1964.

MacDonald, Donald Stone. *U.S.-Korean Relations from Liberation to Self-reliance: The Twenty-year Record: An Interpretative Summary of the Archives of the U.S. Department of State for the Period 1945 to 1965*. Boulder, CO: Westview Press, 1992.

MacDonald, Douglas J. *Adventures in Chaos: American Intervention for Reform in the Third World*. Cambridge, MA: Harvard University Press, 1992.

Maddison, Angus. *Statistics on World Population, GDP, and Per Capita GDP, 1—2008 AD*. n.d. Accessed March 26, 2013. http://www.ggdc.net/maddison/oriindex.htm

Maier, Charles S. *Among Empires: American Ascendancy and Its Predecessors*. Cambridge, MA: Harvard University Press, 2006.

Mandelbaum, Michael. *The Nuclear Revolution: International Politics before and after Hiroshima.* Cambridge, UK: Cambridge University Press, 1981.

Mandelbaum, Michael. *The Case for Goliath: How America Acts as the World's Government in the Twenty-first Century.* New York: Public Affairs, 2005.

Mann, Jim. "Baker Tells Japan: Take Global Role: Policy: Move beyond 'Checkbook Diplomacy.'" *Los Angeles Times.* November 11, 1991. Accessed November 1, 2015. http://articles.latimes.com/1991–11–11/news/mn-996_1_foreign-policy

Manyin, Mark E., Stephen Daggett, Ben Dolven, Susan V. Lawrence, Michael F. Martin, Ronald O'Rourke, and Bruce Vaughn. "Pivot to the Pacific? The Obama Administration's 'Rebalancing' Toward Asia." Congressional Research Service Report for Congress. March 28, 2012. Accessed October 3, 2014. http://fpc.state.gov/documents/organization/187389.pdf

Marshall, Monty G., and Keith Jaggers. "Polity IV Project: Political Regime Characteristics and Transitions, 1800—2012." June 6, 2014. Accessed March 25, 2013. http://systemicpeace.org/polity/polity4.htm.

Martin, Lisa. "The Rational State Choice of Multilateralism." In *Multilateralism Matters: The Theory and Praxis of an Institutional Form*, edited by John G. Ruggie, 91–121. New York: Columbia University Press, 1993.

Martin, Lisa L., and Beth A. Simmons. "Theories and Empirical Studies of International Institutions." *International Organization* 52, no. 4 (Autumn 1998): 729–57.

Mastanduno, Michael. *Unipolar Politics: Realism and State Strategies after the Cold War.* Edited by Ethan B. Kapstein. New York: Columbia University Press, 1999.

Mastanduno, Michael. "System Maker and Privilege Taker: U.S. Power and the International Political Economy." In *International Relations Theory and the Consequences of Unipolarity*, edited by G. John Ikenberry, Michael Mastanduno, and William Wohlforth, 140–77. Cambridge, UK: Cambridge University Press, 2011.

Maswood, Javed. "The Rise of the Asia-Pacific." In *Asia-Pacific in the New World Order*, edited by Anthony G. McGrew and Christopher Brooks, 57–66. London: Routledge, 1998.

Mattes, Michaela. "Democratic Reliability, Precommitment of Successor Governments, and the Choice of Alliance Commitment." *International Organization* 66, no. 1 (January 2012): 153–72.

Mattes, Michaela. "Reputation, Symmetry, and Alliance Design." *International Organization* 66, no. 4 (Fall 2012): 679–707.

Maydew, Randall C. *America's Lost H-Bomb! Palomares, Spain, 1966.* Manhattan, KS: Sunflower University Press, 1997.

Mayer, Michael S. *The Eisenhower Years.* New York: Facts on File, 2009.

McGrew, Anthony G., and Christopher Brooks, eds. *Asia-Pacific in the New World Order.* London: Routledge, 1998.

McKinzie, Richard D. "Oral History Interview with John J. Muccio." December 7, 1973, Washington, DC. Accessed February 4, 2016. http://www.trumanlibrary.org/oralhist/muccio3.htm

Mearsheimer, John J. *The Tragedy of Great Power Politics.* New York: W.W. Norton, 2001.

Mearsheimer, John J., and Stephen M. Walt. *The Israel Lobby and U.S. Foreign Policy.* New York: Farrar, Straus and Giroux, 2007.

Mercer, Jonathan. *Reputation in International Policies*. Ithaca, NY: Cornell University Press, 1996.

Mercer, Jonathan. "Emotion and Strategy in the Korean War." *International Organization* 67, no. 2 (Spring 2013): 221–52.

Merrill, Dennis, ed. *The Documentary History of the Truman Presidency, vol. 32: The Emergence of an Asian Pacific Rim in American Foreign Policy*. Bethesda, MD: University Publications of America, 2001.

Midford, Paul. "Japan's Leadership Role in East Asian Security Multilateralism: The Nakayama Proposal and the Logic of Reassurance." *Pacific Review* 13, no. 3 (2000): 367–97.

Morgan, T. Clifton. "A Spatial Model of Crisis Bargaining." *International Studies Quarterly* 28 (1984): 407–26.

Morgenthau, Hans J. "Alliances in Theory and Practice." In *Alliance Policy in the Cold War*, edited by Arnold Wolfers, 184–212. Baltimore: Johns Hopkins University Press, 1959.

Morrow, James D. "Alliances and Asymmetry: An Alternative to the Capability Aggregation Model of Alliances." *American Journal of Political Science* 35, no. 4 (November 1991): 904–33.

Morrow, James D. "Arms versus Allies: Trade-offs in the Search for Security." *International Organization* 47, no. 2 (Spring 1993): 207–33.

Morrow, James D. "Alliances: Why Write Them Down?" *Annual Review of Political Science* 3, no. 1 (June 2000): 63–83.

Motyl, Alexander J. *Imperial Ends: The Decay, Collapse, and Revival of Empires*. New York: Columbia University Press, 2001.

Motyl, Alexander J. "Empire Falls: Washington May Be Imperious, but It Is Not Imperial." *Foreign Affairs* 85, no. 4 (July/August 2006): 190–94.

Mu, Chunshan. "What Is CICA (and Why Does China Care about It?)." *The Diplomat*. May 17, 2014. Accessed October 18, 2015. http://thediplomat.com/2014/05/what-is-cica-and-why-does-china-care-about-it/

Nanto, Dick K. "East Asian Regional Architecture." Congressional Research Service. Report for Congress. April 15, 2010. Accessed October 3, 2014. http://fpc.state.gov/documents/organization/142760.pdf

National Military Capabilities (v4.0). The Correlates of War Project. January 1, 2013. Accessed December 9, 2014. http://www.correlatesofwar.org/COW2 Data/Capabilities/nmc4.htm

Nester, William R. *Power across the Pacific: A Diplomatic History of American Relations with Japan*. London: MacMillan Press, 1996.

Newman, Robert P. "Clandestine Chinese Nationalist Efforts to Punish Their American Detractors." *Diplomatic History* 7, no. 3 (1983): 205–22.

New York Daily News. "Will Live up to Pledges." June 24, 1953. Excerpts from Editorial Comment on President's State of the Union Message. *New York Times* (1923–current file).

New York Journal American. "First Energetic Step." *ProQuest Historical Newspapers: New York Times* (1851–2010).

Nexon, Daniel H. "What's This, Then? 'Romanes Eunt Domus?'" *International Studies Perspective* 9, no. 3 (August 2008): 300–308.

Nexon, Daniel H., and Thomas Wright. "What's at Stake in The American Empire Debate." *American Political Science Review* 101, no. 2 (May 2007): 253–71.

Newsweek. "Japan's Future: Interview with John Foster Dulles." September 10, 1951.

Nitze, Paul H. *From Hiroshima to Glasnost: At the Centre of Decision, A Memoir.* London: Weidenfeld & Nicolson, 1989.

Nye, Joseph S. "East Asian Security: The Case for Deep Engagement." *Foreign Affairs* 74, no. 4 (July/August 1995): 90–102.

Nye, Joseph S. "The Nye Report: Six Years Later." *International Relations of Asia-Pacific* 1, no. 1 (2001): 95–103.

Nye, Joseph S. *The Paradox of American Power: Why the World's Only Superpower Can't Go It Alone.* Oxford: Oxford University Press, 2002.

Office of the Press Secretary, The White House. "Address to a Joint Session of Congress and the American People." September 20, 2001. Accessed November 1, 2015. http://georgewbush-whitehouse.archives.gov/news/releases/2001 /09/20010920–8.html

Office of the Press Secretary, The White House. "President Bush Signs H.R. 7081, the United States-India Nuclear Cooperation Approval and Nonproliferation Enhancement Act." October 8, 2008. Accessed October 2, 2014. http:// georgewbush-whitehouse.archives.gov/news/releases/2008/10/20081008–4 .html

Office of the Press Secretary, The White House. "Remarks by President Barack Obama, 'Hradcany Square, Prague, Czech Republic.'"April 5, 2009. Accessed December 30, 2009. https://www.whitehouse.gov/the_press_office/Remarks -By-President-Barack-Obama-In-Prague-As-Delivered

Office of the Press Secretary, The White House. "Joint Vision for the Alliance of the United States of America and the Republic of Korea." June 16, 2009. Accessed October 5, 2014. https://www.whitehouse.gov/the_press_office/Joint -vision-for-the-alliance-of-the-United-States-of-America-and-the-Republic-of -Korea/

Office of the Press Secretary, The White House. "Remarks by President Obama and Prime Minister Gillard of Australia in Joint Press Conference." November 16, 2011. Accessed October 2, 2014. https://www.whitehouse.gov/the -press-office/2011/11/16/remarks-president-obama-and-prime-minister-gillard -australia-joint-press

Office of the Press Secretary, The White House. "United States-Japan Joint Statement: A Shared Vision for the Future." April 30, 2012. Accessed October 3, 2014. https://www.whitehouse.gov/the-press-office/2012/04/30/united-states -japan-joint-statement-shared-vision-future

Office of the Press Secretary, The White House. "Remarks by President Obama at the University of Yangon." November 19, 2012. Accessed October 3, 2014. https://www.whitehouse.gov/the-press-office/2012/11/19/remarks-president -obama-university-yangon

Office of the Press Secretary, The White House. "Joint Statement by the United States and Japan." February 22, 2013. Accessed October 2, 2014. https://www .whitehouse.gov/the-press-office/2013/02/22/joint-statement-united-states -and-japan

Office of the Press Secretary, The White House. "Joint Declaration in Commemoration of the 60th Anniversary of the Alliance between the Republic of Korea and the United States of America." May 7, 2013. Accessed October 3, 2014. https://www.whitehouse.gov/the-press-office/2013/05/07/joint -declaration-commemoration-60th-anniversary-alliance-between-republ

Office of the Press Secretary, The White House. "Message to the Congress— Agreement for Cooperation Between the American Institute in Taiwan and the Taipei Economic and Cultural Representative Office Concerning Peaceful Uses of Nuclear Energy." January 7, 2014. Accessed October 2, 2014. https://www.whitehouse.gov/the-press-office/2014/01/07/message-congress -agreement-cooperation-between-american-institute-taiwan

Office of the Press Secretary, The White House. "Remarks by President Obama and President Benigno Aquino III of the Philippines in Joint Press Conference." April 28, 2014. Accessed October 3, 2014. https://www.whitehouse.gov /the-press-office/2014/04/28/remarks-president-obama-and-president-benigno -aquino-iii-philippines-joi

Office of the Press Secretary, The White House. "Remarks by President Obama and Prime Minister Abe of Japan in Joint Press Conference." April 28, 2015. https://www.whitehouse.gov/the-press-office/2015/04/28/remarks-president -obama-and-prime-minister-abe-japan-joint-press-confere

Office of the Press Secretary, The White House. "Remarks by President Obama and President Park of the Republic of Korea in Joint Press Conference." October 16, 2015. https://www.whitehouse.gov/the-press-office/2015/10/16 /remarks-president-obama-and-president-park-republic-korea-joint-press

Ogata, Sadako. "The Business Community and Japanese Foreign Policy." In *The Foreign Policy of Modern Japan*, edited by Robert Scalapino, 175–203. Berkeley: University of California Press, 1977.

Oldenziel, Ruth. "Islands: The United States as a Networked Empire." In *Entangled Geographies: Empire and Technopolitics in the Global Cold War*, edited by Gabrielle Hecht, 13–42. Cambridge, MA: MIT Press, 2011.

Oliver, Robert Tarbell. *Syngman Rhee and American Involvement in Korea, 1942– 1960: A Personal Narrative*. Seoul, Korea: Panmun Book, 1978.

Olson, Mancur, and Richard Zeckhauser. "An Economic Theory of Alliances." *Review of Economics and Statistics* 48 (1966): 266–79.

Osgood, Robert. *Alliances in American Foreign Policy*. Baltimore: Johns Hopkins University Press, 1968.

Oudenaren, John V. "What Is 'Multilateral'?" *Policy Review* 117 (2003): 33–48.

Oudenaren, John V. "Unipolar versus Unilateral." *Policy Review* 124 (2004): 63–74.

Oye, Kenneth A. *Cooperation under Anarchy*. Princeton, NJ: Princeton University Press, 1986.

Packard, George R. *Protest in Tokyo: The Security Treaty Crisis of 1960*. Princeton, NJ: Princeton University Press, 1966.

Paige, Glenn D. *The Korean Decision: June 24–30, 1950*. New York: Free Press, 1968.

Pape, Robert A. "Soft Balancing Against the United States." *International Security* 30, no. 1 (Summer 2005): 7–45.

Park, Chang Jin. "The Influence of Small States upon the Superpowers: United States-South Korean Relations as a Case Study, 1950–53." *World Politics* 28, no. 1 (October 1975): 97–117.

Park, Tae-gyun. *An Ally and Empire: Two Myths of South Korea-United States Relations, 1945–1980*. Seoul, Korea: Academy of Korean Studies Press, 2012.

Paul, Thazha Varkey. *Power versus Prudence: Why Nations Forgo Nuclear Weapons*. Montreal and Kingston: McGill-Queen's University Press, 2000.

Paul, Thazha Varkey. "Soft Balancing in the Age of U.S. Primacy." *International Security* 30, no. 1 (Summer 2005): 46–71.

Peters, Gerhard, and John T. Woolley. "Republican Party Platform of 1952." July 7, 1952. *The American Presidency Project*. Accessed October 21, 2011. http://www.presidency.ucsb.edu/ws/?pid=25837

Posen, Barry. *The Sources of Military Doctrine: France, Britain, and Germany between the World Wars*. Ithaca, NY: Cornell University Press, 1984.

Potsdam Declaration. National Diet Library. July 26, 1945. Accessed August 15, 2011. http://www.ndl.go.jp/constitution/e/etc/c06.html.

Presidential Papers of the United States: Harry S. Truman, 1950. Washington, DC: U.S. Government Printing Office, 1965.

Press-Barnathan, Galia. *Organizing the World: The United States and Regional Cooperation in Asia and Europe*. New York: Routledge, 2003.

Press-Barnathan, Galia. "The Impact of Regional Dynamics on U.S. Policy toward Regional Security Arrangements in East Asia." *International Relations of the Asia-Pacific* 14, no. 3 (September 2014): 369–71.

Pressman, Jeremy. *Warring Friends: Alliance Restraint in International Politics*. Ithaca, NY: Cornell University Press, 2008.

Prime Minister of Japan and his Cabinet. "The Outline of the Basic Plan regarding Response Measures Based on the Law Concerning the Special Measures on Humanitarian and Reconstruction Assistance in Iraq." December 9, 2003. Accessed November 1, 2015. http://japan.kantei.go.jp/policy/2003/031209housin_e.html.

Pruessen, Ronald W. *John Foster Dulles: The Road to Power*. New York: Free Press, 1982.

Pyle, Kenneth B. *Japan Rising: The Resurgence of Japanese Power and Purpose*. New York: Public Affairs, 2007.

Rankin, Karl L. *China Assignment*. Seattle: University of Washington Press, 1964.

Rathbun, Brian C. "Before Hegemony: Generalized Trust and the Creation and Design of International Security Organizations." *International Organization* 65, no. 2 (Spring 2011): 243–73.

Reischauer, Edwin O. *The United States and Japan*. 3rd ed. Cambridge, MA: Harvard University Press, 1965.

Rice, Susan E. "America's Future in Asia: Remarks as Prepared for Delivery by National Security Advisor Susan E. Rice." November 20, 2013, Georgetown University, Gaston Hall, Washington, DC. https://www.whitehouse.gov/the-press-office/2013/11/21/remarks-prepared-delivery-national-security-advisor-susan-e-rice

Ridgway, Matthew. *The Korean War: How We Met the Challenge, How All-Out Asian War Was Averted, Why MacArthur Was Dismissed, Why Today's War Objectives Must Be Limited*. Garden City, NY: Doubleday, 1967.

"Robertson, Walter Spencer (1893–1970)." In *U.S. Leadership in Wartime: Clashes, Controversy, and Compromise*, edited by Spencer C. Tucker, 729–30. Santa Barbara, CA: ABC-CLIO, 2009.

Rosendorff, B. Peter, and Helen V. Milner. "The Optimal Design of International Trade Institutions: Uncertainty and Escape." *International Organization* 55, no. 4 (Autumn 2001): 829–57.

Rothstein, Robert L. *Alliances and Small Powers*. New York: Columbia University Press, 1968.

Rotter, Andrew. *The Path to Vietnam*. Ithaca, NY: Cornell University Press, 1987.

Royall, Kenneth C. "Speech by Kenneth C. Royall, Secretary of the Army, on the United States Policy for Japan." January 6, 1948, San Francisco. Accessed October 11, 2011. http://www.ioc.u-tokyo.ac.jp/~worldjpn/documents/texts/JPUS/19480106.S1E.html

Rubinstein, Alvin Z. *Red Star on the Nile: The Soviet-Egyptian Influence Relationship Since the June War*. Princeton, NJ: Princeton University Press, 1977.

Ruggie, John G. "Multilateralism: The Anatomy of an Institution." In *Multilateralism Matters: The Theory and Praxis of an Institutional Form*, edited by John G. Ruggie, 3–48. New York: Columbia University Press, 1993.

Ruggie, John G. "The Past as Prologue? Interests, Identity, and American Foreign Policy." *International Security* 21, no. 4 (Spring 1997): 89–125.

Ruggie, John G. "What Makes the World Hang Together? Neo-Utilitarianism and the Social Constructivist Challenge." *International Organization* 52, no. 4 (Autumn 1998): 855–85.

Russ, Martin. *Breakout: The Chosin Reservoir Campaign, Korea 1950*. New York: Fromm International, 1999.

Saunders, Phillip C. "The United States and East Asia after Iraq." *Survival* 49, no. 1 (2007): 141–52.

Sayuri, Shimizu. "Perennial Anxiety: Japan-U.S. Controversy over Recognition of the PRC, 1952–58." *Journal of American-East Asian Relations* 4, no. 3 (Fall 1995): 223–48.

Schaller, Michael. *The American Occupation of Japan: The Origins of the Cold War in Asia*. New York: Oxford University Press, 1985.

Schaller, Michael. *Altered States: The United States and Japan since the Occupation*. New York: Oxford University Press, 1997.

Schaller, Michael. "America's Favorite War Criminal: Kishi Nobusuke and the Transformation of U.S.-Japan Relations." *Japan Policy Research Institute* Working Paper 11 (1995). Accessed March 9, 2009. http://www.jpri.org/publications/workingpapers/wp11.html

Schelling, Thomas C. *Arms and Influence*. New Haven, CT: Yale University Press, 1966.

Schnabel, James F., and Robert J. Watson. *The History of the Joint Chiefs of Staff: The Joint Chiefs of Staff and National Policy: The Korean War, Vol. 3, Part I*. Wilmington, DE: Scholarly Resources, 1979.

Schnabel, James F., and Robert J. Watson. *The Joint Chiefs of Staff and National Policy, Vol. 3, 1950–1951*. Washington, DC: Office of the Joint History, 1998.

Schonberger, Howard B. *Aftermath of War: Americans and the Remaking of Japan, 1945–1952*. Kent, OH: Kent State University Press, 1989.

Schroeder, Paul. "Alliances, 1815–1945: Weapons of Power and Tools of Management." In *Historical Dimensions of National Security Problems*, edited by Klaus Knorr, 227–62. Lawrence: University Press of Kansas, 1976.

Schroeder, Paul. "Alliances as Tools of Management." In *Economic Issues and National Security*, edited by Klaus Knorr, 230. Lawrence: Regent's Press of Kansas, 1977.

Schweller, Randall L. "Tripolarity and the Second World War." *International Studies Quarterly* 37, no. 1 (March 1993): 73–103.

Schweller, Randall L. *Deadly Imbalances: Tripolarity and Hitler's Strategy of World Conquest*. New York: Columbia University Press, 1998.

Schweller, Randall L., and Xiaoyu Pu. "After Unipolarity: China's Visions of International Order in an Era of U.S. Decline." *International Security* 36, no. 1 (Summer 2011): 41–72.

Seraphim, Franziska, and Gerrit W. Gong. "Memory and History in East and Southeast Asia: Issues of Identity in International Relations." *Journal of Asian Studies* 62, no. 2 (2003): 560–62.

Shambaugh, David L. "China Engages Asia: Reshaping the Regional Order." *International Security* 29, no. 3 (Winter 2004/05): 64–99.

Shim, J. Y. "Roh Says NK Nuke Talks Big Factor in Troop Dispatch." *Korea Times*. October 1, 2003.

Sil, Rudra, and Peter J. Katzenstein. *Beyond Paradigms: Analytic Eclecticism in the Study of World Politics*. New York: Palgrave Macmillan, 2010.

Sim, S. T. "Opposition Mounts against Dispatching Combat Troops." *Korea Herald*. September 18, 2003.

Sim, S. T. "Foreign Ministry's US Policy Bureau Faces Major Reshuffle." *Korea Herald*. January 16, 2004.

Siverson, Randolph M., and Juliann Emmons. "Birds of a Feather: Democratic Political Systems and Alliance Choices in the Twentieth Century." *Journal of Conflict Resolution* 35 (June 1991): 285–306.

Siverson, Randolph M., and Joel King. "Alliances and the Expansion of War." In *To Augur Well: Early Warning Indicators in World Politics*, edited by J. David Singer and Michael D. Wallace, 37–49. Beverly Hills, CA: Sage Publications, 1979.

Smith, Alastair. "Alliance Formation and War." *International Studies Quarterly* 39, no. 4 (December 1995): 405–25.

Smith, Beverly. "The White House Story: Why We Went to War in Korea." *Saturday Evening Post*. November 10, 1951.

Snyder, Glenn H. "The Security Dilemma in Alliance Politics." *World Politics* 36, no. 4 (July 1984): 461–95.

Snyder, Glenn H. *Alliance Politics*. Ithaca, NY: Cornell University Press, 1997.

Snyder, Jack L. *The Ideology of the Offensive: Military Decision Making and the Disasters of 1914*. Ithaca, NY: Cornell University Press, 1984.

Snyder, Jack L. *Myths of Empire: Domestic Politics and International Ambition*. Ithaca, NY: Cornell University Press, 1991.

Snyder, Jack L. "Imperial Temptations." *National Interest* 71 (Spring 2003): 29–40.

Snyder, Scott, and Jung-yeop Woo. "The U.S. Rebalance and the Seoul Process: How to Align U.S. and ROK Visions for Cooperation in East Asia." *Council on Foreign Relations*, January 2015. http://www.cfr.org/asia-and-pacific/us-rebalance-seoul-process-align-us-rok-visions-cooperation-east-asia/p35926

Solingen, Etel. *Regional Orders at Century's Dawn: Global and Domestic Influences on Grand Strategy*. Princeton, NJ: Princeton University Press, 1998.

Spender, Percy. *Exercises in Diplomacy: The ANZUS Treaty and the Colombo Plan.* Sydney: Sydney University Press, 1969.

Statistics Bureau—Ministry of International Affairs and Communications (Japan). Accessed August 16, 2011. http://www.stat.go.jp/english

Stevenson, Adlai E. "Korea in Perspective." *Foreign Affairs* 30, no. 3 (April 1952).

Stiles, David. "A Fusion Bomb over Andalucia: US Information Policy and the 1966 Palomares Incident." *Journal of Cold War Studies* 8, no. 1 (Winter 2006): 49–673.

Straits Times. "Interested in Pact." March 23, 1949. Accessed November 27, 2011. http://newspapers.nl.sg/Digitised/Page/straitstimes19490323.1.1.aspx

Straits Times. "Reds Won't Hold Asia." March 24, 1949. Accessed November 27, 2011. http://newspapers.nl.sg/Digitised/Page/straitstimes19490324.1.1.aspx

Straits Times. "Pacific Union—President Quirino." July 5, 1949. Accessed January 1, 2015. http://newspapers.nl.sg/Digitised/Page/straitstimes19490705.1.1.aspx

Straits Times. "Chiang Files to Manila for Anti-Red Talks." July 11, 1949. Accessed November 21, 2011. http://newspapers.nl.sg/Digitised/Page/straitstimes19490711.1.1.aspx

Straits Times. "Chiang-Quirino United Front: Starting a Pacific Pact." July 12, 1949. Accessed November 21, 2011. http://newspapers.nl.sg/Digitised/Page/straitstimes19490712.1.1.aspx

Straits Times. "Pacific Union Pact Talks." July 19, 1949. Accessed November 28, 2011. http://newspapers.nl.sg/Digitised/Page/straitstimes19490719.1.1.aspx

Straits Times. "Far East's Share of U.S. Arms Aid." July 27, 1949. Accessed December 11, 2011. http://newspapers.nl.sg/Digitised/Page/straitstimes19490727.1.1.aspx

Straits Times. "Key Thrown in Pacific." July 29, 1949. Accessed December 11, 2011. http://newspapers.nl.sg/Digitised/Page/straitstimes19490729.1.1.aspx

Straits Times. "No More U.S. Aid for Chiang." July 30, 1949. Accessed December 12, 2011. http://newspapers.nl.sg/Digitised/Page/straitstimes19490730.1.1.aspx

Straits Times. "Anti-Red Talks in the U.S." August 8, 1949. Accessed December 13, 2011. http://newspapers.nl.sg/Digitised/Page/straitstimes19490808.1.1.aspx

Straits Times. "Appeal Cabled to Quirino." August 9, 1949. Accessed November 12, 2011. http://newspapers.nl.sg/Digitised/Page/straitstimes19490810.1.1.aspx

Straits Times. "Chiang-Rhee Anti-Red Pact Plea." August 9, 1949. Accessed November 21, 2011. http://newspapers.nl.sg/Digitised/Page/straitstimes19490809.1.1.aspx

Straits Times. "Quirino Will Not Go Home with Nothing." August 11, 1949. Accessed January 9, 2012. http://newspapers.nl.sg/Digitised/Page/straitstimes19490811.1.1.aspx

Straits Times. "U.S. May Aid Alliance." August 13, 1949. Accessed January 30, 2012. http://newspapers.nl.sg/Digitised/Page/straitstimes19490813.1.1.aspx

Straits Times. "U.S. Aid Proposal for Far Eastern Union." August 15, 1949. Accessed January 30, 2012. http://newspapers.nl.sg/Digitised/Page/straitstimes19490815.1.1.aspx

Straits Times. "U.S. Told Watch the Back Door." August 17, 1949. Accessed January 31, 2012. http://newspapers.nl.sg/Digitised/Page/straitstimes19490817.1.1.aspx

Straits Times. "Korean Claim." October 1, 1949. Accessed February 12, 2012. http://newspapers.nl.sg/Digitised/Page/straitstimes19491001.1.6.aspx

Straits Times. "S. Korea Accused before UN." October 3, 1949. Accessed February 13, 2012. http://newspapers.nl.sg/Digitised/Page/straitstimes19491003.1.2.aspx

Straits Times. "Biggest Pacific Naval Exercises This Month." October 4, 1949. Accessed February 13, 2012. http://newspapers.nl.sg/Digitised/Page/straits times19491004.1.1.aspx

Straits Times. "Manila Cool on Pact Plan." October 10, 1949. Accessed February 13, 2012. http://newspapers.nl.sg/Digitised/Page/straitstimes19491010.1.1.aspx

Straits Times. "U.S. Told Keep Reds Out of Asia." October 12, 1949. Accessed February 13, 2012. http://newspapers.nl.sg/Digitised/Page/straitstimes19491012.1 .1.aspx

Straits Times. "U.S. Accused, Advertising at ECAFE." October 18, 1949. Accessed February 13, 2012. http://newspapers.nl.sg/Digitised/Page/straitstimes19491018 .1.1.aspx

Straits Times. "'Threats to Asia' Warns Wavell." October 21, 1949. Accessed February 18, 2012. http://newspapers.nl.sg/Digitised/Page/straitstimes19491021.1 .1.aspx

Straits Times. "South Korea's Hopes." November 3, 1949. Accessed March 13, 2012. http://newspapers.nl.sg/Digitised/Page/straitstimes19491103.1.6.aspx

Straits Times. "T.U.C. of Asian Countries." November 3, 1949. Accessed May 16, 2012. http://newspapers.nl.sg/Digitised/Page/straitstimes19491103.1.1.aspx

Straits Times. "U.S. Resumes Marshall Aid to Indonesia." November 9, 1949. Accessed May 18, 2012. http://newspapers.nl.sg/Digitised/Page/straitstimes19491109.1.1 .aspx

Straits Times. "Asian Cominform to be Set Up." December 3, 1949. Accessed June 22, 2012. http://newspapers.nl.sg/Digitised/Page/straitstimes19491203.1 .1.aspx

Stubbs, Richard. "ASEAN Plus Three: Emerging East Asian Regionalism?" *Asian Survey* 42, no. 3 (2002): 440–55.

Stueck, William. *The Road to Confrontation: American Policy toward Korea and China, 1947–1950.* Chapel Hill: University of North Carolina Press, 1981.

Stueck, William. *The Korean War: An International History.* Princeton, NJ: Princeton University Press, 1997.

Sullivan, Rohan. "Bush Ally Howard Defeated in Australia: Next Prime Minister Promises New Course on Iraq Warning." *Washington Post.* November 25, 2007.

Syngman Rhee through Western Eyes. Seoul, Korea: Office of Public Information, Republic of Korea, 1954.

Tanter, Richard. "Japan's Indian Ocean Naval Deployment: Blue Water Militarization in a 'Normal Country.'" *Japan Focus.* May 15, 2006. Accessed November 1, 2015. http://japanfocus.org/-Richard-Tanter/1700/article.html

Terada, Takashi. "Constructing an 'East Asian' Concept and Growing Regional Identity: From EAEC to ASEAN + 3." *Pacific Review* 16, no. 2 (2003): 251–77.

The Constitution of the Empire of Japan (1889). Hanover.edu. Accessed July 31, 2011. http://history.hanover.edu/texts/1889con.html.

The Situation in the Far East. Testimony of Dean Acheson, Senate Foreign Relations Committee, 12 October 1949." In *Executive Sessions of the Senate Foreign Relations Committee,* 87. Washington, DC: Government Printing Office, 1976.

Tilley, Charles. "How Empires End." In *After Empire: Multiethnic Societies and Nation-Building. The Soviet Union and the Russian, Ottoman, and Habsburg Empires*, edited by Karen Barkey and Mark Von Hagen, 1–11. Boulder, CO: Westview Press, 1997.

Tow, William. "Assessing the Trilateral Strategic Dialogue." East Asia Forum. February 12, 2009. Accessed August 30, 2009. http://www.eastasiaforum.org /2009/02/12/assessing-the-trilateral-strategic-dialogue/

Tow, William, Michael Auslin, Rory Medcalf, Akihiko Tanaka, Feng Zhu, and Sheldon W. Simon. "Assessing the Trilateral Strategic Dialogue." Special Report #16. December 1, 2008. Accessed September 21, 2009. http://www.nbr .org/publications/specialreport/pdf/SR16.pdf

Trachtenberg, Marc. *A Constructed Peace: The Making of the European Settlement, 1945–1963.* Princeton, NJ: Princeton University Press, 1999.

Treaty of Mutual Cooperation and Security between Japan and the United States of America. January 19, 1960. Accessed August 17, 2011. http://www.ioc.u -tokyo.ac.jp/~worldjpn/documents/texts/docs/19600119.T1E.html

Truman, Harry S. "Address in San Francisco at the Opening of the Conference on the Japanese Peace Treaty." September 4, 1951. Accessed August 16, 2011. http://www.presidency.ucsb.edu/ws/index.php?pid=13906#axzz1VE2n6VTg

Truman, Harry S. "Address to the Nation, 11 April 1951." *Dulles Papers*, "Duplicate Correspondence." Box 56.

Truman, Harry S. *Memoirs: Volume II, Years of Trial and Hope.* Garden City, NY: Smithmark Publishers, 1956.

Trussell, C. P. "Congress Praises Eisenhower Talk: But 7th Fleet Decision Brings Fear of War Extension and Deeper U.S. Involvement." February 3, 1953, Special to the *New York Times* (1923–Current file).

Tucker, Nancy Bernkopf. "Nationalist China's Decline and Its Impact on Sino-American Relations, 1949–1950." In *Uncertain Years: Chinese-American Relations, 1947–50*, edited by Dorothy Borg and Waldo Heinrichs, 131–71. New York: Columbia University Press, 1980.

Tucker, Nancy Bernkopf. "John Foster Dulles and the Taiwan Roots of the Two Chinas Policy." In *John Foster Dulles and the Diplomacy of the Cold War*, edited by Richard Immerman, 235–63. Princeton, NJ: Princeton University Press, 1989.

Tucker, Nancy Bernkopf. *Taiwan, Hong Kong, and the United States: Uncertain Friendships.* New York: Twayne Publishers, 1994.

Tucker, Spencer C. *Encyclopedia of the Korean War: A Political, Social, and Military History.* Santa Barbara, CA: ABC-CLIO, 2000.

Twining, Daniel. "America's Grand Design in Asia." *Washington Quarterly* 30, no. 3 (Summer 2007): 79–94.

Twomey, Christopher. *The Military Lens: Doctrinal Difference and Deterrence Failure in Sino-American Relations.* Ithaca, NY: Cornell University Press, 2010.

United Nations. *Statistical Yearbook, 1960.* New York: United Nations, 1960.

United Nations. *Statistical Yearbook, 1961.* New York: United Nations, 1961.

United Nations. *Yearbook of International Trade Statistics, 1955.* New York: United Nations, 1956.

United Nations. *Yearbook of International Trade Statistics, 1958.* New York: United Nations, 1959.

United Nations. *Yearbook of International Trade Statistics, 1960*. New York: United Nations, 1962.

UN Security Council—Members. UN.org. January 1, 2011. Accessed August 17, 2011. http://www.un.org/sc/members.asp

US Agency for International Development. "U.S. Overseas Loans and Grants: Obligations and Loan Authorizations." July 1–September 30, 2012. Accessed November 4, 2014. http://pdf.usaid.gov/pdf_docs/pnaec300.pdf

US Central Intelligence Agency. "Consequences of U.S. Troop Withdrawal from Korea in Spring 1949." February 28, 1949. http://www.foia.cia.gov/sites /default/files/document_conversions/89801/DOC_0000258388.pdf

US Department of Commerce. "National Economic Accounts." Bureau of Economic Analysis. January 1, 2011. Accessed August 16, 2011. http://www.bea /gov/national/index.htm

US Department of Commerce. *Statistical Abstract of the United States, 1954*. Washington, DC: U.S. Department of Commerce, 1954.

US Department of State. *Foreign Relations of the United States, 1946, The Far East, Vol. VIII*. Washington, DC: Government Printing Office, 1971.

US Department of State. *Foreign Relations of the United States, 1947, The Far East, Vol. VI*. Washington, DC: Government Printing Office, 1972.

US Department of State. *Foreign Relations of the United States, 1947, General; the United Nations, Vol. I*. Washington, DC: Government Printing Office, 1973.

US Department of State. *Foreign Relations of the United States, 1948, The Far East and Australasia, Vol. VI*. Washington, DC: Government Printing Office, 1974.

US Department of State. *Foreign Relations of the United States, 1949, The Far East and Australasia, Vol. VII*. Washington, DC: Government Printing Office, 1975.

US Department of State. *Foreign Relations of the United States, 1949, The Far East: China, Vol. IX*. Washington, DC: Government Printing Office, 1974.

U.S. Department of State. *Foreign Relations of the United States, 1950, East Asia and the Pacific, Vol. VI*. Washington, DC: Government Printing Office, 1976.

US Department of State. *Foreign Relations of the United States, 1950, Korea, Vol. VII*. Washington, DC: Government Printing Office, 1976.

US Department of State. *Foreign Relations of the United States, 1951, Asia and the Pacific, Vol. VI*. Washington, DC: Government Printing Office, 1978.

US Department of State. *Foreign Relations of the United States, 1951, Korea and China, Vol. VII*. Washington, DC: Government Printing Office, 1983.

US Department of State. *Foreign Relations of the United States, 1952–1954, East Asia and the Pacific, Vol. XII*. Washington, DC: Government Printing Office, 1984.

US Department of State. *Foreign Relations of the United States, 1952–1954, China and Japan, Vol. XIV*. Washington, DC: Government Printing Office, 1985.

U.S. Department of State. *Foreign Relations of the United States, 1952–1954, Korea, Vol. XV*. Washington, DC: Government Printing Office, 1984.

US Department of State. *Foreign Relations of the United States, 1952–54, Western Europe and Canada, Vol. XVI*. Washington, DC: Government Printing Office, 1985.

US Department of State. *Foreign Relations of the United States, 1955–57, China, Vol. III*. Washington, DC: Government Printing Office, 1985.

US Department of State. *Foreign Relations of the United States, 1958–1960, Japan, Korea, Vol. XVIII.* Washington, DC: Government Printing Office, 1994.

US Department of State. *Foreign Relations of the United States, 1958–1960, China, Vol. XIX.* Washington, DC: Government Printing Office, 1996.

U.S. Department of State. *Foreign Relations of the United States, 1961–63, North-east Asia, Vol. XXII.* Washington, DC: Government Printing Office, 1996.

US Department of State. "Mutual Defense Treaty between the Republic of Korea and the United States of America. (1953, October 1.)" Accessed August 2, 2013. http://photos.state.gov/libraries/korea/49271/p_int_docs/p_rok_60th _int_14.pdf

US Department of State. "United States Relations with China, With Special Reference to the Period 1944–1949." Publication no. 3573, Far Eastern Series 30.Washington, DC: Government Printing Office, 1949.

US Department of State. "United States Accedes to the Treaty of Amity and Co-operation in Southeast Asia." July 22, 2009. Accessed October 25, 2015. http:// www.state.gov/r/pa/prs/ps/2009/july/126294.htm

US Department of State. "Joint Statement of the United States-Singapore Strategic Partners Dialogue." January 18, 2012. Accessed October 3, 2014. http:// www.state.gov/r/pa/prs/ps/2012/01/181488.htm

US Department of State. "Trilateral Strategic Dialogue Joint Statement." October 4, 2013. Accessed October 2, 2014. http://www.state.gov/r/pa/prs/ps/2013 /10/215133.htm

US Department of State. "Proliferation Security Initiative." Accessed October 3, 2014. http://www.state.gov/t/isn/c10390.htm

US Department of Veteran Affairs. "America's Wars." Accessed November 4, 2014. http://www.va.gov/opa/publications/factsheets/fs_americas_wars.pdf

US National Security Council. "NSC-68: United States Objectives and Programs for National Security." April 14, 1950. Accessed August 17, 2011. http://fas.org /irp/offdocs/nsc-hst/nsc-68.htm

US Trade Representative. Overview of the Trans Pacific Partnership. Accessed October 3, 2014. http://www.ustr.gov/tpp/overview-of-the-TPP

United States Treaties and Other International Agreements, vol. 6, part 1. Washington, DC: Government Printing Office, 1956.

United States-India Nuclear Cooperation Approval and Nonproliferation Enhancement Act (2008—H.R. 7081). GovTrack.us. October 8, 2008. Accessed October 2, 2014. https://www.govtrack.us/congress/bills/110/hr7081.

Urata, Shujiro. "Constructing and Multilateralizing the Regional Comprehensive Economic Partnership." *ADBI Working Paper* 449 (2013). http://www.adbi .org/files/2013.12.02.wp449.regional.economic.partnership.asia.pdf

Van Ness, Peter. "Taiwan and Sino-American Relations." In *Dragon and Eagle: United States-China Relations: Past and Future,* edited by Michel Oksenberg and Robert B. Oxnam, 261–81. New York: Basic Books, 1973.

Vatikiotis, Michael, and Murray Hiebert. "How China Is Building an Empire." *Far Eastern Economic Review.* November 20, 2003.

Vaughn, Bruce. "East Asia Summit (EAS): Issues for Congress." Congressional Research Service Report for Congress. December 9, 2005. Accessed October 2, 2014. http://fpc.state.gov/documents/organization/58236.pdf

Wade, Robert. "The US Role in the Long Asian Crisis of 1990–2000." In *The Political Economy of the East Asian Crisis and Its Aftermath: Tigers in Distress*, edited by Arvid J. Lukanskas and Francisco L. Rivera-Batiz, 195–226. Cheltenham, UK: Edward Elgar, 2001.

Walt, Stephen M. *The Origins of Alliances*. Ithaca, NY: Cornell University Press, 1987.

Walt, Stephen M. "Testing Theories of Alliance Formation: The Case of Southwest Asia." *International Organization* 42, no. 2 (Spring 1988): 275–316.

Walt, Stephen M. *Taming American Power: The Global Response to U.S. Primacy*. New York: W.W. Norton, 2005.

Walt, Stephen M., G. John Ikenberry, Michael Mastanduno, and William C. Wohlforth. "Alliances in a Unipolar World." In *International Relations Theory and the Consequences of Unipolarity*. Cambridge, UK: Cambridge University Press, 2011.

Walter, Barbara F. *Reputation and Civil War: Why Separatist Conflicts Are So Violent*. Cambridge, UK: Cambridge University Press, 2009.

Waltz, Kenneth N. "Nuclear Myths and Political Realities." *American Political Science Review* 84, no. 3 (September 1990): 731–45.

Washington Post. "Taipeh hails Formosa Policy; Europe, India press unhappy." February 4, 1954. (1923–1954).

Webber, Douglas. "Two Funerals and a Wedding? The Ups and Downs of Regionalism in East Asia and Asia-Pacific after the Asian Crisis." *Pacific Review* 14, no. 3 (2001): 339–72.

Weber, Katja. "Hierarchy amidst Anarchy: A Transaction Costs Approach to International Security Cooperation." *International Studies Quarterly* 41, no. 2 (1997): 321–40.

Weber, Max. "The Profession and Vocation of Politics." In *Weber: Political Writings*, edited by Peter Lassman and Ronald Speirs, 309–69. Cambridge, UK: Cambridge University Press, 1994.

Weber, Steve. *Multilateralism in NATO: Shaping the Postwar Balance of Power, 1945–1961*. Berkeley: University of California Press, 1991.

Weiner, Tim. "CIA Spent Millions to Support Japanese Right in 50's and 60's." *New York Times*, October 9, 1994. Accessed October 3, 2014. http://www.nytimes.com/1994/10/09/world/cia-spent-millions-to-support-japanese-right-in-50-s-and-60-s.html?pagewanted=all

Weinstein, Franklin B. "The Concept of a Commitment in International Relations." *Journal of Conflict Resolution* 13, no. 3 (March 1969): 39–56.

Weitsman, Patricia A. *Dangerous Alliances: Proponents of Peace, Weapons of War*. Stanford, CA: Stanford University Press, 2004.

Welfield, John B. *An Empire in Eclipse: Japan in the Postwar American Alliance System: A Study in the Interaction of Domestic Politics and Foreign Policy*. London: Athlone Press, 1988.

Wellman, Barry, and S.D. Berkowitz. *Social Structures: A Network Approach*. New York: Cambridge University Press, 1998.

Wendt, Alexander. *Social Theory of International Politics*. Cambridge, UK: Cambridge University Press, 1999.

Wendt, Alexander, and Daniel Friedheim. "Hierarchy under Anarchy: Informal Empire and the East German State." *International Organization* 49, no. 4 (1995): 689–721.

Whitaker, Preston. *Spain and Defense of the West; Ally and Liability.* New York: Harper, 1961.

White, Stacey, Charles W. Freeman, and Michael J. Green. "Disaster Management in Asia: The Promise of Regional Architecture." In *Asia's Response to Climate Change and Natural Disasters: Implications for an Evolving Regional Architecture*, 61–98. Washington, DC: Center for Strategic and International Studies, 2010.

White, William S. "Senate Democrats Hit Formosa Plan: Admiral Radford Is Urging Eisenhower to Blockade Red China." February 7, 1953. Special to the *New York Times* (1923–current file).

Whiting, Allen S. "New Light on Mao: Quemoy 1958: Mao's Miscalculations." *China Quarterly* 62 (June 1975): 263–70.

Wohlforth, William C. "The Stability of a Unipolar World." *International Security* 24, no. 1 (Summer 1999): 5–41.

Wohlforth, William C. "Unipolarity, Status Competition, and Great Power War." In *International Relations Theory and the Consequences of Unipolarity*, edited by G. John Ikenberry, Michael Mastanduno, and William C. Wohlforth, 33–66. Cambridge, UK: Cambridge University Press, 2011.

World Bank. "Japan." World Bank Data. January 1, 2011. Accessed August 16, 2011. http://data.worldbank.org/country/japan.

Yasuyo, Sakata. "The Western Pacific Collective Security Concept and Korea in the Eisenhower Years: The US-ROK Alliance as an Asia-Pacific Alliance." *Journal of Kanda University of International Studies* 20 (2008): 1–30.

Yomiuri Shimbun. "53% of Japanese Do Not Trust the U.S.: Dissatisfaction on Iraq." December 16, 2004.

Yoshida, Shigeru. "Japan and the Crisis in Asia." *Foreign Affairs* 29, no. 2 (January 1951): 171–81.

Yoshitsu, Michael. *Japan and the San Francisco Peace Settlement.* New York: Columbia University Press, 1983.

Zakaria, Fareed. "Our Way: The Trouble with Being the World's Only Superpower." *New Yorker* 14 (October 2002): 72–81.

Zelikow, Philip. "American Engagement in Asia." In *America's Asian Alliances*, edited by Robert D. Blackwill and Paul Dibb, 19–30. Cambridge, MA: MIT Press, 2000.

INDEX

abandonment, 70, 20–21, 25, 36–37, 92, 134

Abe, Shinzo, 211, 216

Acharya, Amitav, 211

Acheson, Dean, 16, 17, 40, 41, 42–45, 52, 54, 168–71, 172, 238n18, 264n74; "defense perimeter" policy, 10, 43–47, 67, 132, 238n17; Japan and, 127, 130, 132, 136, 140, 147–48, 196, 262n43; Korea and, 45, 57, 59, 63, 105, 107, 113; Pacific Ocean Pact and, 177–83; Taiwan and, 42, 62, 66, 72–75, 171, 174

Adenauer, Konrad, 192–94

adhesion strategies, 20, 27, 28, 32, 35–36

Afghanistan, 31, 194

alliances: business model, 214–15, 291n101; control strategies, 27–36, 227n2, 233n44, 235n66; effectiveness studies, 36–37, 234n59; historical examples, 30–31; motives and goals, 3–4, 19–20, 26–28, 37, 228n5, 235n61; as *pactum de contrahendo*, 19; pathological reactions to, 20–27, 37, 61–62, 92, 229n6; recent examples, 198–206

Allison, John M., 78, 135, 137, 157, 178–79, 181

Alsop, Joseph, 61, 71

Alsop, Stewart, 71

Alter, Karen, 214

Altfeld, Michael F., 27

anti-communism, 3, 4, 8, 15, 52, 58–59, 61, 68. *See also* domino theory; Truman Doctrine

ANZUS, 147, 182, 184

ASEAN (Association of Southeast Asian Nations), 29, 30, 39, 196, 199, 204, 206, 207–8, 211, 215, 216; ASEAN Regional Forum (ARF), 3, 199, 207, 208; Code of Conduct, 39, 208

Asian Infrastructure Investment Bank (AIIB), 200–203, 212, 213, 216, 217

Asian-Pacific Council (ASPAC), 13

Asia-Pacific Economic Cooperation Council (APEC), 1–2, 3, 211

Attlee, Clement, 63

Australia, 1–2, 8, 177–79, 198, 226n53; Japan and, 44, 138–39, 141, 146, 149, 181–84; Middle Eastern wars and, 194, 195; regional distrust of, 171, 186. *See also* ANZUS

Babcock, Stanton, 137

Badger, Oscar, 72

Bajpai, Girja Shankar, 76

Baker, James, 289n89

Barak, Ehud, 35, 191

Barnett, A. Doak, 85

Barzel, Rainer, 193

Beckley, Michael, 26, 37

Bell, Coral, 226n51

Berendsen, Carl, 147

Bevin, Ernest, 177, 178

bilateralism, 3–5, 7–12, 14, 17, 19, 28–32, 115, 121, 140–41, 161–64, 173, 175, 177, 181–84, 185, 187; continued relevance of, 7, 196–98, 204, 209–10, 218

Bismarck, Otto von, 28, 30, 31

Blum, Robert, 8, 16, 68

Bowie, Robert, 107

Bradley, Omar, 60
Bridges, Styles, 71
Briggs, Ellis O., 108
Brown, Michael, 227n3
Bundy, McGeorge, 193
Burke, Arleigh, 90
Burma (Myanmar), 75, 77–78, 92, 152,
    171, 198, 247n74, 248n77
Bush, George W., 31, 195
Butterworth, W. Walton, 43, 71,
    264n74
Byrnes, James, 42

Cairo Declaration, 67
Calder, Kent E., 172–73
Calwell, Arthur, 171
checkbook diplomacy, 195
Chen, Cheng, 73
Chennault, Claire, 72
Cheonan sinking, 118
Chiang, Ching-kuo, 78, 93
Chiang, Kai-shek, 4, 43, 52–53, 61,
    67–93 passim, 104, 107, 121,
    163–64, 173–76, 186; Kennedy and,
    253n135; Pacific Pact and, 165–68,
    170–72, 176, 273n19
Chiang Kai-shek, Madame (Soong
    Mei-ling), 71–72
Chiang, Wei-kuo, 75
China (mainland), 4, 5, 10, 18, 23,
    29, 65–93 passim, 162–63, 168–69,
    191–92, 213–16; bilateral prefer-
    ence, 30, 38–39, 199; CCP victory
    (1949), 47, 65–66, 162, 169, 173, 177,
    243n14; current regional archi-
    tecture, 199–206, 212–13; during
    Korean War, 55–63, 97–102, 104,
    109; Israel and, 34–35; Japan and,
    133, 149–53, 158, 270n58; US atti-
    tudes toward, 42, 43, 46–47, 52, 54,
    126–27, 215–16
China, Republic of. *See* Taiwan
CHINCOM, 151, 269n149
Chinhae, 167, 172, 176
Chou, En-lai, 76, 245n32
Christensen, Thomas J., 52, 63, 199,
    240n50, 244n23

CIA: Burma and, 247n74, 248n77;
    Japan and, 144–45, 267n117;
    Taiwan and, 66, 67, 71, 77–78, 88,
    245n44; Vietnam and, 50
CICA (Conference on Interaction and
    Confidence-Building Measures in
    Asia), 199–204, 206, 212, 216
Clark, Mark W.: Japan and, 127;
    Korea and, 95, 99–100, 102, 103,
    106, 108, 110, 113, 121, 174
Clayton, Will, 16
COCOM, 151
Cohen, Warren, 42
Collins, J. Lawton, 107
Combined Forces Command (CFC),
    118
"complex patchworks," 206, 214–19
constraint and containment, 4, 5, 19,
    161
constructivism, 15–16, 188
Cooley, Alexander, 191
Cooper, John Sherman, 264n74
Copenhagen Criteria, 215
Cultural Revolution, 270n158
Cumings, Bruce, 126, 282n5

David, Stephen, 31
Davies, John Patton, 43, 45, 61, 65
De Gaulle, Charles, 192–93
Dening, Esler, 157
Dewey, Thomas, 169
distancing strategies, 7, 25–28, 32–35,
    92, 163–63, 192, 272n2
Dodge, Joseph M., 130, 154
Doidge, Frederick, 138, 141, 181, 182,
    183
domino theory, 8, 11, 23, 55, 57–59,
    80, 92, 105, 121, 161–63, 185–86
Dooman, Eugene, 145
Downer, Alexander, 1
Draper, William H., 126
Drumright, Everett F., 83
Dulles, Janet Pomeroy Avery, 137
Dulles, John Foster, 15, 30, 40, 57,
    60, 61, 185, 240n48, 245n32,
    264n74, 278n91; Japan and, 122,
    134–43, 146–51 passim, 157, 158,

183, 263n66, 280n114; Korea and, 106, 107, 109, 111–13, 175, 242n96; Pacific Ocean Pact and, 177–84, 226n53; SEATO and, 176–77; Taiwan and, 78–86 passim, 92, 101, 247n68, 252n133
Duncan, Charles K., 107

East Asia Summit (EAS), 1–2, 196, 199, 200, 207–8, 216, 218–19, 221n1
Economic Commission for Asia and the Far East (ECAFE), 170, 274n40
Egypt, 29–30, 31
Eisenhower, Dwight D., 27, 48, 56, 59, 64, 163, 186–87, 219; Japan and, 122, 135, 156, 158; Korea and, 102–4, 106, 108, 113, 116, 119; Taiwan and, 69, 71, 74–75, 78–81, 83–85, 90–93, 164
empire-building, 3, 6–7, 28, 37–38, 98, 185
enmeshment, 218
England, 13, 29, 41–42, 178–79; Korea and, 63; Japan and, 132, 133, 135, 140, 141, 150, 152
entrapment, 35, 54, 59–64, 65–66, 72–73, 77, 80–81, 104, 106, 120–21, 161–62, 173, 175–76, 181, 187–88, 192, 235n64
European Coal and Steel Community, 12
EVERREADY plan, 106, 115–16

Fairbank, John King, 58, 162–63
Fang, Songying, 37
Far Eastern Commission (FEC), 141–42
Feary, Robert, 137
Flying Tigers, 70, 72
Formosa. *See* Taiwan
Formosa Resolution, 69
Forrestal, James, 49, 134
Foster, John W., 137
Franco, Francisco, 189–91, 282n8

Gaddis, John Lewis, 47, 55
Garver, John W., 250n110

Gates, Robert M., 213
GATT (General Agreement on Trade and Tariffs), 13, 154
Gelpi, Christopher, 36–37, 236n73
Germany, 5, 9–11, 13, 15, 18, 127, 138, 164, 192–94
Gerzoy, Gene, 194
Gilpin, Robert, 14
gobanken-sama, 160
Goh, Evelyn, 218
Goldstein, Steven, 70, 83
Great Leap Forward, 91, 153, 250n107
Greece, 22, 65
Green, Owen Mortimer, 169
Griswold, A. Whitney, 41
Grossman, Marc, 208
Guam, 41

Harriman, Averell, 62, 76, 174–75
Hatoyama, Ichiro, 157, 158
Hatoyama, Yukio, 214
Hawaii, 41, 150
He, Kai, 217
Heer, Paul, 131
Heinrichs, Waldo, 42
Hemmer, Christopher, 16–17, 226n50
Herter, Christian, 90, 119
Hickerson, John, 57
hierarchical order, 5–6, 20, 185, 216
Hirohito, 125
Ho, Chi Minh, 50
Hodge, John R., 96, 240n62
Hong Kong, 178, 180, 181
Hoover, Herbert, 61, 72, 139, 261n23
Hornbeck, Stanley, 71
Howard, John, 1, 194–95
Huber, Walter, 169
Humphrey, George M., 79, 135

Ikenberry, John, 14, 26, 28, 38
India, 59, 171, 198, 208
Indochina, 50, 53, 58, 59, 62, 69, 162, 180, 181. *See also* Vietnam
Indonesia, 123, 171, 173, 176, 179, 208
international relations theory, 7, 197
Iran, 22
Iraq, 31, 194–95

Ishibashi, Tanzen, 158
Israel, 22, 30, 34–35, 189, 191–92

Jansen, Marius, 154
Japan, 12, 41, 44, 46, 47, 122–60,
    164–65, 185, 187–88, 194–95, 196,
    198, 211, 213; alpha strategy, 134,
    264n71; anti-Americanism in,
    156–58; beta strategy, 132, 135,
    141; China and, 133, 149–53, 158,
    269n149, 270n58; communist
    perceived threat to, 110, 122, 126,
    134, 135, 143, 146–47; economic
    issues, 11–12, 125–26, 128, 129–30,
    139, 140, 143–45, 149–55, 269n149,
    270nn158–59; gamma strategy,
    134; Japanese workers in Korea,
    100–101; LDP, 144, 145, 267n117;
    Pacific Ocean Pact and, 179–82;
    postwar situation, 17–18, 122–31;
    regional distrust of, 13, 15, 18,
    58, 95, 133, 165, 183, 185–86, 205;
    Ryukyu Islands, 44, 47, 143, 183;
    treaties, 8, 131, 136–37, 138–40,
    143, 146–49, 157–59, 183; US
    troops in, 6, 44, 110, 123–26, 128,
    130, 131, 143, 149, 155–59 passim
Javits, Jacob, 169, 226n49
Jervis, Robert, 35, 41, 54, 72
Jessup, Philip C., 43, 177–78
Johnson, Chalmers A., 149
Johnson, Earl D., 137
Johnson, Jesse C., 37
Johnson, Louis, 47, 53, 57, 60, 75, 134,
    136, 247n68
Johnson, Lyndon, 192–94
Judd, Walter, 61, 71, 111, 168

Kagan, Robert, 30
Kahler, Miles, 15, 38
Katzenstein, Peter J., 16–17, 226n50
Kennan, George F., 40, 43, 45–46,
    49–50, 65, 113, 178, 238n18; Japan
    and, 122, 123, 127–29, 131, 133,
    134, 141, 147, 149, 268n126; Korea
    and, 55, 59, 60, 109, 242n91; Tai-
    wan and, 67, 243n14

Kennedy, John F., 71, 91, 93, 192–94,
    253n135
Keohane, Robert O., 23
Key, David, 248n77
Khrushchev, Nikita, 135
Kim, Il-sung, 55, 240n50
Kirk, Allan, 275n50
Kishi, Nobusuke, 145, 158
Knowland, William, 61, 71, 111, 150,
    168
Kohlberg, Alfred, 61, 72
Koizumi, Junichiro, 194–95
Koo, Wellington, 73, 78
Korea. *See* Korea, North; Korea,
    South
Korean War, 10–11, 22–23, 55–64, 94,
    97–104, 106, 113, 117–18, 161, 173–
    76, 187, 242n91; Incheon landing,
    59, 61, 97–98, 242n91; Japan and,
    131, 143, 144, 149; prisoners of war
    release, 103; rollback doctrine, 59,
    62–63, 76, 98, 242n91, 242n96,
    254n17; Taiwan and, 58, 60–62,
    67–68, 69, 75–77, 81, 82, 173–74,
    244n23
Koremenos, Barbara, 32
Kuomintang (KMT), 43, 61, 65–66, 67,
    70, 71, 73, 79

LaFeber, Walter, 145–46
Lake, David A., 26
Lansing, Robert, 137
Lattimore, Owen, 72
League of Nations, 95
Leeds, Brett A., 37
Leffler, Melvyn, 62
liberalism, 5, 11–14, 28–29, 187
Lilliputian strategy of control, 29,
    200, 218
Li, Mi, 77–78, 247n74
Lippmann, Walter, 60
Lipson, Charles, 32
Lodge, John Davis, 71
Loeb, William, 72
Luce, Clare Boothe, 71
Luce, Henry, 61, 71
Lucky Dragon, 157

MacArthur, Douglas, 52–53, 57, 282n5; Japan and, 122, 123–26, 128, 129, 133, 136, 141, 226n56; Korea and, 61–62, 97, 98, 117, 173–75; Taiwan and, 67, 71, 75–76, 81, 247n68

Madrid Pact, 188–91

Magruder, Carter B., 137

Mahathir, Mohamad, 211, 214

Mahbubani, Kishore, 207

Mao, Zedong, 52, 66, 163, 240n50, 243n8

Marshall, George C., 42, 45, 65–67, 71, 72, 128, 174, 184, 238n18

Marshall Plan, 11, 42, 50, 65, 129, 171, 189; in Asia, 173, 276n64

"massive retaliation" doctrine, 101–2

Mastanduno, Michael, 196

Mattes, Michaela, 37, 236n76

McCarran, Patrick, 71

McCarthy, Joseph, 61, 81, 242n89

McKee, Frederick, 61, 72

McNamara, Robert, 193

Menzies, Robert, 138, 178

Merchant, Livingston, 73

Metternich, Klemens von, 30, 31

Meunier, Sophie, 214

micropolitics, 6, 186

minilateralization, 198, 206, 208–9, 213, 218

Miyazawa, Kiichi, 148

Morrow, James D., 26, 27, 232n41

Muccio, John, 62, 94, 96–97, 105, 113, 115

Multilateral Force (MLF), 193

multilateralism, 4–5, 8–14, 16–18, 28–32, 121, 140, 161–62, 166, 172–73, 176, 184, 187, 204, 209–10, 213

Nasser, Gamal Abdel, 30

National Security Council reports: NSC 7, 113; NSC 8, 240n61; NSC 13/2, 128, 130, 134, 142; NSC 13/3, 131; NSC 48/1 and 48/2, 50, 55, 67; NSC 48/5, 68, 69; NSC 68, 49, 55–56, 60, 63; NSC 125/2, 152, 155; NSC 146/2, 69, 79, 80, 84; NSC 167/2, 116; NSC 170/1, 116, 119–20; NCS 5418/1, 190; NCS 5817, 119, 120; NSC, 5907

NATO, 2, 3, 5, 8–9, 11, 13, 15, 29, 42, 168, 170, 179–80, 187, 240n48

NEAPSM (Northeast Asian Peace and Security Mechanism), 209

NEATO concept, 281n121

Nehru, Jawaharlal, 171

Neri, Felino, 138

neutralization of Taiwan Straits, 68, 70, 73, 74, 84

"New Look" doctrine, 10, 156, 176

New York Yankees, 145

New Zealand, 8, 123, 138, 139, 141, 171, 177–79, 181–84, 186, 226n53. *See also* ANZUS

Nitze, Paul, 60, 61

Nixon, Richard, 116–17, 156, 164

Noel-Baker, Philip, 169

Non-Proliferation Treaty, 193

Norstad, Lauris, 174

North Korea (DPRK), 4, 18, 23, 44, 94, 96–97, 105, 119, 209. *See also* Korean War

nuclear weapons, 10, 41, 48–49, 59, 90, 96, 101, 106; in Germany, 192–94; in Japan, 157, 158; in Spain, 189

Obama, Barack, 213–14

Okinawa, 77, 128, 139, 143, 156, 158

"One Belt, One Road" initiative, 200, 212, 216

operational control, 106, 110, 111, 117–18, 120, 196, 257n67, 260n106

Operation Paper, 77

overdependence, 19–27, 59, 61, 81, 92, 121, 122, 186, 230n17, 247n68

Pacific Ocean Pact, 123, 177–84, 207, 279n102

Pacific Pact proposal, 140–41, 164–73, 177, 207

Pakistan, 59, 176

Panikkar, K. M., 76

Park, Chung-hee, 168

Park, Geun-hye, 213–14
Parsons, Graham, 158
Phibun, Songgram, 168
Philippines, 8, 12, 41, 44, 58, 59, 73, 123, 138, 139, 147, 165, 171–72, 176, 177, 179, 182, 198
pivot (or rebalance) to Asia, 198, 206, 213
Plato, 139
postcolonialism, 13, 58, 181, 185
Potsdam Declaration, 262n43
Pound, Roscoe, 72
powerplay strategy, 3–8, 18, 19–20, 26–39, 54, 64, 161–62, 173, 180–84, 186–88, 190, 194; "back end" of, 73–74, 81, 83, 146, 159; China's use of, 200, 204; continued relevance of, 195–206; "front end" strategy, 73, 81, 146, 159; in Germany, 192–94; in Iraq, 194–95; in Israel, 191–92; in Japan, 3, 4–5, 122–23, 132, 135–36, 146–49, 153, 156, 158–60; in Korea, 3, 4, 104–15, 120–21, 122, 175; in Spain, 188–91; in Taiwan, 3, 4, 73–74, 81, 83, 85, 86–88, 92–93, 120–21, 122, 163
Press-Barnathan, Galia, 176, 211–12
Pressman, Jeremy, 30, 191–92, 283n25
Princeton Theological Seminary, 95
Proliferation Security Initiative (PSI), 210–11, 288nn80–81
Pukch'in T'ongil policy, 94, 109, 117
Pyle, Kenneth, 124

Quarles, Donald, 90
Quemoy crisis. *See* Taiwan: offshore islands
Quirino, Elpidio, 138, 139, 147, 165–68, 170–72, 273n22

racism, 15–17, 135, 187–88, 248n88, 282n5
Rankin, Karl, 78
realism, 129, 187
regime theory, 13
regional architecture in Asia: China as hub, 199–204, 212–13, 214;

security dilemma, 216–19; US as hub, 204–6
regional initiatives and institutions, 211–18
Reischauer, Edwin O., 143, 146
"reverse course" (Japanese occupation), 129, 131, 132, 133, 134, 138, 141, 143
Rhee, Syngman, 4, 61, 62, 75, 82, 94–121, 163–64, 175–76, 186; Pacific Pact and, 165, 166–68, 170–72, 176; plans to depose, 100, 106–7, 116, 119
Rice, Condoleezza, 209
Ridgway, Matthew, 101–2, 134, 137, 174, 238n17
risk management, 20, 93, 161, 196
Riverdale, 71
Robertson, Walter, 84, 109–13, 251n112
Rockefeller, John D., III, 137
Roh, Moo-hyun, 194
Roosevelt, Eleanor, 72
Roosevelt, Theodore, 95
Rostow, Walt, 193
Royall, Kenneth C., 96, 129
Rudd, Kevin, 195
Ruggie, John, 14
Russia, 9, 10, 27, 31, 41–42, 45–47, 60, 127, 128, 162; China and, 58–59, 66–67; Japan and, 95, 132–35, 136, 147; Korea and, 96; postwar expansion, 169
Rusk, Dean, 42, 53, 73, 147, 177–78, 181, 192–93, 247n68, 264n74, 279n102

San Francisco Peace Treaty, 139–40, 147
Sato, Eisaku, 145
SCAP, 52, 123–30 passim, 134, 136, 141–42, 148, 151–52, 266n105
Schroeder, Gerhard, 192–93
Schroeder, Paul, 19, 27, 227n2
Schumann, Robert, 13
September 11 attacks, 194
Service, John, 72

Seventh Fleet, 68, 70, 73–75, 277, 279, 280, 297
Sharon, Ariel, 35, 191
Shigemitsu, Mamoru, 157
Singapore, 2, 140, 178, 198
Six Party Talks, 196, 209, 215
Smith, H. Alexander, 61, 71, 111, 150
Snidal, Duncan, 32
Snyder, Glenn H., 20, 27, 35
Snyder, Jack, 197
social network theory, 6–7, 38
Solomon, Richard, 289n89
South China Sea disputes, 30, 39, 199
Southeast Asian Treaty Organization (SEATO), 8–9, 176, 223n12, 278n86
South Korea (ROK), 15, 22–23, 47, 94–121, 180, 184, 185–86, 194, 195, 196, 198, 213; China and, 39, 213–14; economic issues, 12, 100–101, 113–14, 163; Japan and, 100–101, 139, 147, 155, 204; political structure, 12, 95; postwar situation, 17–18, 95; recent tensions in, 118; treaty negotiations with, 8, 108–17; US troops in, 6, 49–50, 52, 55–57, 118, 240n62. *See also* Korean War
Soviet Union. *See* Russia
Spain, 22, 188–91, 282n8
Sparkman, John, 150–51
Spender, Percy, 138, 140–41, 147, 182, 184
Stalin, Joseph, 41, 52, 66, 240n50, 243n8
Stevenson, Adlai, 10
Sun, Li-jen, 75

Taft, Robert, 61, 71
Taiwan (ROC), 6, 12, 8, 15, 17–18, 43, 45, 47, 52–53, 65–93, 172, 180, 184, 185–86, 192, 196, 199; economic issues, 12, 150, 163; Korean War and, 58, 60–62, 173–74, 244n23; lobbying efforts, 22, 71–72; offshore islands, 71, 77, 78–79, 82–85, 88, 90–92, 162; treaties, 8, 83–85, 90–91. *See also* Kuomintang

Tasca, Henry J., 114–15
Thailand, 12, 78, 152, 168, 176
Thucydides, 130
Titoism, 66, 68
Tong, Hollington, 73
Trans-Pacific Partnership (TPP), 3, 211, 213, 218
Treaty of Amity and Cooperation, 221n1
Trilateral Cooperation Oversight Group (TCOG), 198, 205, 209, 217
Trilateral Strategic Dialogue (TSD), 198, 209, 215, 288n76
Truman, Harry S., 41–42, 46, 48–49, 136, 147, 163, 166, 168–69, 172, 184, 186–87, 219, 264n74; Japan and, 122, 129, 134, 137, 147; Korea and, 55–64 passim, 97; Taiwan and, 66, 67, 69, 71, 73–77 passim, 80, 93, 174, 247n62
Truman Doctrine, 10, 49, 61, 63, 65, 187
Tsingtao, 72
Tsunami Core Group, 208, 209, 210, 217
Tucker, Nancy, 67–68
Turkey, 31, 42, 46, 65

undercommitment, 20–21, 23, 230n21
unilateralism, 5, 19, 29, 31, 88, 141, 176–77; Korean, 100, 104, 106–8, 112, 115–20 passim
United Nations, 29, 36, 44, 48, 56–57, 78, 96, 155; UN Commission on Korea, 96
United Nations Command (UNC), 101, 107, 108, 113, 116, 118, 257n67, 258n83
United States: credibility concerns, 56–57, 242n91; early attitudes toward Asia, 40–55; European focus, 40–42, 47, 50–54, 63, 65–66, 104, 165, 168–69; postwar hegemony in Asia, 6–7, 9–10, 14, 31, 39
"unsinkable aircraft carrier" metaphor, 53, 81

Vandenberg, Arthur H., 66, 240n48, 264n74

Van Fleet, James, 111

Vietnam, 50, 245n32

Vietnam War, 13, 143, 207

Vorys, John, 71

Walt, Stephen, 197

Wilson, Charles, 79, 107

Xi Jinping, 204, 214

Yalu River, 59, 61, 97, 98, 101–2

Yeh, George, 74, 82, 84–85

Yoshida, Shigeru, 101, 132, 144, 147, 148–52, 156–58, 267n111

zaibatsu, 126

Zaytun Division, 194